2008
The Supreme Court Review

2008
The

"Judges as persons, or courts as institutions, are entitled to
no greater immunity from criticism than other persons
or institutions . . . [J]udges must be kept mindful of their limitations and
of their ultimate public responsibility by a vigorous
stream of criticism expressed with candor however blunt."
—*Felix Frankfurter*

". . . while it is proper that people should find fault when
their judges fail, it is only reasonable that they should recognize the
difficulties. . . . Let them be severely brought to book,
when they go wrong, but by those who will take the trouble
to understand them."
—*Learned Hand*

THE LAW SCHOOL

THE UNIVERSITY OF CHICAGO

Supreme Court Review

EDITED BY

DENNIS J. HUTCHINSON

DAVID A. STRAUSS

AND GEOFFREY R. STONE

 THE UNIVERSITY OF CHICAGO PRESS

CHICAGO AND LONDON

INTERNATIONAL STANDARD BOOK NUMBER: 978-0-226-36253-3

LIBRARY OF CONGRESS CATALOG CARD NUMBER: 60-14353

THE UNIVERSITY OF CHICAGO PRESS, CHICAGO 60637

THE UNIVERSITY OF CHICAGO PRESS, LTD., LONDON

© 2009 BY THE UNIVERSITY OF CHICAGO, ALL RIGHTS RESERVED, PUBLISHED 2009

PRINTED IN THE UNITED STATES OF AMERICA

The paper used in this publication meets the minimum requirements of American National Standard for Information Sciences–Permanence of Paper for Printed Library Materials, ANSI Z39.48-1984. ⊗

TO RICHARD A. EPSTEIN

*Master teacher, scholar,
and institutional citizen—hail,
but never farewell*

CONTENTS

DANIEL J. MELTZER

HABEAS CORPUS, SUSPENSION, AND GUANTÁNAMO: THE BOUMEDIENE DECISION

Boumediene v Bush[1] was a momentous decision along many dimensions. The Supreme Court, for the first time in its history, invalidated a federal statute that purported to restrict the jurisdiction of the federal courts.[2] In so ruling, the Supreme Court, also for the first time, clearly held, as distinguished from strongly suggesting, that the Constitution's Suspension Clause,[3] despite its indirect wording, affirmatively guarantees access to the courts to seek the writ of habeas corpus (or an adequate substitute) in order to test the legality of executive detention. In determining the reach of the Suspension Clause's guarantee, the Court held—still another first— that it extends beyond the sovereign territory of the United States to protect aliens detained at the American naval base at Guantánamo

---

Daniel J. Meltzer is Professor of Law, Harvard Law School.

AUTHOR'S NOTE: I am grateful to Dick Fallon for characteristically insightful comments.

[1] 128 S Ct 2229 (2008).

[2] The decision in *United States v Klein*, 80 US (13 Wall) 128 (1872), did invalidate a statute phrased in jurisdictional terms, but the Court's Delphic ruling is best understood as holding that Congress may not use jurisdictional regulation to require the Supreme Court, or any federal court, to decide a case in violation of the Constitution. See generally Daniel J. Meltzer, *Congress, Courts, and Constitutional Remedies*, 86 Georgetown L J 2537, 2538–49 (1998).

[3] US Const, Art I, § 9, cl 2 ("The Privilege of the Writ of Habeas Corpus shall not be suspended, unless when in Cases of Rebellion or Invasion the public Safety may require it.").

Bay, Cuba. Finally, in determining the breadth of judicial inquiry that the Suspension Clause guarantees, the Court ruled that a statutory judicial review mechanism that Congress had established as a substitute for habeas corpus was constitutionally inadequate, and thus found, again for the first time, that federal legislation violated the Suspension Clause.

The majority's decision triggered protests from the four dissenters that the Court was arrogating to itself a role better left to the political branches.[4] Since 2004, the Supreme Court has handed down six decisions concerning the detention of persons related in some way to the war on terror. From the Executive's perspective, the scorecard is at best mixed. In only two of those six cases did the Executive prevail—in one case only on a technical and ultimately minor question of venue (though thereby avoiding the risk of a defeat on the merits)[5] and in the other, only after losing an important ruling along the way.[6] But some of the "defeats" were limited[7] or, while rejecting the government's broadest claims, nonetheless gave the government half a loaf,[8] or could be (and were) cured by congressional action.[9]

---

[4] See 128 S Ct at 2279–80, 2293 (Roberts dissenting); id at 2295–96 (Scalia dissenting).

[5] *Rumsfeld v Padilla*, 542 US 426 (2004).

[6] In *Munaf v Geren*, 128 S Ct 2207 (2008), the Court rejected the government's argument that habeas corpus jurisdiction does not extend to a petition filed on behalf of American citizens held in Iraq by American forces operating there under multinational auspices. The Court proceeded, however, to rule for the government in denying the relief sought— an order barring the transfer of those individuals to Iraqi custody, where they feared they would be tortured—on the basis that a sovereign nation like Iraq generally has jurisdiction to punish offenses committed within its borders and that it is for the U.S. political branches to consider petitioners' allegations that they would face torture by Iraq.

[7] Thus, while in *Rasul v Bush*, 542 US 466 (2004), the Court rejected the government's position that the habeas statute, as it then stood, did not extend to detainees at Guantánamo Bay, it did not indicate what rights, if any, the detainees had or how deferential the scope of habeas review would be.

[8] In *Hamdi v Rumsfeld*, 542 US 507 (2004), the government did not contest jurisdiction as such, but asserted that the habeas court could not review individual determinations by the military of enemy combatant status. Eight of nine Justices rejected that view, and at the time the decision seemed like a large defeat for the administration's strategy. From today's perspective the holding is quite modest. The Court treated the case as arising out of a war, and hence recognized the presumptive availability of wartime detention, while rejecting arguments that detention of a *citizen* was not authorized by or indeed violated congressional enactments. The plurality stated that the review to which the petitioner was entitled might be provided by a properly constituted military tribunal, thereby implying that the role of habeas corpus review would be at most quite limited. See text accompanying notes 158–61.

[9] In *Hamdan v Rumsfeld*, 548 US 557 (2006), the Court invalidated the system of military commissions established by President Bush to try war crimes, but the Justices indicated

Boumediene was a clear defeat for the Executive. On the threshold issue before the Court—whether the Constitution required the exercise of habeas corpus jurisdiction over detainees at Guantánamo Bay—the decision rejected a key element of the antiterrorist legal strategy of the Bush Administration, which had assumed (perhaps too confidently, but hardly unreasonably) that Guantánamo Bay was beyond the reach of the writ. Moreover, the Court did not merely uphold habeas jurisdiction, but conveyed, albeit by implication, mistrust of the military hearings that the government has provided to detainees, while providing a sketch of habeas procedure that involves significant judicial intrusion into matters that the Executive had contended were committed to it for decision. But how serious a defeat this decision represents in practice will depend on answers to a broad range of questions, left to the future, about how the habeas jurisdiction will operate. It remains to be seen whether, as Chief Justice Roberts suggested in his dissent, the habeas regime, when fleshed out, will look very much like the statutory scheme that the Court held to be constitutionally inadequate—in which case the Court's intervention may have little practical impact—or, whether, as Justice Scalia predicted in his dissent, the decision will have "disastrous consequences" that will be "devastating" and "will almost certainly cause more Americans to be killed."[10] (Oddly, all four dissenters joined both dissents, despite their sharply conflicting assessments of the consequences of the Court's ruling.) At the same time, whatever legal battles the Executive has lost, neither *Boumediene* nor any of the Supreme Court's prior decisions required the release of any detainees,[11] and so if one measures success not

---

that Congress could fix the defects. Congress accepted that invitation by enacting the Military Commissions Act of 2006, Pub L No 109-366, 120 Stat 2600, codified in relevant part at 28 USC § 2241(e) (Supp 2007).

[10] 128 S Ct at 2294. Compare Paul A. Freund, *On Presidential Privilege*, 88 Harv L Rev 13, 35 (1974) ("History has a way of mocking these specters of disaster forecast from judicial decisions.").

[11] See Jenny S. Martinez, *Process and Substance in the "War on Terror*,*"* 108 Colum L Rev 1013 (2008) (stressing that point while criticizing what she views as the excessively procedural focus of the Supreme Court's decisions). A federal district judge ordered the government to bring a group of seventeen Chinese Muslims detained at Guantánamo to his courtroom, for release in the D.C. area, after the D.C. Circuit found no adequate basis for detaining one of them. See *Parhat v Gates*, 532 F3d 834 (DC Cir 2008). The government asserted that it had been unable to find a country other than China (where the detainees feared they would be tortured) that would accept them upon release, and succeeded in having the district court orders reversed on the ground that the habeas court lacked power to order otherwise inadmissible aliens to be released into the United States. See *Kiyemba v Obama*, 2009 WL 383618 (Feb 18, 2009).

by prevailing in court but by prevailing on the ground, the administration could be viewed as successful.

Whatever its ultimate practical significance, the *Boumediene* decision had a distinctive legal significance. For it was the only one of the recent terrorism decisions in which the Executive's position was plainly authorized by congressional legislation. Thus, the ruling is notable for still another reason—as the Supreme Court's only clear invalidation, during wartime,[12] of executive action that had clear-cut congressional support. The political branches were aligned in purporting to withdraw habeas corpus jurisdiction, yet the Court nonetheless, if unusually, found that action to be unconstitutional.[13]

This article seeks to assess the significance of the *Boumediene* decision. Section I describes the background to the decision and the basis for the Court's ruling. Section II discusses the Court's analysis of the Suspension Clause. It highlights the significance of the Court's holding that that clause confers an affirmative right to habeas corpus review, assesses the distinct holding that that right extends to alien enemy combatants detained at the U.S. Naval Base at Guantánamo Bay, and discusses the implications of the latter holding for the broader question of the extraterritorial reach of habeas corpus jurisdiction. Section III analyzes, and raises questions about, the persuasiveness of the Court's reasoning that the statutory judicial review mechanism that Congress had established as a substitute for habeas corpus was constitutionally inadequate. In turn, Section IV discusses the interplay between the administrative re-

---

[12] Although "war" is a controversial description, see, for example, Bruce Ackerman, *This Is Not a War*, 113 Yale L J 1871 (2004), and Benjamin Wittes, *Law and the Long War* 13 (Penguin, 2008), the Court's cases have not challenged it to date.

[13] Thus, Professors Pildes and Issacharoff argue that during wartime, courts have typically not made first-order decisions about individual liberty, but instead have focused on second-order questions about whether the correct institutional process has been followed. In particular, they suggest that an important question is whether Congress has authorized executive action, and that when it has, courts will uphold the action in question. See Samuel Issacharoff and Richard H. Pildes, *Between Civil Libertarianism and Executive Unilateralism: An Institutional Process Approach to Rights During Wartime*, 5 Theoretical Inquiries L 1 (2004). See also Cass R. Sunstein, *Minimalism at War*, 2004 Supreme Court Review 47, 50–51 (finding that American courts confronting national security issues characteristically take a minimalist approach, one element of which is a requirement of "clear congressional authorization for executive action intruding on interests with a claim to constitutional protection"). As Professors Pildes and Issacharoff explicitly recognize, the general argument is complicated by the frequent open-endedness of the determination whether Congress has in fact authorized a particular executive action. See 5 Theoretical Inquiries L at 36–43. But that problem did not exist in *Boumediene*, where § 7 of the MCA plainly supported the Executive's position that Congress has attempted to preclude the exercise of habeas corpus jurisdiction.

gime established by the Executive and Congress—involving military adjudication followed by limited judicial review—and the tradition of judicial inquiry in habeas corpus, in the broader context of the dissenters' accusation that the majority was engaged in judicial aggrandizement. While noting that the administrative model is not necessarily deficient as a substitute for judicial inquiry on habeas corpus, I suggest that the Court appears to have been motivated by concerns, largely unexpressed, that in practice the system of military adjudication was not structured to provide fair and prompt determinations of enemy combatant status. I also suggest that these concerns about military practice, when set against the Executive's broad assertions of executive power and its limited respect for international law, very likely motivated the Court's invalidation of the judicial review regime established by Congress. Finally, Section V concludes by highlighting some of the issues left open by the decision.

I. The Background and the Ruling

The petitioners in *Boumediene*, all citizens of nations at peace with the United States, were detained at Guantánamo Bay as suspected enemy combatants. Some had been apprehended on Afghan battlefields, others in foreign nations far from any theater of battle. Administration officials had selected Guantánamo as a detention zone because it afforded a secure site that, they believed, would be outside the jurisdiction of the federal courts. But habeas corpus actions filed by such detainees tested the administration's assumption, giving rise to the 2004 decision in *Rasul v Bush*.[14] There the Supreme Court, reversing the D.C. Circuit, held that the basic statutory grant of habeas corpus jurisdiction, 28 USC § 2241, did confer jurisdiction on the federal courts to entertain petitions filed by detainees at Guantánamo Bay. The *Rasul* decision left a number of questions unanswered—with respect to both the scope of substantive rights that the detainees could assert in their habeas actions and the implications of the decision for persons detained in foreign locales lacking the distinctive features of Guantánamo Bay.[15] For present purposes, the key point is that the *Rasul* decision did not

[14] 542 US 466 (2004).

[15] See Richard H. Fallon, Jr. and Daniel J. Meltzer, *Habeas Corpus Jurisdiction, Substantive Rights, and the War on Terror*, 120 Harv L Rev 2029, 2059 n 116 (2007).

rest on the Constitution but only on an interpretation of the statute granting habeas corpus jurisdiction to the federal courts.

A different decision handed down the same day, *Hamdi v Rumsfeld*,[16] affirmed that Congress had authorized the Executive to engage in nonpunitive detention at least of those persons who were "'part of or supporting forces hostile to the United States or coalition partners' in Afghanistan and who 'engaged in an armed conflict against the United States there'"[17]—a form of detention that the Court found to be a "fundamental and accepted . . . incident of war."[18] (Some but not all of the detainees in *Boumediene* fell within that description.) The *Hamdi* decision proceeded to address the constitutional rights of an American citizen detained on that basis in the United States, and found that due process required more robust procedural protections in determining enemy combatant status than the Executive had provided.

The responses of the Executive and the Congress to those decisions set the stage for the decision in *Boumediene*. Within less than two weeks, the Executive constituted and established procedures for Combatant Status Review Tribunals (CSRT), military bodies charged with reviewing initial military determinations that aliens detained at Guantánamo Bay were properly held as enemy combatants.[19] These detainees eventually had the opportunity to have a CSRT hearing to determine whether the evidence supported their continued detention. The following year, Congress enacted the Detainee Treatment Act of 2005 (DTA),[20] which amended the habeas corpus statute to eliminate the jurisdiction that *Rasul* had recognized, establishing in its place a limited statutory review procedure in the D.C. Circuit. Under that procedure, the D.C. Circuit was given jurisdiction to assess "whether the status determination of the [CSRT] . . . was consistent with the standards and procedures spec-

---

[16] 542 US 507 (2004).

[17] Id at 516, quoting the Brief for Respondents, *Hamdi v Rumsfeld*, No 03-6696, *3 (filed Mar 29, 2004) (available on Westlaw at 2004 WL 724020). The outer boundaries of this category are quite uncertain, but on the facts alleged by the government, Hamdi undoubtedly fell within it.

[18] 542 US at 518.

[19] See Memorandum from Paul Wolfowitz, Deputy Secretary of Defense, to the Secretary of the Navy (July 7, 2004) [hereinafter Wolfowitz Memorandum], online at http://www.defenselink.mil/news/Jul2004/d20040707review.pdf (regarding an "Order Establishing Combatant Status Review Tribunal").

[20] 119 Stat 2739.

ified by the Secretary of Defense . . . and (ii) to the extent the Constitution and laws of the United States are applicable, whether the use of such standards and procedures to make the determination is consistent with the Constitution and laws of the United States."[21] And then in 2006, after the Supreme Court had invalidated the military commissions that the President had constituted to conduct war crimes prosecutions, the Military Commissions Act of 2006 (MCA)[22] reiterated and broadened the preclusion of habeas jurisdiction contained in the DTA, while making clear that the statutory limitation of jurisdiction applied retroactively to pending actions.[23] The combined effect of those statutes was to eliminate the jurisdiction of federal (and state) courts to entertain habeas corpus or other forms of actions filed by any alien determined by the military to be an enemy combatant (or awaiting such a determination)— except for review under the DTA.

The habeas cases of the *Boumediene* petitioners, pending in the lower courts after the *Rasul* decision, were dismissed by the D.C. Circuit in light of the elimination of statutory habeas jurisdiction by the MCA. Reasoning that aliens held outside the sovereign territory of the United States lacked any constitutional rights (including rights under the Suspension Clause), the court of appeals found no constitutional infirmity in the elimination of habeas jurisdiction and held that the only form of judicial review available was the statutory review procedure established by the DTA.[24]

Decisions about certiorari rarely merit discussion, but here, too, *Boumediene* is an exceptional case. On April 2, 2007, the Supreme Court denied the petition for certiorari filed by the detainees—over the dissent of Justice Breyer, joined by Justice Souter and in part by Justice Ginsburg.[25] Justices Stevens and Kennedy wrote a statement respecting the denial, invoking the traditional policy of re-

---

[21] § 1005(e)(2)(C) of the DTA, 119 Stat 2742.

[22] Pub L No 109-366, 120 Stat 2600, codified in relevant part at 28 USC § 2241(e) (Supp 2007).

[23] The MCA thus overrode the Court's ruling in *Hamdan v Rumsfeld*, 548 US 557, 576–77 (2006), that the DTA's preclusion of judicial review (other than under the DTA itself) did not apply to pending cases. See § 7(b) of the MCA, 120 Stat 2636. The MCA also extended the preclusion of non-DTA review to all aliens determined to be enemy combatants (or awaiting such a determination), wherever held; the DTA had applied only to those (like the *Boumediene* petitioners) detained at Guantánamo Bay. See § 7(a) of the MCA, 120 Stat 2636.

[24] 476 F3d 981 (DC Cir 2007).

[25] 127 S Ct 1478 (2007).

quiring exhaustion of available remedies (here, judicial review under the DTA) before invoking habeas jurisdiction. At the same time, they noted that exhaustion of inadequate remedies is not required, and added a warning that should the government unreasonably delay proceedings under the DTA, the Court had other means of reviewing the petitioners' contentions.[26] But as Justice Breyer noted in his dissenting opinion, the argument for exhaustion was problematic: the D.C. Circuit had held categorically that the petitioners lacked any constitutional rights, and so insofar as the habeas petitions claimed that the CSRT procedures were unconstitutional, exhaustion of DTA review could not address that question.[27]

After the denial of certiorari, the D.C. Circuit did have an opportunity, its first, to consider the scope of review available to detainees under the DTA. In *Bismullah v Gates*,[28] the government took a reasonably tough position on the scope of DTA review. As described in the Petitioners' Petition for Rehearing on their Petition for Certiorari in *Boumediene*, the government asserted that DTA review was limited to the record assembled before the CSRT, thus precluding the introduction of new documentary or testimonial evidence that a petitioner (or, more realistically, his lawyer) might otherwise proffer; that a detainee should have only three visits with counsel; that even counsel with security clearances could be denied access to classified information; and (contrary to representations made in oral argument in the D.C. Circuit in *Boumediene*) that under the DTA the only remedy available if a CSRT determination were successfully challenged would be a remand to another CSRT (rather than, for example, an order of release).[29] On that view, no court would ever have the power to order a detainee released.

The detainees sought rehearing on the petition for certiorari, and before the Court acted, more fuel was added to the fire. In their Reply Brief on Rehearing, the petitioners relied heavily on an affidavit from a military officer, described in more detail below,[30] that

---

[26] Id.

[27] Id at 1480–81.

[28] 501 F3d 178 (DC Cir 2007) (*Bismullah I*), reh'g denied, 503 F3d 137 (DC Cir 2007) (*Bismullah II*), reh'g en banc denied, 514 F3d 1291 (2008) (*Bismullah III*), vacated and remanded in light of *Boumediene v Bush*, 128 S Ct 2960 (2008), dismissed on remand, 2009 WL 48149 (DC Cir 2009).

[29] Petition for Rehearing on the Petition for Certiorari, *Boumediene v Bush*, No 06-1195 (filed Apr 27, 2007) (available on Westlaw at 2007 WL 1279631).

[30] See text accompanying note 189.

cast doubt on the fairness of the CSRT hearings.[31] All in all, the submissions on rehearing cast doubt on the adequacy of the CSRT/DTA process and on the capacity of the judiciary, were habeas jurisdiction not available, to do anything about it. And if Paul Freund was right that in what he once called the Newtonian world of Constitution, "excessive force in one direction is apt to produce a corresponding counterforce,"[32] it may be that the excessive force of the government's claim to be able to act without judicial oversight—a claim it had also made, but that had been rejected, at least in part, in earlier cases[33]—produced a counterforce sufficient to change the votes of some of the Justices on whether to grant certiorari. In any event, at the very end of the 2006–07 Term, in an extraordinary reversal, the Court granted rehearing in *Boumediene* of its decision on certiorari, vacated the April 2 order of denial, and granted certiorari.[34]

After the proceedings on certiorari, it was perhaps not a surprise that the Court again reversed the D.C. Circuit, ruling that the Suspension Clause does extend protections to aliens detained at Guantánamo Bay as enemy combatants. The Court proceeded to reach an issue that the D.C. Circuit had had no occasion to decide—whether, under the Suspension Clause, the judicial review procedures of the DTA were an adequate substitute for the writ of habeas corpus. Finding that they were not, the Court held § 7 of the MCA, insofar as it purported to eliminate habeas corpus jurisdiction for these petitioners, to be unconstitutional.

II. THE IMPORT OF THE SUSPENSION CLAUSE

The petitioners' constitutional challenge to § 7 of the MCA raised the question whether the protections of the Suspension Clause, however robust they are, extend to persons held as enemy combatants outside the sovereign territory of the United States. That question provoked a lengthy debate between Justice Kennedy's majority opinion and Justice Scalia's dissent. But it is important to note that that debate took as its premise—explicitly in the majority,

---

[31] Petitioners' Reply to Opposition to Petition for Rehearing, *Boumediene v Bush*, Nos 06-1195 and 06-1196 (filed June 22, 2007) (available on Westlaw at 2007 WL 4790792).

[32] See Freund, 88 Harv L Rev at 20 (cited in note 10).

[33] See notes 7–8.

[34] 127 S Ct 3078 (2007).

and, at least arguably, implicitly in the dissent—that the Suspension Clause provides an affirmative guarantee of the right to habeas corpus (or an adequate substitute) for those who fall within its scope.

That premise had never been authoritatively established in the Supreme Court. Indeed, given the uncertainty whether the Obama Administration will maintain the detention center at Guantánamo, or more generally will fashion a quite different set of policies for dealing with suspected terrorists, the significance of this ruling about the Suspension Clause could prove to be as great as, or greater than, the decision's implications for the treatment of detainees. Accordingly, this aspect of the decision merits attention of its own.

A. THE MEANING OF THE SUSPENSION CLAUSE

Habeas corpus has a long and complex history as a protection of individual liberty.[35] Some of that history was known to the Founders, who enshrined the writ in the Constitution. But consider the Suspension Clause's puzzling wording: "The Privilege of the Writ of Habeas Corpus shall not be suspended, unless when in Cases of Rebellion or Invasion the public Safety may require it." The language (unlike the initial version proposed at the Constitutional Convention[36] and the guarantees found in some of the founding states' constitutions[37]) does not explicitly guarantee the availability of habeas corpus,[38] in the way that the Bill of Rights guarantees particular protections. Rather, the Suspension Clause appears in a list of provisions in Article I, Section 9 that limit the power of the government (and specifically of Congress, in some cases explicitly and in others implicitly) to enact certain kinds of

---

[35] A recent and comprehensive review, with references to much of the earlier commentary, is Paul D. Halliday and G. Edward White, *The Suspension Clause: English Text, Imperial Contexts, and American Implications*, 94 Va L Rev 575 (2008).

[36] See Max Farrand, ed, 2 *The Records of the Federal Convention of 1787* 334 (Yale, 1937) (Journal August 20, 1787) ("The privileges and benefit of the writ of habeas corpus shall be enjoyed in this government in the most expeditious and ample manner: and shall not be suspended by the Legislature except upon the most urgent and pressing occasions, and for a limited time not exceeding months.").

[37] See, for example, Massachusetts Constitution of 1780, pt 2, ch 6, Art VII ("The privilege and benefit of the writ of *habeas corpus* shall be enjoyed in this commonwealth, in the most free, easy, cheap, expeditious, and ample manner; and shall not be suspended by the legislature, except upon the most urgent and pressing occasions, and for a limited time, not exceeding twelve months.").

[38] See William F. Duker, *A Constitutional History of Habeas Corpus* 126–29 (Greenwood, 1980).

laws. Thus, the Suspension Clause limits the occasions on which the writ may be suspended,[39] without, however, expressly guaranteeing that the writ will exist. Justice Kennedy's opinion for the Court in *Boumediene* cited two remarks in the Ratification Debates that had, nonetheless, interpreted the Suspension Clause as conferring an affirmative right to habeas corpus review,[40] but it is far from clear that there was a widely shared understanding to that effect. Indeed, some criticized the Constitution precisely because of its failure directly and expressly to guarantee the right to habeas corpus.[41]

Instead, the Suspension Clause seems to presuppose that in the United States, habeas corpus jurisdiction, as traditionally provided in England, the colonies,[42] and the American states,[43] would exist.[44] The role of habeas corpus as an affirmative remedy against official action was clearly understood.[45] At the same time, in the Founding era, questions about the relationship, in the novel constitutional republic being created, of various sources of law—constitution versus statute versus common law; federal law versus state law—had not been fully thought through.[46] Habeas corpus was a recognized common law remedy, and as Professor Casto has noted, lawyers of the era believed that the common law "existed independently of the state."[47] It seems more than plausible to suggest that it would have astonished the Framers to think that they had protected the writ against suspension (presumably by Congress)—

---

[39] See Halliday and White, 94 Va L Rev at 583, 701 (cited in note 35) (the privilege was taken by the Framers and their contemporaries to be self-evident).

[40] See 128 S Ct at 2246–57.

[41] See Rex A. Collings, Jr., *Habeas Corpus for Convicts—Constitutional Right or Legislative Grace?* 40 Cal L Rev 335, 342 (1952) (assembling criticism of the negative wording of the clause).

[42] The writ was used, albeit sparsely, in the colonies. See Halliday and White, 94 Va L Rev at 672 (cited in note 35); Duker, *Constitutional History* at 98–115 (cited in note 38).

[43] See Dallin H. Oaks, *Habeas Corpus in the States—1776–1865*, 32 U Chi L Rev 243, 248–49 (1965).

[44] See id at 248–49 (stating that because every state made the writ available, the Founders may not have focused on whether the Suspension Clause guaranteed the privilege of the writ).

[45] See Halliday and White, 94 Va L Rev at 629–30 (cited in note 35).

[46] See G. Edward White, 3–4 *History of the Supreme Court of the United States: The Marshall Court and Cultural Change, 1815–35* at 112–13 (Oxford, 1988); Meltzer, 86 Georgetown L J at 2553 (cited in note 2).

[47] William R. Casto, *The Supreme Court in the Early Republic: The Chief Justiceships of John Jay and Oliver Ellsworth* 34 (University of South Carolina, 1995).

but that Congress could achieve the same result, not by suspending a writ it had otherwise made available, but instead simply by precluding the federal courts from making it available in the first place. But, again, that is not what the text directly states.

Understanding the meaning of the Suspension Clause is complicated by a distinctive feature of Article III's organization of the new federal judiciary, often known as the Madisonian Compromise—that the inferior federal courts are courts of limited, not general, jurisdiction, and indeed, that under the constitutional plan, their existence and the scope of their jurisdiction is left to Congress.[48] That feature poses a difficulty for arguments that the federal courts had inherent power—whether based on the common law, on some conception of natural law, or on an imperative drawn from the Suspension Clause itself—to entertain habeas petitions. It poses a similar problem for related but distinct arguments that Congress was obliged to provide the federal courts with habeas jurisdiction, or that inferior federal courts, if and when created by Congress, were obliged to make the writ available. For if Congress need not create federal courts at all, or may confer on them only such portions of the categories of jurisdiction set forth in Article III, Section 2, as it thinks advisable, then it might seem to follow that there could be no inherent right to habeas corpus review *in federal court*.[49] The relationship of assumptions underlying the Suspension Clause to the power of Congress to control federal court jurisdiction—and, more specifically, to the possibility that the scope of federal judicial power otherwise conferred by positive law would not permit adequate exercise of the writ—was

---

[48] See generally Richard H. Fallon, Jr., Daniel J. Meltzer, and David L. Shapiro, *Hart and Wechsler's The Federal Courts and the Federal System* 7–9 (Foundation, 5th ed 2003) (hereafter *Hart and Wechsler*). The Madisonian Compromise had settled the issue of congressional control over the inferior federal courts eight days before Charles Pinckney, on August 20, 1787, proposed what eventually became the Suspension Clause. See Duker, *Constitutional History* at 128 (cited in note 38).

[49] Not everyone has accepted this point in the context of habeas corpus. Thus, Francis Paschal, *The Constitution and Habeas Corpus*, 1970 Duke L J 605, 607, asserts that the clause "is a direction to all superior courts of record, state as well as federal, to make the habeas privilege routinely available." On this view, the clause qualifies the general understanding of the Madisonian Compromise—if not of the notion that Congress has broad discretion whether to create lower federal courts, then surely of the accompanying notion, see, for example, *Sheldon v Sill*, 49 US (8 How) 441, 448–49 (1850), that Congress's discretion extends to how broadly to confer jurisdiction on such inferior courts as it does create.

not fully worked out.[50] And, one might wonder, what is left of the Suspension Clause if its limits on the power (presumably, of Congress[51]) to suspend the writ were beside the point in any situation in which Congress had never conferred jurisdiction to award the writ in the first place?

That question had not been squarely faced prior to *Boumediene* because Congress did confer a freestanding grant of habeas jurisdiction on the federal courts in § 14 of the Judiciary Act of 1789[52]—as least under the interpretation of that provision announced by Chief Justice Marshall in *Ex parte Bollman*[53] and followed ever since. At the same time, Marshall denied any claim of inherent judicial power, stating instead that the power of the federal courts to issue the writ must be given by written law.[54] In view of *Bollman*'s statutory holding, the observation about inherent power was unnecessary. Indeed, a recent comprehensive history of the writ argues that the 1789 Act "explicitly conferred habeas jurisdiction on the federal courts, but that those courts were already assumed to have habeas powers at common law, as had courts in colonial British America."[55] And Marshall was at the least aware of lurking problems, for he added: "Acting under the immediate influence of [the Suspension Clause, the members of the First Congress] must have felt, with peculiar force, the obligation of providing efficient means by which this great constitutional privilege should receive life and activity; for if the means be not in existence, the privilege itself would be lost, although no law for its suspension should be enacted. Under the impression of this obligation, they give to all the courts the power of awarding writs of habeas corpus."[56] This passage does not quite say that the Clause itself requires the vesting of jurisdiction, but it highlights the flip

---

[50] The *Boumediene* Court does cite one Founder, Edmund Randolph, who in the Virginia Ratifying Convention appeared to understand the tension, stating that the Suspension Clause was an "exception" to the power of Congress to regulate the courts. 128 S Ct at 2246, quoting 3 Jonathan Elliot, ed, *Debates in the Several State Conventions on the Adoption of the Federal Constitution* 460–64 (J. B. Lippincott, 2d ed 1876).

[51] For discussion of the powerful arguments that only the legislature may suspend the writ, see Jeffrey D. Jackson, *The Power to Suspend Habeas Corpus: An Answer from the Arguments Surrounding Ex parte Merryman*, 34 U Balt L Rev 11 (2004).

[52] Act of Sept 24, 1789, 1 Stat 73, 81–82.

[53] 8 US (4 Cranch) 75 (1807).

[54] Id at 93–94.

[55] See Halliday and White, 94 Va L Rev at 680 (cited in note 35).

[56] 8 US (4 Cranch) at 95.

side of the coin from Marshall's insistence that habeas jurisdiction depends upon the written law.

Beyond the apparent assumption of the Founders that habeas jurisdiction would (absent suspension) be operative, other considerations argue for reading the Suspension Clause as an affirmative guarantee of habeas relief. As David Shapiro has argued, "the habeas corpus remedy is essential to the full realization of certain other guarantees, most particularly that of due process of law in the Fifth Amendment. True, the Bill of Rights followed ratification, but there was a widespread understanding that it would follow, and the development of the writ in England was closely linked with the need to make effective the guarantees of the Magna Carta, especially that of due process of law. Indeed, the notion that a remedy of this kind is essential to the realization of the due process rights of those in custody might well support the conclusion that, had there been no Suspension Clause, such a remedy would still be implicitly mandated by the Constitution."[57]

Nonetheless, *Bollman* long stood as the Court's authoritative pronouncement on this subject. The few subsequent cases considering the Suspension Clause shed little light on the problem, as they concern statutes (*a*) that when limiting federal court habeas corpus jurisdiction, substituted statutory judicial review procedures designed to be essentially equivalent to habeas corpus (but considered in some respect to be more efficient) and (*b*) that also included a safety valve, permitting resort to the writ in the exceptional case in which the substitute review procedure was deemed to be inadequate.[58] Thus, it was not until 2001 that the

---

[57] David L. Shapiro, *Habeas Corpus, Suspension, and Detention: Another View*, 82 Notre Dame L Rev 59, 64–65 (2006). For sources noting the close connection between the writ, as it evolved in the battle against English despotism, and notions of due process, see Robert S. Walker, *The Constitutional and Legal Development of Habeas Corpus as the Writ of Liberty* 88 (Oklahoma State University, 1960); Daniel John Meador, *Habeas Corpus and Magna Carta* (University of Virginia, 1966). Justice Scalia, in his dissenting opinion in *Hamdi v Rumsfeld*, 542 US 507 (2004), a case in which the existence of federal court habeas jurisdiction was uncontested, stressed that habeas corpus was the means for protecting the due process rights of a citizen suspected of a crime—specifically, of the right, in his view, not to be deprived of liberty except by criminal charge and trial. See id at 556–57 (Scalia dissenting).

[58] See *Swain v Pressley*, 430 US 372 (1977) (substituting for federal habeas corpus a collateral review procedure in the D.C. local courts, in part to relieve the burdens on the federal court); *United States v Hayman*, 346 US 205 (1952) (substituting for federal habeas corpus a postconviction review procedure under 28 USC § 2255, primarily to redirect cases from overcrowded federal districts in which federal penitentiaries were located to the districts in which prisoners had been convicted and sentenced). The statutory remedy

Supreme Court decided a case in which it appeared that Congress might have precluded the exercise of habeas corpus jurisdiction without having supplied a substitute review procedure.[59]

That case was *INS v St. Cyr*,[60] which involved complex provisions of amendments to the immigration laws, whose plain meaning pushed strongly in the direction of eliminating all forms of judicial review—appellate review of agency decisions, habeas corpus review, and any other form of judicial inquiry—in a specified category of removal proceedings (into which St. Cyr's case fell). But the Court strained to read statutory provisions as leaving open the general grant of habeas corpus jurisdiction in § 2241 as a means by which St. Cyr could obtain judicial review. And in doing so, the Court suggested that such a reading was necessary to avoid the difficult question whether preclusion of all judicial review would violate the Suspension Clause.[61] In explaining its constitutional reasoning, the Court said that "at the absolute minimum, the Suspension Clause protects the writ 'as it existed in 1789.'"[62]

---

in *Swain* substituted, for Article III judges, local judges who lack Article III's tenure and salary protection, but the Supreme Court reasoned that if the untenured local judges may conduct criminal trials in the first place, they may also entertain collateral review proceedings. 430 US at 382–83. (The Court might have added that the Constitution did not guarantee that habeas corpus would be exercised by the federal courts. See text accompanying notes 69–71.)

[59] In *Felker v Turpin*, 518 US 651 (1996), the Court upheld a 1996 statutory amendment that restricted the ability of state prisoners detained pursuant to a criminal conviction to file more than one habeas petition in federal court. Chief Justice Rehnquist's opinion for a unanimous Court, after noting that before 1867 federal habeas corpus jurisdiction did not generally extend to persons in state custody and that collateral attacks on judgments of conviction rendered by courts of competent jurisdiction were not permitted until well into the twentieth century, nonetheless "assume[d], for purposes of decision here, that the Suspension Clause of the Constitution refers to the writ as it exists today, rather than as it existed in 1789." Id at 663. He proceeded to find no suspension, quoting *Bollman* for the proposition that a federal court's power to award the writ must be given by positive law, declaring that judgments about the proper scope of the writ are normally for Congress to make, and concluding that the restrictions on filing multiple petitions "are well within the compass of" the evolutionary process by which habeas jurisdiction had developed. Id at 664.

[60] 533 US 289 (2001).

[61] Id at 301 n 13.

[62] Id at 301. The year 1789 is a puzzling constitutional baseline; either 1787 (when the drafting was completed) or 1788 (when nine states had ratified the Constitution) seems more appropriate. The First Judiciary Act was enacted in 1789, but since Congress may extend habeas jurisdiction more broadly than the Constitution demands, the scope of the writ under that Act, except insofar as it reflects constitutional understandings, should not govern interpretation of the Suspension Clause.

The 1789 baseline may have entered the Court's decisions though carelessness. In *Swain v Pressley*, 430 US 372, 384 (1977), which upheld Congress's substitution, for habeas review of convictions obtained in the local D.C. courts, a postconviction proceeding in the local

That proposition drew a vigorous dissent from Justice Scalia (joined by Chief Justice Rehnquist and Justice Thomas), who disputed that the Suspension Clause "guarantee[s] any particular habeas right that enjoys immunity from suspension"[63] and contended instead that it requires only that whatever privilege of habeas corpus may exist at any particular time not be suspended except in cases of rebellion or invasion.[64] That position was supported, Justice Scalia argued, by *Bollman*'s insistence that federal court jurisdiction must rest on the written law; that being so, there could be no guarantee that federal courts would possess jurisdiction to issue the writ.[65] He acknowledged that the failure to vest habeas jurisdiction in the federal courts was subject to majoritarian abuse, but contended that it "is not the majoritarian abuse against which the Suspension Clause was directed."[66]

That was the state of play on the meaning of the Suspension Clause prior to *Boumediene*. Justice Kennedy's opinion for the Court essentially took the constitutional reasoning that had informed the statutory construction in *St. Cyr* and transformed it into a constitutional holding—that the Suspension Clause affirmatively confers a right to habeas corpus review and that, accordingly, the preclusion of habeas jurisdiction in § 7 of the MCA is unconstitutional. Many issues in the *Boumediene* case were the subject of dispute between majority and dissent, but unlike in *St. Cyr*, none of the dissenters in *Boumediene* objected that the Suspension Clause simply was not implicated if Congress permanently withdrew habeas jurisdiction over a particular set of cases. To be

---

courts themselves, see note 58, Chief Justice Burger's concurring opinion interpreted the Suspension Clause in light of the Framers' understanding and concluded that "[t]he writ *in 1789* was not considered 'a means by which one court of general jurisdiction exercises post-conviction review over the judgment of another court of like authority.'" Id at 385 (Burger concurring) (emphasis added), quoting Dallin Oaks, *Legal History in the High Court: Habeas Corpus*, 64 Mich L Rev 451 (1966). His opinion makes no reference to the scope of the jurisdiction conferred in the First Judiciary Act, instead stating that "'the writ protected by the suspension clause is the writ as known to the framers, not as Congress may have chosen to expand it.'" Id, quoting Henry J. Friendly, *Is Innocence Irrelevant? Collateral Attack on Criminal Judgements*, 38 U Chi L Rev 142, 170 (1970).

Subsequent decisions have echoed Chief Justice Burger's seemingly careless reference to 1789. See, for example, *St. Cyr*, 533 US at 301 (affirming that "at the absolute minimum, the Suspension Clause protects the writ 'as it existed in 1789'"), quoting *Felker v Turpin*, 518 US at 663–64.

[63] 533 US at 338 (Scalia dissenting).

[64] Id at 339–40.

[65] Id at 337.

[66] Id at 338.

sure, because the dissenters thought that, for other reasons, there
was no violation of the Suspension Clause in any event, that was
not a point on which they were obliged to take issue. But the way
that they phrased their conclusions is nonetheless suggestive: Justice Scalia said "[t]he writ as preserved in the Constitution would
not possibly extend farther than the common law provided when
that Clause was written,"[67] while Chief Justice Roberts acknowledged the holding in *St. Cyr* that as an absolute minimum, the
Suspension Clause protects the writ as it existed in 1789.[68]

Much of the attention to the *Boumediene* decision has focused
on the points on which the dissenters did take issue—the scope
of the writ along various dimensions, as well as broader questions
about the relationship of the courts to the political branches in
matters relating to national security. As a result, the Court's holding that the Suspension Clause confers an affirmative right to
habeas relief has not received the attention that it deserves. That
holding is not, of course, a surprise in light of *St. Cyr*. But the
puzzle of how to construe the unusual guarantee found in the
Suspension Clause had been the subject of considerable debate
and had not received an authoritative answer for more than two
centuries into our nation's history.

But even on that understanding, a subtler question remained:
If the Founders presupposed that the writ would be available, in
what courts would it be available? Some have argued that if federal
courts have only that jurisdiction (including habeas jurisdiction)
given them by Congress, then the Constitution cannot guarantee
the right of access to a *federal* court, for habeas corpus or any
other purpose. In a general version of this argument, Henry Hart
famously contended both that it is a premise of the Constitution
that some court must be open to hear a claim that the Constitution
entitles a litigant to judicial redress and that, given the Madisonian
Compromise, the state courts, which are courts of general jurisdiction, are the ultimate guardians of constitutional rights.[69] In

---

[67] 128 S Ct at 2297 (Scalia dissenting). In *Hamdi v United States*, 542 US 507 (2004),
no one disputed that the federal courts possessed habeas jurisdiction. Yet in his dissent,
some of Justice Scalia's reasoning was at least in tension with his position in *St. Cyr*. See
542 US at 558 ("The writ of habeas corpus was preserved in the Constitution—the only
common-law writ to be explicitly mentioned.").

[68] 128 S Ct at 2287 (Roberts dissenting).

[69] Henry M. Hart, Jr., *The Power of Congress to Limit the Jurisdiction of Federal Courts:
An Exercise in Dialectic*, 66 Harv L Rev 1362, 1364–65, 1401 (1953).

the more specific context of habeas corpus, this view suggests that the Suspension Clause, rather than guaranteeing *federal court* habeas corpus jurisdiction, instead restricts the power of Congress to interfere with *state court* habeas jurisdiction.[70] William Duker, who has advocated this position, notes among other things that the Clause appears in Article I, Section 9, other provisions of which also limit Congress's power vis-à-vis the states.[71]

In *Boumediene*, the Court appears to have passed entirely over this set of questions, simply assuming that if the congressional regime denied the detainees a constitutionally guaranteed right of access to habeas review, that constitutionally required review should be undertaken in federal court.[72] But even accepting Hart's general position—a position that, at least among commentators, is anything but uncontroversial,[73] and that poses special challenges in the unusual context of extraterritorial detention[74]—the Court's

---

[70] See Duker, *Constitutional History* at 126–80 (cited in note 38). See also Akhil Reed Amar, *Of Sovereignty and Federalism*, 96 Yale L J 1425, 1509 (1987). In discussing where the ultimate right to relief might reside if Congress failed to vest habeas jurisdiction in the federal courts, Duker's view would not preclude Congress from displacing state court habeas jurisdiction by making a grant of federal court habeas jurisdiction exclusive.

[71] See Duker, *Constitutional History* at 131–32 (cited in note 38). One might also note that state court judges, while they lack Article III's tenure and salary protection, are not under the influence of the federal political branches. See Daniel J. Meltzer, *Legislative Courts, Legislative Power, and the Constitution*, 65 Ind L J 291, 300 (1990).

[72] The Court does say that the Suspension Clause guarantees that, absent suspension, "the Judiciary will have . . . the writ, to maintain the 'delicate balance of governance.'" 128 S Ct at 2247 (quoting *Hamdi v United States*, 542 US at 536) (plurality). The capitalization of "Judiciary" might be taken to refer to the federal judiciary rather than the courts generally, but that is anything but evident, and surely this passage does not clearly express a constitutional requirement rather than an assumption about the appropriate outcome of this case.

[73] Numerous decisions have cited the observation of Professors Landis and Frankfurter that, as a result of statutory changes in Reconstruction, the federal courts "became the *primary* and powerful reliances for vindicating every right given by the Constitution, the laws, and treaties of the United States." See Felix Frankfurter and James Landis, *The Business of the Supreme Court: A Study in the Federal Judicial System* 65 (Macmillan ed, 1927), quoted, for example, in *Zwickler v Koota*, 389 US 241, 247 (1967). And numerous contemporary theories have been offered suggesting that state courts are not necessarily a *constitutionally* adequate substitute for federal courts in adjudicating federal rights. See, for example, Hart and Wechsler at 330–45 (cited in note 48). My own views are found in Daniel J. Meltzer, *The History and Structure of Article III*, 138 U Pa L Rev 1569 (1990).

[74] One might question whether state courts have extraterritorial jurisdiction to reach detentions at Guantánamo Bay and, if not, whether that problem exposes a flaw in Hart's premise. A plausible response is that state courts could assert jurisdiction over a custodian found within a state, and the local District of Columbia courts could do so over a custodian found within the District. There is a risk, however, that multiple courts (e.g., those of Virginia, Maryland, and the District of Columbia) might each assert jurisdiction over federal custodians found in each jurisdiction. To be sure, a similar problem could arise were multiple federal courts (those in Virginia, Maryland, and the District of Columbia)

assumption seems to be well grounded. First, the decisions in *Ableman v Booth*[75] and particularly in *Tarble's Case*,[76] much criticized[77] but never overruled, at the very least cast doubt upon the constitutional power of the state courts to issue habeas relief against federal custodians. Second, even if those decisions are read more narrowly as resting on an implied congressional preclusion of jurisdiction rather than on the state courts' lack of constitutional power,[78] the *Boumediene* Court's assumption that any constitutionally required relief should be provided in federal court still rests on solid ground. Assume that access to either federal court or state court would suffice to provide the constitutionally required review. Section 7 of the Military Commissions Act, in precluding all courts (other than the D.C. Circuit operating under the DTA) from exercising habeas or any other jurisdiction, could be viewed as having two subrules: (1) no federal court shall exercise such jurisdiction, and (2) no state court shall exercise such jurisdiction.[79] On the assumption that constitutionally adequate redress could be provided by either a federal or a state court, either subrule would be valid without the other. The issue then becomes a matter of statutory severability: if Congress could not constitutionally satisfy its first-order preference of precluding all review outside of the DTA, what second-order preference should the Court ascribe to Congress: eliminating the barrier to federal court jurisdiction or the barrier to state court jurisdiction?

The Court's unstated assumption that it was the barrier to federal court jurisdiction that should fall is entirely sound. To be sure, the Founders might not have shared that assumption; some have argued that they expected habeas jurisdiction to be exercised by the state courts,[80] and indeed that the Suspension Clause presupposed rather than guaranteed the writ because of the unquestioned

---

each to exercise jurisdiction, but in that case there are relatively good mechanisms for coordination and transfer.

[75] 62 US (21 How) 506 (1859).

[76] 80 US (13 Wall) 397, 411–12 (1872).

[77] Representative criticisms are collected in Todd Pettys, *State Habeas Relief for Federal Extrajudicial Detainees*, 92 Minn L Rev 265, 295–96 nn 172–75 (2007).

[78] See *Hart and Wechsler* at 437–39 (cited in note 48). For criticism of the implied preemption rationale, see Pettys, 92 Minn L Rev at 297–307 (cited in note 77).

[79] I take the terminology from Richard H. Fallon, Jr., *As-Applied and Facial Challenges and Third-Party Standing*, 113 Harv L Rev 1321 (2000).

[80] See Amar, 96 Yale L J at 1509 (cited in note 70); Pettys, 92 Minn L Rev at 309–10 (cited in note 77).

power of the state courts to issue it.[81] But here the decisions in *Ableman v Booth* and *Tarble's Case* become relevant insofar as they recognize a concern, born of experience rather than constitutional originalism, about the appropriateness of state court control of federal official action. That concern is also recognized by the broad provision of removal jurisdiction in 28 USC § 1442, permitting federal officers to remove state court actions—including state court actions that could not have been filed in the first instance in federal court. And most broadly of all, the aftermath of the Civil War and Reconstruction left us with a conception of federalism different from that embodied in the original Constitution,[82] one in which the role of the federal courts in protecting individual rights assumes far greater prominence. Relatedly, insofar as there has been judicial review of habeas petitions brought by enemy combatants detained by the United States, both before and after 9/11, that review has generally been in federal court.[83] And in sensitive matters of foreign relations, there is no reason to believe that Congress would have wished to have state rather than federal courts involved.

Thus, if one of the two subrules contained in § 7 must yield, it should be the one barring federal court review. And if that portion of § 7 of the MCA is held to be void, the federal courts, though courts of limited jurisdiction, could fall back upon the preexisting general grant of habeas jurisdiction under § 2241 as it previously stood, thereby avoiding any need to consider the more difficult situation in which the Suspension Clause applies but there is no background congressional grant of federal court jurisdiction on which to rely.

For all of these reasons, the Court's basic premise about where constitutionally required relief must be provided seems correct. Also correct, and of more fundamental importance, is the holding that the Suspension Clause affirmatively guarantees the right to habeas corpus review.

---

[81] See Collings, 40 Cal L Rev at 345 (cited in note 41); Meador, *Habeas Corpus* at 33 (cited in note 57).

[82] See Richard H. Fallon, Jr., *Reflections on the Hart and Wechsler Paradigm*, 47 Vand L Rev 953, 980–83 (1994).

[83] See, for example, *In re Yamashita*, 327 US 1 (1946); *Ex parte Endo*, 323 US 283 (1944); *Ex parte Quirin*, 317 US 1 (1942); *Ex parte Milligan*, 71 US (4 Wall) 2 (1866).

B. DID THE MCA SUSPEND THE WRIT?

The Government did not argue that the MCA constituted a congressional suspension of the privilege of the writ. On one view, that failure seems surprising. While one might doubt that the 9/11 attacks were an invasion or rebellion, it was at least arguable that those words should be given a broad construction, extending generally to warlike actions, both internal and external. If the government had taken that somewhat aggressive view, it could have added that Congress surely knew that it was curtailing habeas corpus for a specified set of potential petitioners and that questions about the constitutionality of that curtailment had been raised as the measure was being debated. Although it is true that the MCA did not expressly state that it was suspending the writ, other congressional legislation has been effective without referring to the constitutional power being exercised; notably, resolutions authorizing the commencement of hostilities (including the Authorization for the Use of Military Force enacted after 9/11,[84] which launched the war in Afghanistan) have been treated as adequate without using the linguistic formula "declaration of war."[85]

But given the legitimate uncertainty about whether the DTA/ MCA regime infringed any constitutional right to habeas possessed by the Guantánamo detainees (and four Justices thought it did not), Congress might have sought to limit what it viewed as a constitutionally gratuitous conferral of statutory jurisdiction (recognized by the *Rasul* decision) without seeking to trench on constitutional rights should its understanding of the Constitution be rejected by the Supreme Court. And there would have been a political price to pay had Congress and the President expressly advocated suspension of the writ. It is one thing to contend that the Guantánamo detainees, hardly a popular group with the voters, have no rights that are being infringed; it is another to contend that a most fundamental protection of liberty is being withdrawn. (That the writ has been suspended on only four previous occasions[86] and that the struggle against terrorism is not a conventional war would only highlight the extraordinary character of treating the MCA as an effort to

---

[84] Pub L No 107-40, 115 Stat 224, 224 (2001), note following 50 USC § 1541 (2000 ed Supp V).

[85] See Curtis Bradley and Jack Goldsmith III, *Congressional Authorization and the War on Terrorism*, 118 Harv L Rev 2047, 2057–66 (2005).

[86] See Duker, *Constitutional History* at 149, 178 n 190 (cited in note 38).

suspend.) The political price highlights an underlying normative point: because suspension of so fundamental a liberty is a rare and solemn act, the Court should impose a clear statement requirement,[87] requiring that Congress plainly seek to suspend the writ (as it has done with respect to all past measures that have been treated as suspensions).[88] Against that background, the Court's assumption that no suspension was intended seems well founded.

C. EXTRATERRITORIALITY AND GUANTÁNAMO BAY

1. *Interpretive methodology: the functional approach.* Even if the Suspension Clause is an affirmative grant of a right to habeas corpus, numerous questions arise, along multiple dimensions, about the scope of that right. Justice Scalia's dissent in *Boumediene* addressed one such issue, the territorial scope of the writ. He relied on an extensive originalist survey to suggest that the writ never had extended to an alien held as an enemy combatant outside the sovereign territory of the United States.[89] And he argued that fidelity to original intent is especially important with respect to the Suspension Clause, "when (as here) the Constitution limits the power of Congress to infringe upon a pre-existing common-law right."[90]

There is no need to rehearse the general debate over originalism, except to note that some of the general concerns about the difficulty of principled application of originalist methodology— including the paucity of reported cases, the variability and indeterminacy of the historical materials, the difficulty of understanding fully the context and set of understandings in which they were embedded, and the uncertainty of how to apply them to current

---

[87] See Cass R. Sunstein, *Interpreting Statutes in the Regulatory State*, 103 Harv L Rev 405 (1989) (advocating canons of construction that would avoid constitutional doubt, promote political accountability, preserve hearing rights, and promote the rule of law); Ernest A. Young, *Constitutional Avoidance, Resistance Norms, and the Preservation of Judicial Review*, 78 Tex L Rev 1549 (2000) (stressing the importance of resistance norms in order to protect enduring public values, including avoiding incursions on the power of judicial review).

[88] Duker, *Constitutional History* at 149, 178 n 190 (cited in note 38).

[89] Oddly, all four dissenters joined both the Chief Justice's dissent and Justice Scalia's dissent. The former says that the question whether the writ runs to Guantánamo is difficult, see 128 S Ct at 2279 (Roberts dissenting), while the latter argues that the obvious answer to the question is no, see id at 2302 (Scalia dissenting).

[90] Id at 2303 (Scalia dissenting).

circumstances[91]—are all in evidence with regard to the Suspension Clause.[92] But it is worth exploring whether there is anything to Justice Scalia's contention that the Suspension Clause is a particularly appropriate domain for originalist analysis.

Arguing against an originalist approach (or what we labeled an "agency" approach), Richard Fallon and I have put forward an alternative vision which we called a common law approach to the writ of habeas corpus.[93] In broad terms, that approach is similar to the "functional approach" endorsed by Justice Kennedy's majority opinion. In advocating a common law approach as against Justice Scalia's position, one can begin (ironically) with a textual point: the writ protected by the Suspension Clause was a common law writ, one that by the time of the Founding had already evolved over the years, primarily as a matter of judicial rather than statutory development.[94] To deny this common law writ the ordinary common law evolution, instead reading the Constitution as freezing in place a snapshot (if one could imagine such a thing) of the writ on a particular moment in this evolutionary course, would be a departure from the history of the writ with which the Founders were familiar. Beyond that textual point, Fallon and I stressed that common law evolution had been the writ's history in American practice (although, admittedly, much of the evolution could be viewed as an elaboration of the scope of the statutory grant of jurisdiction rather than of the constitutional guarantee).[95] A notable example is the Court's decision to extend habeas corpus to American citizens detained overseas in the military justice system—rejecting a long-standing rule that a district court lacked jurisdiction over petitioners who were not in custody within the court's territorial jurisdiction.[96] Hence, we rested in part upon "a

---

[91] See generally David A. Strauss, *Why Conservatives Shouldn't Be Originalists*, 31 Harv J L & Pub Pol 969, 970–72 (2008). A fine summary of key objections to originalism and citations is found in an article attempting, in my judgment unpersuasively, to respond to them. See Richard S. Kay, *Adherence to the Original Intentions in Constitutional Adjudication: Three Objections and Responses*, 82 Nw U L Rev 226 (1988).

[92] See Halliday and White, 94 Va L Rev at 588–93 (cited in note 35); Shapiro, 82 Notre Dame L Rev at 65–68 (cited in note 57).

[93] Fallon and Meltzer, 120 Harv L Rev (cited in note 15).

[94] That theme is stressed in Halliday and White, 94 Va L Rev at 608–13 (cited in note 35).

[95] Fallon and Meltzer, 120 Harv L Rev at 2044 (cited in note 15).

[96] See *Toth v Quarles*, 350 US 11 (1955); *Burns v Wilson*, 346 US 137 (1953). Justice Scalia's insistence that habeas corpus lacks extraterritorial application fits poorly with these

Burkean recognition of the wisdom of adhering to traditional practices of decisionmaking and allocations of power that have worked
well, and in part upon the desirability of courts' acknowledging
and confronting issues presented by new and challenging circumstances, within the framework of the traditions established by the
common law evolution."[97]

The problems posed by American efforts after 9/11 to combat
terrorism in some ways make an especially appropriate case for
such evolution.[98] The current challenges differ from those posed
by conventional wars. (Many, though not all, commentators also
argue that they differ from efforts to address conventional criminal
activity.[99]) We are confronting not a nation but residents of many
nations, with all but one of which (Afghanistan) we are at peace.
The enemy fights not in uniforms on battlefields but through
stealth, targeting primarily civilians, operating in loosely affiliated
transnational networks, motivated not by territorial ambition but
by ideological or religious opposition. There is no representative
of the enemy with the capacity to surrender or to sign an armistice,
and hence no end to this battle is in sight. The U.S. response to
the threat consists not merely of the deployment of force but also
of the use of sophisticated intelligence apparatuses to piece together information. Because the enemy is not obviously identifiable and sometimes suspicion is based on information that is incomplete or of uncertain reliability, the risk of mistaken
assessments of whether an individual is connected to terrorist activity is high, and the harm from false positives (detention of the
innocent, potentially indefinitely) or false negatives (failure to in-

decisions. In his dissent in *Rasul*, he suggested they represented an "atextual exception
thought to be required by the Constitution." 542 US at 497 (Scalia dissenting). In *Boumediene*, he said, the common law writ received into our constitutional republic "took on
such changes as were demanded by a system in which rule is derived from the consent of
the governed, and in which citizens (not 'subjects') are afforded defined protections against
the Government." 128 S Ct at 2306. But, of course, noncitizens also enjoy constitutional
rights, and so his discussion merely begs the question whether aliens detained at Guantánamo Bay, like aliens in the United States, or citizens detained abroad, enjoy rights
under the Suspension Clause.

[97] For a powerful elaboration of such an approach to constitutional interpretation generally, see David A. Strauss, *Common Law Constitutional Interpretation*, 63 U Chi L Rev
877 (1996). For skepticism, see Adrian Vermeule, *Common Law Constitutionalism and the
Limits of Reason*, 107 Colum L Rev 1482 (2007).

[98] Fallon and Meltzer, 120 Harv L Rev at 2033 (cited in note 15).

[99] See, for example, Robert Chesney and Jack Goldsmith, *Terrorism and the Convergence
of the Criminal and Military Detention Models*, 60 Stan L Rev 1079 (2008); Bradley and
Goldsmith, 118 Harv L Rev at 2068 (cited in note 85).

capacitate dangerous terrorists) is great.[100] This set of circumstances has led to a broad range of differing prescriptions, but
there is a "widely shared belief that the present situation urgently
demands legal and constitutional adaptation."[101] Accordingly, an
evolutionary or common law approach to the writ in especially
attractive.

Justice Scalia's dissent nonetheless argues that fidelity to original
intent is especially important with respect to the Suspension
Clause, "when (as here) the Constitution limits the power of Congress to infringe upon a pre-existing common-law right."[102] The
basis for that contention is not entirely clear. But if a key argument
for originalism is the claim that it cabins the power of courts,
when exercising the power of judicial review, to place matters
beyond the control of the political branches, then Justice Scalia
seems to have it backwards. That argument for originalism, at
least, has less, not more, grip with respect to the Suspension Clause
than with respect to other constitutional provisions, in view of the
unique quality of the Suspension Clause—that it recognizes a legislative power to suspend the constitutional right that it confers.
There is always a question whether legal adaptation should be
undertaken by the courts, when interpreting the Constitution, or
by the legislature as a matter of policy. But a key argument against
constitutional adaptation is sharply muted when constitutional rulings may be overridden by simple legislation rather than only by
the extraordinarily difficult process of constitutional amendment.
As a result, the Suspension Clause, rather than calling for special
judicial hesitance about permitting constitutional evolution, if anything might tolerate such evolution more easily than would other
constitutional provisions.[103]

---

[100] See Bradley and Goldsmith, 118 Harv L Rev at 2124 (cited in note 85).

[101] Fallon and Meltzer, 120 Harv L Rev at 2033 (cited in note 15); accord, Wittes, *Law and the Long War* at 154–68 (cited in note 12).

[102] 128 S Ct at 2303.

[103] See Fallon and Meltzer, 120 Harv L Rev at 2045 (cited in note 15). This characterization of the Suspension Clause assumes that a valid suspension does not merely
withdraw the privilege of the writ—which is, after all, only one particular remedy for
unlawful detention—while leaving detainees free to seek other remedies, such as damages,
but instead immunizes the covered executive action from judicial redress generally. For a
defense of that assumption, see Shapiro, 82 Notre Dame L Rev (cited in note 57); Amanda
Tyler, *Suspension as an Emergency Power*, 118 Yale L J (2008–2009). The opposing view is
argued forcefully, but in my judgment unconvincingly, in Trevor Morrison, *Hamdi's Habeas
Puzzle: Suspension as Authorization?* 91 Cornell L Rev 411 (2006), and Trevor Morrison,
Suspension and the Extrajudicial Constitution, 107 Colum L Rev 1533 (2007).

In any event, the opinions spilled a great deal of ink about the status of habeas corpus in English and American history leading up to the Founding, and Justice Scalia succeeded in part in inducing Justice Kennedy to address matters on these terms. The difficulty with the resulting debate, as already suggested, is the absence of applicable precedents—in this case, of eighteenth-century decisions addressing the detention of persons who were (*a*) deemed by the government to be enemies but who were not members of official armed forces or citizens of hostile nations, (*b*) held in a location with the characteristics of the naval base at Guantánamo Bay, (*c*) under modern conditions of transportation and communication.[104] Whether or not his review of the historical materials is entirely convincing,[105] Justice Kennedy is at least relatively straightforward in acknowledging these difficulties.[106] And in the end, there is something more than a bit strange in trying to determine from the scanty available records whether the modern American naval base at Guantánamo Bay is more like eighteenth-century Scotland, Berwick-upon-Tweed, Ireland, or areas in the Indian subcontinent in which the East India Company operated but which remained under the formal sovereignty of the Moghul Emperor.

Justice Kennedy's opinion makes clear, persuasively in my judg-

---

[104] See 128 S Ct at 2262.

[105] He has to wrestle, in particular, with the English decisions that the writ does not run to Scotland. His suggestion that this limitation arose from the difficulties, in eighteenth-century conditions, of extending the writ to such a distant location, see id at 2250, is unconvincing, as Justice Scalia notes, id at 2206 (Scalia dissenting), given that the Channel Islands presented similar difficulties but were within the scope of the writ. Justice Kennedy's further argument that the English courts were resting on a kind of abstention in favor of the Scottish court system is ingenious but made quite hesitantly. See id at 2250 ("we cannot disregard the possibility that the common-law courts' refusal to issue the writ to these places was motivated not by formal legal constructs but by what we would think of as prudential concerns"). The hesitance may be appropriate, as the importation of modern abstention concerns is perhaps anachronistic, and he was unable to point to contemporary sources articulating this basis for the refusal to extend the writ to Scotland.
In other respects, however, Justice Kennedy is relatively cautious in his evaluation of the historical materials. For example, he declines to endorse the conclusion of a leading article that viewed the extension of the English writ to territory in the Indian subcontinent that was not part of the British empire as supporting a broad conception of the writ's territorial reach. See Halliday and White, 94 Va L Rev at 593–613, 700, 704–05 (cited in note 35). Instead, Justice Kennedy noted that because the court exercising that jurisdiction was created by a special English statute and was located in the Indian subcontinent, its example does not necessarily indicate the jurisdictional scope of a common law court in England exercising the traditional common law habeas corpus jurisdiction. 128 S Ct at 2249.

[106] Id at 2251.

ment, that the precedents provide little guidance for the distinctive question before the Court. But despite Justice Scalia's criticism of the majority for lack of clarity on this point,[107] the Court does not express a clear view on the important question whether the Suspension Clause protects only the scope of the writ at the time of the Founding (insofar as that can be ascertained) or instead is appropriately viewed as subject to common law evolution. Justice Kennedy says only that "[t]he Court has been careful not to foreclose the possibility that the protections of the Suspension Clause have expanded" since the Founding and, quoting the *St. Cyr* decision, that "the analysis may begin with precedents as of 1789, for the Court has said that 'at the absolute minimum' the Clause protects the writ as it existed when the Constitution was drafted and ratified."[108]

The Justices in the majority may not have seen eye to eye on this question, thus requiring ambiguity to garner consensus, or may simply have wished to advance a minimalist rationale.[109] But in the end, the implication of the majority's opinion, it seems to me, is that the Suspension Clause, like other constitutional provisions, is not frozen in time. For the majority consults not only the founding era history but also a broader "historical narrative of the writ and its function" in promoting the separation of powers.[110] And in ascertaining the scope of the writ, it makes clear that the reach of the Suspension Clause depends on functional assessments of a broad range of prudential and practical considerations.[111] That cluster of factors will have quite different significance today than two centuries ago. Consider, for example, simply the practicality of the exercise of jurisdiction by the federal district court in the District of Columbia over Guantánamo Bay.

---

[107] Id at 2297 n 2 (Scalia dissenting).

[108] Id at 2248. Note that the Chief Justice's dissent, after discussing the scope of the writ for prisoners of war at the time of the Founding, proceeds to argue that even "[a]ssuming the constitutional baseline is more robust," there is no constitutional violation. Id at 2287 (Roberts dissenting).

[109] See generally Sunstein, 2004 Supreme Court Review 47 (cited in note 13) (arguing that courts encountering national security issues have characteristically followed a particular form of minimalist decision making).

[110] 128 S Ct at 2248.

[111] See id at 2253–62. Of course, one might respond that the opinion could be read as holding that the original understanding of the Suspension Clause was a functional one that contemplated the kind of evolution evidenced by *Boumediene*. Such a version of originalism, however logical, is clearly not how that term is ordinarily used.

Whatever difficulties may be encountered today pale in significance compared to those that would have existed under eighteenth-century transportation and communication conditions.
The Court also stressed that the writ, as an "indispensable mechanism for monitoring the separation of powers," cannot be subject
to manipulation by the Executive, "whose power it is designed to
restrain."[112] That observation, too, suggests a forward-looking,
purposive approach.

2. *The open-ended quality of the functional approach.* Justice Scalia
complained that the Court's functional approach was open ended,
a fair characterization illustrated by the application of that approach to the question whether the Suspension Clause ever requires the availability of the writ when sought by aliens detained
at locations outside American territory, over which the United
States lacks the rather extraordinary de facto control that it has
at Guantánamo Bay. Functional approaches can be applied in a
more or less fine-grained way: Justice Scalia's view in dissent that
the Suspension Clause does not protect aliens anywhere outside
of American sovereign territory (including Guantánamo) could be
defended on the functional ground that efforts to exercise habeas
jurisdiction over detentions beyond American territory will often
encounter practical problems[113] and will concern aliens whose
claims on American courts are not especially strong. Exceptions
to that generalization exist, but rules by their nature may be overinclusive or underinclusive with respect to their underlying purposes, and yet there are functional reasons that favor rules.[114] The
majority's framing of the functional approach is more fine-grained,
subdividing the nonsovereign category into two: (i) areas, like
Guantánamo, that are under exclusive de facto American control
and (ii) areas abroad that are outside our de facto control. A still
more fine-grained functional analysis would reject any use of categories in favor of applying functional criteria directly to the particular circumstances of each case.[115]

---

[112] Id at 2259.

[113] Id at 2299 (Scalia, J, dissenting).

[114] See Kathleen M. Sullivan, *Foreword: The Justices of Rules and Standards*, 106 Harv L
Rev 22, 58 (1992).

[115] The problem is similar to a familiar one in First Amendment law, the difference
between definitional and ad hoc balancing. See, for example, Wallace Mendelson, *The
First Amendment and the Judicial Process: A Reply to Mr. Frantz*, 17 Vand L Rev 479 (1964);
Melville B. Nimmer, *The Right to Speak from Times to Time: First Amendment Theory Applied
to Libel and Misapplied to Privacy*, 56 Cal L Rev 935 (1968).

The varying readings given to the leading precedent of *Johnson v Eisentrager*[116] highlight the open-endedness of the functional approach. In *Eisentrager*, the Court rejected habeas petitions from German nationals who were held in an American prison in occupied Germany, after having been convicted by a U.S. military commission in China of violating the laws of war by continuing military action against the United States following Germany's surrender in 1945. Justice Jackson's opinion does not make clear whether the dismissal rested on a determination that the federal courts lacked jurisdiction, that the petitioners lacked constitutional or other rights on the basis of which to challenge the legality of their detention, or that, because there had been no violation of the petitioners' rights (perhaps because they had none), no constitutional question was raised by dismissing for lack of jurisdiction.[117] But whatever the precise holding, the Court rested in part on the practical difficulties of an effort to exercise habeas jurisdiction across oceans and even potentially during hostilities.[118] In *Boumediene*, Justice Scalia viewed Justice Jackson's argument about practicalities as part of a categorical balancing analysis, whose conclusion was that the writ never extends extraterritorially—at least as to alien petitioners.[119] For the majority in *Boumediene*, Justice Jackson's argument called for a more fine-grained functional analysis, and the Court explained why exercise of the writ would be more practical with respect to the detainees at Guantánamo than it was with respect to the German prisoners in *Eisentrager*.[120] Thus, mere endorsement of a functional approach does not answer the question of how broad the extraterritorial reach of the writ will be.

There are surely some statements in the majority opinion from which one could construct an argument that the Court is moving

---

[116] 339 US 763 (1950).

[117] See Fallon and Meltzer, 120 Harv L Rev at 2056 (cited in note 15).

[118] 339 US at 778–79.

[119] 128 S Ct at 2299 (Scalia dissenting). The qualification is required by the post-*Eisentrager* decisions in *Toth v Quarles*, 350 US 11 (1955), and *Burns v Wilson*, 346 US 137 (1953), in which the Court exercised jurisdiction over petitions by American citizens detained abroad by military authorities.

[120] 128 S Ct at 2252. The Court's recognition that separation-of-powers principles protect aliens as well as citizens was qualified by the statement that those principles may be asserted by foreign nationals "who have the privilege of litigating in our courts." Id at 2246.

in the direction of a broader, extraterritorial reach for the writ with respect to detentions of aliens overseas.[121] For example, the Court finds in *Eisentrager* and the *Insular Cases*[122] a common thread: "the idea that questions of extraterritoriality turn on objective factors and practical concerns, not formalism."[123] And the Court expresses concern that the government might by manipulation seek to defeat the protections of the writ,[124] a concern that might be triggered if the United States could avoid habeas jurisdiction by detaining aliens in a foreign country rather than at Guantánamo Bay. Finally, Justice Kennedy gives little emphasis to a central part of Justice Jackson's reasoning in *Eisentrager*—that aliens who lack prior connection to the United States, and indeed, who are enemies of America, lack a claim to have rights extended to them by our nation.[125]

Despite these portions of the opinion, I doubt that *Boumediene* will end up standing for the proposition that the writ protected by the Suspension Clause extends worldwide. Such a prophecy is hazardous, for the meaning of a precedent depends not simply on its words but also, when (as is ordinarily true, and certainty true of *Boumediene*) multiple characterizations are possible, on the readings given by future courts.[126] Still, I doubt that *Boumediene* will have broad application outside of Guantánamo Bay. The Court, in its historical analysis, states that it could find no authorities involving detention of enemy combatants "held in a territory, like Guantánamo, over which the Government has total military and civil control."[127] Then, in distinguishing the English courts' withholding of the writ from persons held in Scotland, on the basis

---

[121] Earlier, in the *Rasul* opinion, the Court sought to limit the scope of *Eisentrager* without squarely reaffirming it, and, in noting that habeas jurisdiction would reach an American citizen detained at Guantánamo, said that "there is little reason to think that Congress intended the geographical coverage of the statute to vary depending on the detainee's citizenship." 542 US at 481. But the *Rasul* decision was an interpretation of the habeas statute as it then stood, not of the Constitution, and, moreover, it was full of conflicting indications about whether aliens detained not at Guantánamo Bay but elsewhere overseas could invoke habeas jurisdiction. See Fallon and Meltzer, 120 Harv L Rev at 2059 n 116 (cited in note 15).

[122] See, for example, *Balzac v Porto Rico*, 258 US 298, 311–12 (1922).

[123] 128 S Ct at 2258–59.

[124] Id.

[125] *Eisentrager*, 339 US at 770–71.

[126] See generally, for example, Frederick Schauer, *Precedent*, 39 Stan L Rev 571 (1987).

[127] 128 S Ct at 2248.

that Scotland applied its own law and that conflicts might otherwise have arisen, the Court notes that no Cuban court and no law other than American law govern Guantánamo.[128] The majority goes on to declare: "Given the *unique* status of Guantánamo Bay and the particular dangers of terrorism in the modern age, the common-law courts simply may not have confronted cases with close parallels to this one."[129] The opinion then emphasizes that the lease agreements with Cuba give the United States complete jurisdiction and control and the right unilaterally to renew the arrangement in perpetuity; as a result, the United States "maintains *de facto* sovereignty" over Guantánamo."[130] Again, the Court says that (unlike the German prison in *Eisentrager*), "Guantánamo Bay . . . is no transient possession. In every practical sense Guantánamo is not abroad; it is within the constant jurisdiction of the United States."[131] There are few if any locations outside of American sovereignty, other than Guantánamo Bay, that share all of the characteristics noted by the Court.

A second perspective on the implications of *Boumediene* for detention overseas would focus less on the language of the majority's opinion and more on underlying policy concerns that are relevant to the kind of functional approach that the majority advanced. In *Boumediene*, the government contended that an effort to distinguish Guantánamo from other areas outside U.S. sovereign territory would launch the courts down a path on which they would be required simply to resolve the threshold question of jurisdiction, to inquire into delicate military, intelligence, or diplomatic considerations.[132] As applied to the situation in Guantánamo that was before the Court in *Boumediene*, the contention seems overdrawn, as the facts about its status were relatively clear, the practical and logistical concerns that Justice Kennedy analyzed did not seem especially troublesome, and assessment of the situation did

---

[128] Id at 2249–51.

[129] Id at 2251 (emphasis added).

[130] Id at 2253.

[131] Id at 2261. And after stressing Guantánamo Bay's uniqueness, the Court adds that "if the United States were answerable to another sovereign for its acts on the naval base, or if the detention were in an active theater of war," "arguments that issuing the writ would be 'impracticable or anomalous' would have more weight." Id at 2261–62, quoting *Reid v Covert*, 354 US 1, 74 (1957) (Harlan concurring).

[132] Brief for Respondents, *Boumediene v Bush*, Nos 06-1195 and 06-1196, *25 (filed Oct 9, 2007) (available on Westlaw at 2007 WL 2972541).

not require evaluation of sensitive military, intelligence, or diplomatic considerations. But the broader concern is a real one—for in many other areas, applying Justice Kennedy's functional test in a highly particularized, case-by-case fashion could produce a very messy jurisdictional inquiry at the threshold.[133] Efforts to establish habeas jurisdiction worldwide, in areas deemed sufficiently within U.S. control, would require the courts to try to assess whether a particular case raises matters relating to espionage so delicate as not to permit judicial inquiry, or to determine whether we might hold so many prisoners abroad in a conventional war as to make judicial intervention, however valuable, simply impracticable.[134] Moreover, what seems practical when a petition is filed might change considerably during the course of litigation

---

[133] This paragraph draws on Fallon and Meltzer, 120 Harv L Rev at 2057–58 (cited in note 15).

Insofar as the question, given the Court's current membership, may turn on Justice Kennedy's vote, it is worth noting that his opinion concurring in the judgment in *Rasul* reaffirmed that *"Eisentrager* indicates that there is a realm of political authority over military affairs where the judicial power may not enter." 542 US at 487 (Kennedy concurring in the judgment). He did not seek to undermine *Eisentrager* but rather to distinguish it on two bases. The former—that here the detainees were being held indefinitely without having received a full military trial—might apply to detainees held anywhere, and indeed would apply a fortiori if persons detained overseas had not even received process equivalent to a CSRT determination. But the second basis of distinction—that Guantánamo Bay is "in every practical respect a United States territory" and is "far removed from any hostilities," id at 487–88—would suggest a more limited reading.

[134] In considering the scope of habeas jurisdiction abroad, one could imagine a more particularized inquiry along a different dimension. Most aliens detained abroad, like those in *Boumediene*, will lack other contacts with the United States. But that will not invariably be the case, and where it is not, a simple rule that aliens truly abroad fall outside the reach of the Suspension Clause could have harsh repercussions. To take a variant of a hypothetical posed by Fallon and Meltzer, 120 Harv L Rev at 2058 (cited in note 15), imagine that a captured terrorist contends, after coercive interrogation, that a person who had been a lawful resident alien in the United States until employed in Iraq by the military as a translator was in fact aiding forces hostile to the United States. Should the translator, if detained by the military, have no right to contest the allegations? Here, as elsewhere, clear rules have their customary virtues. But the number of such cases is likely to be small, and the particularized inquiry necessary at the threshold would concern prior contacts with the United States rather than military or diplomatic considerations bearing on the degree of American control, and hence would be far less intrusive or sensitive. A basis for conducting such an inquiry seems fairly rooted both in *Eisentrager* and in other cases that recognize the constitutional significance of an alien's prior contacts with the United States. See *Eisentrager,* 339 US at 770 ("The alien, to whom the United States has been traditionally hospitable, has been accorded a generous and ascending scale of rights as he increases his identity with our society. Mere lawful presence in the country creates an implied assurance of safe conduct and gives him certain rights"); *Landon v Plasencia,* 459 US 21, 32–34 (1982) (despite the long-standing doctrine that aliens excluded at the border lack due process rights, permitting a lawful permanent resident alien, stopped at the border when seeking to reenter the United States after a brief absence, to assert a due process claim).

in locales, unlike Guantánamo, in which there is less assurance of long-term stability. As Richard Fallon and I have written, "[n]otwithstanding modern transportation and communications, there could be considerable difficulties in litigating, in the United States, claims pertaining to detentions in distant areas over which American control rests on a temporary and possibly fragile military balance. (Imagine moving detainees, witnesses, or lawyers around in Baghdad today to develop evidence for a habeas proceeding.)"[135] Thoughtful arguments have been offered that these kinds of concerns can be addressed by adopting a deferential standard of review, rather than treating these matters as beyond the jurisdiction of American courts.[136] But the question remains how to assess the costs and benefits of even starting down the path. There are so many imponderables as to make confident assessment difficult. The point here is simply that there are plausible reasons to support a narrow reading of the opinion as extending habeas jurisdiction to Guantánamo Bay but not generally to detentions of aliens anywhere in the world.[137]

A final perspective on the territorial scope of the Suspension

---

[135] Fallon and Meltzer, 120 Harv L Rev at 2057 (cited in note 15).

[136] See, for example, David A. Martin, *Offshore Detainees and the Role of Courts After Rasul v Bush: The Underappreciated Virtues of Deferential Review*, 25 BC Third World L J 125 (2005).

[137] Any geographic limitation to habeas jurisdiction could create incentives for officials to hold detainees in some places and not others in order to avoid the risk of judicial review. If aliens "truly" abroad are outside habeas jurisdiction, military officials may hesitate to bring them from foreign countries to Guantánamo or the United States, where the conditions of confinement might be more secure or humane but where habeas jurisdiction would attach.

The only way to avoid some kind of perverse incentive is to establish a fully worldwide jurisdiction, and even that would not eliminate incentives to escape judicial review—for the United States could still engage in extraordinary rendition, for example, so that detainees are no longer in American custody. We know that the government already has engaged in such actions, sometimes with horrifying results. See generally Jane Mayer, *The Dark Side* (Doubleday, 2008). There is, in short, no simple solution to the incentives problem.

Whether detainees, once having been detained in Guantánamo, would lose their rights under the Suspension Clause if transported abroad and detained there by the United States raises distinct questions. It surely is relevant that the Habeas Corpus Act of 1679, 31 Car 2, c 2 (1679), in order to prevent the king from defeating the jurisdiction of the English courts, forbade transporting prisoners "into any Parts Garrisons Islands or Places beyond the Seas." See Helen A. Nutting, *The Most Wholesome Law—The Habeas Corpus Act of 1679*, 65 Am Hist Rev 527 (1960). And at least as to detainees who had filed petitions prior to being moved, the decision in *Ex parte Endo*, 323 US 283 (1944), provides that a district court that initially has jurisdiction over a habeas petition does not lose it when the government transfers the petitioner outside the court's territorial jurisdiction. (*Endo*, to be sure, involved a transfer to a different district within the United States rather than abroad.)

Clause would be more in the tradition of legal realism, and would focus on possible motivations for the decision not expressed in the opinion—motivations that would explain both why habeas jurisdiction was recognized over Guantánamo and why the Court might not take the further step of holding that the Suspension Clause extends worldwide. One might view the majority's ruling here (as well as in *Rasul*, *Hamdi*, and *Hamdan*) as influenced by general concerns, extending beyond any particular case, that the Bush Administration was claiming an excessive degree of unilateral Executive power, that it was disregarding international law, that its actions had brought the United States into disrepute with many foreign nations, and that a judicial attempt to redress those problems was important to righting the ship of state. Not everyone will agree with the asserted premises, and it is difficult to know how many Justices might have been swayed by the concerns just described, but there is at least a hint of them in the concurring opinion of Justice Souter (joined by Justices Ginsburg and Breyer), which describes the Court's intervention as "an act of perseverance in trying to make habeas review, and the obligation of the courts to provide it, mean something of value both to prisoners and to the Nation."[138] If at least some Justices were moved by the concerns just described, the impulse to extend habeas jurisdiction beyond sovereign boundaries may be less strong if the Obama Administration, and others to follow, adopt a less aggressive view of executive power, a more respectful view of international law, and a less harsh set of policies concerning the detention of suspects and adjudication of their status as enemy combatants.

III. The Adequacy of DTA Review

In my judgment, the most difficult issue in *Boumediene* arose on the premise that the Suspension Clause does apply to Guantánamo Bay. On that premise, the detainees had a constitutional right to habeas corpus or to an adequate substitute therefor. But at least with respect to the claims at issue in *Boumediene*—claims going to the legality of detention rather than to, for example, the conditions of confinement—Congress did provide a substitute: review by the D.C. Circuit under the Detainee Treatment Act. The hard and interesting question is the adequacy of that substitute.

---

[138] 128 S Ct at 2279 (Souter concurring).

In considering that question, the Court was entering new territory, for as noted, the few prior decisions evaluating Acts of Congress that substitute a statutory review procedure for habeas corpus involved substitutes that not only were closely modeled on habeas but also preserved access to the writ itself in instances in which the substitute procedure proved inadequate.[139] By contrast, the DTA included neither of those features, and thus required the Court to address the minimal constitutional requirements for an adequate substitute.

A. THE MAJORITY'S HOLDING

The Court's reasoning, in very summary form, went like this: (a) because the purpose of the DTA was to limit judicial review, it must be narrower than habeas review, for otherwise the statute would not accomplish its purpose of limiting judicial intervention; (b) the Suspension Clause requires at least (i) a meaningful opportunity to contend that custody rests on "'the erroneous application or interpretation' of relevant law"[140] and (ii) the power in appropriate cases to obtain an order of conditional release; (c) the scope of habeas review historically was inversely correlated to the scope and reliability of earlier judicial proceedings; and (d) nineteenth-century authority suggests that prisoners were permitted in habeas proceedings to introduce exculpatory evidence not previously known or available. The Court then listed a number of key limits, stressed by the petitioners, on the inquiry undertaken in CSRT proceedings—most importantly, the detainee's limited ability to rebut the government's factual claims about enemy combatant status, given his limited ability, while detained, to obtain evidence; the lack of counsel; the lack of notice of classified portions of the charges; and the limits of confrontation rights given the admissibility of hearsay. The Court did not judge whether CSRT hearings provided due process, but noted that the risk of error was considerable and that the consequences of error—indefinite detention for a generation or more—are great.[141]

The Court then turned to the scope of judicial review of CSRT determinations under the DTA. Even assuming, the Court said,

---

[139] See text accompanying notes 58–59.

[140] 128 S Ct at 2266, quoting *St. Cyr*, 533 US at 302.

[141] Id at 2269–71.

that the uncertainty about the D.C. Circuit's power to review CSRT factual determinations and all pertinent legal issues, and about the court's authority to order conditional release, were resolved in the petitioners' favor,[142] there was no way to construe the DTA to permit presentation to the D.C. Circuit of relevant exculpatory evidence not in the record of the CSRT proceeding. While the Defense Department's regulations permitted the military to open a new CSRT proceeding when new evidence was proffered, the decision whether to do so was vested in the unreviewable discretion of the Deputy Secretary of Defense and could not be reviewed by the D.C. Circuit. Thus, the CSRT/DTA regime denied petitioners a right, protected by the Suspension Clause, to have a court consider exculpatory evidence.

B. THE DIFFICULTIES WITH THE MAJORITY'S REASONING

The Court's basis for decision seems flimsy when considered in isolation. First, not every petition from a detainee will involve an effort to introduce exculpatory evidence. To be sure, Justice Kennedy noted that at least one of the petitioners in *Boumediene* wished to present such evidence.[143] And certainly that situation may not be unusual: if a detainee learns details of the government's basis for detention (for example, the identity of his accuser(s), or with whom he is suspected of having associated) only after the CSRT's determination, then any testimony offered by the detainee to rebut the accusations against him could be considered exculpatory evidence not previously available. But some detainees have not contested the government's allegations,[144] and others who deny the allegations may be lying and may not have exculpatory evidence to present. At least, then, as to a good number of detainees, the inability to present exculpatory evidence would not seem to be a relevant procedural defect. Chief Justice Roberts, then, had a fair objection in dissent that the Court was in effect adopting an overbreadth methodology, finding § 7 of the MCA facially unconsti-

---

[142] Only eight days after the *Boumediene* decision, the D.C. Circuit, in exercising review under the DTA, interpreted that Act as permitting it to order the release of a detainee if there was not an adequate basis for detaining him. See *Parhat v Gates*, 532 F3d 834 (DC Cir 2008).

[143] 128 S Ct at 2273.

[144] See Wittes, *Law and the Long War* at 86–87 (cited in note 12).

tutional because in a subset of cases (those involving exculpatory evidence), DTA review would be inadequate.[145]

Moreover, when a petitioner does seek to introduce exculpatory evidence, it is far from clear that the Court had to read the CSRT/DTA regime as precluding the introduction of such evidence. Although the Court was correct that the Defense Department's regulation leaves the decision when to open a new CSRT proceeding to consider such evidence entirely within the Department's unreviewable discretion,[146] a key question was not the meaning of the regulation as drafted but rather the meaning of the DTA—and whether the regulations promulgated by the government were consistent with the Act. Section 1005(a)(3) of that Act declares that CSRT procedures "shall provide for periodic review of any new evidence that may become available relating to the enemy combatant status of a detainee."[147] Perhaps the DTA could not be interpreted as authorizing the court of appeals to admit exculpatory evidence.[148] But it is not clear why § 1005(a)(3) could not have been interpreted—particularly in light of the constitutional avoidance canon—as giving petitioners a statutory right to periodic review before a CSRT, and hence a right to have the D.C. Circuit, when exercising its jurisdiction under the DTA, to review whether the status determination (and the failure to reopen it) was consistent with "the laws of the United States"—that is, with § 1005(a)(3).

In perhaps its weakest argument on this point, the majority contrasts the habeas statute—which permits appellate judges to transfer cases to the district court when factfinding is needed[149]—with the DTA's grant of exclusive jurisdiction to the D.C. Circuit, a grant that, the Court says, foreclosed the option of transfer. But the source of the foreclosure is anything but obvious. Rule 48 of the Federal Rules of Appellate Procedure specifically authorizes a court of appeals to appoint a special master to recommend factual findings in matters ancillary to proceedings in the court, and ex-

---

[145] See 128 S Ct at 2291 (Roberts dissenting).

[146] See id at 2273.

[147] 119 Stat 2741.

[148] Some statements in the legislative record suggested that the court of appeals could not take evidence. See, for example, 152 Cong Rec, S 10,268 (daily ed, Sept 27, 2006) (statement of Sen Kyl); id at S 10,403 (daily ed, Sept 28, 2006) (statement of Sen. Cornyn).

[149] See 28 USC § 2241(b).

pressly contemplates that the master can be a judge. There is little reason to think that the exclusivity of the court of appeals' jurisdiction under the DTA plainly forecloses reliance on the normal rules of appellate procedure—especially, again, if such foreclosure would raise constitutional concerns. Nor would invocation of Rule 48 render the DTA's provision for exclusive jurisdiction meaningless, as that provision would still exclude the state courts, other federal circuits, and the federal district courts from exercising jurisdiction over any action seeking to review CSRT determinations.

The Court refused nonetheless to read the DTA as permitting the D.C. Circuit to consider exculpatory evidence, contending that doing so would come close to duplicating the scope of habeas review under § 2241, whereas Congress was trying to displace habeas corpus with a more limited procedure. The general point is surely correct, but nonetheless not fully satisfying. First, it is important to recall that the statutory writ conferring habeas corpus jurisdiction may be broader than the writ that the Constitution requires.[150] That point is evident in the area of postconviction review, where it is uncertain that the Constitution requires a plenary system of federal collateral review of convictions rendered by competent state courts,[151] and where the scope of review today is in many respects narrower than it was during the Warren Court.[152] Thus, at a minimum the DTA could have the purpose of instructing the courts that some constitutionally gratuitous review that the habeas statute might have authorized would not be provided by the DTA. Moreover, reading the DTA to permit the introduction of exculpatory evidence would not make it identical to habeas corpus; at a minimum it would shift venue from the district courts to a particular circuit court. The objective of avoiding constitutional questions has led to stranger constructions of statutes than would have been required to permit the consideration, one way or another, of exculpatory evidence. And thus, there was something to the Chief Justice's lament that the Court was rejecting an interpretation of the statute that would make it constitutional because Congress could not have intended to enact an adequate substitute for habeas.[153]

---

[150] See Fallon and Meltzer, 120 Harv L Rev at 2037 (cited in note 15).

[151] See generally *Hart and Wechsler* at 1290–92 (cited in note 48).

[152] See id at 1302–99.

[153] See 128 S Ct at 2292 (Roberts dissenting).

Despite having found the DTA regime to be constitutionally inadequate, the Court stated that its only holding was that § 7 of the MCA, purporting to withdraw federal court habeas jurisdiction, was unconstitutional; "[a]ccordingly, both the DTA and the CSRT process remain intact."[154] The resulting dual system of review seems very awkward. Despite Congress's evident desire to create a single, streamlined system of judicial review, under *Boumediene* a detainee might seem to be able both to seek review in the D.C. Circuit under the DTA—as has been done since *Boumediene*, and with success[155]—and then, if unsuccessful in obtaining the relief desired, to file a separate habeas corpus action. Given possible differences in the evidentiary record and scope of review in DTA and habeas proceedings, it is far from clear that an adverse decision to a detainee in one would preclude relitigation in the other. There is, I believe, force to the government's argument that once the preclusion of habeas corpus jurisdiction found in the DTA and MCA was held to be unconstitutional, the DTA's judicial review procedure should have been viewed as inseparable from the jurisdiction-stripping provision—leaving habeas corpus in place as the only mechanism for review of CSRT decisions. And six months after the *Boumediene* decision, the D.C. Circuit accepted this argument in a review proceeding brought under the DTA.[156] It remains to be seen whether the Supreme Court, when it squarely faces that question, will agree.

In my judgment, then, there are manifold respects in which the Court's evaluation of the DTA review scheme was not convincing. But there were deeper issues involved in the substitution of DTA review for habeas review, which involved the intersection of several circumstances: concerns about the quality of CSRT proceedings, probable doubts about the capacity or willingness of the military to redress any deficiencies in those proceedings, and the problem of delay. These issues, which the majority discussed only briefly, required more careful analysis.

IV. THE LIMITS OF THE ADMINISTRATIVE MODEL

In *Boumediene*, the Court confronted two different models

---

[154] See id at 2275.

[155] See, for example, *Parhat v Gates*, 532 F3d 834 (DC Cir 2008).

[156] See *Bismullah v Gates*, 2009 WL 48149 (DC Cir 2009).

of review for the determination of enemy combatant status: (i) an administrative model, with initial determinations by an executive decision maker (the CSRT) and then judicial review based on the administrative record, and (ii) a judicial model, in which the habeas court, even if it defers to a prior determination by the military, views itself as the decision maker and as not being bounded by what happened before the CSRT. In opting for the judicial model, the majority was accused by the dissenters of seeking to aggrandize judicial power.[157] But the question of which model to embrace—or, more specifically, whether the Constitution is satisfied by one model or another—is far more complex and difficult than simple accusations of aggrandizement would suggest.

A. THE ANALOGY TO ARTICLE V TRIBUNALS

The government framed the issue in *Boumediene* by comparing CSRT proceedings to the proceedings historically afforded to prisoners of war. And one must recall the discussion in the *Hamdi* decision of the appropriate procedure to use in determining enemy combatant status to understand the basis on which the government's argument rested. In *Hamdi*, the plurality had insisted that Mr. Hamdi, an American detained by the military, was entitled to notice of the factual basis for his classification as an enemy combatant and to a "fair opportunity to rebut the Government's factual assertion before a neutral decisionmaker."[158] The plurality added that "exigencies" may call for acceptance of hearsay as "the most reliable available evidence" and that the Constitution would permit a presumption in favor of credible evidence presented by the government, requiring the petitioner to rebut it with "more persuasive" evidence.[159] Having outlined those procedural requisites, the plurality stated that "there remains the possibility that the standards we have articulated could be met by an appropriately authorized and properly constituted military tribunal,[160] noting that a military regulation already provides for such process in the related situation in which military tribunals determine the status of

---

[157] Id at 2279–80, 2293 (Roberts dissenting); id at 2296, 2302–03 (Scalia dissenting).

[158] 542 US at 533.

[159] Id at 534.

[160] Id at 538.

detainees who claim to be prisoners of war protected under Article V of the Geneva Convention.[161]

In *Boumediene*, the government contended that the CSRTs were modeled on the very Army Regulation cited by the *Hamdi* plurality.[162] The government noted numerous similarities between the two procedures, and indeed argued that CSRTs include protections not afforded by the so-called Article V tribunals, including (i) explicit provisions to ensure the tribunal's independence, (ii) provision of a personal representative to assist the detainee in presenting his case, (iii) a requirement that the "Recorder" (a nonvoting officer) provide "evidence to suggest that the detainee should not be designated as an enemy combatant," (iv) advance provision to the detainee of an unclassified summary of the evidence against him, (v) express authorization for the detainee to provide documentary evidence, and (vi) automatic review of CSRT decisions by higher military authorities.[163] In response, the petitioners disputed some aspects of that comparison and noted respects in which the CSRTs were less protective of detainees than Article V tribunals: the latter, unlike CSRTs, do not presume that the government's evidence is genuine and accurate; they prohibit the use of torture and coercion; they are convened promptly, near the location of capture, thus maximizing the availability of witnesses; and while they do not confer a right to counsel, they do not expressly forbid it—and had in fact permitted counsel at hearings held during the Vietnam War.[164]

The *Boumediene* Court largely ignored these competing assessments of the analogy to Article V tribunals. In dissent, Chief Justice Roberts pressed the argument that the CSRT process satisfied the requirements set forth by the *Hamdi* plurality and that the DTA went further by providing significant Article III review, which *Hamdi* had not clearly said would be required. Congress,

---

[161] Id.

[162] See Brief for the Respondents, *Boumediene v Bush*, Nos 06-1195 and 06-1196, *3–4, 50–52 (available on Westlaw at 2007 WL 2972541) (citing U.S. Department of the Army et al, *Regulation 190–8, Enemy Prisoners of War, Retained Personnel, Civilian Internees and Other Detainees* (Nov 1, 1997)).

[163] Id at *50–52. See also Wittes at 100–01 (cited in note 12).

[164] See Reply Brief for Boumediene Petitioners, *Boumediene v Bush*, No 06-1195, *13–14 (Nov 13, 2007) (available on Westlaw at 2007 WL 3440934).

he said, "followed the Court's lead, only to find itself the victim of a constitutional bait and switch."[165]

Justice Kennedy offered a somewhat feeble response. *Hamdi*, he said, did not have a majority opinion.[166] True enough, but Justice Thomas, whose dissent in *Hamdi* argued that the procedures suggested by the plurality were constitutionally unnecessary, surely would count as a fifth vote that they were constitutionally sufficient. Justice Kennedy also contended that the *Hamdi* case did not involve any effort to withdraw habeas corpus, so that the question before the Court in *Boumediene* had simply not been presented.[167] Also true enough, but the implication of the *Hamdi* plurality was that review of enemy combatant status could be made by a military tribunal—and that if such review were properly conducted, no separate inquiry by a habeas court would be necessary (except to ensure that the military tribunal complied with the due process requirements that the plurality set forth). If the CSRTs in fact satisfied those requirements, that would be the end of the matter— and the scope of review under the DTA seemed more than adequate to make the necessary determination.

Justice Kennedy then offered a different line of argument: that habeas corpus "exists, in Justice Holmes's words, to 'cu[t] through all forms and g[o] to the very tissue of the structure. It comes in from the outside, not in subordination to the proceedings, and although every form may have been preserved opens the inquiry whether they have been more than an empty shell.'"[168] That phrasing at least could be read to suggest that the majority viewed the CSRT proceedings as an empty shell, not worthy of the respect that the *Hamdi* plurality appeared to believe such military proceedings could merit. And Justice Kennedy proceeded to express some uneasiness about the quality of CSRT determinations: "Although we make no judgment as to whether the CSRTs, as currently constituted, satisfy due process standards, we agree with petitioners that, even when all the parties involved in this process act with diligence and in good faith, there is considerable risk of error in the tribunal's findings of fact."[169]

[165] Id at 2285 (Roberts dissenting).
[166] Id at 2269.
[167] Id at 2269–70.
[168] Id at 2270, quoting *Frank v Mangum*, 237 US 309, 346 (1915) (Holmes dissenting).
[169] Id at 2270.

Despite its refusal to declare whether hearings conducted before CSRTs comported with due process,[170] the majority's discussion suggests a lack of faith in CSRTs. One possible reason for a lack of faith would be the belief that the CSRTs did not, in fact, provide the procedural protections set forth by the *Hamdi* plurality. For example, the government's desire to preserve the confidentiality of classified information might have prevented some detainees from obtaining adequately detailed notice of the basis for the charges, which the plurality had said was a due process requirement. (One of the petitioners in *Boumediene* had been accused of associating with an al Qaeda operative in Bosnia but was not told the identity of the operative, making it difficult to respond to the accusation by providing an innocent explanation for any association.[171]) Alternatively, decisions by particular CSRTs about whether evidence that detainees sought to obtain and introduce was "reasonably available" might have been so restrictive as not to satisfy *Hamdi*'s requirement of a fair procedure.[172] The Court might also have been concerned that CSRTs could admit not only hearsay evidence (as the *Hamdi* plurality had contemplated) but also testimony obtained as a result of torture or coercion, with the only limitation being that the CSRT in its discretion "tak[e] into account the reliability of such evidence in the circumstances."[173] And, finally, the *Boumediene* Court may have been concerned about allegations that the CSRTs were subject to command influence.[174]

Substantively, the CSRT's definition of enemy combatant was considerably broader than that applied in *Hamdi*, where the plurality had upheld the legality of detention on the basis Hamdi was "'part of or supporting forces hostile to the United States or coalition partners in Afghanistan'" and who "'engaged in an armed

---

[170] Id.

[171] See Brief for the Boumediene Petitioners, *Boumediene v Bush*, No 06-1195, *4–5 (filed August 24, 2007) (available on Westlaw at 2007 WL 2441590).

[172] See id at 5 (noting one CSRT's determination that a Bosnian Supreme Court decision ordering one of the petitioners released was not "reasonably available," even though it had been filed in a district court proceeding and served on government counsel, and another CSRT's determination that testimony from a person in Sarajevo was unavailable even though the petitioner's counsel later easily located him by looking in the Sarajevo telephone book).

[173] See Memorandum at 3 (cited in note 19).

[174] See Brief for the Boumediene Petitioners, *Boumediene v Bush*, No 06-1195, *30 (filed August 24, 2007) (available on Westlaw at 2007 WL 2441590).

conflict against the United States' there."[175] The CSRT definition, by comparison, was not limited to those who were involved in the 9/11 attacks or who were fighting in Afghanistan, but instead reached anyone who was "part of or supporting Taliban or al Qaeda forces, or associated forces that are engaged in hostilities against the United States or its coalition partners."[176]

Whatever the merits of the petitioners' objections to the standards and procedures followed in CSRT proceedings, a plausible response—one implicit in the Chief Justice's dissent—is that any legal deficiency could be remedied by the D.C. Circuit on review under the DTA. The majority responded that such an approach would inject further delay for detainees who had yet to obtain a full hearing on their effort to obtain release.[177] To this, too, the Chief Justice had a rejoinder—that launching habeas actions with many questions left open about the procedural and substantive rules to be applied would not necessarily expedite resolution of matters, particularly given that DTA review begins in the D.C. Circuit, while habeas cases begin in the district court but surely would be appealed to the D.C. Circuit.[178]

Who was right on the issue of delay is not obvious in the abstract. But the Chief Justice had a fair point that the majority did seem to be distancing itself from the analysis of the plurality in *Hamdi*. One explanation for that stance is that the Court had before it more experience with military adjudication of enemy combatant status. In *Hamdi*, eight Justices agreed that the rudimentary procedure there used to determine enemy combatant status denied due process, but the Court had not seen how a fuller military process, similar to that under Article V, would operate in the context of the war on terror. By the time *Boumediene* was decided, there was considerable experience with such a model, and that experience may have made at least some of the Justices (notably Justices Breyer and Kennedy, who joined both the *Hamdi* plurality and the *Boumediene* majority) less sanguine about its fairness than they had been four years earlier. The passage of time may also have been significant, as by 2008, the threat of imminent

---

[175] 542 US at 516, quoting Brief for Respondents, *Hamdi v Rumsfeld*, No 03-6696, *3 (filed Mar 29, 2004) (available on Westlaw at 2004 WL 724020).

[176] See Memorandum at 1 (cited in note 19).

[177] 128 S Ct at 2275.

[178] Id at 2282 (Roberts dissenting).

terrorist attacks may have seemed to be considerably smaller than it appeared to be four years earlier.

Whatever the reason, the Court's discussion of CSRTs in *Boumediene* seemed more skeptical of military adjudication than the *Hamdi* plurality had been. The majority in *Boumediene* noted that the likelihood of error was significant,[179] and, the Court might have said, far greater in general than in determinations made by most Article V tribunals. Hamdi, like many other suspected enemy combatants, was captured not directly by American forces but by local forces allied with the United States, and those allies may not only be less disciplined than American soldiers but may also have been less discriminating because of the promise of reward.[180] Other detainees were captured fleeing rather than while in battle, and were apprehended in civilian clothes rather than recognizable uniforms of enemy armies. And by the time of the *Boumediene* decision, many of those detained had been captured far from any battle, on the basis of evidence obtained in coercive interrogations or on circumstantial evidence from multiple intelligence sources of varying quality and specificity. Indeed, one study concluded that only 5 percent of detainees were captured directly by U.S. forces.[181]

In something like half of the cases heard by CSRTs, more or less plausible denials, or silence, on the part of the detainee was pitted against more or less plausible inferences drawn from intelligence sources.[182] Such cases raise questions of great difficulty, but the CSRT panels did not necessarily have expertise in assessing intelligence[183] or in determining whether the evidence satisfies the legal standard of enemy combatant—which in the end is not a military but a legal judgment, requiring the articulation and application of standards appropriate to this context.[184] The judgments are difficult ones for any decision maker—far more difficult,

---

[179] Id at 2270.

[180] See Wittes, *Law and the Long War* at 80–81 (cited in note 12).

[181] See Mark Denbeaux and Joshua Denbeaux, *Report on Guantanamo Detainees: A Profile of 517 Detainees Through Analysis of Department of Defense Data* 4 (Seton Hall Pub Law Research Paper No 46, 2006), available at http://law.shu.edu/aaafinal.pdf.

[182] See Wittes, *Law and the Long War* at 72–99 (cited in note 12).

[183] See Fallon and Meltzer, 120 Harv L Rev at 2098 (cited in note 15) (noting the importance, in determining the appropriate scope of habeas review, of the comparative expertise of executive and judicial decision makers, and contending that the military is not necessarily more competent than the courts in making factual determinations).

[184] Id at 2110.

for example, than routine determinations in World War II that a German soldier in uniform was an enemy combatant.[185] And in making these difficult decisions, there is ample reason to fear that the assessment by military officials of the relative risks of false negatives and false positives may be skewed.

If the risk of error before CSRTs was higher than before Article V tribunals, so, too, was the seriousness of error. As the Court noted, a mistaken decision could result in detaining an innocent and harmless person for the duration of a struggle without apparent prospect of termination.[186] And the detainee might be subjected to harsh conditions and harsh interrogation techniques that the Geneva Convention prohibits with respect to conventional prisoners of war. (While in *Hamdi*, only Justices Souter and Ginsburg took the view that the administration could not avail itself of the power to detain that is an accepted incident of war without observing the limits imposed by the Geneva Convention,[187] all of the Justices were surely aware of the government's practices vis-à-vis the detainees.) To be sure, if a CSRT's false positive on enemy combatant status had unusually serious consequences, so, too, might a false negative; mistaken release of a genuine terrorist may pose a far more serious threat than mistaken release of a German or Japanese or North Vietnamese soldier during a conventional war. But the Court, perhaps not implausibly, gave more attention to the consequences of mistaken detention.

If one revisits the *Mathews v Eldridge* balance embraced by the *Hamdi* plurality, a final factor is the extent of the burden that the government would face if required to provide more elaborate process. The burden of the Court's ruling is surely considerable, but it extends only to the two hundred plus individuals detained at Guantánamo Bay. And by the time of *Boumediene*, it may have been clearer than it was in 2004 that the number of detainees potentially filing habeas petitions would make the exercise of habeas jurisdiction more feasible than it would have been, for example, for all of the enemy soldiers captured during World War II.

The Chief Justice was surely correct that there was considerable

---

[185] See Chesney and Goldsmith, 60 Stan L Rev at 1081, 1099–1100 (cited in note 99).

[186] 128 S Ct at 2270. Accord, Chesney and Goldsmith, 60 Stan L Rev at 1100 (cited in note 99).

[187] See 542 US at 549–51 (Souter concurring in part, dissenting in part, and concurring in the judgment).

tension between the Court's opinion and the views of the plurality in *Hamdi* four years earlier. The Court could, in my judgment, have acknowledged that tension more directly, and responded to it by stating that experience had cast doubt upon the soundness of the suggestions in *Hamdi* about the proper due process balance. And the more one delves into the operation of the CSRTs, the more serious those doubts may have been.

B. THE SHORTCOMINGS OF CSRTS

Still, the point remains that if the Court thought that the Constitution requires fuller procedural safeguards for those detained at Guantánamo Bay than for prisoners of war captured in conventional conflicts, any constitutional shortcoming in the CSRT proceedings could have been remedied by review under the DTA by the D.C. Circuit, which plainly extended to that question. Why, one might ask (and Chief Justice Roberts did ask), would such review not suffice to cure any constitutional defects?

My own view is that both to explain the Court's decision and to assess whether it is justified, one has to explore circumstances known to the Court but not emphasized in the *Boumediene* opinion. The Court had before it reports of how the CSRTs had been operating. Those reports might have created deep-seated misgivings about whether military hearings, at least as being conducted, could satisfy the Constitution. To draw on Justice Holmes's famous aphorism,[188] whatever the apparent logic of that position in 2004 when *Hamdi* was decided, the experience revealed by 2008 may have put the question in a different light.

The Court had before it a declaration from Lt. Col. Stephen Abraham, an intelligence officer assigned to the Office for the Administrative Review of the Detention of Enemy Combatants, that raised serious questions about the fairness of CSRT proceedings. Colonel Abraham asserted that (1) the information used to prepare files for CSRT proceedings was often generic, outdated intelligence not relating to individual detainees; (2) the officials responsible for processing intelligence reports for CSRT proceedings sometimes lacked access to pertinent information and often lacked the capacity to evaluate the information they did have;

---

[188] Oliver Wendell Holmes, Jr., *The Common Law* 5 (Little, Brown 1881) ("The life of the law has not been logic; it has been experience.").

(3) there was reason to doubt whether other government agencies met their obligation to furnish exculpatory information for use before the CSRTs; (4) when he sat on one CSRT panel, "[w]hat were purported to be specific statements of fact lacked even the most fundamental earmarks of objectively credible evidence. Statements allegedly made by percipient witnesses lacked detail. Reports presented generalized statements in indirect and passive forms without stating the source of the information. . . . The personal representative did not participate in any meaningful way"; and (5) his CSRT panel, after failing to find that the detainee was an enemy combatant, was questioned by military superiors (a practice followed in other cases) and ordered to reopen the hearing to permit further argument from the government in favor of enemy combatant status.[189]

Also cited in a number of briefs in *Boumediene* was another critical review of CSRT proceedings. This study, which was based on publicly available documents, asserted, inter alia, that "the Government did not produce any witnesses in any hearing and did not present any documentary evidence to the detainee prior to the hearing in 96% of the cases"; detainees generally are provided with only a conclusory summary of classified evidence; "the Government's classified evidence was always presumed to be reliable and valid" and all requests by detainees to inspect it were denied; detainees' requests for witnesses were always denied when the witness was not detained in Guantánamo, and for witnesses in Guantánamo, were denied in 74% of the cases; in the three cases (of 102) in which a CSRT found the detainee not to be, or no longer to be, an enemy combatant, the government convened a new CSRT (and in one case, a third CSRT after two negative determinations), and the second (or third) CSRT found the detainee to be an enemy combatant.[190]

The Petitioners' Brief added fuel to the fire by highlighting some of the more extreme actions taken by the government. It noted the claim of one government lawyer before the district court, in one of the habeas proceedings consolidated before the Court

---

[189] See Reply to Opposition to Petition for Rehearing, *Al Odah v United States*, No 06-1196, Appendix (DC Cir June 22, 2007) (Declaration of Stephen Abraham).

[190] Denbeaux et al, *No-Hearing Hearings—CSRT: The Modern Habeas Corpus? An Analysis of the Proceedings of the Government's Combatant Status Review Tribunals at Guantánamo* 2–3, available online at http://law.shu.edu/news/final_no_hearing_hearings_report.pdf.

in *Boumediene*, that the government could detain, indefinitely, "[a] little old lady in Switzerland who writes checks to what she thinks is a charity that helps orphans in Afghanistan but [which] really is a front to finance al-Qaeda activities."[191] And the appendix quoted from a Kafkaesque CSRT transcript in which a detainee, charged with associating with a known al Qaeda operative, asked the operative's name so that he could determine if he knew him and offer what he asserted would have been an innocent association, but was told that the operative's name could not be revealed because it was classified.[192]

One interpretation of the *Boumediene* decision is that the Court simply lacked faith that military officials serving on CSRTs possessed the combination of capacity and will needed to make judgments that struck reasonable accommodations between the contending interests at play. The Court did not say as much directly, but it did describe the "myriad deficiencies" that the petitioners ascribed to the CSRT process.[193] Moreover, as the Chief Justice complained, the majority opinion "hints darkly" that the DTA may have defects other than the failure to authorize the introduction of exculpatory evidence.[194] I do not think it is too much to read into the Court's opinion something it did not state—a fundamental mistrust of the Executive's capacity or willingness to provide fair hearings.

If indeed the majority harbored such concerns about the CSRT process, it might have feared that the structure set up by the DTA was simply not up to the task of ensuring that detainees would be afforded a fair hearing—or of ensuring that the detainees (many of whom had been held for six years) would obtain such a hearing with reasonable promptness. The problem here would lie in the administrative agency model of review apparently established by the DTA. Under that Act, an administrative body—the CSRT— makes an initial determination. If that determination is found by the D.C. Circuit, on review under the DTA, to be unlawful in some way, the ordinary remedy is to remand the matter to the

---

[191] See Brief for the Boumediene Petitioners, *Boumediene v Bush*, No 06-1195, *3–4 (filed August 24, 2007) (available on Westlaw at 2007 WL 2441590) (quoting Guantánamo Detainee Cases, 355 F Supp 2d 443, 475 (DDC 2005)).

[192] See id at *4–5.

[193] 128 S Ct at 2270.

[194] Id at 2289 (Roberts dissenting).

administrative body for a new hearing that corrects whatever defect was identified. A purely administrative model of review would
have endorsed the position taken by the government in its argument in the *Bismullah* case—a review proceeding in the D.C.
Circuit, brought under the DTA—that the only remedy the court
of appeals could provide, should it find that the CSRT hearing
was in some way unlawful, was a remand back to the agency (the
military) for a new hearing.[195]

Indeed, the Government argued that even when a habeas court
finds that detention is unlawful, the remedy ordered often is not
immediate release, but rather a conditional order requiring release
only if the government fails to provide a future hearing that cures
a prior procedural defect.[196] That limited remedy was particularly
appropriate here, the government suggested, given the Executive's
primary role in determining when detention is necessary and in
addressing the sensitive diplomatic concerns surrounding release.[197] But if the Court simply had lost faith in the fairness of
the military, if it feared command influence, or if it feared that a
determined Executive would find one way or another to continue
holding detainees without having provided adequate proof to justify detention, the Court might have feared that any remand to
cure one or more identified defects was likely to lead only to a
new CSRT determination that would be infected with other procedural problems. The Court might also have feared, in light of
the Abraham affidavit, that if a new hearing resulted in a finding
that the individual was not an enemy combatant, the military
would simply convene still another CSRT until a different finding
was made. And all the while, the detainee would remain at Guantánamo. If some of this is speculation, the Court was very direct
in expressing its concern about the length of time that the petitioners already had been detained without having been given an
adequate hearing.[198]

In *Boumediene*, the Court did suggest that perhaps review under
the DTA departed from the traditional model of administrative
review. For the Court suggested, without quite holding, that the

---

[195] See, for example, *Florida Power and Light Co. v Lorion*, 470 US 729, 744 (1985).

[196] Brief for Respondents, *Boumediene v Bush*, Nos 06-1195 and 06-1196, *60 (filed Oct
9, 2007) (available on Westlaw at 2007 WL 2972541).

[197] Id at *60–61.

[198] See, for example, id at 2275; id at 2277–78 (Souter concurring).

DTA could be read (particularly if necessary to preserve its constitutionality) as giving the D.C. Circuit the power not merely to remand for a new hearing but also to order release, immediate or conditional.[199] But even if this suggestion were followed, relying on the power to release on account of defects in the CSRT proceedings would put the courts in a very troubling predicament. I have already noted the significant risk of false negatives and false positives in making enemy combatant determinations. But the risk of false negatives is magnified if a court is driven to release suspects, not because the government tried to make its proof at a fair hearing and failed, but because of the failure to have provided an administrative hearing that met constitutional requirements. Relatedly, the courts might have found themselves in a particularly unwelcome position if forced to take responsibility for releasing suspected terrorists on the basis that there were defects in the CSRT proceedings.

And the likelihood of finding such defects was considerable, for already a number of different kinds of shortcomings in the CSRT/DTA process had emerged. The one on which the majority focused, in concluding that the DTA was not an adequate substitute for habeas corpus, pertained to exculpatory evidence. Ordinarily in an administrative hearing, the parties have a reasonable opportunity to put the relevant evidence into the agency record. The discovery of new and material evidence after completion of the agency adjudication, although always a possibility, is the exception rather than the rule. But in enemy combatant status determinations, the likelihood that a petitioner, if given access to judicial review, might have such evidence is considerably magnified. The detainee is, to say the least, in unfamiliar surroundings and at best has been isolated and interrogated; at worst, the prisoner may have been subject to abusive treatment. The personal representative is not an advocate and, as already noted, may be quite passive, leaving the detainee largely on his own. It is also worth noting that the CSRT hearing will in most cases require the use of translation into a foreign language, which may be quite imperfect. The detainee in some cases will not even have been given a full explanation of the nature of the charge. When these circumstances are combined with the limited rights under the CSRT regulations to

---

[199] 128 S Ct at 2271–72.

compel the production of evidence (it is all too easy for the tribunal to rule that evidence sought is not reasonably available),[200] it is extraordinarily difficult for someone locked up at Guantánamo to obtain access to witnesses or documents, some located thousands of miles away, that might cast doubt on the allegation that he is an enemy combatant. In such circumstances, the likelihood that in a judicial review proceeding, a petitioner, who for the first time is afforded counsel, may be able to proffer additional exculpatory evidence begins to look far less exceptional.

In considering the likely judicial reaction to CSRT proceedings in light of the evidence of their shortcomings, one might draw an analogy to the debates about structural injunctions in the 1970s and 1980s. A familiar objection to judicial intervention was that the courts do not know how to run prisons or mental hospitals, that judicial intervention can interfere with the government's ability to effectively manage public institutions and with important choices about resource allocation, and that judicial involvement may have unintended consequences.[201] But, at the same time, courts ultimately determined that if public administrators were unwilling or unable to redress serious and ongoing constitutional violations, there comes a point when the judiciary, whatever its limitations as compared to responsible administrators, feels compelled to step in.[202] A similar point could be made here, and if the aspect of executive operations into which the courts were intervening concerned matters of national security, where judicial expertise is often thought to be very limited, at the same time it concerned a system of adjudication, something that judges know a good deal about. And if courts are not especially good at resolving the particularly knotty problems concerning classified information, it may be that military officials—at least those who were dispatched to sit on and assist before CSRTs—also lacked such competence, and may not have been disinterested to boot.

There was another awkwardness in the administrative model,

[200] See, for example, id at 2273; see also the cases of Bismullah and of the Uighur detainees, set forth in the Brief in Opposition to the Petition for Certiorari in *Gates v Bismullah and Parhat v Gates*, No 07-1054 (Supreme Court, filed Nov 3, 2008).

[201] See, for example, Peter Schuck, *Suing Government: Citizen Remedies for Official Wrongs* 24 (Yale, 1983); William A. Fletcher, *The Discretionary Constitution: Institutional Remedies and Judicial Legitimacy*, 91 Yale L J 635, 635–37, 642–49 (1982); Robert Nagel, *Separation of Powers and the Scope of Federal Equitable Remedies*, 30 Stan L Rev 661, 710–11 (1978).

[202] See Fletcher, 91 Yale L J at 693 (cited in note 201).

which had been revealed by the *Bismullah* decision. The Defense Department's procedures for the conduct of CSRT hearings tasked a nonvoting officer, called the Recorder, with presenting evidence to the Tribunal. Though analogous in some respects to a prosecutor, the Recorder was required to request the production of "Government Information": all reasonably available information possessed throughout the government "bearing on the issue of whether the detainee meets the criteria to be designated as an enemy combatant."[203] The detainee's Personal Representative, though not an advocate, apparently was to have the opportunity to review the Government Information.[204] Given the petitioner's evident incapacity to gather evidence and the absence of counsel, the Recorder and Personal Representative were together to assume, in theory, a role somewhat more like a continental investigating magistrate. In turn, the D.C. Circuit ruled that in order for it to carry out its statutory obligation under the DTA to determine whether the government had complied with the standards and procedures specified by the Secretary of Defense, it was required to have before it on appeal "all the information a Tribunal is authorized to obtain and consider"[205]—not only the evidence presented to the CSRT, but all of the "reasonably available information in the possession of the U.S. Government bearing on the issue of whether the detainee meets the criteria to be designated as an enemy combatant."[206]

The government, in seeking rehearing and later certiorari, contended, not implausibly, that the D.C. Circuit's holding would impose extraordinary burdens, as well as security risks. The D.C. Circuit denied a petition for rehearing en banc, dividing 5–5. But the five judges who favored rehearing objected that the panel's opinion departed from what they deemed to be the agency model of review; viewing the CSRT as the agency, Judge Henderson argued that a reviewing court has "no license to 'create' a record

[203] See Secretary of the Navy, Memorandum on Implementation of Combatant Status Review Tribunal Procedures for Enemy Combatants detained at Guantánamo Bay Naval Base, Cuba, Combatant Status Review Tribunal Process, Paragraphs E(3), H(4); Recorder Qualifications, Roles, and Responsibilities, Paragraph C (July 29, 2004), available at http://www.defenseclink.mil/news/Jul2004/d20040730comb.pdf.

[204] See id, Combatant Status Review Tribunal Process, §§ E(1), F(8), G(4).

[205] *Bismullah v Gates (Bismullah I)*, 501 F3d 178, 181 (DC Cir 2007).

[206] *Bismullah v Gates (Bismullah II)*, 514 F3d 137, 138–39 (DC Cir 2007).

consisting of more than the agency itself had before it."[207]

It is not obvious just who was the "agency" in a CSRT proceeding, or how to define the record before the agency, but the panel's decision surely was extraordinary in some respects. It would require review of a potentially huge volume of information that was not directly relied upon by those making the adjudication below. It also promised enormous further delay, for the government had quite reasonably not thought it was under the obligation that the D.C. Circuit recognized. (Indeed, as the court of appeals acknowledged, many of the CSRT hearings preceded enactment of the DTA.[208]) No matter, the D.C. Circuit said; if the government cannot effectively recreate the Government Information, it has the option of convening a new CSRT and maintaining the Government Information therein.

The duty imposed could be viewed as extraordinary quite apart from questions of burden and delay. In civil cases—and detention of enemy combatants is viewed as civil, rather than criminal, detention—the government generally lacks the obligation that it has in criminal cases to turn over exculpatory evidence,[209] and even in the criminal cases, defendants have no right to discovery of the government's files to test whether it has met its obligation to provide exculpatory evidence.[210]

Yet if the panel's decision exceeded the norm for administrative review or for civil detention, the problem it confronted highlighted shortcomings of the administrative model for determining enemy combatant status. On the one hand, if the panel's approach were to prevail, the consequent delays would have been considerable. (The *Boumediene* petitioners pointed out in their Reply Brief, filed in November of 2007, that although the first petition had been filed for review under the DTA twenty-two months earlier, no record had yet been filed in the D.C. Circuit in any DTA cases, and the government had acknowledged its inability to

---

[207] *Bismullah v Gates (Bismullah II)*, 514 F3d 1291, 1300 (DC Cir 2008) (Henderson dissenting from the denial of rehearing en banc). See generally *Florida Power & Light v Lorion*, 470 US 729, 740 (1985); *United States v Carlo Biahchi and Co.*, 470 US 709, 714–15 (1963).

[208] *Bismullah v Gates (Bismullah I)*, 503 F3d 137, 141 (DC Cir 2007).

[209] See *Brady v Maryland*, 373 US 83 (1963).

[210] See *Weatherford v Bursey*, 429 US 545 (1977).

produce the required records in a timely fashion.[211]) On the other hand, if the panel was wrong, the resulting system—reliance upon an administrative record only of the evidence introduced before the CSRT, in a proceeding in which, for all the reasons already noted, the detainee would often have lacked any effective way to test the government's evidence or to adduce pertinent evidence—ran serious risks of resulting in indefinite detention of individuals without adequate justification.

The point is not that the administrative model cannot be used when personal liberty is at stake; it is widely used, to take just one example, in the immigration context. But in that context not only are the issues often quite clear-cut (more often the question is the availability of discretionary relief from deportation rather than deportability); in addition, the deportee in the administrative hearing may be represented by counsel, has access to the pertinent evidence presented by the government, has a greater capacity to confront the government's evidence and to present evidence,[212] has a right to a decision maker with statutory protections against prosecutorial influence,[213] and is protected by a requirement that the government establish deportability by clear and convincing evidence.[214] By contrast, as Chief Judge Ginsburg noted in the *Bismullah* proceedings, "[u]nlike the final decision rendered in a criminal or an agency proceeding, which is the product of an open and adversarial process before an independent decisionmaker, a CSRT's status determination is the product of a necessarily closed and accusatorial process in which the detainee seeking review will have had little or no access to the evidence the Recorder presented to the Tribunal, little ability to gather his own evidence, no right to confront the witnesses against him, and no lawyer to help him prepare his case, and in which the decisionmaker is employed and chosen by the detainee's accuser."[215]

The foregoing problems were only hinted at in the *Boumediene* opinion. If I am correct, however, in speculating about the mo-

[211] See Reply Brief for Boumediene Petitioners, *Boumediene v Bush*, No 06-1195, *18–19 (Nov 13, 2007) (available on Westlaw at 2007 WL 3440934).

[212] 8 USC § 1229a(b)(4)(B).

[213] 8 USC § 1101(b)(4).

[214] 8 USC § 1229a(c)(3)(A).

[215] 514 F3d 1291, 1296 (DC Cir 2008) (Ginsburg concurring in the denial of rehearing en banc).

tivations of at least some of the Justices in the majority, would it have been better for them to have discussed more directly the adequacy of the CSRT/DTA model? To have done so would have been awkward, potentially embarrassing to the administration, and might have had to rest on a small amount of evidence and a large degree of situation sense. At the same time, a discussion along these lines might have provided a more adequate response to the Chief Justice's contention that the DTA provided an adequate substitute process as well as a stronger response to the accusations of judicial aggrandizement voiced in both dissents.

C. EXHAUSTION AND EXPEDITION

There was one aspect of the CSRT/DTA model, however, about which the Court's concerns were directly stated, and that concerned expedition.[216] One can find numerous references in the case law to the importance of habeas corpus as a speedy remedy,[217] but little authority dealing with how such a requirement might be implemented in a situation as complex as that involving detention of suspected enemy combatants and in which Congress has enacted an alternative judicial review mechanism. Exhaustion requirements are common in habeas corpus proceedings, both in postconviction cases[218] and in court-martial proceedings,[219] and in both situations they delay access to habeas by requiring resort to other remedies that ordinarily are, but in a particular case may not be, adequate to provide relief. The Court's opinion in *Boumediene* could be read as resting on a constitutional requirement of expedition. Alternatively, one could read it as holding that the Suspension Clause protects these petitioners, that Congress (not having anticipated that constitutional protection) did not expressly make exhaustion of DTA review a prerequisite to habeas corpus jurisdiction, and

---

[216] See text accompanying note 177.

[217] See, for example, *Carafas v LaVallee*, 391 US 234, 238 (1969); *Fay v Noia*, 372 US 391, 400 (1963), overruled on other grounds in *Coleman v Thompson*, 504 US 722 (1991). One purpose of the enactment by Parliament of the Habeas Corpus Act of 1679, 31 Car 2, c 2 (1679), was to provide "more speedy relief of all persons imprisoned for any such criminal or supposed criminal matters" by requiring that the jailer file a return to the writ within three days unless great distances were involved. The Act also required that persons detained for treason or felony be brought to trial, upon their motion, within two terms of court or released on bail.

[218] See, for example, 28 USC § 2254(b–c) (2006).

[219] See, for example, *Schlesinger v Councilman*, 420 US 738 (1975).

that the equitable considerations from which the exhaustion re-quirement initially flowed[220] did not support exhaustion given the delays these petitioners had already encountered. However read, the Court's opinion surely supports the notion that speed is an important aspect of the habeas remedy, but the exact nature of any constitutional requirement of expedition remains to be seen.

V. CONCLUSION

In its holding that the Suspension Clause is an affirmative guarantee of habeas corpus review, and its invalidation of govern-ment practices during "wartime" that had the clear sanction of both the President and Congress, *Boumediene* is surely a momen-tous decision as a matter of constitutional doctrine. Yet its practical effect, like the practical effect of the Court's earlier war on terror decisions, may be quite limited. The decision affirms that habeas corpus jurisdiction must be made available to those persons de-tained at Guantánamo, but aside from indicating that detainees must have some ability to introduce exculpatory evidence in habeas proceedings, it does not tell us how the habeas jurisdiction is to be exercised. We still know little about the scope of the substantive power to detain persons classified by the government as enemy combatants but who, unlike Mr. Hamdi, were not captured on or near a battlefield. Does the legality of detention depend upon the Authorization of the Use of Military Force enacted by Congress, which authorizes force "against those nations, organizations, or persons [the President] determines planned, authorized, commit-ted, or aided the terrorist attacks that occurred on September 11, 2001, or harbored such organizations or persons, in order to pre-vent any future acts of international terrorism against the United States by such nations, organizations or persons"? What are the limits of authority to detain persons who rendered aid that was minimal or unknowing, or, more generally, to detain suspected terrorists not captured on or near a conventional battlefield? Where detention is authorized, is there any limit on its duration?

Similar questions arise with regard to the procedural protections that CSRT hearings must afford. The plurality in *Hamdi* provided some suggestions in dictum on this score, but as already suggested,

---

[220] See *Ex parte Royall*, 117 US 241 (1886).

the tone of *Boumediene* is quite different in this regard.[221]

Finally, there remain unresolved questions relating to the appropriate role of the courts in reviewing CSRT determinations of enemy combatant status. Habeas courts will face a complex of questions falling under the general heading of "scope of review"— the deference (if any) that they should give to various determinations by CSRTs of fact, law, or application of law to fact.[222] And in cases in which a habeas court determines that detention is unlawful, there can arise difficult questions about the appropriate remedy—for example, if no nation is willing to accept the detainee (or if the only one that will is expected to torture him), must the detainee be released into the United States?

Of course, President Obama has said that he wishes to close the prison at Guantánamo Bay,[223] but such a closure would still leave open the question what to do with the more than two hundred persons still detained there. A decision by the next administration that all detainees must either be tried in Article III courts or released could moot the need for courts to resolve questions about the permissible bounds of nonpunitive detention of terrorists. But prosecution (whether by military or civilian courts) may not be a feasible path with respect to some detainees—even those thought to be most dangerous—when concerns about the confidentiality or the reliability of the evidence against them precludes making the requisite showing of proof beyond a reasonable doubt according to the normal processes of criminal trial. Thus, it is highly possible that the government will continue to detain at least some individuals, in which event their challenges to detention will provide the occasion for litigation of the open issues noted above.

The resolution of many of those open questions may depend importantly, however, not only on whether detention remains as a legal response to terrorism, but also on whether the next administration alters the process for military adjudication of the lawfulness of detention. From both a doctrinal and a legal realist

---

[221] For a brief discussion of some of these questions, written before *Boumediene*, see Fallon and Meltzer, 120 Harv L Rev at 2089–95 (cited in note 15).

[222] Richard Fallon and I have previously tried to sketch an approach to such problems. See id at 2096–2111.

[223] See Obama for America, http://obama.3cdn.net/417b7e6036dd852384_luzxmvl09 .pdf.

perspective, the scope of judicial inquiry on habeas is likely to turn importantly on the quality of the administrative proceedings that precede it.[224] As already noted, courts often provide a countervailing force to extreme claims by the political branches.[225]

But, at the same time, the judicial counterforce is a limited one. Seven years after 9/11, although the Court's decisions have repeatedly rejected the government's legal position, from the perspective of detainees seeking their liberty, the results of judicial intervention have been quite limited.[226] That fact is a reminder that even when rendering dramatic and doctrinally significant decisions, the judiciary is, in the end, the least dangerous, because the least powerful, branch.

---

[224] For an elaboration of this theme from a doctrinal perspective, see Fallon and Meltzer, 120 Harv L Rev at 2097–98 (cited in note 15).

[225] See text accompanying notes 22–23.

[226] See generally Martinez, 108 Colum L Rev (cited in note 11).

MARK TUSHNET

HELLER AND THE CRITIQUE OF JUDGMENT

I. Introduction

In 2005 when Justice Stephen Breyer observed in his concurring opinion in *Van Orden v Perry* that in "difficult borderline cases," he saw "no test-related substitute for the exercise of legal judgment,"[1] no one took much note, except perhaps to observe that the distinction he drew—in exercising legal judgment—between the display of the Ten Commandments on the grounds of the Texas statehouse and a display of the Ten Commandments in the McCreary County courthouse seemed thin. Three years later, though, his invocation of "legal judgment" in *Medellin v Texas* and *District of Columbia v Heller* drew rebuttals from Chief Justice Roberts and Justice Scalia.

In *Medellin* Justice Breyer found a number of questions embedded in case law and basic principle to help judges decide whether a treaty was self-executing. And, as in *Van Orden*, he contrasted his "practical, context-specific judicial approach, seeking to separate run-of-the-mill judicial matters from other matters, sometimes more politically charged" with "a simple test, let alone a magic

Mark Tushnet is William Nelson Cromwell Professor of Law, Harvard Law School.

Author's note: I thank Todd Rakoff for extremely helpful comments on an earlier version of this article. A point of clarification: I do not believe that I have ever read Kant's *Critique of Judgment* but if I have, I certainly have no recollection of having done so. The title of this article is therefore not intended to evoke anything associated with that work.

[1] *Van Orden v Perry*, 545 US 677, 700 (2005) (Breyer, J, concurring in the judgment).

978-0-226-36253-3/2009/2008-0002$10.00

formula."² Chief Justice Roberts's response was scornful: "In this case, the dissent—for a grab bag of no less than seven reasons—would tell us that this *particular* ICJ judgment is federal law. That is no sort of guidance."³

Justice Breyer's dissent in *Heller* again referred to judgment, this time judicial judgment: "[A]nswering questions such as the questions in this case requires judgment—judicial judgment exercised within a framework for constitutional analysis that guides that judgment and which makes its exercise transparent."⁴ He specified what judicial judgment required as "an interest-balancing inquiry,"⁵ a phrase that I believe unfortunately obscures what I think Justice Breyer means—or should mean—by "legal" or "judicial judgment." Justice Scalia picked up on the reference to interest balancing, but not on the reference to judgment, and described as "judge-empowering" the inquiry Justice Breyer would engage in.⁶

I believe that Justice Breyer's reference to legal or judicial judgment opens an important line of inquiry into, well, legal and judicial judgment. After Section II of this article describes the competing interpretive methods used by the majority and Justice Scalia in *Heller*, Section III tries to clear away some underbrush. Legal and judicial judgment is something different from judgment according to rules, tests, or formulas, but it is not, or at least is not necessarily, judgment according to standards or interest balancing, itself a formula. The difference is perhaps ironically signaled by the "grab bag of no less than seven reasons" Justice Breyer produced: seven is far too large a number to be usefully expressed in a standard or an interest-balancing formula. Justice Breyer correctly identifies transparency as a virtue of his approach, and I will contrast that transparency with what is I believe necessarily opaque in Justice Scalia's majority opinion in *Heller*.

With those matters out of the way, Section IV turns in a more constructive direction. I attempt to make sense of the idea that "legal and judicial judgment" is a distinctive mental faculty, in the

---

² *Medellin v Texas*, 128 S Ct 1346, 1382 (2008) (Breyer, J, dissenting). For a broader discussion of *Medellin*, see Curtis A. Bradley, *Self-Execution and Treaty Duality*, 2008 Supreme Court Review (in this volume).

³ 128 S Ct at 1363.

⁴ *District of Columbia v Heller*, 128 S Ct 2783, 2870 (2008) (Breyer, J, dissenting).

⁵ Id at 2852.

⁶ 128 S Ct at 2821.

same family of faculties as is the ability to sense the external world, without relying too heavily on deep accounts of mind and brain.[7] Relying on arguments made by others, especially Tony Kronman, I suggest that the way in which lawyers are trained helps the best lawyers develop the faculty of legal judgment. I conclude, though, with some worries about the extent to which what is regarded at any one time as good or sound legal judgment will reflect not the exercise of some internal mental faculty but rather some external social judgments of a sort that those not embedded in a particular social setting—in particular, nonlawyers and lawyers who see themselves marginalized by "the Establishment"—will find questionable. And, pervading the constructive account is a nagging sense that talk of a distinctive mental faculty does not quite get at what Justice Breyer means, or should mean, by legal or judicial judgment. Still, perhaps even a speculative and flawed discussion will provoke others into developing Justice Breyer's account more astutely than I can.

II. Interpretive Method in District of Columbia v Heller

The majority opinion in *Heller*, written by Justice Scalia, exemplifies the "new originalism."[8] Examining the use of the terms *arms*, *keep*, and *bear* in the years leading up to the Second Amendment's adoption and the use of those terms afterward, Justice Scalia concluded that the right protected by the Second Amendment was an individual right to keep common weapons in the home for the purpose of self defense against intruders.[9] The amendment's introductory clause explained one of the reasons for protecting such a right against legislative invasion, but its reference to "a well-regulated Militia" would not have been understood at the time to limit the right conferred in the amendment's operative clause. Other interpretive modes appear in the majority opinion only as targets of criticism. For example, precedent-based adjudication is insufficient to overcome what originalist analysis shows because the rel-

---

[7] The mental faculty of legal and judicial judgment is deployed in reaching discrete judgments, and the distinction between such judgments and the faculty itself is, I think, important.

[8] For a discussion of this aspect of the decision, see Mark Tushnet, *Heller and the New Originalism*, 69 Ohio St L J 609 (2008).

[9] 128 S Ct at 2822 (asserting that the Second Amendment "takes . . . off the table" an "absolute prohibition of handguns held and used for self-defense in the home.").

evant precedents are inadequate.[10] Justice Stevens's dissent com-
bines originalism with precedent. His opinion takes different lessons
from the historical inquiry,[11] and approaches precedent differently.[12]

Justice Breyer joined Justice Stevens's dissent, and supplemented
it with some historical inquiry of his own.[13] The heart of his opinion,
though, was a discussion of the interest-balancing approach he
thought the better way to approach the question of interpreting the
Second Amendment. That interest-balancing approach flowed naturally, Justice Breyer argued, from the standard form of constitutional analysis, which subjects challenged legislation to different
degrees of scrutiny depending on the individual interest adversely
affected by the legislation. Justice Breyer asserted, in my view correctly, that the purpose for gun regulation was "a 'primary concern
of every government—a concern for the safety and indeed the lives
of its citizens.'"[14] He then invoked the language of strict scrutiny,
the standard most likely to lead to invalidating regulation. Legislation can survive strict scrutiny only if it serves a "compelling"
interest. But, he noted, the interest in citizen safety was surely
compelling. The next step in strict scrutiny involves determining
whether the regulation serves the compelling interest well enough—
is "narrowly tailored," and the like. But that, Justice Breyer said,
was just what an interest-balancing approach requires—determining

[10] See id at 2814–15 (discussing *United States v Miller*, 307 US 174 (1939), and observing,
inter alia, that the decision dealt only with "the type of weapon" covered by the Second
Amendment (emphasis omitted); that it "did not even purport to be a thorough examination
of the Second Amendment"; that the "respondent made no appearance in the case" and
that the Court was therefore "presented with no counterdiscussion" to the government's
assertions about the Second Amendment's history).

[11] I do not believe that Justice Stevens's opinion must be read as exemplifying the old
rather than the new originalism. See Tushnet, quoted above in note 8, for a discussion.

[12] Having examined and dismissed the relevant Supreme Court decisions, Justice Scalia's
opinion treats lower court opinions reaching a result contrary to the *Heller* majority as
founded on sand. In contrast, Justice Stevens gives the line of precedents weight. His
position is confounded by the fact that he treats the Supreme Court's precedents as already
having resolved the question at hand, but I think it possible to read his opinion as defending
the proposition that a line of precedents can gain weight on its own even if the cases at
its foundation do not provide the strongest support one might imagine, and might indeed
not provide much support at all. And, in some sense, only such a reading gives the precedents weight as precedents rather than as correctly decided cases. The basic point here
is made by Fredrick Schauer, *Precedent*, 39 Stan L Rev 571 (1989).

[13] 128 S Ct at 2849 (Breyer, J, dissenting) (discussing colonial-era ordinances in the
cities of Boston, Philadelphia, and New York requiring that gunpowder be stored safely
to avoid danger to firefighters).

[14] Id at 2851 (Breyer, J, dissenting) (quoting *United States v Salerno*, 481 US 739, 755
(1987)).

"whether the regulation at issue impermissibly burdens the ['interests protected by the Second Amendment'] in the course of advancing the ['governmental public-safety concerns']."[15] The Court should ask "whether the statute burdens a protected interest in a way or to an extent that is out of proportion to the statute's salutary effects upon other important governmental interests."[16] Invoking some of his prior opinions,[17] Justice Breyer then said that the standard he described should be applied by courts that deferred "to a legislature's empirical judgment in matters where a legislature is likely to have greater expertise and greater institutional factfinding capacity," but the courts ultimately must make the "impermissible burden" determination for themselves.[18]

Justice Breyer's own application of his standard was divided into two parts, one assessing the District's ban from the perspective of the District's city council when it adopted the ban in 1976 and the other doing the same from the perspective of a court in 2008.[19] As to the former: Justice Breyer summarized the facts reported by a committee of the District's city council, detailing the role of guns in crime and violence nationwide and in the District. The report found that handguns had "a particularly strong link to undesirable activities in the District's exclusively urban environment."[20] As to the view from the courts today, Justice Breyer summarized statistics "that tell much the same story that the committee report told 30

---

[15] Id at 2852 (Breyer, J, dissenting). Justice Scalia's response to this argument involves an excursion into an area of constitutional theory—how to conceptualize the "core" rights protected by constitutional provisions—the exploration of which would take us too far afield. For a brief discussion, see Mark Tushnet, *Heller and the Perils of Compromise*, Lewis & Clark L Rev (2009).

[16] 128 S Ct at 2852 (Breyer, J, dissenting).

[17] Justice Breyer cited *Turner Broadcasting System, Inc. v FCC*, 520 US 180, 195–96 (1997), and *Nixon v Shrink Missouri Government PAC*, 528 US 377, 403 (2000) (Breyer, J, concurring).

[18] 128 S Ct at 2852 (Breyer, J, dissenting).

[19] Although Justice Breyer does not spell out his reasons for taking the two perspectives, I assume that he does so because legislation that did not impermissibly burden a protected interest when it was adopted might come to do so as circumstances change. I note one implication of this position: The precedential weight given a decision upholding a statute against constitutional challenge shortly after its adoption should decrease over time. For a related thought, see Alexander M. Bickel, *The Least Dangerous Branch: The Supreme Court at the Bar of Politics* 133–43 (1962) (discussing a decision rejecting a facial challenge to a licensing statute when brought shortly after the statute's enactment, and arguing that that decision should not preclude as-applied and facial challenges brought later).

[20] 128 S Ct at 2855 (Breyer, J, dissenting).

years ago."[21] Noting that opponents of the District's regulation did not quarrel substantially with the statistics he reported, Justice Breyer then turned to an evaluation of their disagreement with the District's view that a handgun ban would do something significant to alleviate crime and violence. He summarized their position: Crime had increased after the handgun ban went into effect, and indeed increased more rapidly in the District than in other cities; statistical studies showed that strict guns laws are not associated with decreases in crime, violence, suicide, or accidental deaths; other studies showed that handgun ownership deters crime. Justice Breyer said that these arguments might convince legislatures to adopt different regulations than the District's, but they were not "strong enough to destroy judicial confidence in the reasonableness of a legislature that rejects them."[22] Correlation is not causation, he said in effect.

A word should be said about Justice Breyer's analysis here. Under his interest-balancing approach, a court should be trying to find out the degree to which a particular regulation actually advances the government's compelling interest in citizen safety—safety from handguns law-abiding citizens own, which can be stolen, misused as in suicides, or accidentally discharged, and safety from lawbreakers who use handguns to commit crimes. Justice Breyer's summary of the studies presented to the Court is policy-based. He concedes that a legislature might find the studies sufficient to establish that stringent gun regulations have only a small effect in advancing the interest in citizen safety. That, though, is not enough for a judge. "[L]egislators, not judges, have primary responsibility for drawing policy conclusions from empirical facts," whereas judges should ask themselves only whether the legislature's inferences from the facts are reasonable.[23] He concluded that "the District's judgment, while open to question, is nevertheless supported by 'substantial evidence.'"[24]

For an inquiry into whether a burden is disproportionate to the goals achieved, this is rather weak tea: Justice Breyer asserts (appropriately) that citizen safety is a compelling interest, and then uses a strong version of judicial deference to a legislature's empirical

[21] Id at 2856 (Breyer, J, dissenting).

[22] Id at 2859 (Breyer, J, dissenting).

[23] Id at 2860 (Breyer, J, dissenting).

[24] Id (quoting *Turner Broadcasting System, Inc. v FCC*, 520 US 180, 195 (1997)).

judgments about the efficacy of the regulations it adopts to advance that interest. Under this analysis, courts would approach the determination of a gun regulation's constitutionality with a presumption one would think difficult to overcome. Recall that Justice Breyer set out on his journey by calling for strict scrutiny of gun regulations. But he ended by applying a test that looks much more suitable for intermediate than strict scrutiny.[25]

Justice Breyer then turned to the burdens the handgun ban placed on constitutionally protected interests. Justice Breyer dismissed the suggestion that the ban had any real impact on a District resident's ability to hunt, but accepted the proposition that the ban placed some burden on a constitutionally protected interest in self-defense in the home.[26] The proportionality inquiry Justice Breyer favored required that he next ask whether there were better—less restrictive—methods of achieving the legislature's goals. Here he observed that "the very attributes that make handguns particularly useful for self-defense are also what make them particularly dangerous."[27] Their ease of use by adults makes them dangerous for children; their size and weight make them useful for self-defense but also easy to steal and hide. Licensing systems do not address the risk of theft and subsequent misuse. His conclusion was that "although there may be less restrictive, *less effective* substitutes for an outright ban, there is no less restrictive *equivalent* of an outright ban."[28]

Once again we see how toothless this segment of the inquiry is. As everyone who has examined the question has concluded, a "less restrictive means" test is vacuous—that is, necessarily leads to upholding a statute against a claim that there is some less restrictive means of accomplishing the government's goals—if the substitute means must achieve exactly what the challenged statute does: One can *always* find something that the less restrictive means does less well than the statute, if only with respect to ease of administration.[29]

---

[25] I should note, though, that Justice Breyer did not purport to be applying strict scrutiny. His proportionality inquiry is in his view the right one for all claims that a statute violates constitutionally protected interests.

[26] In light of the attention paid to that interest by the majority, Justice Breyer's acceptance of this proposition seems rather grudging.

[27] 128 S Ct at 2864 (Breyer, J, dissenting).

[28] Id.

[29] For a succinct statement, see Laurence H. Tribe, *American Constitutional Law* 722–23 (1978) ("Implicit in any such holding . . . is a judgment that the reduced effectiveness entailed by a less restrictive alternative is outweighed by the increment in . . . protection gained by demanding such an alternative.").

Justice Breyer then wrapped up, although there was little more to say. Formally, he asked whether the handgun ban disproportionately burdened constitutionally protected interests. It was appropriately tailored, in the sense that it addressed a problem distinctively associated with urban crime and violence. And, although it did burden an interest in self-defense in the home, that interest was not, according to Justice Breyer, the primary interest protected by the Second Amendment. Notably, we cannot tell from Justice Breyer's opinion how the proportionality question would be answered had he agreed with the majority that self-protection in the home was the Second Amendment's "core."

III. Transparency, Rules, Standards, and Legal Judgment

Justice Breyer's defenses of legal or judicial judgment have been telegraphic at best, and some of his formulations and those of his critical colleagues on the Supreme Court are a bit misleading. Justice Breyer says, accurately, that his approach produces greater transparency in Supreme Court opinions, but I believe that transparency is a collateral benefit of the deployment of legal or judicial judgment. And his reference to interest balancing, which is the primary target of Justice Scalia's response in *Heller*, obscures the deeper meaning of legal or judicial judgment.

A. TRANSPARENCY

Justice Breyer defends his approach as transparent. By listing the things he takes into account when making a decision, he opens his opinion to public evaluation and criticism. So, for example, in *Heller* he refers to a number of studies of gun violence and its effects in cities as compared to rural areas,[30] and identifies problems he thinks infect studies purporting (in his view) to show the ineffectiveness of various gun regulations.[31] Those who read his opinion can examine the sources and assess whether Justice Breyer has presented them fairly. His opinion does indeed lay out a great deal of what he builds into his judgment, although the high degree of deference he gives to legislative judgments makes that transparency less significant as to his own judgment: An opinion that

---

[30] 128 S Ct at 2857 (Breyer, J, dissenting).

[31] Id at 2859 (Breyer, J, dissenting).

said that deference must be high and merely sketched the evidence the legislature might have relied on would have been equally transparent as to Justice Breyer's exercise of judicial judgment.

At least in legal settings, transparency is a comparative. How transparent is the majority's analysis in *Heller*?[32] After one concludes that the Second Amendment protects an individual right to keep and bear arms, that the word *arms* means "all instruments that constitute bearable arms" (which could include shoulder-launched Stinger missiles, one would think),[33] and that some regulations of bearable arms are constitutionally permissible, one has to decide whether the stringent regulations in the District of Columbia are permissible or not. Here Justice Scalia offers a two-part analysis. He enumerates a number of reasons why "a citizen may prefer a handgun for home defense"—ease of access and use, for example.[34] But, more important,[35] "the American people have considered the handgun to be the quintessential self-defense weapon," and "handguns are the most popular weapon chosen by Americans for self-defense in the home."[36] The connection between popularity or widespread preference and the rest of the majority's analysis is obscure. The majority's originalism suggests that the structure of the analysis should be something like this: At the time of the Second Amendment's adoption, Americans understood that it guaranteed that they could keep and bear those bearable arms that were most popular at the time. Projecting that understanding forward, the Second Amendment today protects the right to keep and bear the most popular weapon for self-defense in the home.[37]

---

[32] Justice Breyer discussed some of the opacities in the majority opinion. Id at 2869–70 (Breyer, J, dissenting).

[33] Id at 2792.

[34] Id at 2818.

[35] Justice Scalia writes, "Whatever the reason" after describing those reasons.

[36] 128 S Ct at 2818.

[37] A similar analysis would—or will—apply to the Court's treatment of what it referred to as presumptively lawful regulations, id at 2816–17 and n 36. Justice Scalia's opinion is ambiguous about what that treatment should be. At one point the opinion suggests that regulations of gun ownership and the like should be assessed according to some "standard of scrutiny" other than rational-basis review. Id at 2817. Elsewhere it suggests that regulations will be assessed according to "the historical justifications for the exceptions." Id at 2821. See also id at 2816 (asserting that "we do not undertake an exhaustive *historical* analysis today of the full scope of the Second Amendment") (emphasis added). On the abstract level at which the Court addressed the issue, a "standard of scrutiny" approach is not obviously different from Justice Breyer's interest-balancing approach, except that

Here two points seem worth making. First, I am constructing an argument out of the seeming logic of the majority's opinion, because the opinion does not provide the argument. To that extent the opinion is opaque. Second, and perhaps more important, why the majority (imputedly) projects the criterion *popularity* forward is unclear. Weapons are popular for reasons, as Justice Scalia's alternative argument suggests. Perhaps, then, we should project forward not popularity directly, but the reasons certain weapons were popular in 1791. Ease of access and use might be the reasons weapons in widespread use were popular. Yet, it might be the case (instead, or as well) that weapons were popular because they had a set of characteristics that provided what was widely believed to be the right balance between utility for self-defense and safety for the community. Justice Scalia's analysis does not explain why he chooses (if he does) to project forward "popularity" rather than the reasons for popularity. I do not doubt that one could defend the result in *Heller* even if some other characteristic were projected forward. The "transparency" argument, though, is that Justice Breyer tells us what he is doing, while Justice Scalia is far less clear.[38]

But, does Justice Breyer really tell us what he is doing? Certainly he tells us what he takes into account in coming to the conclusion he does. Listing a number of factors tells us what Justice Breyer thinks is important, but it does not tell us how much one factor matters relative to another, or why the factors taken together produce the result. It is as if the opinion reads, "Taking all these things into consideration, the regulation is constitutionally permissible (or the treaty is self-executing)." The first part of the analysis is transparent, the second substantially less so.

There are, I believe, two ways for Justice Breyer to respond to that observation. One, which he seems to adopt in *Heller*, is to adopt an "interest-balancing inquiry."[39] Such an inquiry might be summarized in a standard like "undue burden" or the propor-

---

some interests carry presumptively heavier weight than others. The "historical justifications" approach therefore seems more consistent with the opinion's tenor, and it is that approach that will involve the projection forward of something about the regulations thought compatible with the Second Amendment at the time of its adoption.

[38] Justice Breyer makes this point as follows: "[I]f tomorrow someone invests a particularly useful, highly dangerous self-defense weapon, Congress and the States had better ban it immediately, for once it becomes popular Congress will no longer possess the constitutional authority to do so." 128 S Ct 2869 (Breyer, J, dissenting).

[39] Id at 2852.

tionality test Justice Breyer proposed in *Heller*: "whether the statute burdens a protected interest in a way or to an extent that is
out of proportion to the statute's salutary effects upon other important government interests."[40] Whatever might be said about a
standard-based approach in *Heller* or *Van Orden*, I do not think
that at its heart Justice Breyer's approach rests on a preference
for standards as against rules. Justice Breyer's list of seven factors
to be considered does not have the feel of a social science inquiry
into facts, proportionality, and government interests. Perhaps we
could say that Justice Breyer would ask whether it would be reasonable all things considered to interpret a treaty to be self-executing, but in my view that does not capture the nature of the
judgment he thinks must be exercised. The next section explains
why the rules-standards debate is not the same as that between
Justice Breyer and his critics on the Court.

The second response takes the idea of "legal or judicial judgment" to be distinct from a standards-based approach. As Justice
Breyer repeatedly says, his approach *is* different from a rules-based
approach, but it is not, I think, a standards-based one. Rather,
under his approach a judge considers all the relevant matters and
then more or less directly apprehends the answer. Part IV of this
article takes up this, I believe better, understanding of Justice
Breyer's approach.

B. OF RULES AND STANDARDS

The rules-standards debate is decades old and I have essentially
nothing to add to it.[41] Justice Scalia in *Heller* asserted that an
interest-balancing standard was "judge-empowering."[42] Justice
Scalia is unfortunately unclear on what he means by "judge-empowering." There are, I think, three candidates for a definition.
(1) Interest balancing may empower judges to exercise complete

---

[40] Id.

[41] Some standard sources on the rules-standards distinction are Kathleen Sullivan, *The Supreme Court, 1991 Term—Foreword: The Justices of Rules and Standards*, 106 Harv L Rev 22 (1992); Duncan Kennedy, *Form and Substance in Private Law Adjudication*, 89 Harv L Rev 1685 (1976); Margaret Jane Radin, *Reconsidering the Rule of Law*, 69 BU L Rev 781 (1989); Carol M. Rose, *Crystals and Mud in Property Law*, 40 Stan L Rev 577 (1988); and Pierre Schlag, *Rules and Standards*, 33 UCLA L Rev 379 (1985).

[42] As I read the opinion, Justice Scalia appears to use this term as a pejorative. This section aims to show that it cannot be fairly so used once we understand that the term describes everything judges do no matter what their interpretive approach.

discretion in reaching their conclusions—or, more pejoratively, it licenses them to do whatever they feel like doing—whereas a rules-based jurisprudence imposes some constraints on judicial discretion. (2) Interest balancing may empower judges relative to legislatures. (3) Or, it may empower them relative to those who wrote and adopted the Constitution. Scholarship on rules and standards establishes that none of these candidates offers a persuasive account of "judge-empowering."

As to the first candidate: Rules and more particularly systems of rules can be judge-empowering relative to standards, depending on how complex the rule system is.[43] And, as to the second, standards can be legislature-empowering relative to rules. The reason is familiar. A court acts for a first-order reason—to accomplish something, such as interpreting the Constitution correctly—and uses a rule in the service of that goal to disempower judges. Constraining the courts, though, is a second-order reason. But, as is well known, rules are inevitably over- and underinclusive with respect to their first-order justifications. An overinclusive rule is legislature-disempowering. A standard, in contrast, can be used to isolate the source of the underinclusiveness and treat it as a consideration relevant to upholding the legislature's action. So, for example, suppose that the first-order reason for the Second Amendment is to ensure that people have the ability to use weapons for self-defense in the home, and to implement that reason the Court adopts the rule that the legislature may not prohibit sales of handguns. The rule is overinclusive, and it disables the legislature from adopting a regulation prohibiting sales of handguns to people who do not certify that they will keep the guns at home and use them only for self-defense.

Establishing that rules and standards can be equivalent through an analysis of *Heller* is necessarily difficult. As applied in *Heller*, Justice Scalia's rule was judge-empowering and Justice Breyer's standard was legislature-empowering. Justice Scalia's concern must therefore have been that Justice Breyer's interest-balancing approach would be legislature-disempowering in some other case where Justice Scalia's rule-based approach would be legislature-

---

[43] A complex rule system allows a judge to invoke a rule or an exception to the rule or a qualification to the exception, for example, to the point where the judge has the same degree of control over the outcome as she would in applying a standard like "undue burden."

empowering. But, again, *Heller* is hardly the case in which to make that claim. Justice Scalia must offer us a case in which Justice Breyer would invalidate a gun regulation that Justice Scalia would uphold. But, as Justice Scalia correctly noted, "Few laws in the history of our Nation have come close to the severe restriction of the District's handgun ban."[44] Justice Breyer would have upheld that ban, and, in light of its "severity," one is hard pressed to imagine any other gun regulation he would strike down.

We could explore this problem further, but it would take us far afield.[45] Instead, I will try to tease out of *Heller* itself some indications that Justice Breyer's standards-based approach is not necessarily more judge-empowering that the Court's rules-based approach. The Court asserted that "nothing in our opinion should be taken to cast doubt on longstanding prohibitions on the possession of firearms by felons. . . ."[46] Assume for the moment that the Court ends up holding felon-in-possession statutes constitutional across the board, either by employing intermediate (or strict) scrutiny or by projecting forward historical bans on gun possession by felons. Martha Stewart is a felon who under current law is forever prohibited from owning a handgun or keeping one in her home or homes for purposes of self-defense.[47] Under the assumed rules-based approach, this does not violate the Second Amendment. In contrast, one can readily imagine an interest-balancing analysis finding the ban unconstitutional: The burden on the constitutionally protected interest in self-defense by means of ordinary weapons is disproportionate to the statute's effect in advancing the government interest in ensuring that weapons of vi-

---

[44] 128 S Ct at 2818.

[45] The most promising direction would be to acknowledge that interest balancing is not judge-empowering in *Heller* or with respect to the Second Amendment generally, but that across the range of constitutional issues to which interest balancing might be applied, the technique is judge-empowering relative to a rules-based approach. To evaluate that claim, we would have to examine not only the structure of interest balancing but its actual application in many areas, as well as the various rule structures employed in those areas. I simply assert here my judgment that that examination would disclose that interest balancing is not systematically more judge-empowering that a rules-based approach.

[46] 128 S Ct at 2816–17.

[47] 18 USC § 922 (g) (1) ("It shall be unlawful for any person who has been convicted in any court of a crime punishable for a term of imprisonment for a term exceeding one year . . . to . . . possess in or affecting commerce, any firearm or ammunition"). Martha Stewart was convicted of a securities fraud offense carrying a potential term of more than one year. *United States v Stewart*, 433 F3d 273 (2d Cir 2005) (affirming conviction for violating 18 USC § 371, which carries a potential sentence of five years).

olence be kept out of the hands of those who have demonstrated a propensity to violence. Here interest balancing is judge-empowering and legislature-disempowering.

Next, consider the existing ban on handgun possession by those who have committed misdemeanor crimes of domestic violence or are under a domestic-violence order of protection.[48] Again under the assumed rules-based approach, these provisions might be unconstitutional because they deny the right to own handguns to people who have not committed felonies (or are otherwise disqualified by some historically rooted justification for a ban on possession). Here the rules-based approach is judge-empowering and legislature-disempowering. And again it is easy to imagine an interest-balancing approach supporting the conclusion that these provisions are constitutionally permissible because they advance the government interest described above without unduly burdening the constitutionally protected interest. Interest balancing then would be legislature-empowering and judge-disempowering.

The preceding are examples of the ways in which an interest-balancing approach might be legislature-empowering relative to a rules-based approach because the interest balancer can take into account features of the problem that the rules screen from judgment. Of course the judge who takes a rules-based approach could develop a response, perhaps along the following lines.[49] The exception allowing bans on gun possession by felons is a projection forward of a historically rooted exception for felons, it is true. But in the 1790s felonies were defined in ways that meant that a felon was almost inevitably a person who had demonstrated a propensity for violence. The historically rooted exception, then, is not for felons as such, but for those convicted of crimes that are defined in ways that ensure that felons were those with the undesirable propensity. Projecting that forward, we have an exception to the rule against banning handgun possession not for felons as such but for those who by their conduct have demonstrated a propensity for violence. Martha Stewart can own a handgun; the person con-

---

[48] 18 USC §§ 922 (g) (8) (domestic-violence protection order provision), (9) (misdemeanor crime of domestic violence).

[49] I must note that I am hypothesizing facts that I suspect historical research would indeed confirm.

victed of misdemeanor domestic violence cannot.[50] At this point, though, we are dealing with a rule system, not a rule. And the examples show that rule systems are no less judge-empowering than are interest-balancing approaches.

Perhaps, though, what Justice Scalia means is that Justice Breyer's approach is judge-empowering not vis-à-vis the legislature, but vis-à-vis the Constitution makers. On this view Justice Scalia's originalism respects the Constitution makers' decisions, and so is power-neutral vis-à-vis contemporary legislatures: It empowers judges when contemporary lawmakers depart from the Constitution makers' design and disempowers them when those lawmakers respect that design. And, again on this view, Justice Breyer's approach is judge-empowering across the board, because whether a decision by contemporary lawmakers survives constitutional scrutiny depends solely on how judges apply Justice Breyer's approach. Note, though, that on this interpretation the conflict is between an approach that empowers the Constitution makers (as judges understand what they did) vis-à-vis contemporary lawmakers and one that empowers judges vis-à-vis contemporary lawmakers. In choosing which approach we ought to take, in the first instance we have to compare the Constitution makers to contemporary decision makers. And the question of relative judicial empowerment is irrelevant to *that* comparison. Only after we have a good account of why decisions made by the Constitution makers ought to prevail over decisions made by contemporary legislatures can we ask whether an approach that gives judges the power to determine what decisions were indeed made by the Constitution makers should be preferred over Justice Breyer's approach. Justice Scalia makes a preference for the Constitution makers axiomatic, but as a large body of scholarship shows, it is not.[51]

Justice Scalia's axiom may be that a preference for the Consti-

---

[50] The "order of protection" provision could be upheld on the ground that the judge who entered the order necessarily made a finding that the person subject to the order had a propensity to commit violence.

[51] For an example of a normative—and plainly contestable—argument for the preference for the Constitution makers, see Randy E. Barnett, *Restoring the Lost Constitution: The Presumption of Liberty* (2004). Every work that defends a nonoriginalist approach to constitutional interpretation and takes the countermajoritarian difficulty seriously argues against the preference for the Constitution makers, because there is no difficulty unless there are reasons to prefer decisions made by contemporary legislatures to those made by the Constitution makers (as judges understand those decisions).

tution makers implemented through originalist methods constrains judges, whereas Justice Breyer's approach does not. And that might be so if "legal or judicial judgment" meant no more than mere personal preference. But, as I argue below, there is a better—or at least more suggestive—interpretation of Justice Breyer's words, and if we adopt that interpretation arriving at a conclusion about whether Justice Scalia's approach or Justice Breyer's is more constraining becomes substantially more difficult.[52]

I have been proceeding in this section as if what Justice Breyer meant by "legal or judicial judgment" was "standards, not rules." That substitution might work in *Van Orden* and *Heller*. In both one might fairly say that Justice Breyer was calling for the use of a standard like "undue burden" or "reasonable under all the circumstances." The substitution is more difficult in *Medellin*, as I observed earlier, because that case involves rules versus judicial judgment in connection with interpreting treaties.[53]

IV. The Idea of Legal Judgment

The idea that there is *something* fairly characterized as legal or judicial judgment is hardly novel. Louis Brandeis spoke of being the lawyer "for the situation,"[54] by which he appears to have meant a practice in which he took into account all the ramifications of the problem at hand and helped devise a solution that addressed the concerns of everyone affected by the problem. Karl Llewellyn described the "situation sense" of good lawyers,[55] and the term he

---

[52] This is particularly so if, as I have argued elsewhere, the claim that Justice Scalia's interpretive approach is substantially constraining is seriously overstated. See Mark Tushnet, *New Originalism*, cited above in note 8.

[53] Further, the majority in *Medellin* held that a treaty is self-executing only if its "terms reflect a determination . . . that the treaty has domestic effect." 128 S Ct at 1366. This holding might raise questions about whether a rather large number of ordinary commercial treaties are enforceable by a treaty beneficiary. The Court gave examples in which such treaties had been held enforceable defensively. Cases where parties seek to enforce such treaties offensively, I suspect, are good candidates for the invocation of an exception to the *Medellin* rule. If so, the distance between Justice Breyer's approach and that of the *Medellin* majority would be reduced just as, and indeed by the same mechanism that, the distance between his approach and the majority's in *Heller* is likely to be reduced.

[54] Richard Painter attributes the phrase to a supporter of Brandeis testifying at Brandeis's Supreme Court confirmation hearings. Richard Painter, *Contracting Around Conflicts in a Family Representation: Louis Brandeis and the Warren Trust*, 8 U Chi L Sch Roundtable 353, 353 n 2 (2001).

[55] Karl Llewellyn, *The Common Law Tradition: Deciding Appeals* 403 (1960).

used resonates with the idea of legal or judicial judgment as a mental capacity. Elsewhere Llewellyn wrote of "the law of singing reason"[56] in a way that—style aside—sounds a great deal like Justice Breyer: Such a rule "wears both a right situation-reason and a clear scope-criterion on its face" and produces "regularity, reckonability, and justice all together."[57] Yet, these formulations are famously vaporous or, more generously, no more than metaphorically evocative.[58] Can we do anything to dissipate the fog?

A. THE BASIC IDEA

What Llewellyn's words evoke is, I believe, the idea that legal or judicial judgment is a mental faculty or capacity. So, Llewellyn writes of good lawyers who have "horse-*sense*," which is a combination of "experience, sense, and intuition."[59] Or, again, the good judge will "*recognize*" the law immanent in a situation.[60] As Anthony Kronman summarizes Llewellyn's position, the good judge "will *see with special clarity* what decision in any particular case is most likely to comport with, and provide support for, the emerging though still undeveloped *ethos* of the situation that the case in question illustrates."[61] When we try to expound Llewellyn's po-

---

[56] Id at 183.

[57] Id. I suspect that it is no accident that Justice Breyer, a leading purposivist in statutory interpretation, echoes Llewellyn, also a purposivist. Compare Stephen Breyer, *On the Uses of Legislative History*, 65 S Cal L Rev 845 (1992), with Karl Llewellyn, *Remarks on the Theory of Appellate Decision and the Rules of Canons About How Statutes are to be Construed*, 3 Vand L Rev 395 (1950).

[58] Anthony Kronman observes that Llewellyn "leaves an essential component of the lawyer-statesman ideal concealed in mystery and therefore vulnerable to attack as a mystical conceit." Anthony T. Kronman, *The Lost Lawyer: Failing Ideals of the Legal Profession* 24 (1993). (In context, I think the "essential component" referred to here is judgment, although it might be the connection between judgment and character.) See also Todd Rakoff, "The Implied Terms of Contracts: Of 'Default Rules' and 'Situation-Sense,'" in Jack Beatson and Daniel Friedmann, eds, *Good Faith and Fault in Contract Law* 202 (1995) ("Llewellyn's . . . exposition of situation-sense has at times a mystical sound to it.").

Sometimes in teaching about what I take to be Justice Breyer's approach, I refer to Robert Heinlein's description of "grokking," which Heinlein defined as "understanding so thoroughly that the observer becomes a part of the observed—to merge, blend, intermarry, lose identity in group experience." Robert Heinlein, *Stranger in a Strange Land* 214 (1961). Joseph Singer asserts that "grok[king] describe[s] accurate intuition." 94 Yale L J 1, 47 n 144 (1984). I believe that Singer is correct to the extent that he treats "grokking" as a mental faculty like intuition or sensory perception, but that "intuition" is not precisely what "grokking" is—and is not what I have in mind when I use the term in my classes to get at what I believe is at work in Justice Breyer's approach.

[59] Llewellyn, *The Common Law Tradition* at 201 (cited in note 55) (emphasis added).

[60] Id at 261.

[61] Kronman, *The Lost Lawyer* at 223 (cited in note 58) (emphasis added).

sition, that is, we end up using terms associated with mental faculties. I suggest only that we should take the association seriously.

Further elaborating his understanding of Llewellyn, Kronman counterposes to Llewellyn's account one in which "abstract theorizing" plays a large role.[62] For Kronman (and Llewellyn), for the good lawyer and judge horse-sense is a habit, not a theory.[63] And habits are acquired by experience and practice, not (primarily) by reflection.[64] For lawyers, the training begins in law school, with the case method, and continues in practice. When done well, teaching through the case method induces prospective lawyers to work their way inside a real-world problem, to see it in all its complexity. That complexity is brought out in traditional Socratic teaching when the instructor offers slight variants on the facts as presented in the case, either as new cases or, more interestingly I think, as suggesting some complexities in the case at hand that were suppressed by the reported decision. It is brought out in other forms of case-related teaching such as clinical legal education through the student's confrontation with an unpurified real-world problem.[65] Asking a student to describe the solution to the problem—and insisting that the solution be untheorized—cultivates the faculty of legal judgment.[66]

---

[62] Id at 217. See also Rakoff, "The Implied Terms of Contracts" at 202 (cited in note 58) ("the particular virtue of judges using this method is not to be smart, as it might be if they were presented with a clear, abstract, and complex algorithm"). Kronman elsewhere describes the capacity he identifies as "deliberative imagination." Kronman, *The Lost Lawyer* at 116 (cited in note 58).

[63] See Karl Llewellyn, *The Bramble Bush: The Classic Lectures on the Law and Law School* 104 (Steve Sheppard, ed, 2008) ("Good hunching power is a resultant of good sense, imagination, and *much* knowledge."). Kronman connects Llewellyn's view of legal or judicial judgment as a mental faculty with Kronman's own interest in the lawyer-statesman ideal, and criticizes Llewellyn for failing to make such a connection. See note 58 above. Whatever the merits of Kronman's position about lawyer-statesmen, I am interested in the possibility of a freestanding faculty of legal or judicial judgment, and so do not examine here what Kronman draws from Llewellyn.

[64] One can consciously direct oneself to engage in something that becomes habitual, but once it does, the conscious direction drops out of the picture.

[65] Kronman takes Socratic instruction as the paradigmatic form of legal education, which requires him to valorize the shifting perspectives Socratic instruction forces on students— first asking them to argue for the plaintiff, then for the defendant, for example. See Kronman, *The Lost Lawyer* at 113–14 (cited in note 58). Again, that analysis, whatever its merit, is more closely connected to Kronman's interest in educating prospective lawyer-statesmen than to Llewellyn's interest in improving the prospective lawyer's ability to exercise the faculty of legal or judicial judgment.

[66] Good teachers will allow gestures in the direction of moral or political philosophy, or of economics, but they will caution students against taking those gestures to be placeholders for philosophy or economics pursued more systematically.

Things change once the student becomes a lawyer, and as Kronman emphasizes not always for the better. Today's new lawyers may find themselves cooped up in a narrow specialty, working on a small part of a large problem under the supervision of senior lawyers who do not give them a larger view of the situation because the senior lawyers find themselves under severe financial and time constraints. Llewellyn's good lawyer—that is, the one who comes to have good legal judgment—finds herself in a different situation. The model lawyer for Llewellyn is the small-town lawyer dealing with the everyday legal problems of ordinary people, or the high-level counselor to a large corporation who has the chief executive's trust and offers legal advice fully informed by knowledge of the corporation's activities.[67] Working in those settings gives the lawyer the opportunity to exercise the faculty of legal judgment, and good lawyers demonstrate their ability to exercise that faculty well.[68]

Treating legal or judicial judgment as a mental faculty has an additional feature. Justice Scalia's concern that Justice Breyer's approach is "judge-empowering" suggests a familiar critique—that interpretive approaches untethered to some larger theoretical construct license judges to implement their personal preferences under the guide of enforcing the law.[69] We might take critics of Justice Breyer's approach as presented here as saying that a judicial judgment in favor of a plaintiff is rather like an everyday "judgment" that vanilla ice cream is better than chocolate ice cream—a statement of personal preference but not the exercise of some interesting mental faculty.

---

[67] Llewellyn's lectures to first-year law students tack back and forth between references to these two practice settings. Llewellyn, *Bramble Bush* at 17–18, 161–62 (cited above in note 63).

[68] Todd Rakoff suggested to me in conversation that the fact that the U.S. Supreme Court is a generalist court, dealing with statutory and common law matters (even in a post-*Erie* world) as well as constitutional interpretation, harmonizes well with the proposition that its judges are to exercise judicial judgment, because their regular exposure to such a wide range of matters cultivates in them the faculty of judicial judgment. And, although the matter is too complex to explore in this article, it may be that judges on specialized constitutional courts elsewhere should exercise a different form of judgment, which, for example, might include more explicit attention to the role politics plays in good constitutional interpretation. For a discussion, see Mark Tushnet, "Comparative Constitutional Law," in Mathias Reimann and Reinhard Zimmerman, eds, *Oxford Handbook of Comparative Law* 1242–46 (2006).

[69] For Justice Scalia, of course, the theoretical construct is originalism, but there are many alternatives: economics, moral or political philosophy, and more.

There is a large philosophical literature on the nature of judgment, and I do not think it likely to be productive to draw on it here (even if I had the expertise to do so credibly, which I do not). All I can do is report that many of us seem to distinguish in our ordinary speech between preferences and judgments: I prefer twentieth-century modern art to medieval art, but I judge that in general Constantin Brancusi is a better sculptor than Jeff Koons.[70] And I am confident that people who have experienced rap and hip-hop music in ways that I have not can distinguish between good and not-as-good rappers and hip-hop artists, all of whom sound pretty much the same to me.

Here Llewellyn's idea of a "situation sense" may be helpful. When we make aesthetic judgments such as those I have just described, one thing we think about is whether some component of the art work fits well into the entire work.[71] The good solutions to which Llewellyn refers have the same characteristic in the legal context: All their components fit the circumstances well. Judgments of this sort seem to lie somewhere between mere preferences and theoretically rationalized conclusions.[72] At the very least, the critical claim that legal or judicial judgment of the sort I believe Justice Breyer to be invoking is not different from mere preferences like those for vanilla or chocolate ice cream needs a defense; asserting the critical claim is insufficient, in light of our ability to understand the difference between preferences and judgments in other contexts.[73] That, I think, is enough to make Justice Breyer's approach interesting enough to become an object of scholarly attention.

---

[70] Which is not to say that I judge every Brancusi sculpture better than any Koons.

[71] I take the artist's effort to construct such a fit to be one major theme in the first act of Stephen Sondheim's *Sunday in the Park with George*.

[72] Rakoff, "The Implied Terms of Contracts" at 216–19 (cited in note 58), describes "Situation-sense as a general method for constructing default rules" (section heading), with "eight distinctive features," id at 216. I am inclined to think that this systematizes situation-sense too much, placing it closer to the pole of theory and rationality than is appropriate.

[73] As I understand the philosophical literature, this point is what philosophers are getting at when they describe (certain) judgments as objective or universal. For examples, see Paul Edwards, *The Logic of Moral Discourse* 108 (1955) (describing the statement, "The steak at Barney's is nice" as "clearly an objective claim"); Nick Zangwill, "Aesthetic Judgment," § 1.5, *Stanford Encyclopedia of Philosophy*, http://plato.stanford.edu/entries/aesthetic-judgment/ ("Judgments of taste are like empirical judgments in that they have universal validity; but, they are unlike empirical judgment [sic] in that they are made on the basis of an inner response."). I thank Robert Justin Lipkin for directing me to Edwards's argument.

B. SOME QUALIFICATIONS

I have referred to legal judgment as a mental faculty. That term resonates with a philosophical tradition, in one of whose incarnations mental faculties are reducible in principle to characteristics of the physical brain.[74] For present purposes I am agnostic on whether the faculty of legal judgment is part of a family of mental faculties ultimately reducible in that way, although I confess to some skepticism about the proposition that it is.[75] In using the term I mean to evoke ideas about preconscious mental operations, or taken-for-granted ways of thinking, which may but need not be tied to anything in the physical brain.[76]

A more important qualification arises in this way: Can legal judgment, understood to be a mental faculty, account for disagreement among lawyers who all assert that they are indeed employing legal judgment in reaching their decisions? Cases like *Medellin* and *Heller* unfortunately do not give us the material for dealing with that question. Although there was disagreement in both cases, only Justice Breyer asserted that he was using legal judgment, a fact that provided the basis for the majority's criticism of his method of decision making. More generally, contemporary disputes over interpretation among U.S. constitutionalists typically involve claims about method entangled with claims about outcomes. Under the circumstances it is exceedingly difficult, and perhaps impossible, to isolate the extent to which the differences in outcome result from differences in method or equivalently and more important in the present context to determine whether judges using the same method could fairly reach different results.

Still, it seems implausible a priori that any interpretive method, even one tied to something like a mental faculty, would eliminate reasonable disagreements among judges. At this point the training that equips good lawyers may be significant. Consider what I take to be another mental faculty, the capacity to perform and appreciate music. Everyone can play music and appreciate it, but those

---

[74] In modern shorthand, on this view mental faculties are hardwired in the brain.

[75] It seems reasonably clear to me that a full account of legal or judicial judgment would treat it not as a freestanding mental faculty but as a version of a more general faculty of judgment. I lack the ability to discuss "judgment" in more general terms, though.

[76] In particular I do not mean to rely on, or even strongly to evoke, the burgeoning literature on neuroscience and ethical judgment, a literature about which I have a great deal of skepticism.

who are trained are better in the exercise of those capacities than those who are not. So too with the capacity to make legal judgments. Nonlawyers have the capacity to exercise legal judgment. Present them with a legal problem and ask for an answer, and most of the time you will get something that is a reasonable reproduction of the lawyer's answer, or is a reasonable alternative to it. Sometimes you will get quite wild answers, of course. And you will almost never get an answer that reflects what a good lawyer might say about the problem. The good lawyer will identify facets of the problem that the nonlawyer overlooks, for example, perhaps because they are not on the problem's surface or because they link this problem to another one such that some answers to the present problem would present difficulties for the other.

At the same time, of course, we know that people well trained in music will disagree about whether a particular piece of music or a specific performance is a good one. Some think that modern atonal music is better than eighteenth-century music, for example, and there obviously are disagreements about whether a specific piece of atonal music is good within that field. What accounts for these disagreements?

Two answers seem plausible. First, training gives people a set of criteria to use in evaluating performances and, in the context of interest here, in evaluating legal arguments. People disagree when they rank the criteria somewhat differently or when they evaluate somewhat differently the significance of facts or nonlegal judgments relevant to one or more criteria.[77] Implicit in this formulation are two thoughts. Good lawyers have a grasp on more criteria than less good lawyers. They have reasons, which they can offer, for ignoring one or more criteria when seeking to resolve a specific problem, whereas the less good lawyers do not even know that they are ignoring such criteria. In addition, and perhaps more important, good lawyers disagree "somewhat" over ranking and applying the criteria. Their disagreements, that is, occur within a restricted range. One good lawyer will not think it accurate to say to another, "I know that you think that criterion extremely important when dealing with this problem, but I find it quite irrelevant here." Rather, the response will be, "I understand

---

[77] An alternative formulation is that people disagree when they place somewhat different weights on different criteria (or on the facts and the like relevant to a particular criterion). I avoid this formulation because it brings us too close to the language of balancing.

that you think it quite important, but in my view you are over-estimating its importance somewhat, but enough to affect your judgment—or, as I see it, misjudgment—about the proper outcome."

The restricted range within which good lawyers disagree leads us to the second response to the question about the origins of disagreement. Put simply, training socializes people into understanding what it means to be a good lawyer.[78] Some possibilities, conceptually available, are taken off the table through socialization.[79] And, of course, what seems to be a good argument at one time might come to seem a bad one at another.[80]

This might seem an unattractive feature of legal judgment. We know, for example, that legal academics in the 1950s evaluated candidates for faculty appointments by asking whether they were "sound," meaning, did they show that they could exercise what then counted as good legal judgment?[81] That had a troublingly homogenizing effect on the legal academy. So too with legal or judicial judgment, understood as I have described it, more generally. Disagreements will occur, but only within the range permitted by the then-prevailing standards of good judgment. Those who construct arguments in seemingly good legal form to support outré conclusions will be regarded as bad lawyers, lacking good legal or judicial judgment. Yet it seems to me implausible that legal or judicial judgment, understood as a mental faculty, could possibly have this kind of "Establishment" tilt.

Again, two responses seem available. The first is a straightforward confession-and-avoidance. All this might be true, but is irrelevant with respect to judges. The processes for selecting judges

---

[78] Edwards, *The Logic of Moral Discourse* (cited in note 73), makes important to his discussion that those who understand the judgments each other makes come from a common background. See id at 106 ("It should be added that both Horn and I are, at any rate as regards food, persons of very average (Western) taste."). My reference to socialization resonates, for me, with that observation.

[79] In classrooms, this occurs, for example, when an instructor asks a student to "talk like a lawyer," meaning, "Put that argument, which you have drawn from somewhere outside the law, into terms familiar to lawyers."

[80] People whose sole training is in appreciating or performing pre-twentieth-century music may find it difficult to say that modern music is good according to any criterion they have at hand, and may even find it impossible to perform such music in a minimally competent way on instruments they know how to use in performing baroque or romantic-era music.

[81] Cf. Laura Kalman, *Yale Law School and the Sixties* 50 (2005) (describing Yale's failure to promote Vern Countryman and David Haber in the 1950s).

will surely screen out almost all of those with eccentric views anyway.[82] The bench will almost inevitably be rather homogeneous with respect to the conclusions judges reach.[83] Given who our judges are quite likely to be, we would benefit from having them exercise legal or judicial judgment even though we know that such judgment operates within a restricted range. Justice Breyer's position, as reconstructed here, is that good lawyers acting as judges exercising such judgment reach better results than bad lawyers purporting to exercise such judgment and than lawyers who mistakenly think that they should not exercise judgment at all.[84]

The second response is perhaps more interesting. I have assumed to this point that training can help a lawyer better exercise the faculty of legal or judicial judgment. There are, of course, other faculties as well, including the ordinary faculty of rational evaluation of arguments and facts. We can imagine a person who has been trained to be a good lawyer in the sense I have been developing, who is also extremely good at using the rational faculty. Such a person might be able to simulate good legal or judicial judgment, so to speak. That is, she could proffer the answer to a legal question that a good lawyer would proffer, and yet know at the same time that radically different answers, and not merely answers within the restricted range common to (ordinary) good lawyers, are rationally available.[85] I think that the most interesting possibility raised by this suggestion is that the simulations of good legal or judicial judgment might have a halo effect: When this lawyer or judge offers a radical answer, the fact that she has heretofore displayed good legal or judicial judgment may give her answer credibility—may make it seem not quite as radical as initially appeared, for example.

---

[82] This is true of both the federal nomination-and-confirmation process and state-level elections, at least for higher state courts.

[83] No one expects any judge in the United States to conclude that the Constitution requires some form of market socialism, for example, even though formally good legal arguments to that conclusion are not hard to come by. (All it takes is a bit of creativity with the state action doctrine, building on *Shelley v Kraemer*, 334 US 1 (1948), and disparate impact doctrine.) Note that homogeneity in the legal academy should be more troubling because it screens out ideas rather than authoritative judgments, which is why the use of "soundness" as a criterion for academic appointments is (or, one hopes, was) a bad practice.

[84] I return below to one problem that Justice Breyer's position as reconstructed here raises.

[85] I imagine Justice William O. Douglas to have been such a person.

V. Implications and Conclusion

That there is a faculty of legal or judicial judgment may have only modest implications for institutional design. It suggests that it is a good idea to staff courts with people trained as lawyers. That does not rule out the possibility of including some people trained in other disciplines on multijudge courts, as recently suggested by Adrian Vermeule, although it does suggest that the lawyers should predominate.[86] Similarly, what may be an emerging "soft" rule that Supreme Court Justices should have experience as appellate judges is obviously consistent with the idea that there is a faculty of judicial judgment. To the extent that lawyers' training and practice experience helps improve their ability to exercise that faculty, perhaps we might seek in our Justices a range of experiences as lawyers—prosecutors and criminal defense attorneys, those who in their legal practices represented large corporations and individual plaintiffs, and (perhaps) lawyers with political experiences that brought them into contact with the problems the legal system posed for ordinary citizens.

Probably the most important modest implication of identifying a faculty of legal or judicial judgment is that doing so is not inconsistent with a practice of adjudication in which rules play a role. Judicial judgment might in some circumstances lead a judge to conclude that a rule rather than a standard is appropriate for the problem at hand. Good lawyers know that sometimes having rules pervade an area is better—because of the guidance the rules give to other important actors in the system, for example—than using standards. What Justice Breyer rejects is the opposition between rules and judicial judgment on the level of method: He would not exclude some solutions a priori because they reject the rule form and require judicial judgment.

This methodological point does not in itself say anything about whether Justice Breyer's opinions overall or in some specific areas demonstrate good judgment. Sometimes his judgment seems to be tied too closely to what are a case's accidental factual features. For example, *Bartnicki v Vopper* found it unconstitutional to hold a person liable for damages under wiretap laws for broadcasting an unlawfully recorded phone call.[87] The phone call occurred dur-

---

[86] Adrian Vermeule, *Should We Have Lay Justices?* 59 Stan L Rev 1569 (2007).

[87] 532 US 514 (2001).

ing collective-bargaining negotiations between a teachers' union and a school board, and in the call the union's negotiator said, "If they're not gonna move for three percent, we're gonna have to go to their, their homes . . . To blow off their front porches, we'll have to do some work on some of those guys." Justice Breyer agreed that the damage award was unconstitutional, but in a concurring opinion suggested that the majority had not been sufficiently sensitive in "strik[ing] a reasonable balance between their speech-restricting and speech-enhancing consequences."[88] He focused on the case's facts: that the speaker was a "limited public figure," for example, and, perhaps more important, that "the speakers had little or no *legitimate* interest in maintaining the privacy of the particular conversation" because its content "rais[ed] a significant concern for the safety of others."[89] Surely, though, the latter was a mere accident. The union representative pretty clearly was letting off steam rather than expressing a real intention to engage in violence, and I doubt that the result should change no matter how forcefully the representative expressed his dissatisfaction with the negotiation's course. Good judgment would have involved understanding the statement on a somewhat higher level of generality than Justice Breyer saw it.[90] In *Bartnicki*, perhaps a rule would have been better than a standard.

Yet, facts do matter to arriving at good judgments, and Justice Breyer's split votes in the two recent Ten Commandments cases illustrate how. He voted to uphold the display of the Ten Commandments on the statehouse grounds in Texas, and to find unconstitutional a display of the Ten Commandments in a county courthouse. His opinion strongly suggested that he found a real distinction between old and new displays with respect to their relation to Establishment Clause values.[91] And such a distinction

---

[88] Id at 536 (Breyer, J, concurring).

[89] Id at 539.

[90] Having criticized Justice Breyer's exercise of judgment in *Bartnicki*, though, I feel compelled to note that my own assessment is that overall his work, including his opinion in *Heller*, displays how a good lawyer goes about embodying good judgment in the law.

[91] See *Van Orden v Perry*, 545 US 677, 702 (2005) (Breyer, J, concurring in the judgment) ("As far as I can tell, 40 years passed in which the presence of this monument, legally speaking, went unchallenged (until the single legal objection raised by petitioner). And I am not aware of any evidence suggesting that this was due to a climate of intimidation. . . . Those 40 years suggest that the public visiting the capitol grounds has considered the religious aspect of the tablets' message as part of what is a broader moral and historical message reflective of a cultural heritage.").

is certainly defensible and perhaps sensible. The fact that a new display provokes immediate controversy signals that the locality is already culturally heterogeneous, and efforts to identify it with a distinctive religious tradition should raise Establishment Clause red flags. And the fact that an old display had not provoked controversy until recently signals that cultural heterogeneity is new to the area and that *eliminating* the display might suggest the disparagement of long-term residents in a way that also should raise red flags.[92]

As I indicated at the outset, I am unsure whether we can make complete sense of the idea of legal or judicial judgment as a distinctive mental faculty. At the same time, there must be *something* to be said in favor of Justice Breyer's approach to adjudication, whether I have said it or not. For, in the end, surely there is something quite peculiar about a criticism of judges for the very fact that they exercise judgment.

---

[92] Although the concept is not directly applicable, the distinction between old and new displays resonates with the tort-law concept of "coming to the nuisance," according to which someone who moves into an area where some existing activity satisfies the criteria for public nuisance may not recover damages from the activity.

NATHANIEL PERSILY

FIG LEAVES AND TEA LEAVES IN THE SUPREME COURT'S RECENT ELECTION LAW DECISIONS

In the field of American election law, political developments and the Supreme Court's docket often progress along parallel tracks. Those tracks rarely intersect with such salience and notoriety as in the 2000 election controversy. More often, the issues the Supreme Court decides have immediate thematic relevance to the ongoing campaign, even when the Court is not actually deciding a case that grows out of the campaign itself. Such was the case with the Supreme Court's election law docket from the 2007–2008 term and the historic 2008 election. The five election law cases the Court decided hinted at ongoing controversies with incarnations in the 2008 campaign.

The election law docket was diverse, including a case on each of the topics that have preoccupied election lawyers and academics in recent years: campaign finance,[1] voter identification,[2] the Voting

Nathaniel Persily is Charles Keller Beekman Professor of Law and Political Science, Columbia Law School.

AUTHOR'S NOTE: Thanks to Jason M. Levy for excellent research assistance, and to Richard Briffault, Guy-Uriel Charles, Christopher Elmendorf, Ned Foley, Heather Gerken, Richard Hasen, Samuel Issacharoff, Pamela Karlan, Richard Pildes, and David Strauss for helpful comments.

[1] *Davis v FEC*, 128 S Ct 2759 (2008).

[2] *Crawford v Marion County Election Bd*, 128 S Ct 1610 (2008).

Rights Act (VRA),[3] and the regulation of political parties.[4] As the Supreme Court considered the constitutionality of a federal law that attempted to mitigate the funding advantages of rich candidates, both John McCain and Barack Obama grappled with legal and political controversies growing out of the acceptance or non-acceptance of public funding designed for that purpose.[5] While the Court attempted to define the constitutional bounds of a political party's power in the nomination process, Democrats in Florida and Michigan were suing their party to force it to seat delegations elected in contravention of party rules.[6] As the parties geared up for the many fights in the fall over voter fraud and voter suppression, the Supreme Court weighed in with its first full opinion concerning voter identification requirements.[7] Finally, as Barack Obama made history as the first successful African American presidential candidate, the Court considered whether to give an expansive or restricted reading to provisions of the Voting Rights Act that, in indirect and direct ways, made that historic event possible.[8]

At the highest levels of abstraction, the themes in these two parallel universes appear well connected, but the cases from the 2007–2008 term, with perhaps one exception, had very little salience with the public. The one exception might be the Court's decision in *Crawford v Marion County*[9] upholding Indiana's law requiring voters to present a photo ID. That case represented the latest chapter in the sordid story of perceived fraud and disenfranchisement (or "integrity" versus "access") that had played out in several states

---

[3] *Riley v Kennedy*, 128 S Ct 1970 (2008).

[4] *Wash. State Grange v Wash. State Republican Party*, 128 S Ct 1184 (2008); *New York v Lopez Torres*, 128 S Ct 791 (2008).

[5] See, for example, Michael Cooper, *McCain to Obama: "Keep Your Word,"* NY Times Polit Blog (Apr 11, 2008), online at http://thecaucus.blogs.nytimes.com/2008/04/11/mccain-to-obama-keep-your-word.

[6] See, for example, Katherine Q. Seelye, *Florida and Michigan May See Delegates Halved*, NY Times (May 29, 2008), online at http://www.nytimes.com/2008/05/29/us/politics/29dems.html?partner = permalink&exprod = permalink; Katherine Q. Seelye, *Clinton Camp's Argument: No Michigan Delegates for You*, NY Times Polit Blog (May 30, 2008), online at http://thecaucus.blogs.nytimes.com/2008/05/30/clinton-camps-argument-no-michigan-delegates-for-you/; Order Granting Motion for Summary Judgment; Motion to Dismiss, *Nelson v Dean*, No 4:07cv427-RH (entered Dec 14, 2007), online at http://moritzlaw.osu.edu/electionlaw/litigation/documents/Nelson-ORDER12-14-07.pdf.

[7] See *Crawford*, 128 S Ct 1610 (2008).

[8] See *Riley*, 128 S Ct 1970.

[9] 128 S Ct 1610.

that passed ID requirements.[10] The Court also considered the case in the midst of the high-profile controversy surrounding the firing of U.S. attorneys unwilling to prosecute voter fraud claims.[11] However, even for *Crawford*, the available data suggest the stakes were much lower than either side had claimed.[12]

The other four cases the Court decided barely attracted attention beyond the election law bar. In *Davis v FEC*,[13] the only five-to-four decision of the bunch, the Court struck down the so-called Millionaire's Amendment provision of the Bipartisan Campaign Reform Act (BCRA).[14] The Court found the law violated the First Amendment rights of some self-financed candidates by allowing their opponents to take advantage of the law's provision that allowed them to raise contributions triple the normal limits.[15] The provision was sufficiently underutilized and below the radar that it drew little criticism despite the deeply divided Court.[16] Similarly, the Court's seven-to-two decision in *Riley v Kennedy*[17] interpreting Section 5 of the Voting Rights Act involved an issue that was difficult to understand and rarely important.[18] The Court held that a preexisting

---

[10] See *Purcell v Gonzalez*, 127 S Ct 5 (2006) (sustaining at a preliminary stage a district court decision upholding a voter ID law); *Common Cause/Georgia v Billups*, No 07-14664 (11th Cir 2009), online at http://www.ca11.uscourts.gov/opinions/ops/200714664.pdf (rejecting challenge to Georgia photo ID law). *Weinschenk v State*, 203 SW3d 201 (Mo 2006) (striking down Missouri voter ID law).

[11] See Siobhan Morrissey, *Newsmaker of the Year*, 94 ABA J 26 (2008) (naming Alberto Gonzales "Newsmaker of the Year," largely for his role in the firing of eight U.S. attorneys); Philip Chignon, *Democrats Were Targets in Inquiries, Panel Is Told*, NY Times (Oct 24, 2007), online at http://www.nytimes.com/2007/10/24/Washington/24prosecute.html?scp=2&sq=gonzales+U.S.+attorney&st=nyt (discussing U.S. attorney firing scandal).

[12] See Stephen Ansolabehere, *Access versus Integrity in Voter Identification Requirements*, 63 NYU Annual Surv Am L 613, 626 (2008) (demonstrating that the claims of both vote fraud and vote suppression were overblown); Michael J. Pitts, *Empirically Assessing the Impact of Photo Identification at the Polls Through an Examination of Provisional Ballots*, 24 J L & Pol (forthcoming 2009) (estimating 400 voters in Indiana cast provisional ballots that went uncounted because of an ID problem).

[13] 128 S Ct 2759 (2008).

[14] Id at 2766.

[15] Id.

[16] But see Editorial, *Millionaires Win*, Wash Post B06 (June 29, 2008); Editorial, *Justices for Free Speech*, Wall St J (June 28, 2008), online at http://online.wsj.com/article/SB121460646723712065.html?mod=googlenews_wsj#printMode; Editorial, *Millionaire's Amendment*, NY Times (Apr 21, 2008), online at http://www.nytimes.com/2008/04/21/opinion/21mon1.html?scp=2&sq=Millionaire%92s%20Amendment%20&st=cse (discussing the case prior to oral argument).

[17] 128 S Ct 1970 (2008).

[18] Id.

state election law need not be precleared for compliance with the VRA once the succeeding state law was ruled unconstitutional by a state court.[19] A similar result held in the Court's unanimous decision in *New York v Lopez Torres*,[20] in which the Court upheld New York's unique method of nominating judicial candidates for the party's line on a general election ballot. Opponents had argued that the law gave too much power to party bosses, who could often structure nominating conventions to ensure that their favorites were guaranteed to win.[21] Finally, in *Washington State Grange v Washington State Republican Party*,[22] the Court (seven to two) upheld against a First Amendment challenge Washington's nonpartisan blanket primary, in which candidates can express a party preference on the ballot even against the wishes of the party itself.

This article reads the fig leaves (how the Court has papered over disagreement to craft apparent consensus) and the tea leaves (what the recent decisions portend for the future) from the Roberts Court's recent election law decisions. The greater consensus in these cases (four of five were decided by supermajorities), even given their lower salience, deserves an explanation. Chief Justice Roberts was the only Justice who joined the controlling opinions in each of the five cases the Court considered during that term. Indeed, he has joined the controlling opinion in all but one election law case his Court has considered.[23] Compared to the Rehnquist Court, for example, the Roberts Court's initial signals are more directly attributable to the Chief Justice's efforts. Part I of this article discusses two such efforts from the 2007–2008 term. In some cases the Court achieved greater consensus by relying on the distinction between as-applied and facial challenges, a distinction that has undergone subtle transformations in the last few years. In others, the Court avoided disagreement by eschewing one of the concerns that had been percolating in prior cases—namely, the fear that election laws might be used as a tool for incumbent or partisan entrenchment. Part II looks at each of these cases as guides for what may lie ahead.

---

[19] Id at 1982.

[20] 128 S Ct 791 (2008).

[21] Id at 799.

[22] 128 S Ct 1184 (2008).

[23] Even in that one case, the Texas gerrymandering case *LULAC v Perry*, he was in the minority on only one aspect of the case: the decision to strike down one district as violating Section 2 of the Voting Rights Act.

In general, these cases suggest the Roberts Court will be quite restrained in its treatment of election laws, with the notable exception of its aggressive review of campaign finance reforms. It may have backed away somewhat from strong arguments concerning political party autonomy that found favor with the Rehnquist Court, while also giving states greater leeway when it comes to regulating voter and candidate access to the ballot. On issues of racial discrimination and the Voting Rights Act, the Roberts Court (which is really the Kennedy Court, in this regard) has yet to provide any clear signals. Part III presents some tentative conclusions.

I. The Fig Leaves That Cloaked the 2007–2008 Term's Election Law Cases

In the post-*Bush v Gore*[24] world, it had become traditional to view election law as one more arena in which the Court was closely divided along ideological lines.[25] Whether the issue was partisan gerrymandering,[26] campaign finance,[27] judicial elections,[28] the Voting Rights Act,[29] or race and redistricting,[30] the Rehnquist Court seemed evenly divided, with either Justice O'Connor or Justice Kennedy casting the decisive vote.[31] In his confirmation hearings, John Roberts hoped things would be different,[32] and the 2007–2008 term

---

[24] 531 US 98 (2000).

[25] See Heather K. Gerken, *Rashomon and the Roberts Court*, 68 Ohio St L J 1213, 1213 (2007) (noting the highly fractured decisions in recent election law cases).

[26] See *Vieth v Jubelirer*, 541 US 267 (2004); *League of United Latin Am. Citizens v Perry*, 548 US 399 (2006) (*"LULAC"*).

[27] See *McConnell v FEC*, 540 US 93 (2003); *FEC v Wis. Right to Life, Inc.*, 127 S Ct 2652 (2007) (*"WRTL"*); *Colo. Republican Fed. Campaign Comm. v FEC*, 533 US 431 (2001) (*"Colorado Republican II"*).

[28] See *Republican Party of Minnesota v White*, 536 US 765 (2002).

[29] See *Georgia v Ashcroft*, 539 US 461 (2003); *LULAC*, 548 US 399.

[30] See *Easley v Cromartie*, 532 US 234 (2001).

[31] There are just a few exceptions to this general pattern of post-*Bush v Gore* election law split decisions. In *Randall v Sorrell*, 548 US 230 (2006), the Court by a vote of six to three struck down Vermont's low contribution limits. In *Clingman v Beaver*, 544 US 581 (2005), the Court, in a fractured decision, upheld a law that prevented the Libertarian Party from allowing other parties' members to vote in its primary. Also, the first opinion in *WRTL*, 546 US 410, 412 (2006), was unanimous, but it merely remanded to the district court to entertain an as-applied challenge.

[32] See Editorial, *The Roberts Court Returns*, NY Times (Sept 30, 2007), online at http://www.nytimes.com/2007/09/30/opinion/30sun1.html ("At his confirmation hearings, Chief Justice John Roberts told the Senate he had 'no agenda,' and famously compared his role to that of an umpire calling balls and strikes. He has also said he wants more consensus on the court, and fewer 5-to-4 decisions.").

showed some promise in that regard.[33]

As previously suggested, the greater consensus in the past term's election law cases derived, in part, from the low stakes—in both partisan and jurisprudential respects—these cases presented. With the exception of *Crawford*, in which the Justices nevertheless split six to three, none of these cases presented an issue the resolution of which would likely favor one party over another or even apply systematically to American elections. These cases were quite different, for example, than ones the Court had recently entertained concerning partisan gerrymandering or core issues of campaign finance. Therefore, the apparent consensus may prove to be a quirky result from an unusual docket limited to last term.

An alternative explanation, though, is that the approach the Court took in several of these cases suggests a move toward a style and type of argument that can gain a broader coalition than may have otherwise existed in such cases.[34] In particular, the heavy reliance on the distinction between as-applied and facial challenges led the Court to decide these cases by larger majorities. Although the decisions are minimalist in appearance and ambiguous in actual meaning, this strategy has the virtue of projecting a spirit of judicial restraint and moderation. It therefore appeals to those on the fence who view siding with the majority as a small and perhaps reversible step, rather than the creation of a sweeping rule of law.

In addition, although the Court had ample opportunity with this docket to hint, as many academics had hoped,[35] in the direction of an election law jurisprudence founded on promoting competition, the Court's opinions were instead quite traditional in their approach. They balanced state interests against rights to vote, to associate, or to speak rather than asking whether the laws at issue represented moves entrenching incumbents or their parties. Several Justices who had voiced such concerns in earlier cases fell silent last

---

[33] Linda Greenhouse, *Supreme Court Memo: At Supreme Court, 5-to-4 Rulings Fade, but Why?* NY Times (May 23, 2008), online at http://www.nytimes.com/2008/05/23/us/23memo .html?pagewanted=print.

[34] See Gerken, 68 Ohio St L J (cited in note 25) (noting the unstable middle on the Court in election law cases which has led to a "doctrinal interregnum").

[35] See Richard H. Pildes, *Foreword: The Constitutionalization of Democratic Politics*, 118 Harv L Rev 28 (2004). I should emphasize that advocates of the markets paradigm, such as Rick Pildes and Sam Issacharoff, do not suggest that competition should be the exclusive and outcome-determinative consideration in election law cases, just that it should play a stronger role. Nor would these scholars necessarily advocate a different result in each of the cases from last term, given the relevance of other considerations.

term. Although one cannot describe this dog-not-barking as a *strategic* move to build broader coalitions, the general lack of attention to this type of argument explains, in just a small way, the muted dissent in some of these cases. It also illustrates the Roberts Court's reticence to question openly the motives of members of the political branches.

A. THE PROMINENCE AND CHANGING NATURE OF AS-APPLIED CHALLENGES IN ELECTION LAW[36]

Even as the body of the Court's term was still warm, commentators noticed a stylistic, if not substantive, shift in how the Court was treating the distinction between as-applied and facial challenges in election cases.[37] Two of the Court's decisions from the term—*Washington Grange* and *Crawford*—upheld laws against facial challenges while explicitly reserving the question whether some as-applied challenge might be appropriate in a subsequent case. This approach is consistent with an earlier campaign finance case from the Roberts Court, *Wisconsin Right to Life v FEC*,[38] which vindicated an as-applied challenge to the Bipartisan Campaign Reform Act, which the Rehnquist Court had upheld on its face only three years earlier.[39] Those cases are also consistent with the Roberts Court's approach in certain nonelection cases, such as the two abortion cases it has decided, in which it upheld laws on their face while leaving open the possibility of later as-applied challenges.[40]

---

[36] A much longer discussion of the changing nature of as-applied doctrine in the recent election law decisions can be found in Nathaniel Persily and Jennifer Rosenberg, *Defacing Democracy*, Minn L Rev (forthcoming 2009).

[37] See Rick L. Hasen, *About Face: The Roberts Court Sets the Stage for Shrinking Voting Rights, Putting Poor and Minority Voters Especially in Danger*, FindLaw (Mar 26, 2008), online at http://writ.lp.findlaw.com/commentary/20080326_hasen.html; Dahlia Lithwick, *Grandma Got Carded*, Slate (Jan 9, 2008), online at http://www.slate.com/id/2181781/pagenum/all/#page_start (discussing oral arguments in *Crawford*, Lithwick notes, "With increasing frequency, the court's conservative wing has been chipping away at facial challenges (the better to bar litigation), and today Scalia takes out a sledgehammer: 'I mean, every facial challenge is an immense dictum on the part of this court, isn't it?' He goes on to characterize all facial challenges as the court 'sitting back and looking at the ceiling and saying, oh, we can envision not the case before us, but other cases . . .'").

[38] *WRTL*, 127 S Ct 2652 (2007).

[39] Id at 2673.

[40] See *Ayotte v Planned Parenthood of Northern New England*, 546 US 320 (2006); *Gonzales v Carhart*, 550 US 124 (2007); Persily and Rosenberg, Minn L Rev (forthcoming 2009) (cited in note 36).

The *Washington Grange* and *Crawford* cases are interesting in this respect because they appear to signal a shift at least in the way the Court discusses as-applied and facial challenges, if not in what the Court means by the distinction. In general, the standard approach to differentiating the two types of constitutional attack concerns whether the challenged law is alleged to be unconstitutional in all of its applications (the so-called *Salerno*[41] standard for facial challenges) or simply as-applied to the plaintiff's unique circumstances. In last term's election law cases, though, the Court seemed to be conflating the as-applied/facial doctrine with doctrines of ripeness and justiciability. In both cases, the Court suggested that the law should be upheld on its face because the true extent of the constitutional burden remained unknown at the time of the litigation. In the future, when the burden of the law could be better understood, a proper as-applied challenge might lie.

In *Washington State Grange v Washington State Republican Party*,[42] the Court upheld a nonpartisan primary law against a facial challenge because it was unclear whether the ballot would infringe on the parties' First Amendment rights.[43] The law specified that any candidate could run in the primary, in which the top two vote-getters, regardless of party, would advance to the general election ballot. But the law allowed the candidates to state a party preference that would appear next to their name on the primary and general election ballot. The parties sued because they would not have any control over which candidates, including some that might not even be party members, could use the parties' names on the ballot. The Supreme Court upheld the law on its face because the ballot would only violate the parties' associational rights if voters would be confused as to whether the "party preference" designation on the ballot signified endorsement of the candidate by the party.[44] Because the ballot had not yet been designed, the Court could not determine that it would necessarily confuse voters into wrongly assuming party endorsement where none existed.[45] It would be possible for the ballot to be especially clear that an "R"

---

[41] *United States v Salerno*, 481 US 739, 744 (1987) ("[T]he challenger must establish that *no set of circumstances exists* under which the Act would be valid.") (emphasis added).

[42] 128 S Ct 1184 (2008).

[43] Id at 1195.

[44] Id.

[45] Id at 1194.

next to a candidate's name, for example, does not signify she is endorsed by the Republican Party. The law, therefore, was facially constitutional, even if it might be unconstitutional once the state had applied it in a concrete case. (As it turned out, the ballot notation for the 2008 election said "Prefers Republican Party" or "Prefers Democratic Party" under the candidate's name.[46])

Washington Grange provided a precedent the *Crawford* Court quickly followed in upholding Indiana's photo ID requirement.[47] Given that no statewide election had been held under the new Indiana law, there was great uncertainty as to the number of people who would be unable to vote as a result of it. Although they alleged that 40,000 Indianans of voting age did not have acceptable forms of ID, the plaintiffs did not find a single person who said that the law would prevent her from voting.[48] In what Justice Scalia's concurrence derided as a "record-based resolution of the case,"[49] Justice Stevens's controlling opinion[50] (joined by Chief Justice Roberts and Justice Kennedy) emphasized that the record was incomplete both as to the number of voters burdened by the ID requirement and as to the severity of the burden on those affected.[51] In this sense, the Court, as in *Washington Grange*, upheld the law on its face because no constitutional injury had yet been proven based on the facts in the legislative or litigation history.[52] If this is the correct way to read *Crawford*, then the voter ID law might be unconstitutional on its face once better evidence emerges

---

[46] See Sample Ballot—Kitsap County, Washington, online at http://www.kitsapgov.com/aud/elections/archive/08/sample%20ballot%20gen%202008.pdf.

[47] See *Crawford v Marion County*, 128 S Ct 1610, 1622 (2008) ("Our reasoning in that case [*Washington Grange*] applies with added force to the arguments advanced by petitioners in these cases.").

[48] 472 F3d 949, 951–52 (7th Cir 2007).

[49] *Crawford*, 128 S Ct at 1626 (Scalia concurring).

[50] The Court split into three equal camps in *Crawford*. Justice Stevens wrote the controlling opinion for himself, Justice Kennedy, and Chief Justice Roberts. Justice Scalia's concurrence was joined by Justices Alito and Thomas. Justices Souter, Ginsburg, and Breyer dissented.

[51] 128 S Ct at 1622.

[52] The Court adopted a similar approach in *Baze v Rees*, 128 S Ct 1520 (2008), rejecting a facial challenge to the three-drug protocol Kentucky uses in its executions. The mere risk that the protocol might be misused in a way that led the condemned to suffer did not justify striking it down on its face. What an as-applied challenge to the method might look like in the future is somewhat difficult to contemplate, given that someone else besides the person "injured" by the misuse of the protocol would then need to bring the case. Perhaps the next person who is to be subjected to the protocol could bring an "as-applied" challenge based on what was learned from the previous mistake.

as to the number of people who cannot or do not vote because of a lack of ID.

Crawford's emphasis on the distinction between facial and as-applied challenges, however, may mean something altogether different from the ripeness-style inquiry coming out of *Washington Grange*. A large section of the controlling opinion appears to apply the traditional view of the doctrine by rejecting plaintiffs' facial challenge but leaving open whether later plaintiffs could show a unique harm that justifies striking the law down as applied to them. The opinion refers to certain classes of voters, such as elderly people born out of state, homeless people, and others who might not have birth certificates, as populations likely to experience a "special burden on their right to vote."[53] For those people, the law might impose an especially severe burden such that the state must make an exception to the ID requirement. The case of the nine elderly nuns who were turned away from the polls (by a fellow nun, incidentally) for lack of ID in the 2008 Indiana presidential primary might serve as an example of potential plaintiffs in a future case.[54] Relying again on the deficiencies in the record, however, the Court suggested "it is not possible to quantify either the magnitude of the burden on this narrow class of voters or the portion of the burden imposed on them that is fully justified."[55]

In this respect, the decision treats the Indiana ID law as the Court treated Title II of the Bipartisan Campaign Reform Act (BCRA) in *McConnell v FEC*[56] and *Wisconsin Right to Life v FEC*

---

[53] 128 S Ct at 1622.

[54] See Associated Press, *Nuns with dated ID turned away at Ind. Polls* (May 6, 2008), online at http://www.msnbc.msn.com/id/24490932/; Michael Scherer, 7 *Things That Could Go Wrong on Election Day*, Time (Oct 26 2008), online at http://www.time.com/time/specials/packages/article/0,28804,1853246_1853243_1853238,00.html?imw=Y. Great disagreement exists as to how many people do not vote or end up voting a provisional ballot as a result of strict voter ID laws. Survey research suggests that ID laws have little effect on turnout. See Ansolabehere, 63 NYU Annual Surv Am L (cited in note 12). Relying on interviews of county election officials, the one study of the effect of voter ID in Indiana estimated that approximately 400 people cast provisional ballots that went uncounted in the 2008 presidential primary because of ID problems. See Pitts, 24 J L & Pol (forthcoming 2009) (cited in note 12). The state does not release data that classify provisional ballots by "cause," nor do they release information as to how many ballots cast because of ID problems go uncounted or how many people are turned away because of ID problems. Therefore, those attempting to establish the ID requirement as a significant barrier to voting or one that has a measurable disparate impact on distinct groups will face great difficulties.

[55] 129 S Ct 1622.

[56] 540 US 93 (2003).

(WRTL).[57] In *McConnell*, the Court rejected a facial challenge to the express advocacy provisions of the BCRA, which prohibited the use of corporate or union treasury money for television advertisements that "refer[red] to a clearly identified candidate" in the period immediately before a federal election. However, the Court left open the possibility in a footnote[58] of later as-applied challenges that demonstrated unique burdens on the speech rights of certain corporate entities. The Court seemed to suggest that a corporate-funded advertisement that ran afoul of the law but was a genuine discussion of issues, rather than an attempt to influence an election, would be exempted from the law. Three years later the Roberts Court sustained such an as-applied challenge in *WRTL* so as to exempt a corporate-sponsored advertisement that mentioned two senators by name (one of whom would appear on the ballot) in the context of an admonition to call them to tell them to confirm Bush's judicial nominees. Most significantly for purposes of assessing the evolution of the "as-applied" jurisprudence, however, the Court did not merely exempt this particular ad. Rather, the as-applied challenge led to a rule that now limited the statute only to advertisements that are "susceptible of no reasonable interpretation other than as an appeal to vote for or against a specific candidate."[59] Given that very few such ads are incapable of some other interpretation, the Court used this as-applied challenge to exempt most of the potential applications of the statute.[60]

---

[57] 127 S Ct 2652 (2007).

[58] *McConnell*, 540 US at 157 n 52.

[59] *WRTL*, 127 S Ct at 2667. This creation of a rule pursuant to an as-applied challenge is all the more peculiar in the context of the BCRA, given that the statute included a backup "secondary definition" of electioneering communications that would be triggered if the primary definition were declared unconstitutional. The effect of *WRTL* was to redefine the primary definition of express advocacy without triggering the secondary definition and in effect rewriting a statute to produce regulatory language for which Congress never voted. See Persily and Rosenberg, Minn L Rev (forthcoming 2009) (cited in note 36).

[60] *WRTL*, 127 S Ct at 2684 n 7 (Scalia, J, concurring in part, concurring in the judgment) (arguing for facial invalidation and describing *WRTL*'s controlling opinion as exercising "faux judicial restraint"). *WRTL* and *Washington Grange*'s discussions of the as-applied/facial distinction are peculiar in another respect. Both constituted First Amendment challenges to election laws. In general, the *Salerno* rule is relaxed in the First Amendment context because of the fear of a chilling effect on speech. See, for example, *Ashcroft v Free Speech Coalition*, 535 US 234 (2002) (suggesting that a law will be facially unconstitutional if it prohibits a "substantial amount of protected speech"). These two cases almost appear to craft an election law exception to the general First Amendment overbreadth exception to facial challenges.

If *Crawford* follows the formula of *McConnell/WRTL*, then discrete groups of individuals who have particular difficulty acquiring ID might be able to receive court-crafted exemptions from the law. Although still viable in theory, there is good reason to think plaintiffs will rarely bring or succeed with such challenges. Indeed, a federal court has already rejected one such as-applied challenge to the Indiana law,[61] and the Eleventh Circuit has upheld a similar Georgia ID law without even mentioning the possibility of an as-applied challenge.[62] Individuals who find it difficult to navigate the hurdles of getting an ID are unlikely to find a federal lawsuit to be an easier course to enfranchisement. And the parties, interest groups, and nonprofits that ordinarily bring such cases have little incentive to do so in this context, when the narrowness of any as-applied relief, especially if granted only after an election, is unlikely to extend to a significant group of people. There are only so many elderly voters who were born out of state, have significant difficulty getting birth certificates, and would prefer not to vote by absentee, for example—and litigation to gain an exception for that narrow class of people is unlikely to provide benefits that outweigh the costs. The chief burden on voting rights the ID requirement imposes is the cost and inconvenience of acquiring the necessary documents and then traveling to and waiting at the Bureau of Motor Vehicles to get an ID. For all practical purposes, the Court appears already to have decided that such a burden is not severe in the abstract, and it is difficult to define a class of people for whom the burden is uniquely severe to the point where the time and cost involved necessarily and inevitably will preclude them from voting.[63] A capacious rule-like exception along the lines of *WRTL* seems already foreclosed by *Crawford*.

The *Crawford* Court's assessment of the burdens the ID law imposed (let alone the state's antifraud justification discussed later in this article) has as much to do with substantive voting rights doctrine as it does with the distinction between as-applied and

---

[61] See *Stewart v Marion County*, 2008 WL 4690984, *3 (SD Ind, Oct 21, 2008).

[62] See *Common Cause/Georgia v Billups*, No 07-14664 (11th Cir 2009), online at http://www.ca11.uscourts.gov/opinions/ops/200714664.pdf.

[63] In other words, the most opponents could hope for is a ruling that strikes down the law, for example, as applied to poor people who find it very difficult to get the required documents, such as a birth certificate, to then get an ID. But "very difficult" is probably not good enough. Most people falling into that category conceivably can get such documents; they just will not do so merely for the trivial benefit of voting.

facial challenges.[64] To be sure, the as-applied ruling, insofar as it makes voting rights litigation more costly and less likely, represents a significant blow for voting rights advocates.[65] Yet the principal problem with that holding, if there is one, would be the evolution away from a conception of the relevant constitutional balance that views hindrances with concentrated impacts on certain groups as the singular and historic inquiry involved in weighing state interests versus deprivations of voting rights. In *Harper v Virginia Board of Elections*, for example, the Supreme Court struck down the poll tax on its face, not merely as applied to poor people.[66] Voting laws that are unconstitutional on their face are usually so because a minority (even a nonsuspect one) is disadvantaged. This is not to say that any law that makes it more difficult for some people to vote is necessarily unconstitutional. Otherwise, voter registration itself, let alone reducing the number of polling places, would be facially unconstitutional.[67] However, the inquiry as to the facial constitutionality of the law must necessarily be about justifying the burdens on the minority for whom the "neutral" law presents a disparate impact.

The *WRTL*, *Washington Grange*, *Crawford* triumvirate may signal a shift in the way the Roberts Court treats the as-applied/facial distinction in election law cases. The distinction between facial and as-applied challenges, which had always been the subject of

[64] See Michael C. Dorf, *Facial Challenges to State and Federal Statutes*, 46 Stan L Rev 235, 294 (1994) (suggesting the distinction between as-applied and facial challenges is largely dependent on the appropriate test determined by substantive doctrine).

[65] The effects may already be seen in *Florida Conference of the NAACP v Browning*, 2008 WL 2567204 (ND Fla 2008) (rejecting facial challenge to Florida's "no match, no vote" law).

[66] See *Harper v Virginia Bd of Elections*, 383 US 663 (1966). The *Crawford* Court tried to distinguish *Harper* by suggesting that, unlike there, an election-related state interest (preventing fraud) justifies the Indiana ID rule and a poll tax was unrelated to voter qualifications. See *Crawford*, 128 S Ct at 1615; see also id at 1624 & n 1 (Scalia, J, concurring) ("[W]e have never held that legislatures must calibrate all election laws, even those totally unrelated to money, for their impacts on poor voters or must otherwise accommodate wealth disparities."). Of course, the proponents of the poll tax thought it was very relevant to voter qualifications. One might also ask whether, as to the state justification, the tax would then be constitutional if used to fund elections. Implicitly, perhaps, the Court is also reaffirming the constitutionality of literacy tests, which it upheld in *Lassiter v Northampton County Board of Elections*, 360 US 45 (1959), and has never repudiated, even though the Voting Rights Act later made such tests illegal. One could easily make arguments as to the importance of literate voters for the integrity of elections.

[67] 128 S Ct at 1626 (Scalia, J, concurring) (discussing the potential implication of striking down voter ID for the constitutionality of all types of election laws).

debate,[68] may simply be breaking down with these cases, as well as others the Court has decided.[69] At times the Court deploys the distinction between the two types of constitutional attack in order to avoid explicitly overturning precedent (*WRTL*); in others it does so to craft greater consensus by focusing on deficiencies in the record (*Crawford*) or the ripeness of the case (*Washington Grange* and *Crawford*). The *WRTL/McConnell* pairing illustrates how judicially crafted "as-applied" exceptions can swallow legislative rules. *Washington Grange* and one interpretation of *Crawford* appear to hold open the promise of a future "as-applied" challenge, which, now based on full knowledge of the law's effects, might lead to a finding of facial unconstitutionality. Finally, the interpretation of *Crawford* that emphasizes a carve-out for potentially disadvantaged groups points toward as-applied challenges that are theoretically available but extremely unlikely.

These three cases, as well as the abortion cases the Court has decided, have delivered ammunition to critics who claim that the "passive virtue" of minimalism through incremental as-applied challenges is sometimes neither passive nor virtuous.[70] The strategy can be quite activist, as *WRTL* illustrates, when employed in a constitutional domain where the opinion's author cares deeply about the rights at issue. In other contexts, where the rights implications are deemed less severe (*Crawford* and *Washington Grange*, perhaps), the illusory promise of future as-applied challenges can be a bone to throw to Justices who might otherwise dissent or to litigants ever hopeful that they might find the extraordinary case with the right set of facts where narrow relief is both desirable and warranted. In each case, the choice made at this branch on the constitutional decision tree almost always reflects some position as to the desired outcome in such cases, in general. Thus, while we may concentrate on the significance of favoring one type of constitutional attack over another, this debate often represents a proxy war of sorts over the central constitutional values at stake.

---

[68] Compare Richard Fallon, *As-Applied and Facial Challenges and Third Party Standing*, 113 Harv L Rev 1321, 1324 (2000) (suggesting all constitutional challenges "are in an important sense, as-applied"), with Matthew D. Adler, *Rights Against Rules*, 97 Mich L Rev 1, 157 (1998) (arguing there is "no such thing as a true as-applied constitutional challenge").

[69] See *Baze v Rees*, 128 S Ct 1520 (2008); *Carhart v Gonzalez*, 127 S Ct 1610, 1639 (2007); *Ayotte v Planned Parenthood of Northern New England*, 546 US 320 (2006).

[70] I am indebted to Pam Karlan for this quip.

B. THE LACK OF CONCERN FOR ANTICOMPETITIVE ELECTION LAWS

One other argument that the *Crawford* majority found irrelevant was the contention that the voter ID law represented an effort by a Republican legislature to place barriers in the way of Democratic voters. Such an argument has been a staple of both election law litigation and academic discussion in recent years (even if rarely commanding a Court majority), with proponents advocating a greater role for courts in reining in efforts at entrenchment by parties and incumbent politicians.[71] In one election law context or another, every Justice on the Roberts or Rehnquist Court has signed on to such a theory, even though none would subscribe to it consistently across election law. The argument, dubbed "politics as markets" by some,[72] maintains that the traditional rights-based focus of election law cases ought to be relaxed in favor of an approach that concentrates on removing barriers to political competition and controlling self-interested moves made by incumbents to entrench themselves. Such concerns were absent from any majority opinion, which is worth recognizing given that at least three cases—*Crawford, Davis*, and *Lopez Torres*[73]—squarely presented the issue.

For those who worry about one party using its monopoly to hobble the competitive position of its adversary by tinkering with voter eligibility, *Crawford* provided a perfect opportunity to express that concern. Indeed, Judge Evans's dissent from the Seventh Circuit panel decision that upheld the ID law made the point bluntly. "Let's not beat around the bush," he wrote. "The Indiana voter photo ID law is a not-too-thinly-veiled attempt to discourage elec-

---

[71] See Nathaniel Persily, *The Place of Competition in American Election Law*, in Michael P. McDonald and John Samples, eds, *The Marketplace of Democracy: Electoral Competition and American Politics* 172–74 (Brookings, 2006) (summarizing academic discussion and caselaw).

[72] See Samuel Issacharoff and Richard H. Pildes, *Politics as Markets: Partisan Lockups of the Democratic Process*, 50 Stan L Rev 643 (1998); Richard H. Pildes, *Foreword: The Constitutionalization of Democratic Politics*, 118 Harv L Rev 28, 55 (2004); Samuel Issacharoff, *Gerrymandering and Political Cartels*, 116 Harv L Rev 593, 642–43 (2002).

[73] See *Lopez Torres v N.Y. State Bd of Elections*, 462 F3d 161 (2d Cir 2006) (observing that "[s]ince 1944 New York's judicial nominating system has been described as exclusionary and boss-dominated; reports and newspaper editorials from that time forward have decried an electoral practice 'that mocks choice,' and criticized a system in which 'voters can never know the candidates and have to accept party slates,' while the 'real choice is left to political bosses . . . who control nominations'").

tion-day turnout by certain folks believed to skew Democratic."[74]
Just as one party might be able to tip the electoral scales in its
favor through partisan gerrymandering or restrictive ballot access
rules, so too it could tailor barriers to entry to ensure some of its
opponents' supporters will have difficulty voting.

The argument did not resonate with anyone on the Supreme
Court, however. Given his frequent expression of this concern in
the context of gerrymandering,[75] ballot access,[76] and regulation of
political parties,[77] Justice Stevens might have been thought to be
receptive to this argument. Yet his opinion in *Crawford*, like Justice
Scalia's concurrence, refused to look behind the state's proffered
antifraud interests to unearth partisan motivation. "[I]f a nondis-
criminatory law is supported by valid neutral justifications," Stevens wrote, "those justifications should not be disregarded simply
because partisan interests may have provided one motivation for
the votes of individual legislators."[78] Because he placed great
weight on the legitimacy of the state's proffered antifraud interest
and therefore did not view partisan interests as the only justification for the ID law, the unanimous support of Republican legislators and unanimous opposition by Democrats was irrelevant
to the constitutionality of the statute. Even the dissenters who
would have struck down the law would not have done so because
of nascent partisan motivation.[79]

[74] See *Crawford v Marion County Election Bd*, 472 F3d 949, 954 (7th Cir 2007) (Evans dissenting).

[75] See *League of United Latin American Citizens v Perry*, 548 US 399, 458 (2006) (Stevens, J, dissenting); *Vieth v Jubelirer*, 541 US 267, 332–33 (2004) (Stevens, J, dissenting) ("when partisanship is the legislature's sole motivation—when any pretense of neutrality is forsaken . . .—the governing body cannot be said to have acted impartially."); *Karcher v Daggett*, 462 US 725 (1983) (Stevens, J, concurring).

[76] See *Timmons v Twin Cities Area New Party*, 520 US 351, 378 (1997) (Stevens, J, dissenting) (arguing that the intent of an antifusion law to promote the two-party system ought to weigh against the constitutionality of the law).

[77] See *Clingman v Beaver*, 544 US 581, 614 (2005) (Stevens, J, dissenting).

[78] *Crawford*, 128 S Ct at 1624. Stevens's position in *Crawford* may not be as surprising as I suggest, given his general aversion to purpose-based tests. See, for example, *Washington v Davis*, 426 US 229, 252, 254 (1976) (Stevens, J, concurring) ("the line between discrim-inatory purpose and discriminatory impact is not nearly as bright, and perhaps not quite as critical, as the reader of the Court's opinion might assume").

[79] Justice Souter emphasized that "[t]ens of thousands of voting-age residents lack the necessary photo identification" and "[a] large proportion of them are likely to be in bad shape economically" yet did not argue that such residents were more likely to be Dem-ocrats. See *Crawford*, 128 S Ct at 1638 (Souter dissenting). Justice Breyer would have found the law unconstitutional because it "imposes a disproportionate burden upon those eligible voters who lack a driver's license or other statutorily valid form of photo ID."

The anticompetitive impact of the nomination method for New York judicial elections was *the* issue in *New York State Board of Elections v Lopez Torres*.[80] The district court and Second Circuit panel that had struck down the hybrid system of a primary election to send delegates to a convention did so because of the determinative and unchecked power wielded by party leaders at the convention to choose the party's judicial nominees.[81] They argued that the election of delegates to those conventions was meaningless given that party bosses ended up wielding their informal, yet coercive, power to force the convention to ratify their wishes. Because virtually all judicial districts favor one party or the other, the nomination exists as the determinative selection process for who will be a trial court judge.

Justice Scalia's opinion for the Court expressly rejected the political markets argument in the context of the judicial nomination system and perhaps more broadly. Both his opinion for the Court and Justice Kennedy's concurrence maintained that the option of running as an independent candidate was an adequate safeguard to protecting the right of a potential candidate to run for office.[82] The Court refused to look at the functionally monopolistic power the parties wielded in selecting judges for each judicial district. The fact that a general election in a politically homogeneous district was almost always a meaningless exercise once the party had selected the nominee did not change the constitutional calculus. The First Amendment, the decision held, "does not call on the federal courts to manage the market [for political ideas] by preventing too many buyers from settling upon a single product."[83]

Campaign finance is the one context in which a majority of the current Court (though not in a single decision) has signed on to the principle that the Constitution requires an inquiry into a reg-

---

[80] 128 S Ct 791 (2008).

[81] *Lopez Torres v N.Y. State Bd of Elections*, 462 F3d 161, 200–01 (2d Cir 2006) ("[T]hrough a byzantine and onerous network of nominating phase regulations employed in areas of one-party rule, New York has transformed a de jure election into a de facto appointment. '[I]n every practical sense,' these regulations preclude all but candidates favored by party leadership 'from seeking the nomination of their chosen party, no matter how qualified they might be, and no matter how broad or enthusiastic their popular support.'") (internal citations omitted); *Lopez Torres v New York State Bd of Elections*, 411 F Supp 2d 212, 255 (EDNY 2006) ("[T]he New York system is designed to freeze the political status quo, in which party leaders, rather than the voters, select the Justices of the Supreme Court.").

[82] *Lopez Torres*, 128 S Ct at 801; id at 803 (Kennedy, J, concurring).

[83] Id at 801.

ulation's effect on political competition. The strongest advocates for the anti-entrenchment approach have been Justices Scalia and Thomas, who repeatedly warn against the risk that incumbents will craft campaign finance laws that insulate themselves from competition.[84] In *Randall v Sorrell*,[85] a controlling opinion for the Court, for the first time, struck down a campaign finance law— Vermont's stringent limit on contributions—because of its anti-competitive impact on challengers.[86] The decision even went so far as to state explicitly that the constitutionality of contribution limits depends on whether they "magnify the advantages of incumbency to the point where they put challengers to a significant disadvantage."[87]

No language similar to that in *Randall* can be found in the Court's opinion in *Davis*. Despite the clunkiness of doing so given the strange character of the Millionaire's Amendment, the *Davis* decision reads like a formulaic campaign finance decision. The Court inquired whether the law was a limitation on contributions or expenditures, the former raising less of a constitutional problem than the latter. Once it concluded that the Millionaire's Amendment restricted expenditures, because it punished self-financed candidates by allowing their opponents (and only their opponents) to raise contributions treble the normal limits,[88] the Court searched and failed to find a compelling state interest to justify it. No interest in preventing corruption or the appearance of corruption justified this law, and the proffered state interest in "level[ling] electoral opportunities" might not even have been le-

---

[84] See *McConnell v FEC*, 540 US 93, 249–50 (2003) (Scalia, J, dissenting) ("As everyone knows, this is an area where evenhandedness is not fairness. . . . [A]ny restriction upon a type of campaign speech that is equally available to challengers and incumbents tends to favor incumbents."); *Colorado Federal Campaign Committee v Federal Election Com'n*, 518 US 604, 644 n 9 (1966) (Thomas, J, dissenting) ("There is good reason to think that campaign reform is an especially inappropriate area for judicial deference to legislative judgment. What the argument for deference fails to acknowledge is the potential for legislators to set the rules of the electoral game so as to keep themselves in power and to keep potential challengers out of it.") (citations omitted).

[85] 548 US 230 (2006).

[86] Id at 237.

[87] Id at 248.

[88] *Davis*, 128 S Ct at 2771 (The BCRA "imposes an unprecedented penalty on any candidate who robustly exercises that First Amendment right [to spend personal funds for campaign speech].").

gitimate, let alone compelling.[89] Therefore, the law violated the First Amendment.

The absence of a discussion of the law's effect on competition is particularly striking because plenty of statements in the legislative record hint at the pro-incumbent bias of the Millionaire's Amendment.[90] As Senator Harry Reid plainly said in the debate over the Amendment: "It has nothing to do with millionaires. It has everything to do with protecting us. It is an incumbent advantage measure in this underlying bill."[91] Or as Congressman Tom Reynolds warned, "My colleagues should live in fear, all 435 of us, that a wealthy American decides to run."[92] Even Senator John McCain, who authored the BCRA and reluctantly accepted the Millionaire's Amendment, admitted the provision would pass because "everyone [was] scared to death of waking up one morning and reading in the newspaper that some Fortune 500 C.E.O. or heiress is going to run against them."[93] Yet for the Court, no word appears about entrenchment; the law simply impaired speech without any good justification.[94]

---

[89] Id at 2773. The Court also rejected the state interest in preventing the perception that offices are for sale to the highest bidder.

[90] Brief of Gene DeRossett and J. Edgar Broyhill II as Amici Curiae Supporting Appellant at 13, 26–27 n 15, *Davis*, 128 S Ct 2759 (No 07-320) (quoting legislative history); Robert Bauer, *The Travails of Reform, in Its Encounters with the Very Wealthy*, More Soft Money Hard Law (Aug 16, 2006), online at http://moresoftmoneyhardlaw.com/moresoftmoneyhardlaw/updates/federal_candidates_officeholders.html?AID=794 ("The Millionaire's Amendment—meant to provide some protection for opponents of the rich, 'self-financed' candidate—is straightforward in purpose and design. It is born of much fretting about the danger presented to incumbency by rich people.").

[91] 147 Cong Rec S 2845-02, S 2852 (Mar 26, 2001) (statement of Sen. Harry Reid in opposition to BCRA).

[92] 148 Cong Rec H 256-03, H 261 (Feb 12, 2002) (statement of Rep. Thomas Reynolds, opposing the House version of BCRA because the Millionaire's Amendment did not go far enough to protect incumbents).

[93] Alison Mitchell, *Senate Votes to Aid Candidates Facing Deep Pockets*, NY Times A16 (Mar 21, 2001).

[94] Professor Richard Pildes suggests that, although it goes unmentioned, the animating force of the majority opinion must be its concern about entrenchment. See Rick Pildes, *When Do Campaign Finance Laws Become a Way to Protect Incumbents?* Balkinization (June 26, 2008), online at http://balkin.blogspot.com/2008/06/sympathy-for-millionaire-self.html ("And a key aspect to this case is only hinted at in the Court's opinion but nonetheless undoubtedly shapes the decision: the enormous risk that this provision—and others like it Congress might adopt—is a way for incumbents to manipulate election laws so as to make it even harder for challengers to take them on."). I am not sure I even see the hints. Nevertheless, it takes great effort to do so, whereas, in other opinions, such as Justice Scalia's dissent in *McConnell*, the point is made explicit. This alleged *sub silentio* adoption of the markets approach is all the more remarkable given that the Court reached out in *Randall v Sorrell* to strike down the law because of its anticompetitive effect, even though

To find some glimmer of the political markets approach, one would need to look to the dissent, not the majority opinion. Writing only for himself, Justice Stevens begins his opinion with a radically authoritarian view of the lack of First Amendment protection available for campaign speech.[95] He would have upheld both the law's contribution limits and its limits on expenditures. In the part of his dissent joined by three others, however, he warns about the effect of wealth on political competition.[96] He views the Millionaire's Amendment as attempting "to reduce the distinct advantages enjoyed by wealthy candidates for congressional office."[97] The provision, under this view, promoted rather than hindered competition by diminishing the ability of wealthy candidates to buy their election. Although the dissent does not speak of incumbency or entrenchment, per se, it does view the measure as quite explicitly promoting a more competitive electoral playing field. For the majority, if anything, that was precisely the problem.

The absence of a majority opinion in these cases that takes the political competition argument seriously is not unique to last term. Apart from *Randall*, the argument remains one more often made in dissent, whether by Justices or academics. Nevertheless, the Court's possibly calculated decision not to peek behind the veil of the proffered state interests to view a background of political avarice and partisanship attests to a strategy of avoiding more open conflict with the political branches. The point may be more stylistic than anything else, but in the post-*Bush v Gore* era (or perhaps the post-Rehnquist Court era) a retreat from aggressively analyzing the motives of politicians is worth noting.

II. Reading the Tea Leaves in the Roberts Court's Election Law Decisions: The Signals from the 2007–2008 Term for What Lies Ahead

Despite its infancy, the Roberts Court has now issued opin-

---

no one plausibly argued the contribution limits there were motivated by incumbent entrenchment.

[95] *Davis*, 128 S Ct at 2779 (Stevens, J, concurring in part, dissenting in part) (arguing that rules for election spending by candidates ought to be similar to rules for speaking by litigants in court).

[96] Id at 2781 ("[W]e have long recognized the strength of an independent governmental interest in reducing both the influence of wealth on the outcomes of elections, and the appearance that wealth alone dictates those results.").

[97] Id at 2782.

ions in each of the major categories of election law: campaign finance, voting rights, regulation of political parties, and redistricting. It also will soon hear major cases dealing with the meaning and constitutionality of the Voting Rights Act,[98] as well as two additional campaign finance cases, one of which also deals with judicial elections.[99] Thus far the Court has only struck down campaign finance laws (all three it has considered) and one district at issue in the Texas gerrymandering case.[100] In all other cases, the Court has upheld the election laws it has reviewed. It should therefore come as no surprise that the future looks bleak for campaign finance regulation, complicated for cases concerning race and redistricting, but hopeful for jurisdictions crafting election laws for most other areas.

A. CAMPAIGN FINANCE

Campaign finance is the area of election law where the Roberts Court has made its most significant mark to date. In particular, the replacement of Chief Justice Rehnquist and Justice O'Connor, who often voted to uphold campaign finance laws, with Chief Justice Roberts and Justice Alito, who have proven to be more libertarian in campaign finance cases, has led to a solid five-member coalition that appears skeptical of campaign finance regulations. The Roberts Court has struck down all three campaign finance laws it has considered: Vermont's contribution and expenditure limits in *Randall*, the application of the BCRA to certain corporate campaign ads in *WRTL*, and the Millionaire's Amendment in *Davis*.

From *Buckley v Valeo*[101] until *Randall v Sorrell*,[102] contribution

---

[98] See *Bartlett v Strickland*, 2009 WL 578634; *Northwest Austin Mun. Util. Dist. No. One v Mukasey*, 573 F Supp 2d 221 (DDC 2008), prob juris noted (US Jan 9, 2009) (No 08-322).

[99] See *Citizens United v Federal Election Commission*, No 07-2240 (probable jurisdiction noted Nov 14, 2008) (addressing whether corporate-sponsored films critical of Hillary Clinton and Barack Obama would violate the "electioneering communications" provision of the BCRA as interpreted by the Court in *McConnell* and *WRTL*); *Caperton v A.T. Massey Coal Co.*, No 08-22 (cert granted Nov 14, 2008) (addressing whether a judge who has accepted donations from an individual or firm involved in a case before his court must be disqualified on due process grounds).

[100] See *Davis v FEC*, 128 S Ct 2759, 2774 (2008); *WRTL*, 127 S Ct 2652 (2007); *Randall v Sorrell*, 548 US 230 (2006); *LULAC*, 548 US 399 (2006).

[101] 424 US 1 (1976).

[102] 548 US 230 (2006).

limits appeared almost untouchable by the Supreme Court. Once the state justified a law as motivated by a desire to combat corruption or its appearance, the only question remained whether the law, in effect, prevented a candidate from "amass[ing] the resources necessary for effective advocacy."[103] Until *Randall*, the Court had little difficulty giving great deference to Congress and state legislatures on both the problem of corruption and the propriety of contribution limits to prevent it. Jurisdictions could feel relatively secure that, even with the flimsiest evidence of corruption or its appearance, contribution limits would be upheld.[104] *Randall*, for the first time, placed an unsteady "lower bound" on how far contribution limits could go, by asking "whether [such limits] magnify the advantages of incumbency to the point where they put challengers to a significant disadvantage."[105] Given that Vermont's limits were the lowest in the nation, as well as a variety of other factors,[106] the controlling opinion for the Court (written by Justice Breyer but joined in full only by Chief Justice Roberts and in part by Justice Alito) found the limits were not "closely drawn" to address the state's interests in preventing corruption or its appearance.

The increased scrutiny of what had been thought to be a safe regulatory option invites inquiry as to whether the fundamental tenets of the *Buckley* framework have become destabilized. In addition to *Randall*, both *Davis* and *WRTL* have challenged some of the assumptions that guided the doctrinal development from *Buckley* through *McConnell*. The pillars of campaign finance doctrine until these recent decisions were judicial acquiescence to limits on individual contributions and to bans on corporate treasury expenditures on candidate campaigns, along with a general skepticism of regulations of individual expenditures.

A majority of the current Court, as with the Rehnquist Court,

---

[103] See *Nixon v Shrink Missouri Gov't PAC*, 528 US 377, 395 (2000) (quoting *Buckley v Valeo*, 424 US 1, 21 (1976)).

[104] See *Nixon*, 528 US 377.

[105] *Randall v Sorrell*, 548 US 230, 248 (2006).

[106] For example, the opinion added that the contribution limits would hinder political parties' ability to target their contributions to competitive races, and would generally reduce the voice of political parties "to a whisper." Id at 253, 254, 256, 257. It also pointed out that the Vermont law did not adjust the contribution limits for inflation, that they were the lowest in the nation, and that many volunteer services were considered contributions. Id at 261, 250.

has stated a desire to overturn *Buckley v Valeo*, but different Justices would overturn it for diametrically opposed reasons. Both Justice Stevens and Justice Ginsburg have written or joined opinions that say the First Amendment ought not stand in the way of regulating individual expenditures, as well as contributions.[107] At least three and possibly four votes exist on the current Court to overturn *Buckley*'s holding regarding the lesser scrutiny applied to contribution limits. In *Randall* itself, as well as earlier cases, Justices Thomas, Scalia, and Kennedy railed against the *Buckley* framework. They would subject both contribution and expenditure limits to strict scrutiny. Justice Alito's position has been slightly more cryptic, but his opinions in *Randall* and in *Davis* point in a skeptical direction. In *Randall*, his separate, partial concurrence went out of its way to emphasize that the parties had not requested the Court to reexamine *Buckley*.[108]

Furthermore, Justice Alito's opinion for the Court in *Davis* had some pretty disparaging things to say about the federal contribution limits. As suggested above, the Court's opinion there tries to take the square peg of the Millionaire's Amendment and fit it into the round hole of the *Buckley* doctrine. That provision did nothing to limit the expenditures of a self-financer, even if it indirectly penalized him by making it easier for his opponent to raise more money. Rather than curtailing the speech rights of candidates—indeed, it enabled more speech—the primary constitutional problem with the Millionaire's Amendment was that it undermined the justification for the contribution limits in an ordinary election. If the contribution limits could be raised when a candidate confronted a self-financer, Justice Alito suggested, then why are those limits closely drawn to prevent corruption in the normal case?[109] In other words, although the constitutionality of the federal limits was not before the Court, the existence of the exception for millionaire opponents was a problem because it re-

---

[107] See *Nixon v Shrink Mo. Govt PAC*, 528 US 377, 398 (Stevens, J, concurring); *Colorado Republican Federal Campaign Committee v Federal Election Commission*, 518 US 604, 648 (1996) (Stevens, J, dissenting).

[108] See id at 263 (Alito, J, concurring).

[109] See *Davis v FEC*, 128 S Ct 2759, 2774 (2008) ("If the normally applicable limits on individual contributions and coordinated party contributions are seriously distorting the electoral process, if they are feeding a 'public perception that wealthy people can buy seats in Congress,' and if those limits are not needed in order to combat corruption, then the obvious remedy is to raise or eliminate those limits.") (internal citation omitted).

quired an explanation for why that exception should not ordinarily be the rule.

Finally, Justice Alito discussed *Buckley* and its progeny as sustaining "the facial constitutionality of limits on discrete and aggregate individual contributions and on coordinated party expenditures."[110] That line would appear gratuitous if not for the strategy of *WRTL* to undo *McConnell* through as-applied challenges. Perhaps it signals some future analogous move to use *Randall* and *Davis* to chip away incrementally at the federal contribution limits. One should note that only Chief Justice Roberts and Justice Alito join together in the as-applied holding of *WRTL*; the three others who help form the majority would have reversed *McConnell* and struck the electioneering communications provisions down on their face. Moreover, Justice Alito also wrote separately in *WRTL* to emphasize that if as-applied litigation proves unworkable, the Court should strike down the electioneering provisions on their face.[111]

If this analysis is correct, then Chief Justice Roberts alone stands in the way of a fundamental alteration of the constitutional doctrine of campaign finance. Only he joined in full the controlling opinions in *WRTL*, *Randall*, and *Davis*. All of those opinions bend over backwards to justify their results in terms of stare decisis,[112] even as critics sometimes pointed out the tortured logic thereby needed to overturn a large amount of the *Buckley* framework while treating other aspects as binding precedent.[113] If followed, his approach would suggest a gradual erosion of the "pro-regulation" aspects of the *Buckley* framework, namely, the lower scrutiny otherwise accorded contribution limits and corporate treasury expenditures in candidate elections. In *Citizens United v FEC*,[114] a case slated for the upcoming term, we may get some answers as to the impact of *WRTL*, as well as some guidance as to its effect on the disclosure regime forced upon organizations that spend corporate treasury funds. That case asks whether a corporate trea-

[110] Id at 2770.

[111] *WRTL*, 127 S Ct 2652, 2674 (2007) (Alito, J, concurring).

[112] Id at 2664–72; *Randall v Sorrell*, 548 US at 243; *Davis v FEC*, 128 S Ct at 2770–74.

[113] *WRTL*, 127 S Ct at 2674–87 (Scalia, J, concurring in part, concurring in the judgment); *Randall*, 548 US at 265–66 (Thomas, J, concurring in the judgment); Richard Hasen, *Beyond Incoherence: The Roberts Court's Deregulatory Turn in FEC v. Wisconsin Right to Life*, 92 Minn L Rev 1064 (2008) (noting the tension between *McConnell* and *WRTL*).

[114] No 07-2240 (probable jurisdiction noted Nov 14, 2008).

sury-funded movie attacking Hillary Clinton during the 2008 primary campaign, as well as television ads marketing the movie, constitute protected issue advocacy or electioneering. The appellants there explicitly ask the Court to overrule its landmark decision in *Austin v Michigan Chamber of Commerce*,[115] which allowed for distinctive regulation of corporate electioneering activities. Moreover, the Republican Party has just filed an as-applied challenge to the soft money ban that was upheld in *McConnell*;[116] if that and the *Citizens United* appeal prove to be successful, then the basics of the post-*Buckley* regime are likely to unravel.

To return to the theme that began this article, it is also likely that the campaign finance developments of the 2008 election will not be lost on the Court. Barack Obama's unprecedented $750 million, 4-million-donor campaign[117] may have broken the stereotypes as to who is favored by a system of private financing of campaigns. The election may curtail further reform efforts, now that an unlikely candidate supported by mass participation has greatly benefited from private contributions, but its effect on the relevant constitutional questions is difficult to predict. The pro-regulationists may point to this election as evidence that a popular candidate can run a competitive campaign even when contributions are capped at relatively low amounts. Campaign finance libertarians, on the other hand, may point to this election as evidence of the irrationality of contribution limits at all. If a candidate can raise hundreds of millions of dollars through the internet, how can it be that contributions in excess of the federal limit of $2,300, for example, present a risk of corruption?

B. REDISTRICTING AND THE VOTING RIGHTS ACT

Redistricting cases rivaled campaign finance to constitute the largest share of the election law docket of the Rehnquist Court. Although occasionally dealing with heretofore unresolved ques-

---

[115] 495 US 652 (1990). According to campaign finance expert Robert Bauer, this case "has the potential to leave a large and ever widening crack in the foundation of contemporary campaign finance regulation." See Robert Bauer, *Citizens United: The Olson Brief*, online at http://www.moresoftmoneyhardlaw.com/updates/outside_groups.html?AID=1404.

[116] See Editorial: *Campaign finance on trial, again*, Wash Times (Nov 13, 2008), online at http://www.washingtontimes.com/news/2008/nov/13/campaign-finance-on-trial-again/ (describing lawsuit).

[117] See Jeanne Cummings, *Obama, the billion dollar man*, Politico (Dec 2, 2008), online at http://www.politico.com/news/stories/1208/16115.html.

tions concerning partisan gerrymandering,[118] the Rehnquist Court considered a broad array of cases concerning the use and overuse of race in the redistricting process. Those cases came in the form of challenges to districting plans based on the Voting Rights Act (VRA)[119] or the constitutional prohibition on excessively race-based districts (the so-called *Shaw* line of cases).[120] The Roberts Court has issued opinions in two such cases, *Riley v Kennedy*[121] from last term, and *LULAC v Perry*,[122] the Texas gerrymandering case from two terms earlier. It will also hear two VRA cases in the upcoming term: *Bartlett v Strickland*,[123] which asks whether the VRA sometimes requires the creation of minority districts where minorities cannot form a majority, and *Northwest Austin Municipal Utility District Number One v Holder*,[124] which challenges the constitutionality of Section 5 of the VRA.

If the Rehnquist Court was really the O'Connor Court when it came to constitutional questions concerning race,[125] then the

---

[118] See *Davis v Bandemer*, 478 US 109 (1986); *Vieth v Jubelirer*, 541 US 267 (2004). Although the Roberts Court considered the issue of partisan gerrymandering in *LULAC*, 548 US 399 (2006), it did not rule such claims nonjusticiable nor did it come up with a standard for when such gerrymanders are unconstitutional. Justice Kennedy's opinion in *Vieth* remains the "law," in that such claims are justiciable but no standard exists to adjudge their constitutionality. The 2006 and 2008 elections probably put a nail in the coffin for future partisan gerrymandering claims, which had never been on more than life support. The fact that the Democrats were able to capture Congress in 2006 and extend their margin in 2008 despite aggressive Republican gerrymanders has added greater credibility to the claims that partisan gerrymanders are self-correcting and judicial venturing into this political thicket is unnecessary and perhaps counterproductive. Some consider partisan gerrymanders to be self-correcting because the more aggressive the line-drawing party is in spreading its supporters, the greater the risk that a small shift in voters leads to a loss of a great number of seats. See *Davis v Bandemer*, 478 US 109, 152–55 (1986) (O'Connor, J, concurring) (making such an argument as a basis for finding such claims nonjusticiable). As it turns out, Democrats picked up seats across states with redistricting plans that presented a variety of partisan or incumbent biases. However, in the face of the Republican gerrymander in Pennsylvania that gave rise to *Vieth*, the Democrats captured five Republican-held seats, such that they now hold twelve of the nineteen seats in the delegation.

[119] See, for example, *Georgia v Ashcroft*, 539 US 461 (2003); *Reno v Bossier Parish School Board*, 528 US 320 (2000); *Johnson v DeGrandy*, 512 US 997 (1994).

[120] See, for example, *Shaw v Reno*, 509 US 630 (1993); *Miller v Johnson*, 515 US 900 (1995); *United States v Hays*, 515 US 737 (1995); *Shaw v Hunt*, 517 US 899 (1996); *Bush v Vera*, 517 US 952 (1996); *Hunt v Cromartie*, 526 US 541 (1999); *Easley v Cromartie*, 532 US 234 (2001).

[121] 128 S Ct 1970 (2008).

[122] 548 US 399 (2006).

[123] 2009 WL 578634.

[124] *Northwest Austin Mun. Util. Dist. No. One v Mukasey*, 573 F Supp 2d 221 (DDC 2008), prob juris noted (US Jan 9, 2009) (No 08-322).

[125] See, for example, *Grutter v Bollinger*, 539 US 306 (2003); *Georgia v Ashcroft*, 539 US

Roberts Court is the Kennedy Court on similar topics.[126] Justice Kennedy cast the decisive vote in the Roberts Court's most recent foray into school desegregation, although no one joined his opinion in full.[127] He did the same in *LULAC*, vindicating one of the claims of impermissible race-based vote dilution, while rejecting another, and ignoring a claim of racial gerrymandering.[128] His opinion there appeared to express genuine discomfort at times with the potential expansiveness of the VRA.[129] Even when he recrafted VRA doctrine in order to strike down one district as diluting the Hispanic vote, he did so by challenging other aspects of the plan that he considered as violating notions of "cultural compactness."[130] The plan diluted the Hispanic vote by taking Hispanic voters out of one district where they "naturally" belonged and were on the verge of political opportunity, but it also tried to compensate with the creation of an "unnatural" district that cobbled together far-flung, culturally distinct Hispanic commu-

---

461 (2003); *Easley v Cromartie*, 532 US 234 (2001); *Shaw v Reno*, 509 US 630 (1993); *Richmond v J.A. Croson Co.*, 488 US 469 (1989); *Adarand Constructors, Inc. v Peña*, 515 US 200 (1995).

[126] See generally Heather Gerken, *Justice Kennedy and the Domains of Equal Protection*, 121 Harv L Rev 104 (2007); Guy-Uriel Charles, *Race, Redistricting, and Representation*, 68 Ohio St L J 1185 (2007). Professors Gerken and Charles view Justice Kennedy's opinions as evolving toward a more complex view of race than expressed here. They consider his recent opinions as softening on the themes of colorblindness and racial essentialism, whereas I see them as relatively consistent with his prior decisions on racial gerrymandering and affirmative action.

[127] See *Parents Involved in Community Schools v Seattle School District No. 1*, 127 S Ct 2738, 2788 (2007) (Kennedy, J, concurring in part and concurring in the judgment).

[128] *LULAC*, 548 US at 424–47.

[129] See id at 446 (worrying about an interpretation of the VRA that "unnecessarily infused race into virtually every redistricting, raising serious constitutional questions"); Nathaniel Persily, *The Promise and Pitfalls of the New Voting Rights Act*, 117 Yale L J 174, 246–47 & n 254 (2007).

[130] *LULAC*, 548 US at 428–43; Daniel R. Ortiz, *Cultural Compactness*, 105 Mich L Rev First Impressions 48 (2006), online at http://www.michiganlawreview.org/firstimpressions/vol105/oritz.pdf. Because Justice Kennedy voted to strike down a district as violating the Voting Rights Act, one might consider him more receptive than he is to claims of race-based vote dilution. I think it is fair to say that Kennedy was less concerned about the district (District 23) that he struck down than he was about a nearby Hispanic district (District 25) that allegedly compensated for its loss. That district, which he viewed as cobbling together distant and distinct Hispanic communities, was subject to a *Shaw* claim of racial predominance. Kennedy could not get a majority to strike down that district as excessively race-based, so instead he sided with the four more liberal Justices to craft an opinion that effectively said such a far-flung district was inadequate compensation for the loss of a different district that was culturally compact. He did not rule on the *Shaw* claim for District 25 because he assumed (correctly) than any remedial plan that addressed the VRA violation in District 23 would require a redrawing of District 25.

nities.[131] Although Justice Kennedy ultimately voted to strike down the relevant district because of its race-based dilutive effects, his opinion is reminiscent of his others where he expressed concern about the excessive use of race in drawing districts.[132]

Last term's VRA case, *Riley v Kennedy*,[133] arose from such a unique set of facts that it is difficult to assess its long-term significance. The precise issue involved whether Section 5 of the VRA requires a covered state to preclear a former voting law that was only brought into effect once a state court struck down a successor statute under the state constitution. The Court ruled that the state did not need to seek preclearance because the unconstitutional law never technically went into effect. Despite the arcane nature of the case, legal academics quickly took to blogs to argue, sometimes acrimoniously, over the legal importance of the decision.[134] The case is significant, if at all, as a window on how the Court views the VRA in general, especially given that it will soon weigh in on its constitutionality. It is somewhat rare for an opinion that limits the reach of the VRA to receive seven votes of support, let alone with Justice Ginsburg as the author. That alone might suggest the stakes were low or the issue was *sui generis*.

---

[131] See *LULAC*, 548 US at 429 ("[T]he State [can] use one majority-minority district to compensate for the absence of another only when the racial group in each area had a § 2 right. . . ."); see also Ortiz, 105 Mich L Rev First Impressions at 49 (cited in note 130) (describing the importance of the Court's move from a geographic to a cultural theory of compactness).

[132] See, for example, *Miller v Johnson*, 515 US 900, 927 (1995) (subjecting Georgia congressional district to strict scrutiny because it was excessively race-based); *Bush v Vera*, 517 US 952, 999 (1996) (Kennedy, J, concurring) ("If, however, the bizarre shape of the district is attributable to race-based districting unjustified by a compelling interest (e.g., gratuitous race-based districting or use of race as a proxy for other interests), such districts may 'cause constitutional harm insofar as they convey the message that political identity is, or should be, predominantly racial.'"); see also *Georgia v Ashcroft*, 539 US 461, 491 (Kennedy, J, concurring) (expressing concern about the necessarily predominant use of race in districts drawn pursuant to the Voting Rights Act).

[133] 128 S Ct 1970 (2008).

[134] See Rick Hills, *Civil Rights Lawyers' Ignorance of Local Government Law*, Prawfsblawg (May 30, 2008), online at http://prawfsblawg.blogs.com/prawfsblawg/2008/05/civil-rights-la.html (arguing that the case represents the trivialization of voting rights litigation); Pamela Karlan, *Rick Hills' Marshall McLuhan Moment*, Balkinization (June 4, 2008), online at http://balkin.blogspot.com/2008/06/rick-hills-marshall-mcluhan-moment.html (providing a pointed critique of Hills's post from the lawyer who argued *Riley*); Mike Pitts, *Pitts on Hills on Riley and the VRA*, Election L Blog (June 2, 2008), online at http://electionlawblog.org/archives/010956.html (refuting Hills's claim that the law at issue benefited minority voters); Rick Pildes, *Pildes on Riley Decision*, Election L Blog (May 27, 2008), online at http://electionlawblog.org/archives/010904.html (arguing that the majority opinion and dissent suggest greater skepticism of the Section 5 regime).

Perhaps the case signifies the fatigue of the Court with the VRA disputes on the jurisprudential periphery and reluctance to expand the scope of the VRA by resolving the remaining open questions in a direction more favorable to civil rights. Chief Justice Roberts signaled quite clearly where he was on such peripheral questions, if not the core impact of the VRA, when in *LULAC* he complained, "It is a sordid business, this divvying us up by race."[135] He and others sounded a similar note in the oral argument in the present term's first VRA case, *Bartlett v Strickland*.[136] That case asks whether Section 2 of the VRA requires jurisdictions to draw districts that may be under 50 percent minority. For the most part, courts have operated under the assumption that a minority community must be able to constitute over 50 percent of a potential district before it can have a viable claim of vote dilution under Section 2 of the VRA.[137] The Court has repeatedly avoided the question until this year[138] and, as with *Riley*, appears poised to block further attempts to venture into uncharted territory concerning race and redistricting. This reticence comes from a general uneasiness concerning both race-consciousness and standardless discretion for rules governing redistricting.

The larger question for the current term is whether this reticence has reached a point that the Court is willing to take the dramatic step of declaring Section 5 of the VRA unconstitutional. The case now on appeal to the Supreme Court asks whether the Section 5 regime, reauthorized in 2006, has become anachronistic to the point of being unconstitutional.[139] Section 5 requires certain

---

[135] *LULAC*, 548 US at 511 (Roberts, CJ, dissenting).

[136] 2009 WL 578634, transcript online at http://www.supremecourtus.gov/oral_arguments/argument_transcripts/07-689.pdf (comments of Chief Justice Roberts, Justice Kennedy, and Justice Alito expressing concern about an interpretation of the VRA that would lead it to apply to a greater number of districts).

[137] See *Pender County v Bartlett*, 649 SE2d 364, 372 (NC 2007), cert granted *Bartlett v Strickland*, No 07-689 (oral arguments heard Oct 14, 2008) ("Although the United States Supreme Court has left open this issue, the majority of federal circuit courts confronting the question have concluded that, when a district must be created pursuant to Section 2, it must be a majority-minority district.").

[138] See *LULAC*, 548 US at 445 (opinion of Kennedy) (rejecting claim that white Democrat constituted African American candidate of choice, in part because of constitutional questions that would be raised). In several other cases the Court has assumed without deciding that districts under 50 percent minority might be protected under Section 2. *Johnson v De Grandy*, 512 US at 1009; *Voinovich v Quilter*, 507 US 146, 154 (1993); *Thornburgh v Gingles*, 478 US 30, 46–47 n 12 (1986).

[139] *Northwest Austin Municipal Utility District Number One v Mukasey*, 557 F Supp 2d 9 (DDC 2008), prob juris noted (US Jan 9, 2009) (No 08-322) ("*NAMUDNO*").

covered jurisdictions to submit their voting laws for preclearance by the Attorney General or the U.S. District Court for the District of Columbia, which decide whether such laws have the purpose or effect of "retrogressing" with respect to minority voting rights.[140] Although it was subsequently amended, the "coverage formula," originally established in 1965, included jurisdictions that had low voter turnout in the 1964 election and employed voting "tests or devices," such as a literacy test.[141] Very few jurisdictions have "bailed out" of coverage, as permitted by the statute,[142] by demonstrating a consistent pattern of voting rights compliance and other factors over a ten-year period. In the current appeal, a municipal utility district in Austin argues that it should not be forced to preclear its voting laws, given its lack of a history of discrimination, simply because the state of Texas is a covered jurisdiction.[143]

It is possible that the concern several members of the Court have expressed regarding race and redistricting, let alone excesses of federal power, will lead them to strike down the VRA. Moreover, the election of Barack Obama may add to their convictions that such a regime is unnecessary and out of date. Section 5 was born out of the frustration of civil rights advocates for whom case-by-case federal court adjudication was an ineffective means of controlling mainly Southern obstructionist jurisdictions. Those jurisdictions would find creative ways to comply with court orders while ensuring the disenfranchisement of African Americans. Even if they were not inclined to do so previously, some Justices may view record African American turnout in the 2008 election, let alone Barack Obama's success in a few covered jurisdictions,[144] as

---

[140] Voting Rights Act (VRA), § 5, 42 USC § 1973c (2000).

[141] See 89 PL 110; 79 Stat 437.

[142] See 42 USC § 1973b(a)(1) (2000). On the history of bailout, see Michael P. McDonald, *Who's Covered? Coverage Formula and Bailout*, in David L. Epstein et al, eds, *The Future of the Voting Rights Act* 255, 257 (2006).

[143] *NAMUDNO*, 557 F Supp 2d 9, 24 (DDC 2008), prob juris noted (US Jan 9, 2009) (No 08-322).

[144] Almost all of Virginia and one-third of North Carolina (two states Obama won) are covered, as are a few localities in New York, California, Florida, New Hampshire, and Michigan. However, Alabama, Alaska, Arizona, Georgia, Louisiana, Mississippi, South Carolina, and Texas (all states Obama lost) are covered in their entirety. See Section 5 Covered Jurisdictions, http://www.usdoj.gov/crt/voting/sec_5/covered.php. It is worth noting that Obama lost all states that are completely covered by Section 5. In an amicus brief filed in the *NAMUDNO* case, Stephen Ansolabehere, Charles Stewart, and I point out that the 2008 election, far from counting against the constitutionality of Section 5,

evidence that the fundamental justification for Section 5 has been removed.[145]

The restraint and minimalism that animates the Court's move toward greater emphasis on as-applied challenges may also come to lead the Court to uphold the VRA against this most recent challenge. Striking down the VRA on federalism grounds, as the plaintiffs request, would constitute the most significant court challenge to Congressional power since the *Lochner* era.[146] More modest courses of action could satisfy the majority's discomfort with the Section 5 regime (assuming it has any) while still upholding the law on its face. In particular, the Court could reject the present challenge to the coverage regime, but allow for later challenges to the criteria for bailout. In other words, as in *McConnell/WRTL*, *Washington Grange*, and *Crawford*, it could uphold the law while recognizing that in a future individual case the Constitution might require that the bar should be lowered for a covered jurisdiction to bail out.[147] It could say that the state of Texas (or other covered

---

actually helps distinguish the covered and uncovered jurisdictions. Using both exit poll and actual election results at the county level, we argue that the gap in the voting preferences of whites and minorities remains much wider in the covered jurisdictions. See Brief Amicus Curiae of Nathaniel Persily, Stephen Ansolabehere, and Charles Stewart in Support of Neither Party, *Northwest Austin Municipal Utility District v Holder* (No 08-322), prob juris noted (US Jan 9, 2009).

[145] Compare Abigail and Stephan Thernstrom, *Racial Gerrymandering Is Unnecessary*, Wall St J (November 11, 2008), available at http://online.wsj.com/article/SB1226373739375 16543.html (suggesting that an Obama victory means that "the doors of electoral opportunity in America are open to all" and arguing that "the Voting Rights Act should therefore be reconsidered") to Kristen Clarke, *The Impact of the 2008 Presidential Election on Efforts to Measure Racially Polarized Voting in Future Voting Rights Act Litigation*, Harvard L & Policy Rev (forthcoming 2009) (arguing that the Obama victory should not fundamentally alter the concerns that undergird the VRA).

[146] See Persily, 117 Yale L J at 251–53 (cited in note 129).

[147] The plaintiffs cleverly anticipated this by phrasing their claim, alternatively and ambiguously, as an as-applied challenge. See *NAMUDNO*, 557 F Supp 2d at 76. It is possible that the Court might take their invitation and declare the law unconstitutional as-applied to such a small jurisdiction or strike down parts of the statute that prevent such a jurisdiction from independently bailing out. Doing so would allow the Court to escape the headlines of striking down the VRA, while chipping away at the coverage regime. There are several problems with this approach that would not be applicable to a later attempt to challenge a refusal of bailout as unconstitutional. First, it is unclear as a threshold matter whether one can launch as-applied challenges to exercises of Congressional power on federalism grounds. See Gillian E. Metzger, *Facial Challenges and Federalism*, 105 Colum L Rev 873 (2005). Second, the Court has already upheld the coverage of subjurisdictions as constitutional and the statute does not contemplate the possibility of every subjurisdiction independently seeking a declaratory judgment in the U.S. District Court for D.C. to escape coverage. See *City of Rome v United States*, 446 US 156 (1980). Instead, the Court may simply say that the remedy for the utility district here is for the state of Texas to attempt to bail out, and if it is denied, the Court can then review and recraft the criteria for bailout.

jurisdictions) should attempt to bail out of coverage first and the criteria used to reject its bailout request should be interpreted in such a way to avoid constitutional difficulty. The bailout regime, itself, operates as an analog to as-applied challenges: allowing those jurisdictions that consider themselves unfairly captured to prove the law should not be applicable to them. Given that the Roberts Court has at least hinted at the continuing constitutionality of the VRA,[148] a majority uncomfortable with the new VRA might prefer a strategy of upholding on its face today while allowing for quasi-as-applied challenges later through lowering the hurdles for bailout.

C. REGULATION OF POLITICAL PARTIES

The Rehnquist Court's decisions concerning the rights of political parties tended to follow two themes. The first was a general disregard for minor parties' claims either for ballot access or other associational rights.[149] The second was robust protection for major parties' rights, as illustrated in decisions striking down laws that infringed on a major party's right to include independents[150] or exclude nonmembers[151] from voting in its primary. For the most part, these cases had a greater impact on academic discussion than on party behavior or policy debate. The cases posed rich theoretical questions about the uniqueness of political parties as quasi-state actors that are at once protected by the First Amendment but also have the capacity to craft election laws to infringe on voters' and other parties' rights.[152]

---

[148] Even the more conservative members of the Court have suggested that the previous incarnation of the VRA was constitutional. See *LULAC*, 548 US at 517 (Scalia, J, dissenting in part) (joined by Roberts, Alito, and Thomas); Nathaniel Persily, *Strict in Theory, Loopy in Fact*, 105 Mich L Rev First Impressions 43 (2006) (highlighting the unprecedented move by Scalia to vote to uphold a racially gerrymandered district on the basis of the compelling state interest of complying with Section 5 of the Voting Rights Act).

[149] See, for example, *Timmons v Twin Cities Area New Party*, 520 US 351 (1997) (rejecting claim by minor party for fusion candidacy); *Munro v Socialist Workers Party*, 479 US 189 (1986) (upholding ballot access requirement); *Clingman v Beaver*, 544 US 581 (2005) (rejecting Libertarian party's right to allow members affiliated with other parties to vote in its primary); *Arkansas Ed. Television Comm'n v Forbes*, 523 US 666 (1997) (rejecting claim of independent candidate to be part of candidate debate on public television). But see *Norman v Reed*, 502 US 279 (1992) (vindicating rights of minor party in Illinois).

[150] See *Tashjian v Republican Party of Conn.*, 479 US 208 (1986).

[151] See *California Democratic Party v Jones*, 530 US 567 (2000); see also *Eu v San Francisco County Democratic Central Comm.*, 489 US 214 (1989).

[152] See Nathaniel Persily, *Toward a Functional Defense of Political Party Autonomy*, 76 NYU

The Roberts Court appears to be hewing close to the Rehnquist Court's line in the two party-related cases it decided in the 2007–2008 term, as well as its discussion of party rights in both *Randall v Sorrell* and *LULAC*. Although too much should not be made from these few cases (especially given the lopsided votes in last term's cases), the placement of most members of the current Court on the relevant themes has now become apparent. In general, the Justices can be arrayed roughly according to their concern for major parties' associational rights claims and for the rights of outsiders (minor parties or insurgent candidates) who seek to challenge the two major parties.

Justices Stevens and Ginsburg are least willing to protect major parties in their claims of associational rights or to grant credence to state interests that mask bias against minor parties. Thus, they (along with Justice Souter) dissented when the Court upheld the antifusion law widely believed to inhibit the growth of minor parties,[153] when it rejected the Libertarian Party's claim to include other parties' members in its primary,[154] and when it upheld the Texas Republican gerrymander.[155] Justice Souter appears to differ with Stevens and Ginsburg in the value he places on the two-party system[156] and in the autonomy rights of all political parties. Stevens and Ginsburg, but not Justice Souter, were therefore willing to uphold the blanket primary in California against claims it invaded parties' associational rights by forcing parties to accept outsiders in their primaries.[157] All three, of course, voted to uphold both the nonpartisan blanket primary in *Washington Grange* and the judicial nomination method in *Lopez Torres*, although Justice Stevens, joined by Souter, went out of his way to criticize the wisdom of the latter.[158]

Justice Breyer differs from the other more liberal members of

---

L Rev 750 (2001); Nathaniel Persily and Bruce E. Cain, *The Legal Status of Political Parties: A Reassessment of Competing Paradigms*, 100 Colum L Rev 775 (2000); Bruce E. Cain, *Point/ Counterpoint: Party Autonomy and Two-Party Electoral Competition*, 149 U Pa L Rev 793 (2001); Samuel Issacharoff, *Private Parties with Public Purpose: Political Parties, Associational Freedoms, and Partisan Competition*, 101 Colum L Rev 274 (2001).

[153] See *Timmons*, 520 US 351, 370 (Stevens, J, dissenting).

[154] *Clingman*, 544 US 581, 608 (Stevens, J, dissenting).

[155] *LULAC*, 548 US at 447 (Stevens, J, dissenting); id at 483 (Souter, J, dissenting).

[156] See *Timmons*, 520 US 351, 382 (Souter, J, dissenting).

[157] *Jones*, 530 US at 590 (Stevens, J, dissenting).

[158] See *New York v Lopez Torres*, 128 S Ct 791, 801 (2008) (Stevens, J, concurring).

the Court in his focus on entrenchment above other concerns. His controlling opinion for the Court in *Randall* (joined only by Chief Justice Roberts and Justice Alito) best exemplifies his thinking. Focusing on the law's effect on challengers attempting to compete against incumbents, he found the restrictions on political party contributions to be an especially disconcerting "danger sign" for the contribution limits at issue.[159] Similarly, his approach to partisan gerrymandering in *Vieth* and *LULAC* focused on whether one party attempts to use its power in the redistricting process to keep itself in power.[160] He also joined separate concurrences in both *Clingman v Beaver*[161] and *Lopez Torres*[162] in order to emphasize an alternative, narrower holding that might allow a minor party or insurgent candidate to have a successful claim were the election law at issue more hostile to competition.[163] However, Breyer also seems more concerned about protecting the rights of major parties than those of minor parties, as exemplified in his willingness to join the Court in both striking down California's blanket primary and upholding Minnesota's ban on fusion candidacies.[164]

Justice Kennedy often shares Breyer's concerns about entrenchment,[165] although in other cases he supplements those concerns with an unsurpassed First Amendment libertarianism to protect party speech and associational rights. His separate concurrence in *California Democratic Party v Jones*,[166] for example, stands out as a

---

[159] See *Randall v Sorrell*, 548 US 230 (2006) (opinion of Breyer).

[160] *LULAC*, 548 US at 491–92 (Breyer, J, concurring in part and dissenting in part); *Vieth v Jubelirer*, 541 US 267, 355–68 (2004) (Breyer, J, dissenting).

[161] See *Clingman*, 544 US at 603 (O'Connor, J, concurring) ("[T]he State itself is controlled by the political party or parties in power, which presumably have an incentive to shape the rules of the electoral game to their own benefit.").

[162] *Lopez Torres*, 128 S Ct at 801 (Kennedy, J, concurring).

[163] The two cases that do not fit this mold are *Timmons*, in which Breyer joins the majority to uphold the antifusion ban, and *Jones*, where Breyer joins the majority to strike down California's blanket primary.

[164] See *Jones*, 530 US 567; *Timmons*, 520 US 351.

[165] Kennedy expressed these concerns in a case before Breyer even joined the Court when he dissented from a decision that upheld Hawaii's ban on write-in voting. See *Burdick v Takushi*, 504 US 428, 442 (Kennedy, J, dissenting) (arguing that the ban on write-in votes alongside restrictive ballot access laws diminished the right to cast a meaningful vote).

[166] *California Democratic Party v Jones*, 530 US 567, 586, 590 (2000) (Kennedy, J, concurring) ("When the State seeks to regulate a political party's nomination process as a means to shape and control political doctrine and the scope of political choice, the First Amendment gives substantial protection to the party from the manipulation. In a free society the State is directed by political doctrine, not the other way around.").

broad condemnation of state attempts to limit party autonomy in both the nomination process and campaign finance. Moreover, his concurrence in *Vieth* urges future challenges to partisan gerrymanders to focus on the potential costs to freedom of association from one party's discrimination against another party's voters.[167] Because he appears to place greater importance on parties' right to speak and associate, he and Breyer also disagree in the party finance cases[168] and in *Washington Grange*, where Kennedy joined Scalia's dissent arguing against the constitutionality of the nonpartisan blanket primary.

Justices Thomas and Scalia, in contrast, tend to side against minor parties, while protecting political parties' rights to exclude nonmembers. The one case that has divided them (as it divided Breyer and Kennedy) was *Washington Grange*, for which Justice Thomas wrote the opinion for the Court and Justice Scalia (joined by Justice Kennedy) vigorously dissented.[169] In that case they simply appeared to disagree as to the likelihood that the nonpartisan blanket primary would blur the difference between a party preference and a party endorsement.

Chief Justice Roberts and Justice Alito have been joined at the hip when it comes to the party cases. In an opinion only for themselves in *LULAC*, they rejected the partisan gerrymandering claim without saying such claims would never be justiciable.[170] In *Randall*, they (and they alone) joined Breyer in the opinion that also emphasized the problems with low limits on party contributions.[171] While joining the majority in *Lopez Torres*, they joined

---

[167] *Vieth*, 541 US at 316 (Kennedy, J, concurring).

[168] See *Colo. Republican Fed. Campaign Comm. v Fec*, 518 US 604 (1996) ("*Colorado Republican I*"); *Colo. Republican Fed. Campaign Comm. v FEC*, 533 US 431 (2001) ("*Colorado Republican II*").

[169] *Wash. State Grange v Wash. State Republican Party*, 128 S Ct 1184 (2008).

[170] *LULAC*, 548 US at 492 (Roberts, J, concurring in the judgment in part, concurring in part, dissenting in part) ("The question whether any such standard [for partisan gerrymandering] exists—that is, whether a challenge to a political gerrymander presents a justiciable case or controversy—has not been argued in these cases."). Roberts's curt treatment of the partisan gerrymandering claim in *LULAC* is bizarre, given that the Court had earlier remanded the case in light of *Vieth*. *Vieth* was *only* about partisan gerrymandering. The district court's post-*Vieth* opinion, which led to the appeal the Supreme Court considered in *LULAC*, was almost exclusively about whether the Texas gerrymander failed any possible standard that could have satisfied Justice Kennedy's opinion in *Vieth*. The justiciability of partisan gerrymandering claims and the presentation of alternative standards were certainly argued in the case.

[171] *Randall*, 548 US at 236.

together (alone again) in Roberts's separate concurrence in *Washington Grange* to emphasize that a showing of the likelihood of confusion would be enough to strike down the nonpartisan blanket primary.

Washington Grange is therefore the tea leaf that deserves reading to surmise what might lie ahead for the Roberts Court in party autonomy cases. Not only because it was a unanimous decision, but also because it falls in line with the Rehnquist Court cases on marginalizing those that challenge the two major parties, *Lopez Torres* was not a surprise.[172] The fact that Justice Scalia could only get Justice Kennedy to join him in dissent in *Washington Grange* may suggest some sort of shift away from the thick autonomy arguments that he wrote for a seven-member majority in *California Democratic Party v Jones*. However, the limited resolution of the facial challenge, as well as the more extreme autonomy argument the parties made in *Washington Grange*, should caution against viewing the case as a sea change. Now that the Court has established the basic contours of a party's right to exclude or include certain classes of voters in its primary, perhaps a case like *Washington Grange* is simply viewed as implicating a peripheral autonomy right concerning the control over the party's brand name. In some respects, the party cases from this past Term may simply be emblematic of the general restraint the Roberts Court has exercised over election laws outside the context of campaign finance. Perhaps Chief Justice Roberts, in particular, viewed *Washington Grange* in the light of *Crawford* that would soon be decided. That case laid the groundwork for the facial holding of *Crawford*, and by upholding both laws the Court could avoid the charge that it was defending the rights of powerful political parties while minimizing the importance of the voting rights of those without photo ID.

D. BARRIERS TO PARTICIPATION

The *Crawford* case was not the Roberts Court's first and only entry into the fray over voter integrity and access. Both before

---

[172] If one views the case more as one about judicial elections, it is even less surprising. The Court has hinted at its discomfort with judicial elections while protecting judicial campaign speech. See *Republican Party of Minnesota v White*, 536 US 765 (2002). The antidemocratic form judicial elections take in New York might be less troublesome to one who believes electing judges is a mistake from the outset.

and after *Crawford*, the Court waded into the debate. In *Purcell v Gonzalez*,[173] a case upholding at a preliminary stage Arizona's ID requirement, the Court forecasted the concerns about perceptions of fraud that Justice Stevens eventually expressed in *Crawford*. *Purcell* emphasized, in particular, that "Voter fraud drives honest citizens out of the democratic process and breeds distrust of our government. Voters who fear their legitimate votes will be outweighed by fraudulent ones will feel disenfranchised."[174] And in a surprising (also interlocutory) opinion less than a month before the 2008 election, a unanimous Court weighed in to establish that the Help America Vote Act does not confer a private right of action to the Republican Party in its attempt to force the Ohio Secretary of State to provide mismatch lists from the voter registration file.[175] The lasting impact of these cases, particularly *Crawford*, will likely be felt in the asymmetric evidentiary burdens they have required for proving actual or perceived fraud, on the one hand, and measurable disenfranchisement on the other.

The Court's holding in *Crawford* that the state interest in preventing actual or perceived fraud justified the ID law is as important a development as its assessment of the burden on voters described earlier. The *Crawford* Court found the lack of evidence of past instances of voter impersonation fraud in Indiana—the kind an ID law would prevent—to be unimportant in justifying the law. Such fraud had occurred at some point in other parts of the country,[176] Justice Stevens's opinion maintained, and Indiana and other states had experienced other types of fraud, such as absentee voter fraud. Drawing from the campaign finance case law recognizing

---

[173] *Purcell v Gonzalez*, 127 S Ct 5 (2006).

[174] Id at 7.

[175] *Brunner v Ohio Republican Party*, 129 S Ct 5 (2008).

[176] The only two instances of in-person fraud the controlling opinion identifies are one case in Washington and one anecdote from the days of Tammany Hall. See *Crawford*, 128 S Ct at 1619 nn 11–12. The Circuit Court opinion suggested that such lack of evidence is likely the result of nonenforcement of minor criminal laws, akin to littering, as well as the inherent difficulties of detecting such fraud. *Crawford*, 472 F3d 949, 953–54. Heated debate may continue over these empirics of voter fraud, but few argue that no ineligible voters end up casting votes in elections. At the same time, concerted efforts by groups to commit fraud by voter impersonation almost never happen. The benefits of such a strategy are too low or too difficult to quantify given that the conspirator must coordinate a number of voters sufficient to overcome the expected margin of loss. And the costs are too high (both in terms of moving from one polling place to the next and potentially getting caught) to make this a smart strategy to rig an election. This is especially true given that other means of fraud, such as through absentee ballots or tampering with vote totals, might require less effort, better avoid detection, and work more effectively.

the state interest in combating perceptions of corruption,[177] the controlling opinion found the ID law further justified as safeguarding voter confidence in the integrity of elections.[178] Even if no actual fraud had occurred or would be prevented, the argument went, a voter ID law might reasonably address voters' fears of electoral mischief.[179]

In a study published in the *Harvard Law Review* the same week as the *Crawford* decision, Stephen Ansolabehere and I presented recent data as to public perceptions of vote fraud.[180] We found that a large share of the public believes voter impersonation occurs very often (9 percent) or somewhat often (32 percent). The same pattern holds for questions about double voting or noncitizen voting. However, we find that, contrary to the contention in *Purcell*, respondents who perceive a great deal of fraud are no less likely to turn out to vote. Nor does there seem to be any difference in perceptions of fraud based on whether the respondent lives in a state with a stricter ID requirement or was personally asked for ID.

Although the available empirical evidence might undermine the strong claims about confidence and voter ID laws, such an argument (as in campaign finance cases) may simply represent "piling on" once the Court has lowered the standard so low for proof of actual fraud. Whether a court relies on opportunities for voter fraud, isolated and perhaps distant instances of actual fraud, or presumed voter perception of fraud, the outcome will still be the same. The central question is whether the state can act prophylactically to avoid an unlikely, even if widely assumed, threat to democracy. The Court has answered "yes" to that question, at least when the number of people who may not then vote as a consequence is difficult to define or identify.

---

[177] See Nathaniel Persily and Kelli Lammie, *Perceptions of Corruption and Campaign Finance: When Public Opinion Determines Constitutional Law*, 153 U Pa L Rev 119, 122–23 (2004).

[178] *Crawford*, 128 S Ct at 1620 ("[P]ublic confidence in the integrity of the electoral process has independent significance, because it encourages citizen participation in the democratic process.").

[179] Indeed, one also must have some sympathy for Justice Stevens's evaluation of the threat of voter fraud: as a Republican growing up in Chicago, election fraud was not a theoretical problem for him; it was a way of life.

[180] See Stephen Ansolabehere and Nathaniel Persily, *Vote Fraud in the Eye of the Beholder: The Role of Public Opinion in the Challenge to Voter Identification Requirements*, 121 Harv L Rev 1737 (2008).

The question then turns to whether the constitutional balance that *Crawford* has struck would tip against such laws if more concrete or substantial evidence of vote hindrance or denial could be demonstrated. Here again, though, the question as to what *Crawford* means with respect to future as-applied challenges becomes critical. One view of *Crawford* dictates that the primary job of courts will be to carve out exceptions for individuals and groups disadvantaged by voting laws. If that represents an accurate reading, then it is difficult to see how most laws of this ilk would not then be justified (or at least *as justified* as the Indiana law) by an appeal to the same antifraud justifications.[181]

The controversy over voter fraud has only intensified and become more politicized since the *Crawford* decision. It manifested itself during the 2008 campaign in the blowup over ACORN's error-prone voter registration drives,[182] as well as efforts in various states to create registration mismatch lists that threatened to lead to challenges to voter qualifications in the polling place. Those threats rarely materialized, but the lawsuits provided a template for what may lie ahead. *Crawford* will continue to serve as the reigning precedent for the next generation of ID laws, such as those requiring proof of citizenship for voting.[183] However, the more prevalent cases pitting claims of fraud against claims of access concern laws that regulate registration drives[184] or that erect hurdles for voters whose registration status is questioned due to discrepancies between the voter registration database and some other database.

The Supreme Court issued an unexpected decision relevant to the last type of case when it held that a political party could not sue the Ohio Secretary of State under the Help America Vote Act

---

[181] In applying *Crawford* so as to uphold a similar photo ID law in Georgia, an Eleventh Circuit panel did not even seem to leave open the possibility of as-applied challenges. See *Common Cause/Georgia v Billups*, 554 F3d 1340 (11th Cir 2009).

[182] See Rotten Acorn, Recent Fraud, online at http://www.rottenacorn.com/activity Map.html.

[183] See Ian Urbina, *Voter ID Battle Shifts to Proof of Citizenship*, New York Times (May 12, 2008), online at http://www.nytimes.com/2008/05/12/us/politics/12vote.html?_r = 1 &hp&oref = login (describing proposed, but as yet unpassed, constitutional amendment in Missouri that would require proof of citizenship from voters and noting similar bills in nineteen others states).

[184] See *League of Women Voters of Florida v Browning*, 575 F Supp 2d 1298 (SD Fla 2008) (citing *Crawford*'s analysis of both fraud and as-applied challenges and upholding regulations of third-party registration drives).

to force her to release a list of mismatches between the state's voter registration database and the motor vehicles and Social Security databases.[185] As a consequence of that holding, great variation will continue to exist between states as to how they handle discrepancies between the HAVA-required statewide voter registration database[186] and other lists, such as the Social Security and department of motor vehicles databases. The cause for concern arises from the large number of errors (sometimes affecting 20 percent of new registrations) that occur because of transcription problems, changed names, or faulty address information in the databases.[187] States that purge mismatched voters from the voter rolls or require them to cure the discrepancy through various steps do so for fraud-prevention or election-integrity reasons similar to those expressed in *Crawford*. At least one court that has considered such a "no-match, no-vote law" concluded that the law was facially constitutional and justified by the state's interest in combating fraud or its appearance.[188] Moreover, like *Crawford*, as-applied challenges were viewed as a sufficient safeguard for mismatched voters who found it particularly difficult to cure the registration defect.

III. Conclusion

Despite changed membership on the Court and the passage of eights years, *Bush v Gore* continues to cast a shadow over the election cases the Supreme Court considers, as well as the elections

---

[185] *Brunner v Ohio Republican Party*, 129 S Ct 5 (2008).

[186] See Title 42 USC § 15483 (2000 ed, Supp V) (describing requirement of statewide voter registration database).

[187] See Justin Levitt, Wendy R. Weiser, and Ana Munoz, *Making the List: Database Matching and Verification Processes for Voter Registration* ii (Brennan Center, 2006).

[188] See *Florida State Conference of the NAACP v Browning*, 569 F Supp 2d 1237 (N D Fla 2008) (upholding Florida's "no-match, no-vote" law). The law required that individuals whose voter registration forms could not be verified against DMV or Social Security databases needed to resolve the discrepancy. They could do so by presenting in person or mailing a copy of their ID to their local board of elections. If they failed to do so before the election, they would be required to cast a provisional ballot, which they could cure by producing an ID to the board shortly afterward. As with *Crawford*, the state justified the law as an antifraud measure that would build public confidence, despite little historical evidence in Florida of fraud occurring, outside the context of absentee ballots. 569 F Supp 2d at 1261. The plaintiffs, as in *Crawford*, could not produce before the election anyone who would not be able to vote as a result. The Court took refuge in *Crawford*'s holding concerning facial and as-applied challenges to suggest that burdened voters could seek a remedy as applied to themselves.

themselves. When parties view the stakes of every legal dispute as if a presidential election might ride on it, no constitutional question regarding the operation of elections or campaigns seems too small for judicial resolution. At the same time, each election case often brings with it risks of accusations of politicization of the judiciary, in general, or partisanship of judges, in particular. Breaking with this legacy requires that the Roberts Court continuously confront a challenge in its election cases to attempt consensus and to proceed incrementally.

The cases from the 2007–2008 term represent concerted effort expended particularly by Chief Justice Roberts to establish an approach to election law that achieves these goals. The controlling opinions of the Court—all joined, but none written, by Roberts—exude restraint and minimalism, while ensuring that courts will remain actively and intimately involved in the minutiae of election law. The frequently expressed preference for as-applied challenges led supermajorities of the Court to uphold election laws today that the Court implies might be unconstitutional tomorrow. Indeed, the redefinition or fudging of the differences between facial and as-applied challenges has allowed the Court to disguise what otherwise seem like more transformative election law holdings. The type of as-applied challenge to ID laws *Crawford* leaves open, for example, might allow for narrow exceptions for especially burdened groups, or a broad invalidation of the law once we learn more about its effects, as with the style of the ballot in *Washington Grange*. Similarly, when as-applied challenges lead to the crafting of legislative-like rules, as in *WRTL*, then the Court can have its cake of preserving precedent while substantially eating it too.

Such an approach also represents a subclass of strategies to avoid open conflict with the political branches. Another is the Court's avoidance of arguments that hint, in effect, at politicians behaving too politically. Even when glaringly obvious from the legislative history, the Court shies away from accusations of partisan bias or incumbent entrenchment. In *Davis*, for example, traditional First Amendment analysis proved ill-suited to striking down the Millionaire's Amendment, when the chief concern arising from the law may have been its underlying incumbent-protection motive. Moreover, whereas the lopsided partisan support for ID laws may persuade lower court judges of their unconstitutionality, even the dissenters in *Crawford* could not bring themselves to make the charge that the law represented an attempt by one party to place obstacles in the way of its opponents' supporters.

Although the low salience of most of the cases from the 2007–2008 term may also explain the surprising degree of consensus, seemingly minor cases engendered heated disagreement for earlier Courts. Furthermore, these cases may prove to be the building blocks for more transformational election law shifts recognizable only in retrospect. With *Davis*, for example, the Court continues its trend of chipping away at prevailing campaign finance doctrine. *Washington Grange* and *Lopez Torres* may prove more significant over the long term if they represent a move away from greater scrutiny both of laws that curtail party autonomy and ones that cement party organizational hegemony. *Crawford*, too, represents a mere introduction to the voter fraud and suppression debate. This past election suggests the ruling in that case, where the stakes have proven to be low, may project broader, more important signals as to the role of courts in defining the limits of partisan attempts to erect barriers to registration and voting. Finally, *Riley*'s unique facts and lopsided resolution ought not to distract from the possibility that the case may be emblematic of a shifting tide against aggressive enforcement of the Voting Rights Act. For all of these cases from the 2007–2008 term, their implications may become evident even sooner than the opinion authors thought. With four or more election law cases accepted for the subsequent term, the Roberts Court has refused to let these controversies cool or fester before it attempts at some partial resolution.

CURTIS A. BRADLEY

SELF-EXECUTION AND TREATY DUALITY

Pursuant to Article II of the Constitution, the President has the power to make treaties with the advice and consent of two-thirds of the Senate, and these treaties uncontroversially become binding on the United States as a matter of international law. The status of such treaties within the U.S. legal system is less clear. The Supremacy Clause states that, along with the Constitution and laws of the United States, treaties made by the United States are part of the "supreme Law of the Land." At least since the Supreme Court's 1829 decision in *Foster v Neilson*, however, it has been understood that treaty provisions are directly enforceable in U.S. courts only if they are "self-executing."[1] The legitimacy and implications of this self-execution requirement have generated substantial controversy and confusion among both courts and commentators.

Much of the debate over self-execution has been fought out, at least in part, on originalist territory, with competing claims about what the constitutional Founders would have understood. Whatever one may think of the virtues of originalist methodology in general, it has not been successful in moving the self-execution debate forward. Among other things, both treaty practice and the nation's

Curtis A. Bradley is the Richard A. Horvitz Professor of Law, Duke Law School.

AUTHOR'S NOTE: I would like to thank Robert Ahdieh, Kathy Bradley, Brad Clark, Martin Flaherty, Jack Goldsmith, Avril Haines, Duncan Hollis, John Parry, Eric Posner, Nick Rosenkranz, Paul Stephan, Ed Swaine, Carlos Vázquez, and participants in a Constitutional Law Workshop at Georgetown Law Center for their helpful comments.

[1] See 27 US (2 Pet) 253, 314–15 (1829).

position in the world have changed so dramatically since the Founding that is difficult for originalism to compel contemporary conclusions. It is noteworthy, for example, that most scholarship on self-execution hardly mentions the phenomenon of congressional-executive agreements (which are ratified by the President with the approval of a majority of both houses of Congress rather than two-thirds of the Senate), even though they constitute the vast majority of international agreements concluded by the United States since the 1930s.[2] Similarly, the development in the modern era of legislative-style multilateral treaties, many of which overlap substantially with domestic legislation, poses issues not contemplated by the Founders.[3]

The Supreme Court's decision last Term in *Medellín v Texas* contains the most extensive discussion of treaty self-execution in the Court's history.[4] In that case, the Court held that a treaty obligation of the United States to comply with a decision of the International Court of Justice (the international adjudicatory arm of the United Nations that sits in The Hague) was not self-executing and thus could not be applied by U.S. courts to override an otherwise valid state rule of criminal procedure. The Court also held that the President lacked the unilateral authority to compel state courts to comply with the International Court's decision. The decision is both controversial and subject to differing interpretations and thus, if anything, is likely to intensify the debate.

My goal in this article is to clear up some conceptual confusion relating to the self-execution doctrine and, in the process, better explain the contemporary practice of the courts and political branches relating to treaty enforcement. To that end, I will make three claims about treaty self-execution. First, the Supremacy Clause does not by itself tell us the extent to which treaties should be judicially enforceable. Second, the relevant intent in discerning self-execution is the intent of the U.S. treaty-makers (that is, the President and Senate), not the collective intent of the various parties to the treaty. Third, even if treaties and statutes have an equivalent status in the U.S. legal system in the abstract, there are important

---

[2] See Oona Hathaway, *Treaties' End: The Past, Present, and Future of International Lawmaking in the United States*, 117 Yale L J 1236 (2008).

[3] See Curtis A. Bradley, *The Treaty Power and American Federalism*, 97 Mich L Rev 390, 396–97 (1998).

[4] See 128 S Ct 1346 (2008).

structural and functional differences between them that are relevant to judicial enforceability.

As will be shown, these three claims are interconnected. The central theme connecting them is that treaties have a dual nature, in that they operate both within the domain of international politics as well as within the domain of law. In addition to having a certain status within international law, and potentially also within domestic law, every treaty is a contract that implicates the U.S. relationship with one or more other nations, and such a relationship inherently includes political as well as legal elements, such as considerations of reciprocity, reputation, and national interest. This duality of treaties is in turn relevant, as I will explain, to their domestic judicial enforceability.[5] The three claims set forth in this article are also complementary, in that each of them is best understood along with the other two, and together they present a relatively coherent explanation for the judicial precedent in the area, including (despite its ambiguities) the *Medellín* decision, as well as the practices of the political branches.

Part I of this article briefly reviews the academic debates over treaty self-execution, some of the uncertainties surrounding the issue, and what is at stake. Part II defends and explains the implications of my first claim: that the Supremacy Clause does not by itself tell us the extent to which treaties should be judicially enforceable. Part III defends the second claim: that the relevant intent concerning self-execution is that of the U.S. treaty-makers. Part IV defends the third claim: that, even if statutes and treaties have equivalent legal status in the abstract, they are different in important ways that relate to judicial enforceability. Finally, Part V explains how *Medellín*, despite its ambiguities, is generally consistent with these three claims.

In staking out these claims, I will refer extensively to the work of Professor Carlos Vázquez, who has been the most prolific and sophisticated theorist about treaty self-execution and who recently

---

[5] There is a long-standing theoretical debate about how to conceive of the relationship between international law and domestic law, a debate that is sometimes framed as one between "monism" and "dualism." The term "dualism" in that debate refers to the view "that international and domestic law are distinct, each nation determines for itself when and to what extent international law is incorporated into its legal system, and the status of international law in the domestic system is determined by domestic law." Curtis A. Bradley, *Breard, Our Dualist Constitution, and the Internationalist Conception*, 51 Stan L Rev 529, 530 (1999). My use of the term "duality" in this article is not intended to engage with that debate.

published an important article on the topic in the *Harvard Law Review*. Although my article will focus primarily on points of disagreement between us, I should emphasize at the outset that there are many points relating to treaty self-execution on which we agree, and I have benefited greatly from his work on the subject.

I. The Self-Execution Debate

As Professor Vázquez has usefully explained, there are a number of possible reasons why a U.S. court might decline to enforce a treaty that has gone through the Article II process.[6] A treaty may call for a governmental action, such as the appropriation of money or the creation of criminal liability, that is thought to lie exclusively within the powers of the full Congress. Some treaty cases, like some constitutional and statutory cases, may be nonjusticiable—for example, because of standing requirements or the political question doctrine. Or the case may depend upon the recognition of a private right of action, and the court may conclude that the treaty does not itself confer such a right of action. Finally, a court may conclude that a treaty was not intended to be judicially enforceable unless and until implemented by a political branch, usually Congress. The *Foster* decision relied on this last proposition, and Professor Vázquez refers to this doctrine as "*Foster*-type non-self-execution."[7] It is this type of non-self-execution that is the focus of this article.

Critics of *Foster*-type non-self-execution contend that it is at odds with, or at least in tension with, the Supremacy Clause, which states that "all" treaties made by the United States shall be the supreme law of the land. *Foster*-type non-self-execution, the argument goes, means that only *some* treaties are given effect as supreme law of the land.[8] In part because they view *Foster*-type non-self-execution as difficult to reconcile with the Supremacy Clause, critics contend that there should at least be a strong presumption in favor of treaty

---

[6] See Carlos Manuel Vázquez, *The Four Doctrines of Self-Executing Treaties*, 89 Am J Intl L 695 (1995).

[7] See Carlos Manuel Vázquez, *Treaties as Law of the Land: The Supremacy Clause and the Judicial Enforcement of Treaties*, 122 Harv L Rev 599, 602 (2008).

[8] See Vázquez, 89 Am J Intl L at 706 (cited in note 6); Vázquez, 122 Harv L Rev at 610 (cited in note 7); Jordan J. Paust, *Self-Executing Treaties*, 82 Am J Intl L 760, 760 (1988); see also Louis Henkin, *Foreign Affairs and the United States Constitution* 199 (2d ed 1996) ("[Chief Justice] Marshall [in *Foster*] . . . felt obligated to read an exception into the Supremacy Clause.").

self-execution. Professor Vázquez has argued, for example, that "the concept of a non-self-executing treaty is in tension with the Supremacy Clause's designation of treaties as 'law'," and that, as a result, "our Constitution should be read to establish a presumption that treaties are self-executing."[9]

The most prominent counterpoint to this view has come from Professor John Yoo. In a lengthy article published in the *Columbia Law Review*, Yoo argued that the original understanding of the constitutional Founders was that treaties would not operate as domestic law when they (as is often the case today) addressed matters falling within the scope of Congress's legislative authority.[10] In a subsequent article, Yoo argued that requiring legislative implementation for many treaties is also supported by constitutional text and structure.[11] As an alternative to his constitutional claim, Yoo contended that there should at least be a presumption against treaty self-execution, such that the treaty-makers would be required to issue a "clear statement" if they wanted a treaty to be self-executing.[12]

At least before *Medellín*, it was unclear to what extent the case law supported one view or the other, although it seems fair to say that it did not implement what Professor Yoo claimed was the original understanding (as he essentially conceded). Courts have often enforced treaties directly without consideration of whether the treaties addressed matters falling within Congress's legislative authority.[13] In particular, as noted in the Restatement (Third) of Foreign Relations Law, "[p]rovisions in treaties of friendship, commerce, and navigation, or other agreements conferring rights on foreign nationals, especially in matters ordinarily governed by State law, have been given effect without any implementing legislation, their

---

[9] Carlos Manuel Vázquez, *Laughing at Treaties*, 99 Colum L Rev 2154, 2157, 2173 (1999).

[10] See John C. Yoo, *Globalism and the Constitution: Treaties, Non-Self-Execution, and the Original Understanding*, 99 Colum L Rev 1955 (1999).

[11] See John C. Yoo, *Treaties and Public Lawmaking: A Textual and Structural Defense of Non-Self-Execution*, 99 Colum L Rev 2218 (1999).

[12] Id at 2255. For critical responses to Yoo's articles, see Martin S. Flaherty, *History Right? Historical Scholarship, Original Understanding, and Treaties as "Supreme Law of the Land,"* 99 Colum L Rev 2095 (1999), and Vázquez, 99 Colum L Rev 2154 (cited in note 9).

[13] See, for example, *Kolovrat v Oregon*, 366 US 187 (1961) (applying treaty with Serbia to allow Yugoslavian nationals to inherit personal property from Oregon decedent); *Asakura v City of Seattle*, 265 US 332 (1924) (applying treaty with Japan to preempt Seattle ordinance that disallowed noncitizens from being licensed as pawnbrokers); *Ware v Hylton*, 3 US 199 (1796) (applying treaty with Great Britain to preempt Virginia statute that restricted ability of British creditors to recover on pre–Revolutionary War debts).

self-executing character assumed without discussion."[14] On the other hand, lower courts in recent years have often been reluctant to allow private judicial enforcement of treaties, especially multi-lateral treaties, so much so that it is arguable that the modern case law suggests a presumption against self-execution.[15]

Modern lower court decisions have also highlighted a number of uncertainties surrounding the self-execution doctrine. One uncertainty concerns the relevant intent that courts should look to in discerning self-execution. If self-execution is like the substantive terms in the treaty, then, as with a domestic contract, a court should attempt to discern the collective intent of the parties.[16] Some courts have in fact suggested that approach, albeit without much analysis.[17] The Restatement, by contrast, takes the position that the relevant intent is that of the U.S. treaty-makers—that is, the Senate and President[18]—and courts have in fact given particular weight to evidence of U.S. intent.[19]

Another, somewhat related uncertainty concerns the materials that courts should look at in discerning the relevant intent. The Court in *Foster* emphasized the treaty text, but it is not clear when treaty text will be deemed to suggest self-execution or non-self-execution. There have also been questions about the extent to which it is proper for courts to take account of nontextual materials, such as drafting or ratification history. In the 1970s and 1980s, some lower courts developed multifactored tests for self-execution. These factors included the following considerations:

---

[14] Restatement (Third) of the Foreign Relations Law of the United States, § 111, reporters' note 5 (1987).

[15] See, for example, *United States v Emuegbunam*, 268 F3d 377, 389 (6th Cir 2001) ("As a general rule, however, international treaties do not create rights that are privately enforceable in the federal courts."); *United States v Li*, 206 F3d 56, 60 (1st Cir 2000) (en banc) ("[T]reaties do not generally create rights that are privately enforceable in the federal courts."); *Goldstar (Panama) S.A. v United States*, 967 F2d 965, 968 (5th Cir 1992) ("International treaties are not presumed to create rights that are privately enforceable.").

[16] See, for example, *Air France v Saks*, 470 US 392, 399 (1985) (noting that, when interpreting the meaning of a treaty, U.S. courts attempt "to give the specific words of the treaty a meaning consistent with the shared expectations of the contracting parties"); *Societe Nationale Industrielle Aerospatiale v United States District Court*, 482 US 522, 533 (1987) ("In interpreting an international treaty, we are mindful that it is 'in the nature of a contract between nations,' to which 'general rules of construction apply.'").

[17] See cases cited in note 66.

[18] See text accompanying note 68.

[19] See David H. Moore, *An Emerging Uniformity for International Law*, 75 Geo Wash L Rev 1, 12–14 (2006); Vázquez, 89 Am J Intl L at 705 n 47 (cited in note 6).

(1) the language and purposes of the agreement as a whole; (2) the circumstances surrounding its execution; (3) the nature of the obligations imposed by the agreement; (4) the availability and feasibility of alternative enforcement mechanisms; (5) the implications of permitting a private right of action; and (6) the capability of the judiciary to resolve the dispute.[20]

Some courts also have suggested that deference should be given to the views of the Executive Branch, at the time of the litigation, with respect to whether a treaty is self-executing.[21]

Courts have also had to address the effect of "non-self-execution declarations" attached by the Senate to its advice and consent to some treaties. Since early in U.S. history, the Senate has had a practice of qualifying its consent to certain treaties through the adoption of reservations and other limitations.[22] Starting in the 1970s, with the support of the Executive Branch, the Senate began considering the adoption of "non-self-execution declarations" in connection with its consent to the ratification of human rights treaties, and it began adopting these declarations in the early 1990s. These declarations have been voted on by the Senate as part of its resolution of advice and consent to the treaties, and have been typically included in the U.S. instrument of ratification that is communicated to the other treaty parties. Before *Medellín*, the Senate had utilized these formal non-self-execution declarations in connection with a few treaties outside the human rights area as well, but such declarations were uncommon. For most treaties, the Senate and Executive Branch either did not express a view about self-execution, or they expressed a view in less formal ratification materials, such as the President's letter of transmittal to the Senate or the report of the Senate Committee on Foreign Relations.

As Professor Jack Goldsmith and I have explained, the U.S. treaty-makers have articulated a number of reasons for using the formal non-self-execution declarations in the human rights area:

First, they believe that, taking into account the substantive reservations and interpretive conditions, U.S. domestic laws and

---

[20] *Frolova v Union of Soviet Socialist Republics*, 761 F2d 370, 373 (7th Cir 1985); see also, for example, *United States v Postal*, 589 F2d 862, 877 (5th Cir 1979).

[21] See, for example, *More v Intelcom Support Services, Inc.*, 960 F2d 466, 472 (5th Cir 1992).

[22] See Curtis A. Bradley and Jack L. Goldsmith, *Treaties, Human Rights, and Conditional Consent*, 149 U Pa L Rev 399, 400–402 (2000).

remedies are sufficient to meet U.S. obligations under human rights treaties. There is thus no additional need, in their view, for domestic implementation. Second, there is concern that the treaty terms, although similar in substance to U.S. law, are not identical in wording and thus might have a destabilizing effect on domestic rights protections if considered self-executing. Third, there is disagreement about which treaty terms, if any, would be self-executing. The declaration is intended to provide certainty about this issue in advance of litigation. Finally, the treatymakers believe that if there is to be a change in the scope of domestic rights protections, it should be done by legislation with the participation of the House of Representatives.[23]

Although courts consistently have treated these declarations as dispositive of the issue of self-execution,[24] some commentators have questioned their validity, arguing, among other things, that they are at odds with the Supremacy Clause.[25]

An important recent addition to the literature on self-execution came from Professor Tim Wu.[26] Professor Wu analyzed the patterns of judicial enforcement of treaties throughout U.S. history and found that courts had consistently enforced treaties in cases involving state breaches of treaty obligations, but that, as a result of institutional deference, they often had not enforced treaties when they perceived that doing so would conflict with the wishes of Congress or, at least in some instances, the Executive Branch. Professor Wu further concluded that, as his institutional deference explanation would predict, the role for direct judicial enforcement of treaties has been eroded by the twentieth-century rise of congressional-executive agreements, since, he argued, these agreements shift implementation authority from the courts to Congress.

Not surprisingly, the Court's decision in *Medellín* is spurring a

---

[23] Id at 419–20.

[24] See, for example, *Renkel v United States*, 456 F3d 640, 644 (6th Cir 2006) (collecting cases); *Auguste v Ridge*, 395 F3d 123, 141 n 17 (3d Cir 2005) (same).

[25] See, for example, Malvina Halberstam, *United States Ratification of the Convention on the Elimination of All Forms of Discrimination Against Women*, 31 Geo Wash J Intl L & Econ 49, 64 (1997); John Quigley, *The International Covenant on Civil and Political Rights and the Supremacy Clause*, 42 DePaul L Rev 1287, 1302–04 (1993); David Sloss, *Non-Self-Executing Treaties: Exposing a Constitutional Fallacy*, 36 UC Davis L Rev 1, 46–55 (2002); cf. Henkin, *Foreign Affairs and the United States Constitution* at 202 (cited in note 8) (arguing that the practice of non-self-execution declarations "is 'anti-Constitutional' in spirit and highly problematic as a matter of law").

[26] See Tim Wu, *Treaties' Domains*, 93 Va L Rev 571 (2007).

new round of debate over treaty self-execution.[27] In a recent article in the *Harvard Law Review*, Professor Vázquez further develops arguments from his past writings on the subject.[28] He contends that, as a result of the Supremacy Clause, there should be a "requirement of equivalent treatment"—that is, that "treaties are presumptively enforceable in court in the same circumstances as constitutional and statutory provisions of like content."[29] In addition, while he accepts that *Foster*-type non-self-execution can be an exception to this requirement, he contends that there should be a presumption in favor of self-execution "that can be overcome only through a clear statement that the obligations in a particular treaty are subject to legislative implementation."[30]

The Senate has also adjusted its practices after *Medellín*, and its adjustments are raising new questions. The Senate is expressing its views about self-execution more frequently than in the past, and it is more consistently doing so in its formal resolution of advice and consent rather than in less formal ratification materials.[31] At the same time, the Senate has not been recommending that these formal declarations be included with the U.S. instrument of ratification that is communicated to the other treaty parties.[32] Finally, the Senate has for the first time been attaching *self-execution* as well as non-self-execution declarations to its advice and consent to some treaties,[33] and there is some question about whether those new decla-

---

[27] For an online debate that occurred shortly after the decision, see *Federalist Society Online Debate, Medellín v. Texas, Part I: Self-Execution* (March 28, 2008) (featuring Ted Cruz, David Sloss, Nick Rosenkranz, and Edwin Williamson), at http://www.fed-soc.org/debates/dbtid.17/default.asp.

[28] See Vázquez, 122 Harv L Rev 599 (cited in note 7).

[29] Id at 602.

[30] Id.

[31] See, for example, Exec Rep 110–12, 110th Cong, 2d Sess, *Extradition Treaties with the European Union* at 9 (Sept 11, 2008) ("Such a statement, while generally included in the documents associated with treaties submitted to the Senate by the executive branch and in committee reports, has not generally been included in Resolutions of advice and consent."), at http://frwebgate.access.gpo.gov/cgi-bin/getdoc.cgi?dbname=110_cong_reports&docid=f:er012.110.pdf.

[32] See, for example, Exec Rept 110–19, 110th Cong, 2d Sess, *International Convention on the Control of Harmful Anti-Fouling Systems on Ships* at 9–10 (Sept 11, 2008) (indicating that a declaration of non-self-execution, unlike a different declaration included in the resolution of advice and consent, would not be included in the instrument of ratification), at http://frwebgate.access.gpo.gov/cgi-bin/getdoc.cgi?dbname=110_cong_reports&docid=f:er019.pdf.

[33] See 154 Cong Rec S9328–S9332 (Sept 23, 2008) (senatorial advice and consent for various mutual legal assistance, extradition, and tax treaties, containing a declaration for each one stating that, "This Treaty is self-executing.").

rations are constitutionally valid.[34]

There are a number of issues at stake in the self-execution debate. As suggested above, one issue concerns the validity of non-self-execution and self-execution declarations attached by the Senate to its advice and consent to some treaties. To the extent that these declarations are valid and binding, their increased use will simplify the self-execution question going forward. The United States is already a party to thousands of treaties, however, that lack such Senate declarations. It seems likely after *Medellín* that treaties that fall within established lines of self-execution precedent, such as bilateral treaties granting aliens property or business rights, will continue to be treated as self-executing. It is uncertain, however, to what extent treaties not covered by existing lines of precedent, and which lack Senate declarations, will be viewed as judicially enforceable. One example is the Vienna Convention on Consular Relations, which gives arrested foreign nationals the right to have their consulate notified of their arrest and to communicate with their consulate.[35] As will be discussed, this treaty provision forms part of the backdrop of the *Medellín* case, although the Supreme Court reserved judgment on whether it was self-executing. The Geneva Conventions governing the treatment of classes of individuals during wartime are another example, as detainees in the war on terrorism have sought to invoke them to challenge their detention, treatment, and trial.[36] Whether these and other treaties will be found to be self-executing will be affected by whatever presumption (if any) that courts apply with respect to self-execution and by the types of materials that courts consider in making the determination.

II. Supreme Law of the Land

In this part, I stake out my first claim: the Supremacy Clause does not by itself tell us the extent to which treaties should be judicially enforceable. The Supremacy Clause states that "all Treaties made, or which shall be made, under the Authority of the United States, shall be the supreme Law of the Land." Critics of non-self-

---

[34] See, for example, Vázquez, 122 Harv L Rev at 685–94 (cited in note 7) (doubting the constitutional validity of self-execution declarations).

[35] See Vienna Convention on Consular Relations, Art 36.

[36] See, for example, *Hamdan v Rumsfeld*, 415 F3d 33, 38–40 (DC Cir 2005) (concluding that the Third Geneva Convention was not judicially enforceable), reversed on other grounds, 548 US 557 (2006).

execution emphasize the word "all" and suggest that non-self-execution is problematic because it means that not all treaties are judicially enforceable. In making this argument, critics incorrectly equate supreme law of the land with automatic judicial enforceability.

A brief consideration of the other forms of supreme federal law—federal statutes and the Constitution—shows that judicial enforceability is not a prerequisite for status as supreme law of the land. Suits by citizens who are not concretely injured by government lawbreaking cannot bring suit, even if it means that no one can ever bring the suit.[37] Certain constitutional questions are considered nonjusticiable political questions.[38] Congress can sometimes deprive the courts of jurisdiction to hear federal statutory claims, such as statutory claims relating to discretionary agency action.[39] States have broad immunity from suit on federal law claims, even though they are obligated to comply with federal law.[40] Conditional spending provisions and statutory delegations of discretionary authority to the Executive are also often not judicially enforceable.[41] In all of these and similar situations we do not think that there is any violation of, or even tension with, the Supremacy Clause.

Even when a statute is judicially enforceable, Congress often uncontroversially regulates the extent to which it is enforced, and how it is enforced, further suggesting that the Supremacy Clause does not deprive the national political branches of flexibility over this issue. Thus, for example, even though the Supremacy Clause makes statutes supreme over state law, Congress sometimes enacts statutes that expressly do not preempt state law.[42] Moreover, it is not un-

---

[37] See, for example, *United States v Richardson*, 418 US 166, 179 (1974) ("[T]he absence of any particular individual or class to litigate these claims gives support to the argument that the subject matter is committed to the surveillance of Congress, and ultimately to the political process.").

[38] See, for example, *Nixon v United States*, 506 US 224 (1993).

[39] See, for example, *Webster v Doe*, 486 US 592 (1988).

[40] See, for example, *Alden v Maine*, 527 US 706 (1999); *Seminole Tribe of Florida v Florida*, 517 US 44 (1996).

[41] See, for example, *Gonzaga University v Doe*, 536 US 273 (2002) (disallowing private enforcement of Family Educational Rights and Privacy Act); *Dept of the Navy v Egan*, 484 US 518, 526–30 (1988) (disallowing review of denial of security clearance).

[42] See, for example, 15 USC § 7707(b)(2) (stating that statute relating to electronic mail "shall not be construed to preempt" certain state laws); 18 USC § 896 (stating that statute relating to extortionate credit transactions "does not preempt any field of law with respect to which State legislation would be permissible in the absence of this [statute]").

common for Congress to limit standing to sue or to expressly or implicitly preclude private rights of action.[43] It is also widely accepted that Congress can limit the domestic enforceability of congressional-executive agreements, which constitute the vast majority of the international agreements concluded by the United States in the modern era (and which constitute binding "treaties" under international law).[44]

Statutes delegating implementation authority to the Executive provide a particularly close analogy to non-self-executing treaties. Consider, for example, the statute at issue in the famous foreign affairs case, *United States v Curtiss-Wright Export Corp*.[45] The statute there authorized President Franklin Roosevelt to criminalize the sale of arms to two countries involved in a conflict in Latin America if he found that such criminalization "may contribute to the reestablishment of peace between those countries." Before Roosevelt implemented this statute, it would not have been judicially enforceable, and yet it still would have been part of the "Laws of the United States" referenced in the Supremacy Clause. In a treaty, the Senate and President might similarly delegate domestic implementation discretion to nonjudicial actors—that is, to either Congress or the Executive Branch. Many statutory provisions are like this, and no one thinks that the Supremacy Clause requires that these provisions create self-executing rules of decision for the judiciary.

Ironically, supporters of broad treaty enforcement should be the last ones to tie law status to judicial enforcement. Judicial review is often unavailable on the international plane to enforce treaty and other legal obligations. That fact, along with the frequent absence of other formal enforcement machinery, has sometimes led people to question whether international law is really "law." The prevailing

---

[43] See, for example, 6 USC § 134 (stating, in information infrastructure statute, that "[n]othing in this part may be construed to create a private right of action for enforcement of any provision of this chapter"); 12 USC § 1831g(d) (stating, in banking statute, that "[t]his section may not be construed as creating any private right of action"). See also Paul B. Stephan, *Private Remedies for Treaty Violations After Sanchez-Llamas*, 11 Lewis & Clark L Rev 65 (2007).

[44] For example, Congress restricted the domestic judicial enforceability of the GATT and NAFTA trade agreements. See 19 USC § 3512; 19 USC § 3312. For acceptance of this congressional authority, see, for example, Henkin, *Foreign Affairs and the United States Constitution* at 217 (cited in note 8); Lori Fisler Damrosch, *The Role of the United States Senate Concerning "Self-Executing" and "Non-Self-Executing" Treaties*, 67 Chi Kent L Rev 515, 525–26 (1991); Stefan A. Riesenfeld and Frederick M. Abbott, *The Scope of U.S. Senate Control Over the Conclusion and Operation of Treaties*, 67 Chi Kent L Rev 571, 641 (1991).

[45] 299 US 304 (1936).

view among international law scholars, however, is that international law can meaningfully be described as law despite the frequent absence of formal enforcement mechanisms, including the absence of judicial review.[46] Supporters of a broad approach to treaty self-execution are particularly likely to hold this view about international law. Yet if international law can be law on the international plane without judicial enforceability, why is that not also true on the domestic plane?

Of course, there is a *relationship* between a law's status as supreme law of the land and judicial enforceability, a relationship highlighted by the statement in the Supremacy Clause that state judges shall be bound by the supreme law of the land, "anything in the Constitution or laws of any State to the contrary notwithstanding." The supreme law of the land takes precedence over conflicting state law, and one method of enforcing that supremacy is through the courts. But this relationship is not a necessary one. If in concluding the treaty the Senate and President have validly precluded judicial enforcement (an issue addressed in the next part), then the state judges clause does not come into play. The inclusion of treaties in the Supremacy Clause simply, but very importantly, allows the U.S. treaty-makers to preempt state law *if they want to*, without the possibility that state legislatures or judges will nullify the preemption.

The argument for more mandatory judicial review of treaty obligations depends on a separation-of-powers-oriented, rather than federalism-oriented, construction of the Clause. Critics of non-self-execution argue that treaties were included in the Supremacy Clause to help avert U.S. treaty violations, something that they contend will be more likely to occur without self-execution.[47] As an initial matter, it is important to remember that U.S. compliance with its treaty obligations generally does not depend on self-execution. There are many ways for a nation to comply with a treaty without

---

[46] See, for example, Thomas M. Franck, *The Power of Legitimacy Among Nations* (1990); Louis Henkin, *How Nations Behave* (2d ed 1979); Harold Hongju Koh, *Why Do Nations Obey International Law?* 106 Yale L J 2599 (1997).

[47] See, for example, Sloss, 36 UC Davis L Rev at 16 (cited in note 25) ("The Framers included treaties in the Supremacy Clause to help promote U.S. compliance with its treaty obligations."); Vázquez, 89 Am J Intl L at 706 (cited in note 6) (contending that treaties were included in the Supremacy Clause "to avert conflicts with other nations that could be expected to result from violations of treaties attributable to the United States"); Vázquez, 122 Harv L Rev at 675 (cited in note 7) ("It was to avoid such friction that the Constitution gave treaties the force of domestic law and instructed judges to give them effect.").

direct judicial application, including preexisting legislation, new legislation, and executive action, and U.S. compliance with most treaties is not in fact accomplished through its courts. As discussed
below in Part III, treaties are never self-executing in some countries,
and yet those countries generally manage to comply. Critics of
political branch flexibility with respect to the issue of self-execution
also neglect to consider the ex ante effects of eliminating such flexibility. Among other things, if the political branches could not regulate the domestic effects of treaties, they would likely enter into
fewer, and less significant, treaty commitments.[48]

In any event, the "compliance" description of the Supremacy
Clause is potentially misleading because it neglects to mention the
breaching parties that the Founders were worried about—the states.
Almost everyone agrees that the inclusion of treaties in the Supremacy Clause was a response to a specific problem under the
Articles of Confederation, which is that the Articles did not give
the national government sufficient authority to ensure state compliance with treaty obligations. This was particularly an issue with
respect to the 1783 peace treaty with Great Britain, which had a
provision requiring that British creditors be allowed to collect on
pre–Revolutionary War debts. Because some states had enacted laws
preventing compliance with that provision, the British refused to
comply with a provision in the treaty obligating them to vacate
military forts in the northwest. The Continental Congress took the
position that the treaty was "part of the law of the land" binding
on the states,[49] but this was not expressly stated in the Articles of
Confederation. Perhaps because of this, the Continental Congress
simply proceeded to *request* that the states repeal any laws inconsistent with the peace treaty, which generated compliance from
some but not all of the states.

During the Constitutional Convention, the "Virginia Plan"
would have addressed the problem of state noncompliance with
federal law by giving the national legislature the power to "negative"
state laws, an idea particularly championed by James Madison. The
proposed negative approach was ultimately rejected at the Con-

---

[48] See, for example, Bradley and Goldsmith, 149 U Pa L Rev at 410–16 (cited in note
22) (documenting how non-self-execution declarations and other conditions helped break
the logjam that had prevented U.S. ratification of human rights treaties).

[49] See 32 Journals of the Continental Congress 124 (March 21, 1787); see also 32 Journals
of the Continental Congress 177 (April 13, 1787).

vention, in part because it was thought to intrude too much on state sovereignty. Instead, the Convention adopted the Supremacy Clause, a version of which was originally set forth in the "New Jersey Plan." As originally proposed, the Supremacy Clause stated that treaties and other federal laws would be "supreme law of the respective States."[50] As submitted to the Committee of Style near the end of the Convention, the Clause still referred to the "supreme law of the several States."[51] The Committee changed the wording of the Clause, without explanation, to the "supreme Law of the Land."[52]

Madison maintained throughout the Convention that the Supremacy Clause approach was inadequate to ensure against state violations of federal law, including treaties.[53] In defending the Constitution in *The Federalist Papers*, however, he argued that including treaties in the Supremacy Clause should be considered unobjectionable given that the Continental Congress could already "make treaties which they themselves have declared and most of the States have recognized, to be the supreme law of the land."[54] As Madison's implicit reference to the British peace treaty experience suggests, the Federalist defense of the Supremacy Clause was framed in terms of the relationship between the national government and the states. For example, Hamilton complained in Federalist No. 22 that, under the Articles of Confederation, treaties were "liable to the infractions of thirteen different legislatures, and as many different courts of final jurisdiction, acting under the authority of those legislatures," with the result that "[t]he faith, the reputation, the peace of the whole Union, are thus continually at the mercy of the prejudices, the passions, and the interests of every member of which it is composed."[55] The state ratification debates, as Professor Julian Ku has observed, similarly "focused on what we would recognize today as the federalism question," and they "appear to confirm that the new

---

[50] I *The Records of the Federal Convention of 1787* at 245 (Max Farrand ed, 1911).

[51] II *The Records of the Federal Convention of 1787* at 572 (Max Farrand ed, 1911).

[52] See generally Christopher R. Drahozal, *The Supremacy Clause: A Reference Guide to the United States Constitution* (2004).

[53] See, for example, I *The Records of the Federal Convention of 1787* at 316 (cited in 50) (expressing concern that the New Jersey Plan would not sufficiently prevent individual states from imposing on the whole country a "rupture with other powers").

[54] Federalist 38 (Madison) in Clinton Rossiter, ed, *The Federalist Papers* 238 (1961).

[55] Federalist 22 (Hamilton) in *The Federalist Papers* at 151 (cited in note 54).

Constitution was intended to prevent the state violations of treaties that had occurred during the Articles period."[56]

These materials suggest that the Founders did not want U.S. compliance with treaties to be dependent on state law. The Founders understandably concluded that, unless it was clear that treaties took precedence over state law, an individual state could enact laws that would impose harmful externalities on the entire nation, and the national government would be powerless to prevent it. As Justice Chase would later explain in a decision applying the British peace treaty to preempt a Virginia statute, "[a] treaty cannot be the supreme law of the land, that is of all the United States, if any act of a state legislature can stand in its way."[57] The Founders *might* have assumed as well that the usual mechanism for ensuring state compliance with treaties would be judicial review, although Professor Yoo has contested this proposition.

Nothing in this history, however, suggests that treaties were included in the Supremacy Clause in order to empower the courts to deter or redress *national government* breaches of treaties, or in any other way limit the national political branches' control over treaty compliance. Indeed, the entire thrust of the adoption of the Supremacy Clause was one of empowering the national government to operate more effectively. As Professor Christopher Drahozal notes in his book on the Supremacy Clause:

> Certainly the Supremacy Clause does away with the question under the Articles of Confederation of whether *states* have to implement treaties before they take effect. That possibility, the subject of debate and federal action in connection with the Treaty of Peace with Great Britain, is conclusively rejected by the Supremacy Clause. Beyond that, however, the resolution of the self-execution debate is less clear, at least with respect to the preemption of state law.[58]

---

[56] Julian G. Ku, *Treaties as Laws: A Defense of the Last-in-Time Rule for Treaties and Federal Statutes*, 80 Ind L J 319, 377 (2005).

[57] *Ware v Hylton*, 3 US (3 Dall) 199, 236 (1796) (Chase, J); see also, for example, Alona E. Evans, *Self-Executing Treaties in the United States of America*, 30 Brit Year Book Intl L 178, 180–81 (1953) ("Experience under the Articles of Confederation lent support to the decision of the Constitutional Convention that, in a federal system, the conclusion of treaties must necessarily be within the exclusive competence of the Central government and that treaties must take precedence over the constitutions and laws of the several States.").

[58] Drahozal, *The Supremacy Clause: A Reference Guide to the United States Constitution* at 160 (cited in note 52). John Jay, a particularly strong supporter of international law among the Founders, denied in Federalist 64 that treaties should be "repealable at pleasure" by

To put it differently, there is no reason to think that the Supremacy Clause removes the international political dimension of treaties, which leaves to national governments the ultimate responsibility for deciding whether and how to comply with treaty obligations, and for accepting whatever international consequences may flow from that decision. The Supremacy Clause simply ensures that in the United States this responsibility rests at the federal rather than state level.

The federalism orientation of the Supremacy Clause is further reflected in the fact that it refers only to state judges and state laws and does not mention the federal political branches. The Constitution addresses the Executive Branch's obligation to comply with federal law not in the Supremacy Clause but rather in the Take Care Clause of Article II.[59] As for Congress, it is well settled that Congress has the authority to override both treaties and statutes, despite their status as supreme law of the land.[60] Congress does of course have an obligation to comply with the Constitution, but the Supreme Court in *Marbury* described this obligation as emanating principally from the nature of a written constitution that assigns limited and enumerated powers to the national government rather than from the Supremacy Clause.[61] The pattern of judicial enforcement of treaties throughout U.S. history also comports with a federalism rather than separation-of-powers understanding of the Supremacy Clause. As Professor Wu has found, most judicial enforcement of treaties has been directed at states and localities, and, even outside that context, courts have tended to "look for

the United States, but he was probably speaking there about the international plane rather than domestic plane, and in fact he remarked that "[t]he proposed Constitution . . . has not in the least extended the obligation of treaties." Federalist 64 (Jay) in *The Federalist Papers* at 394 (cited in note 54); see also Ku, 80 Ind L J at 378 (cited in note 56) ("Jay's claim that treaties could never be cancelled without agreement by the other treaty party reveals that he was probably analyzing treaties in their international character without taking into account the complications of how to carry out treaties under municipal law.").

[59] See US Const, Art II, § 3 (stating that the President "shall take Care that the Laws be faithfully executed").

[60] Congress obviously has the ability to override earlier congressional enactments. As for overriding earlier treaties, see, for example, *Whitney v Robertson*, 124 US 190, 195 (1888) (reasoning that Congress can override a treaty and explaining that "[t]he duty of the courts is to construe and give effect to the latest expression of the sovereign will").

[61] *Marbury v Madison*, 5 US (1 Cranch) 137, 176–78 (1803). The Court did note at the end of its opinion, however, that it was not "entirely unworthy of observation" that the Constitution is listed before the "Laws of the United States" in the Supremacy Clause and that the phrase "Laws of the United States" in that Clause is qualified by the requirement that they be "made in Pursuance" of the Constitution. See id at 180.

signals from Congress or the Executive that might show who is meant to be responsible for enforcing a given treaty."[62]

Once the concept of supreme law of the land is viewed as potentially separate from automatic judicial enforceability, it is easier to understand contemporary judicial and political branch practice relating to treaties. Consider, for example, the non-self-execution declarations that the Senate and President sometimes include with their consent to treaties. These declarations are not an effort to turn off the Supremacy Clause, as some critics contend. They are simply an effort by the U.S. treaty-makers to regulate the separable issue of judicial enforceability. I will say more about these declarations in the next part, and I will address in that discussion other constitutional objections that might be raised against them. For now, it is important to note that, in order to conclude that they violate the Supremacy Clause, one would need to read that Clause as not only mandating direct judicial enforceability, but doing so even when the Senate and President expressly do not desire judicial enforceability, and even when they have concluded that other U.S. laws already place the United States in compliance with the treaty. Again, there is nothing in the history of the Supremacy Clause that suggests such a mandate.

More generally, if there is no inherent conflict between non-self-execution and the Supremacy Clause, it is more difficult to justify a general presumption in favor of self-execution, at least one premised on the purported policies of that Clause. Critics of non-self-execution typically describe the non-self-execution doctrine announced in *Foster v Neilson* as a problematic deviation from the Supremacy Clause. Although most critics are willing to accept that *Foster* has precedential force, they argue that its scope should be kept to a minimum given what the critics describe as its constitutionally dubious origins. Professor Vázquez contends, for example, that although "it is too late to reject *Foster*-type non-self-execution entirely[,] . . . *Foster* is reconcilable with the constitutional text only if accompanied by a strong presumption of self-execution."[63] But if non-self-execution is not in fact at odds with the Supremacy Clause, then at least this argument for a presumption in favor of self-execution loses force.

---

[62] Wu, 93 Va L Rev at 595 (cited in note 26).
[63] Vázquez, 122 Harv L Rev at 610, 643 (cited in note 7).

III. Relevant Intent

My second claim is that, in discerning whether a treaty is self-executing, the relevant intent is that of the U.S. treaty-makers (i.e., the Senate and President), not the collective intent of the treaty parties. As I will explain, my claim does not depend on any particular view about the relevance of ratification history or other nontextual materials in the self-execution analysis. Indeed, my claim is compatible even with a pure "public meaning" approach to interpretation.[64]

As Professor Vázquez has noted, "Courts and commentators seem to agree that a treaty's self-executing character is largely, if not entirely, a matter of intent."[65] There has been substantial uncertainty, however, over whose intent counts—the collective intent of the parties to the treaty, or just the intent of the U.S. Senate and President. Before *Medellín*, some lower courts had suggested, without analysis, that the collective intent of the parties is what matters,[66] and this is also the view of some commentators.[67] By contrast, the Restatement (Third) of Foreign Relations Law reasons that the intent of the U.S. treaty-makers should be dispositive. As the Restatement explains:

> In the absence of special agreement, it is ordinarily for the United States to decide how it will carry out its international obligations.

---

[64] If it were appropriate to apply a public meaning approach to the issue of self-execution rather than an approach focused on intent, my claim would be that it should be the U.S. public meaning, not the international public meaning, that should be controlling, and that the materials relevant to the public meaning would include the declarations included by the Senate in its resolution of advice and consent. I do not explore here the precise implications of such an approach, since courts and scholars have to date framed the self-execution issue as one of intent, and that is how the issue is described in *Medellín*.

[65] Vázquez, 89 Am J Intl L at 704 (cited in note 6). See also, for example, Edwin D. Dickinson, *Are the Liquor Treaties Self-Executing?* 20 Am J Intl L 444, 449 (1926).

[66] See, for example, *United States v Postal*, 589 F2d 862, 876 (5th Cir 1979) ("The question whether a treaty is self-executing is a matter of interpretation for the courts when the issue presents itself in litigation, . . . and, as in the case of all matters of interpretation, the courts attempt to discern the intent of the parties to the agreement so as to carry out their manifest purpose."); *Diggs v Richardson*, 555 F2d 848, 851 (DC Cir 1976) ("In determining whether a treaty is self-executing courts look to the intent of the signatory parties as manifested by the language of the instrument, and, if the instrument is uncertain, recourse must be had to the circumstances surrounding its execution.").

[67] See, for example, Riesenfeld and Abbott, 67 Chi Kent L Rev at 608–09 (cited in note 44); Vázquez, 122 Harv L Rev at 638–41 (cited in note 7). The Supreme Court's 1833 decision in *United States v Percheman*, discussed in Part IV, also could be read to suggest an intent-of-the-parties approach, since the Court there looked to a foreign language version of the treaty in discerning self-execution. See text accompanying note 104.

> Accordingly, the intention of the United States determines whether an agreement is to be self-executing in the United States or should await implementation by legislation or appropriate executive or administrative action.[68]

Although I do not always agree with the Restatement's claims, on this issue the Restatement is persuasive. Nations have widely varying approaches to the domestic status of treaties, with some nations (such as Great Britain) always requiring legislative implementation before treaties can be enforced by domestic courts, other nations allowing most or all treaties to be enforced directly by their courts, and still other nations allowing only some treaties to be enforced in this way.[69] Furthermore, international law generally does not concern itself with the particular institutions a nation uses to implement international obligations; nations are simply required to comply with their treaty obligations, and it does not matter whether they do so through their courts or through some other mechanism. As a leading international law casebook notes, "International law requires a state to carry out its international obligations but, in general, how a state accomplishes that result is not of concern to international law or to the state system."[70] For these reasons, nations almost never negotiate about treaty self-execution, especially for multilateral treaties. Moreover, parties negotiating a treaty are typically indifferent to the issue, so even tools used for contract gap filling would not work here. If the search for self-execution turned on the collective intent of the parties, it would almost always be a meaningless exercise.

Although some advocates of the intent-of-the-parties approach recognize that there will almost never be any collective intent with respect to self-execution,[71] they argue that allowing senatorial and

---

[68] Restatement (Third) of the Foreign Relations Law of the United States, § 111, cmt. h (cited in note 14); see also John H. Jackson, *Status of Treaties in Domestic Legal Systems: A Policy Analysis*, 86 Am J Intl L 310, 329 (1992) ("It seems safe to conclude that the U.S. constitutional practice and status is that the treaty-making officials, as a unilateral matter, will control the determination of 'self-executing' in the domestic legal system.").

[69] See Thomas Buergenthal, *Self-Executing and Non-Self-Executing Treaties in National and International Law*, 235 Recueil des Cours 303, 315–19 (1992 IV); Duncan B. Hollis, *A Comparative Approach to Treaty Law and Practice*, in Duncan B. Hollis, Merritt R. Blakeslee, and L. Benjamin Ederington, eds, *National Treaty Law and Practice* 1, 40–47 (2005).

[70] Lori F. Damrosch et al, *International Law: Cases and Materials* 160–61 (4th ed 2001).

[71] See, for example, Vázquez, 122 Harv L Rev at 607 (cited in note 7) ("[E]xcept in the rarest of cases, courts searching for a common intent of the parties regarding the need for implementing legislation do so in vain.").

presidential intent to control on this issue would be unconstitutional because it would give the Senate and President a lawmaking power outside of the Article II Treaty Clause.[72] While the Constitution allows the Senate and President to make law in the form of treaties, these commentators contend that this is true only when they do so in conjunction with one or more other nations. Therefore, the argument goes, if the regulation of self-execution is not done in conjunction with other nations, it is an unconstitutional exercise of lawmaking authority.

One problem with this constitutional argument is that it fails to distinguish between the making of substantive treaty commitments, which is governed by international law, and the self-execution issue, which, at least under current practice, concerns an issue of domestic law. The making of substantive treaty commitments requires the consent of one or more other nations because this is what is required by international law in order for there to be a binding treaty. Nations naturally bargain over those substantive terms, and, just as with domestic contracts, the relevant intent for those terms is the collective intent of the parties. Moreover, there is an interest in having relatively uniform interpretations of these terms among the parties, in part for reciprocity reasons. Self-execution, by contrast, is not a matter of international law—the United States would not violate international law by either having, or not having, self-execution. Nor is there any particular need or desire for uniformity in the approaches to self-execution. While one could imagine nations bargaining over whether to require direct judicial enforcement of a treaty, it almost never happens.

Although the regulation of self-execution could be described as a type of lawmaking power (and, as discussed below, the Supreme Court did refer to it this way in *Medellín*), it is not a constitutionally problematic lawmaking power when exercised by two-thirds of the Senate and the President. It is not a freestanding power, but rather is simply an adjunct to the treaty-making power set forth in Article II, and it only comes up if the full process for making a treaty has been satisfied. Moreover, it is not a power to create any new obligations for the United States, but rather is simply a power to regulate how those obligations are implemented internally. It can therefore reasonably be viewed as a lesser-included power of the

---

[72] See, for example, id at 639; Riesenfeld and Abbott, 67 Chi Kent L Rev at 599 (cited in note 44).

Senate and President's authority not to ratify the treaty at all, which would also prevent judicial enforcement of the treaty.[73] The principal argument against such a lesser-included power is that the Supremacy Clause forces the U.S. treaty-makers to accept judicial enforceability whenever they ratify a treaty susceptible to judicial enforcement. But, as discussed above in Part II, nothing in the text or history of the Clause, or in judicial precedent, suggests that the Clause operates in that way.

There is one lower court decision from the 1950s that offers support for the Treaty Clause argument, but it is poorly reasoned, was vacated as moot by the Supreme Court, and has had no influence since it was decided. That decision, *Power Authority of New York v Federal Power Commission*,[74] involved a treaty between the United States and Canada pursuant to which the two countries agreed to share water on the Niagara River. A preexisting federal statute gave the Federal Power Commission the authority to issue licenses concerning the use of U.S. waters. In approving the treaty with Canada, however, the Senate had attached to its advice and consent what it referred to as a "reservation" stating that "no project for redevelopment of the United States' share of such [Niagara River] waters shall be undertaken until it be specifically authorized by Act of Congress." As a result of this reservation, the commission concluded that it lacked authority to issue a license concerning the use of the Niagara River water.

In a 2–1 decision, the D.C. Circuit reversed the commission. The majority concluded that the Senate's reservation was constitutionally problematic, and the court therefore assumed that the Senate did not intend it to be binding. The court reasoned that the Constitution gives the Senate and President only the power to make a "Treaty," and that a treaty must concern matters of mutual concern to the other treaty parties. The court suggested, however, that the Senate's reservation was not part of the treaty because it "makes no change in the relationship between the United States and Canada under the treaty and has nothing at all to do with the rights or obligations of either party."[75] The court cited, with apparent ap-

---

[73] See Restatement (Third) of the Foreign Relations Law of the United States, § 303, reporters' note 4 (cited in note 14).

[74] 247 F2d 538 (DC Cir), vacated as moot sub nom, *American Public Power Association v Power Authority of New York*, 355 US 64 (1957).

[75] Id at 541.

proval, occasional statements by officials and courts suggesting that the Article II treaty power might be limited to matters of international concern.

The majority's analysis is questionable. There may be genuine reasons to be concerned about the scope of the treaty power, and I have myself highlighted some of those reasons in prior writings.[76] Among other things, the treaty power might be used to circumvent federalism restraints that would otherwise apply to Congress. But a decision by the Senate and President simply to defer an internal policy question for resolution by the full Congress, as in *Power Authority*, does not implicate these concerns. As the dissent explained in that case:

> It may well be that, no matter how broad the power to make treaties, it is not without limits; and that, like any other power, it can be abused. This case, however, does not pose an abuse of the treaty power. The reservation in question is an instance of self-denial, not usurpation. It does not subvert our constitutional system. It was motivated by a desire that the treaty power should not be used in a manner which would exclude the Congress at large and the President from playing their normal roles in making domestic law.[77]

Professor Henkin, in a trenchant article criticizing the decision, similarly explained that "[t]here has been no *mala fides*, no 'repeal' of legislation, no 'colorable use of the treaty-making power' for an extraneous, improper purpose. The President and Senate have merely refused to throw new and valuable resources into an old established system of development which Congress may not have intended and may not now desire."[78]

In any event, the decision has had essentially no influence. Not a single court has relied on this decision since it was issued more than fifty years ago.[79] Nor has the decision affected political branch practice, which, since the decision, has developed to include the use

---

[76] See Bradley, 97 Mich L Rev at 390 (cited in note 3); Curtis A. Bradley, *The Treaty Power and American Federalism, Part II*, 99 Mich L Rev 98 (2000). See also Nicholas Quinn Rosenkranz, *Executing the Treaty Power*, 118 Harv L Rev 1867 (2005).

[77] 247 F2d at 552 (Bastian dissenting).

[78] Louis Henkin, *The Treaty Makers and the Law Makers: The Niagara Reservation*, 56 Colum L Rev 1151, 1173 (1956).

[79] One dissenting judge relied on it. See *Igartua-de la Rosa v United States*, 417 F3d 145, 191 (1st Cir 2005) (Howard dissenting).

of non-self-execution declarations. These declarations have consistently been upheld by the lower courts, and the Supreme Court recently suggested that they are valid.[80] Even in academic writings, the *Power Authority* decision has not been invoked extensively. One likely reason is that its suggestion that the treaty power might be limited to matters of international rather than domestic concern is a difficult distinction to apply in practice and could easily lead to undesirable consequences. If applied stringently, this distinction might render invalid the U.S. ratification of a variety of important treaties, including many human rights treaties, since those treaties do not involve reciprocal promises in the traditional sense. (The U.S. government does not condition its promise to respect the human rights of its citizens on other countries' respect for the human rights of their citizens.) Probably in part for this reason, the Restatement (Third) of Foreign Relations rejects any effort to have treaty validity turn on the domestic-versus-international distinction.[81]

The intent-of-the-U.S. approach is not only constitutionally valid; it also best explains judicial and political branch practice. Unlike an intent-of-the-parties approach, this approach has an easy time explaining the consistent deference that courts have given to non-self-execution declarations attached by the Senate and accepted by the President. Under the intent-of-the-U.S. approach, these declarations are clear evidence of senatorial and presidential intent concerning self-execution, which is the relevant intent for this issue. Commentators who argue for an intent-of-the-parties approach, by contrast, either find these declarations unconstitutional or have a difficult time explaining their validity.[82] Moreover, the intent-of-the-U.S. approach would find valid the recent *self-execution* decla-

---

[80] See *Sosa v Alvarez-Machain*, 542 US 692, 735 (2004) (noting that the United States ratified the International Covenant on Civil and Political Rights "on the express understanding that it was not self-executing *and so did not itself create obligations enforceable in the federal courts*") (emphasis added).

[81] See Restatement (Third) of the Foreign Relations Law of the United States, § 302, cmt. c and reporters' note 2 (cited in note 14).

[82] See, for example, Riesenfeld and Abbott, 67 Chi Kent L Rev at 296 (cited in note 44) (arguing that "the Senate lacks the constitutional authority to declare the non-self-executing character of a treaty with binding effect on U.S. courts"); Sloss, 36 UC Davis L Rev at 41–43 (cited in note 25) (arguing that the declarations are invalid when used in certain ways); Vázquez, 122 Harv L Rev at 672–85 (cited in note 7) (struggling with the issue and ultimately concluding that the declarations are valid based on a complicated analysis of the international law validity of a hypothetical reservation of non-self-execution).

rations attached by the Senate, as long as the treaty was otherwise susceptible to judicial application. An intent-of-the-parties approach, by contrast, would likely see these declarations as unconstitutionally expanding the international obligations of the United States.[83] It is also worth noting that, outside of the human rights area, declarations concerning self-execution have not typically been included in the instruments of ratification that are communicated to the other treaty parties, and the Senate has not been recommending their inclusion in these instruments after *Medellín*.[84] Such communication would presumably be a constitutional prerequisite, however, under an intent-of-the-parties approach. [85] All of this purported unconstitutionality should at least give us pause before committing to the intent-of-the-parties approach.[86]

The intent-of-the-U.S. approach also explains why it is perfectly appropriate for courts to consider treaty text when discerning self-execution, as they have done since *Foster*. Treaty text is relevant under this approach because it is what the Senate and President specifically approve when agreeing to the treaty, just as statutory text is relevant in discerning congressional intent with respect to whether and to what extent a statute is to be judicially enforceable. This is true, under the intent-of-the-U.S. approach, regardless of whether the treaty text would mean something different to other treaty parties on this question of self-execution (or mean nothing at all to them on this question). The textual question under the intent-of-the-U.S. approach is, simply, did the Senate and President intend in agreeing to this language that the treaty would be directly enforceable in U.S. courts? As discussed below, this is precisely the reasoning of the Supreme Court in *Medellín*. Supporters of the intent-of-the-parties approach, by contrast, have a difficult time

---

[83] See Vázquez, 122 Harv L Rev at 687–88 (cited in note 7). Professor Vázquez attempts to use the purported unconstitutionality of such declarations as a reason for a presumption in favor of self-execution. See id at 690–91. If the self-execution declarations are in fact constitutional, that reason goes away.

[84] See text accompanying note 32.

[85] See, for example, Vázquez, 122 Harv L Rev at 641 (cited in note 7) (arguing for such a requirement).

[86] *Congress*'s ability to regulate self-execution may also be at stake. Compare Carlos Manuel Vázquez, *The Military Commissions Act, the Geneva Conventions, and the Courts: A Critical Guide*, 101 Am J Intl L 73, 89–91 (2007) (arguing that a congressional restriction on judicial enforcement of the Geneva Conventions would be unconstitutional), with Curtis A. Bradley, *The Military Commissions Act, Habeas Corpus, and the Geneva Conventions*, 101 Am J Intl L 322, 339–41 (2007) (challenging that claim).

explaining why text is relevant. Professor Vázquez, for example, criticizes judicial reliance on treaty text in discerning whether treaties are self-executing:

> Because nations negotiating treaties rarely, if ever, select the wording of a treaty with the question of legislative implementation in mind, judges who draw conclusions about this question from treaty text are very likely attributing to the words a meaning *that was not intended by the parties.*[87]

As made clear by the italicized language, this argument only holds if the relevant intent is that of the parties, which, as I have argued, it is not.

Contrary to what some commentators appear to assume, an endorsement of the intent-of-the-U.S. approach, by allowing for unilateral declarations of self-execution or non-self-execution, does not require acceptance of something akin to legislative history in the statutory context. Unlike legislative history, declarations regarding self-execution are subject to the same domestic process as the underlying enactment: the declarations are voted on by the Senate as part of its resolution of advice and consent and take effect only if the President decides to proceed with ratification after being presented with them. These declarations are therefore in effect part of the relevant text, not a mere piece of legislative history.[88] The extent to which a court should look at *other* materials in discerning the intent of the U.S. treaty-makers, such as ratification history, depends on one's theory of interpretation, and no particular conclusion on this is compelled by the intent-of-the-U.S. approach. That said, even hard-line textualists who resist the use of legislative history might accept the relevance of certain considerations beyond the words of the treaty, to the extent that those considerations shed light on how the text would likely be understood by the U.S. treaty-makers (or the relevant domestic public) with respect to the issue of self-execution. These considerations might include the extent to

---

[87] Vázquez, 122 Harv L Rev at 635 (cited in note 7) (emphasis added); see also id at 640 ("[T]he treaty itself will almost never have any relevant content on the question of direct enforceability."); id at 660 ("[V]irtually all treaties have no relevant content on the question of direct versus indirect judicial enforceability.").

[88] The Senate Foreign Relations Committee sometimes expresses a view about self-execution in the ratification materials rather than in a formal declaration included with the Senate's resolution of advice and consent. I am referring here only to the formal declarations.

which Congress has already regulated the subject covered by the treaty, the existence or nonexistence of a history of domestic judicial enforcement of similar treaty terms, and perhaps even the structural or functional consequences of self-execution or non-self-execution. As a result, there are likely to be materials for courts to work with beyond the words of the treaty regardless of whether they consider statements made in the ratification history.

In sum, when the United States enters into a treaty, one of the decisions it can make concerns whether and to what extent the treaty is to be implemented directly by its courts. Although this decision may have international consequences, it does not typically involve an international bargain, and it is not determined by international law. Instead, it concerns a political decision about how the nation will address its treaty obligations, a decision that may be influenced by a mix of structural, diplomatic, and policy considerations. The proper institutions to make this decision are the political institutions involved in committing the United States to the underlying treaty obligations, and it is therefore their intent that it is relevant.

IV. Statutes and Treaties

As discussed in Part II, there are a variety of situations in which federal statutes are not judicially enforceable, even though statutes are part of the supreme law of the land. Proponents of a broad doctrine of treaty self-execution respond that, even if this is so, treaties should be no *less* enforceable than federal statutes, something that Professor Vázquez calls "the requirement of equivalent treatment."[89] My third claim, which I defend in this part, is that there are important differences between statutes and treaties that are relevant to judicial enforceability, and these differences suggest less of a judicial role for enforcing treaties than for statutes, especially in the modern (i.e., post–New Deal and World War II) era.

One difference between statutes and treaties concerns the way that they are drafted. Because treaties are international bargains that reflect the input of other nations, they are less likely than statutes to be drafted with either extant U.S. law or the U.S. legal system in mind. As a result, it is not uncommon for treaties to use legal terms and concepts that are different from those typically used in the United States, even when the policies of the treaties are

---

[89] Vázquez, 122 Harv L Rev at 602 (cited in note 7).

otherwise in accord with U.S. law. In addition, while treaties are increasingly drafted to achieve statute-like objectives, the need to find common ground among countries with widely varied legal systems, cultures, and preferences often results in a lack of linguistic precision. These drafting differences between statutes and treaties are likely to be particularly evident for multilateral treaties that have numerous parties.

Another difference between statutes and treaties is that treaties are less likely to envision domestic courts, or even judicial review more generally, as the vehicle of their enforcement. Whereas U.S. statutes are enacted against the backdrop of a well-developed practice of judicial review that includes a centralized national court system, treaties are negotiated against the backdrop of a decentralized system with a wide variety of legal systems, and the drafters often envision different enforcement mechanisms than statutes, most commonly diplomacy, but sometimes (as in the case of the United Nations Charter provision at issue in *Medellín*) coordinated international sanctions. While it may seem strange in this country to think of law as divorced from judicial review, as explained in Part II, this is not at all strange on the international stage, and international lawyers have long insisted that international law is law despite the absence of judicial enforceability.

Unlike statutes, treaties are also a hybrid of contract and law. Treaties inherently involve contractual commitments to other nations and thus implicate considerations of international politics and diplomacy, considerations that are particularly the domain of the Executive Branch. To be sure, proponents of presumptive self-execution understandably bristle when courts (including the Court in *Medellín*) quote from the *Head Money Cases* for the proposition that "[a] treaty is primarily a compact between independent nations" that "depends for the enforcement of its provisions on the interest and the honor of the governments which are parties to it."[90] Proponents correctly note that the Court further observed in that case that "a treaty may also contain provisions which confer certain rights upon the citizens or subjects of one of the nations residing in the territorial limits of the other, which partake of the nature of municipal law and which are capable of enforcement as between private

---

[90] *Edye v Robertson* (*Head Money Cases*), 112 US 580, 598 (1884).

parties in the courts of the country."[91] Nevertheless, the language from the *Head Money Cases* reflects an important truth, which is that, unlike statutes, treaties operate not only within the domain of law, but also within the domain of international politics. The hybrid nature of treaties helps explain why they are probably subject to termination by the President unilaterally,[92] whereas this is of course not true for statutes.[93] It also explains why courts tend to give greater deference to Executive interpretations of treaties than they give to Executive interpretations of statutes (even taking into account the *Chevron* deference doctrine in administrative law).[94]

Treaties and statutes also differ in the way that they engage with the U.S. democratic process. Statutes are enacted after two houses of Congress deliberate on and approve them, often with much wrangling over the text, and they are signed by the President or passed with enough votes to override the President's veto. Treaties, by contrast, are negotiated by the President and then approved by a supermajority of the Senate, which as a matter of practice has little if any involvement in negotiating the treaty's text and, subject to an ability in some instances to decline consent to particular treaty provisions, has no authority to amend the product of the negotiation. By leaving out the House of Representatives entirely and leaving even the Senate out of the negotiation and drafting process, treaty-making involves less of the machinery of representative U.S. democracy than do statutes. Indeed, this is a principal point cited by supporters of the use of congressional-executive agreements, which involve the full Congress.[95] Even if there are advantages to

---

[91] Id.

[92] See *Goldwater v Carter*, 617 F2d 697 (DC Cir 1979), vacated, 444 US 886 (1979).

[93] Professor Vázquez spends considerable effort seeking to rebut the proposition that the contractual nature of treaties prevents them from being enforced through domestic courts. See Vázquez, 122 Harv L Rev at 623–27 (cited in note 7). That proposition is not a serious one, however, and it is not my contention here. Nor does Professor Vázquez's rebuttal of that proposition establish, as he ultimately asserts, that the contractual nature of treaties is "irrelevant" to the self-execution issue. See id at 626 (referring to the purported "irrelevance" of the fact that treaties are contracts between nations).

[94] See, for example, *Sumitomo Shoji America, Inc. v Avagliano*, 457 US 176, 184–85 (1982) ("Although not conclusive, the meaning attributed to treaty provisions by the Government agencies charged with their negotiation and enforcement is entitled to great weight."); see also *Medellín v Texas*, 128 S Ct 1346, 1361 (2008). Unlike *Chevron* deference, courts defer to Executive interpretations of treaties even when expressed for the first time in litigation. See, for example, *De Los Santos Mora v New York*, 524 F3d 183, 204 (2d Cir 2008).

[95] See, for example, Hathaway, 117 Yale L J 1236 (cited in note 2).

having a less transparent and populist process for concluding agreements with other nations (as the constitutional Founders believed), from a democratic theory perspective treaties are probably a less attractive vehicle than statutes *for making domestic law*.[96] This is presumably part of the reason that it has long been assumed that, unlike statutes, treaties may not by themselves create criminal liability in the United States.[97]

Defenders of self-execution equivalency for statutes and treaties often point to the "last-in-time doctrine," which holds that, when there is a conflict between a federal statute and a self-executing treaty, U.S. courts will apply the later in time of the two enactments.[98] This doctrine, however, makes no claim about the extent to which treaties and statutes should be judicially enforceable, but rather simply holds that when both are enforceable the later in time is controlling. In any event, despite the doctrine, it appears that courts have been quite reluctant to allow treaties to displace statutes. There is only one Supreme Court decision that has clearly allowed a treaty to supersede a statute, *Cook v United States*, and in that case the Executive Branch pushed for this outcome and thus sought to overturn the actions of its own Coast Guard.[99] Moreover, as Professor Tim Wu has noted, "because non-self-execution or other doctrines of deference can be, and are, used to prevent a later-in-time treaty from abrogating an earlier statute, the last-in-time rule is not a full or accurate portrayal of judicial practice."[100]

The reluctance of U.S. courts to allow treaties to supersede federal statutes can be traced back to the decision that is said to be

---

[96] In many instances it is likely to turn out that the concurrence of two-thirds of the Senate will represent a majority of the country's population, but this will not necessarily be the case. If large states are in dissent, two-thirds of the Senate can represent substantially less than a majority of the population, given that small and large states have equal representation in the Senate. See Yoo, *Treaties and Public Lawmaking*, 99 Colum L Rev at 2240 n 79 (cited in note 11). Senators also of course have much longer terms than members of the House, which (by design) may make them less responsive to democratic majorities.

[97] See, for example, *Hopson v Krebs*, 622 F2d 1375, 1380 (9th Cir 1980); *United States v Postal*, 589 F2d 862, 877 (5th Cir 1979); *The Over the Top*, 5 F2d 838, 845 (D Conn 1925).

[98] See, for example, *Whitney v Robertson*, 124 US 190, 194 (1888); *Cook v United States*, 282 US 102, 118–19 (1933). There is debate among commentators over whether the last-in-time rule is consistent with Founding understandings, with some commentators claiming that treaties should always trump statutes, other commentators claiming that statutes should always trump treaties, and still other commentators defending the status quo.

[99] See 288 US 102 (1933); Wu, 93 Va L Rev at 597 (cited in note 26).

[100] Wu, 93 Va L Rev at 595–96 (cited in note 26).

the genesis of the self-execution doctrine, *Foster v Neilson*.[101] *Foster* involved an 1819 treaty between the United States and Spain that ceded certain disputed territory east of the Mississippi River to the United States. The petitioners claimed title to a tract of land within the territory based on an 1804 grant from Spain, and on that basis sought to eject the respondent from the tract. The English-language version of the treaty provided in relevant part that all grants of land made by Spain in the ceded territory prior to the treaty "shall be ratified and confirmed to the persons in possession of the lands to the same extent that the same grants would be valid if the territories had remained under the dominion" of Spain. The Court famously concluded that this provision was in "the language of contract" and therefore "addresse[d] itself to the political, not the judicial department; and the legislature must execute the contract before it can become a rule for the Court."[102]

What many descriptions of this decision fail to note is that, before concluding the treaty with Spain, the U.S. government had taken the position that the area encompassing the tract at issue in the case had already been ceded by Spain to France in 1800, and that France had conveyed it to the United States in 1803 as part of the Louisiana Purchase. This view, moreover, was reflected in several federal statutes enacted prior to the treaty. It was against that backdrop that the Supreme Court concluded that "the legislature must execute the contract before it can become a rule for the Court" and that, in the meantime, the Court was *not at liberty to disregard the existing laws on the subject.*[103]

Critics of *Foster* often point out that the Court changed its view about the enforceability of the treaty provision several years later in *United States v Percheman*, after examining the Spanish version of the treaty.[104] Critics contend that *Percheman* shows the weakness of the *Foster* precedent and provides support for a presumption in favor of self-execution.[105] Importantly, however, the land at issue in *Percheman* was indisputably within Spanish territory at the time of

---

[101] See 27 US at 314–15. The concept of non-self-executing treaties predated *Foster*. Justice Iredell discussed the concept, for example, in his circuit court decision in the *Ware v Hylton* case in the 1790s. See 3 US 199, 272 (1796) (Iredell).

[102] 27 US at 314–15.

[103] Id at 314–15 (emphasis added).

[104] 32 US (7 Pet) 51 (1833).

[105] See, for example, Vázquez, 122 Harv L Rev at 607–08, 644–45 (cited in note 7).

the 1819 treaty and thus, unlike in *Foster*, the grant in question did not pose a potential conflict with preexisting statutes.[106] This pair of decisions, therefore, can be seen as an early marker of judicial reluctance to allow treaties to displace Congress's legislative role (a reluctance also confirmed by Professor Wu's work).

The *Power Authority* decision, discussed in the last part, may be another example of this reluctance. In reversing the Federal Power Commission and declining to give effect to the purported reservation, the *Power Authority* decision is said to undermine the legitimacy of non-self-execution declarations sometimes attached by the Senate today to its advice and consent to treaties. As discussed above, to the extent that it does indict such declarations, its reasoning is unpersuasive, and it has had essentially no influence on subsequent practice. The decision can reasonably be read more narrowly, however, in light of the statutory backdrop in that case, which by its terms appeared to give the commission licensing authority over the newly acquired water. In that light, the decision can be seen as reflecting the reluctance of a court to allow a treaty provision (or treaty reservation) to override a federal statutory scheme, which was in fact the thrust of an important academic brief submitted on behalf of the petitioner in that case.[107] Indeed, as Professor Henkin noted in commenting on the *Power Authority* decision, "it seems doubtful . . . that anyone would have challenged the power of the Senate and President to append a provision that development of the waters of the Niagara was to await congressional action, had there been no applicable legislation."[108]

Assuming this reluctance to allow treaties to displace Congress's legislative role is justified, it suggests a greater potential scope for non-self-execution today than might have been true in the past. In the modern era, both statutes and treaties have proliferated, and the content and structure of treaty-making has changed such that treaties are often the vehicle for broad-based legislative efforts.

---

[106] See 32 US (7 Pet) at 88–89; see also *Garcia v Lee*, 37 US 511, 520 (1838) (noting this distinction between *Foster* and *Percheman* and stating that "the case of Foster and Elam v. Neilson must, in all other respects, be considered as affirmed by that of The United States v. Percheman"); Buergenthal, 235 Recueil des Cours at 373 (cited in note 69) (also noting this distinction).

[107] See *Opinion of Philip C. Jessup & Oliver J. Lissitzyn for the Power Authority of the State of New York* (Dec 1955) (on file with author); see also Bradley and Goldsmith, 149 U Pa L Rev at 453 (cited in note 22) (discussing this point).

[108] Henkin, 56 Colum L Rev at 1172 (cited in note 78).

These developments mean, among other things, that statutes and treaties are much more likely to overlap with one another and to express potentially different policy choices. Even when treaties reflect policies similar to those in existing U.S. statutes, treaties (as noted above) tend to use different language than is used in the statutes and thus, if enforced directly, may require significant litigation to work out the implications of this language. (As discussed in Part I, this is one reason the Senate routinely includes non-self-execution declarations with its advice and consent to human rights treaties.)[109] One should expect, therefore, that in the modern era courts would become less willing to apply treaties directly as rules of decision, and this is precisely what appears to have happened. As discussed earlier, the lower courts in the post–World War II period have come close to presuming against self-execution, at least for multilateral treaties and other treaties not covered by prior lines of precedent.[110]

The rise of congressional-executive agreements also may reduce the need for and desirability of direct judicial application of treaties.[111] As the overlap between treaty-making and legislating has increased, so has the number of congressional-executive agreements, such that now they constitute the vast majority of inter-

---

[109] See text accompanying note 23.

[110] See text accompanying note 15; see also Restatement (Third) of the Foreign Relations Law of the United States, § 111, reporters' note 5 (cited in note 14) ("Treaties on subjects that Congress has regulated extensively are more likely to be interpreted as non-self-executing.").

[111] Professor Vázquez attempts to invoke the phenomenon of congressional-executive agreements as support for treaty self-execution, arguing that if an international agreement is not likely to be self-executing, the President would have no reason to use the Article II process instead of the congressional-executive agreement process, and thus the choice of the Article II process must suggest a desire for self-execution. See Vázquez, 122 Harv L Rev at 691–92 (cited in note 7). This argument is questionable on a number of levels. As a legal matter, it is far from clear that congressional-executive agreements benefit from the *Missouri v Holland* rule that allows Article II treaties (and legislation implementing them) to regulate matters beyond the scope of Congress's authority. See, for example, Hathaway, 117 Yale L J at 1339 (cited in note 2) (concluding that *Missouri v Holland* does not apply to congressional-executive agreements). If not, that would constitute an independent legal reason for the President to use the Article II treaty process in some instances, regardless of whether the treaty will be self-executing. In addition, there might be all sorts of nonlegal reasons why the President would continue to use the Article II process for certain agreements that have nothing to do with self-execution, such as the avoidance of likely political resistance from the Senate. This appears to be the case, for example, in the arms control area, see Curtis A. Bradley and Jack L. Goldsmith, *Foreign Relations Law: Cases and Materials* 554–55, 558 (3d ed 2009) (documenting successful Senate insistence on use of Article II process for arms control treaties), and yet it is unlikely that arms control treaties are generally self-executing.

national agreements concluded by the United States. As supporters of this development emphasize, these agreements have the virtue of including the full Congress in considering whether to approve a treaty, and in deciding how the treaty should be accommodated within the framework of existing U.S. law. The shift to these agreements also reduces the issue of self-execution, since Congress often specifies the level of judicial enforceability that it wants when approving the agreements (sometimes substantially limiting such enforceability).[112] Furthermore, it is easier to analogize these congressional-executive agreements to statutes for purposes of judicial enforceability because they actually are statutes.

V. MEDELLÍN AND ITS AMBIGUITIES

The Supreme Court's decision last Term in *Medellín v Texas*, despite some ambiguities, is generally consistent with the three claims defended above.[113] Under the Vienna Convention on Consular Relations, a treaty that the United States ratified in 1969, when foreign nationals are arrested in the United States, the arresting authorities are obligated to inform the foreign nationals that they have the right to have their consulate notified of the arrest and to communicate with the consulate.[114] Under a separate Optional Protocol to the Vienna Convention that it also ratified in 1969, the United States further agreed to have disputes arising under the Vienna Convention heard by the International Court of Justice (ICJ).

In a 2004 decision, *Case Concerning Avena and Other Mexican Nationals*, the ICJ concluded that the United States had violated the consular notice rights of fifty-one Mexican nationals on death row in various states, and that it was obligated to provide these nationals with "review and reconsideration" of their convictions and sentences in light of the violations, notwithstanding any procedural defaults that might otherwise bar such review and reconsideration.[115] Under a provision in another treaty—Article 94 of the United Nations Charter—a member of the United Nations (such

---

[112] See Hathaway, 117 Yale L J at 1321 (cited in note 2); Wu, 93 Va L Rev at 648 (cited in note 26).

[113] My analysis in this part draws upon an earlier article. See Curtis A. Bradley, *Intent, Presumptions, and Non-Self-Executing Treaties*, 102 Am J Intl L 540 (2008).

[114] See Vienna Convention on Consular Relations, Art 36.

[115] 2004 ICJ Rep 12 (March 31), reprinted in 43 ILM 581 (2004).

as the United States) "undertakes to comply with the decision of the International Court of Justice in any case to which it is a party."[116]

After the ICJ's decision in *Avena*, the U.S. government took the position that the ICJ had erred in concluding that the Vienna Convention overrode domestic rules of procedural default, and the Supreme Court agreed with the government in a 2006 decision, *Sanchez-Llamas v Oregon*, that did not involve any of the fifty-one Mexican nationals covered by the *Avena* decision.[117] The government also took the position that, although an ICJ decision to which the United States is a party is binding on the United States as a matter of international law, it does not "provide a free-standing source of law on which a private party may rely in domestic judicial proceedings."[118] Despite taking these positions, President Bush issued a memorandum to his attorney general in February 2005 stating that the United States would comply with the *Avena* decision by having its state courts give effect to the decision "in accordance with general principles of comity" in the fifty-one cases covered by the decision, and the government took the position that this memorandum was binding on state courts. Shortly thereafter, the United States withdrew from the Optional Protocol, which had been the basis for the ICJ's jurisdiction in *Avena*.

Jose Ernesto Medellín, one of the fifty-one Mexican nationals covered by the *Avena* decision, was convicted of murder and sentenced to death in Texas in 1994. He first raised a Vienna Convention claim in state postconviction proceedings, and the state courts held that the claim was procedurally defaulted because it had not been raised on direct review. Medellín subsequently sought federal habeas corpus relief, which was denied. After President Bush issued the memorandum concerning compliance with *Avena*, Medellín once against initiated state postconviction proceedings. The Texas Court of Criminal Appeals denied relief, concluding that neither the *Avena* decision nor the President's memorandum operated to displace Texas's law of procedural default.

---

[116] United Nations Charter, Art 94(1).

[117] See *Sanchez-Llamas v Oregon*, 548 US 331 (2006).

[118] Brief for the United States as Amicus Curiae, *Ex parte Jose Ernesto Medellín*, at 14 (Tex Ct Crim App Sept 2, 2005), at http://www.debevoise.com/publications/pdf/CCA %20US%20Amicus.PDF.

In *Medellín v Texas*, the Supreme Court affirmed.[119] The Court, in an opinion by Chief Justice Roberts, first held that the U.S. obligation to comply with the ICJ's decision in *Avena* was not self-executing and thus did not override Texas's law of procedural default. The Court examined Article 94 and the other treaty provisions to determine whether they "convey[ed] an intention" of self-execution,[120] and concluded that they did not. Endorsing the U.S. government's argument on this point, the Court explained that the phrase "undertakes to comply" in Article 94 does not constitute "a directive to domestic courts" but rather constitutes a commitment to take future political branch action.[121] The Court noted that Article 94 "does not provide that the United States 'shall' or 'must' comply with an ICJ decision, nor indicate that the Senate that ratified the U.N. Charter intended to vest ICJ decisions with immediate legal effect in domestic courts."[122] Rather, the Court understood the language of Article 94 as "confirm[ing] that further action to give effect to an ICJ judgment was contemplated."[123] In a concurrence, Justice Stevens similarly reasoned that the phrase "undertakes to comply," especially when read in context, is best construed as "contemplat[ing] future action by the political branches."[124]

In addition to relying on the "undertakes to comply" language, the Court noted that the remainder of Article 94 expressly set forth an enforcement mechanism for noncompliance with ICJ decisions— reference of the matter to the UN Security Council for possible sanctions. The Court reasoned that "[t]he U.N. Charter's provision of an express diplomatic—that is, nonjudicial—remedy is itself evidence that ICJ judgments were not meant to be enforceable in domestic courts."[125] The Court also cited evidence suggesting that, when it submitted the UN Charter to the Senate, the Executive Branch envisioned that the Security Council would be the only

---

[119] See 128 S Ct 1346 (2008).

[120] Id at 1356 (quoting *Igartua-De La Rosa v United States*, 417 F3d 145, 150 (1st Cir 2005) (en banc)).

[121] Id at 1358.

[122] Id.

[123] Id at 1359 n 5.

[124] Id at 1373 (Stevens, J, concurring).

[125] Id at 1359.

avenue for enforcement of ICJ decisions.[126] More generally, the Court accorded deference to the Executive Branch's views about the treaties, noting that the Executive Branch had "unfailingly adhered to its view that the relevant treaties do not create domestically enforceable federal law."[127] The Court further emphasized particular features of the ICJ adjudicatory system, including the fact that the ICJ can only hear disputes involving nations, not individuals.[128]

Finally, the Court observed that the consequences of giving direct effect to ICJ judgments "give pause."[129] The Court expressed particular concern that, under such a regime, even erroneous ICJ decisions could override state law, and potentially even federal law.[130] The Court also worried that the ICJ would have the ability to bind U.S. courts to extreme remedies, such as "annul[ling] criminal convictions and sentences, for any reason deemed sufficient by the ICJ."[131] For these reasons, the Court suggested that it was unlikely that the U.S. political branches had intended for the obligation to comply with ICJ judgments to be self-executing.

In reaching its conclusion, the Court rejected what it called the "multifactor, judgment by judgment" approach to self-execution suggested by Justice Breyer in dissent, whereby courts would consider not only treaty text and drafting history, but also the treaty's subject matter, whether the treaty provision confers specific individual rights, and whether direct enforcement of the treaty would require the courts to create a new cause of action.[132] The Court reasoned that such an approach would be too indeterminate and would give the courts too much discretion, thereby "assign[ing] to the courts—not the political branches—the primary role in deciding when and how international agreements will be enforced."[133] The Court particularly objected that, under the dissent's proposed approach, a treaty provision could be self-executing in some cases and non-self-executing in others. The Court thought it "hard to believe that the United States would enter into treaties that are sometimes

---

[126] Id at 1359–60.

[127] Id at 1361.

[128] Id at 1360.

[129] Id at 1364.

[130] Id.

[131] Id.

[132] See id at 1362–63; id at 1382–83 (Breyer, J, dissenting).

[133] Id at 1363.

enforceable and sometimes not,"[134] and it expressed concern that allowing courts to make such case-by-case judgments would give the judiciary "the power not only to interpret but also to create the law."[135]

In addition to its finding of non-self-execution, the Court held that the President's memorandum did not have the effect of overriding Texas's law of procedural default. The Court reasoned that the conversion of a non-self-executing treaty obligation into self-executing federal law is an act of lawmaking that falls to Congress, not the President.[136] The Court further reasoned that, "[w]hen the President asserts the power to 'enforce' a non-self-executing treaty by unilaterally creating domestic law, he acts in conflict with the implicit understanding of the ratifying Senate," and therefore his action falls into the lowest category of presidential power under Justice Jackson's framework from the *Youngstown* steel seizure case.[137]

As discussed below, the Court's decision in *Medellín* is generally consistent with the three claims defended above: that the inclusion of treaties in the Supremacy Clause does not by itself tell us the extent to which treaties are judicially enforceable; that the relevant intent in discerning self-execution is that of the U.S. treaty-makers; and that there are important differences between statutes and treaties that are relevant to their judicial enforceability.

A. SUPREME LAW OF THE LAND

Consider first the relationship between Supremacy Clause and judicial enforceability. The Court obviously saw no contradiction between that Clause and the concept of non-self-execution. It cited *Foster* with approval and did not treat it as some deviation from the Constitution that had to be grudgingly accommodated because of stare decisis.

Nor did the Court view the Supremacy Clause as mandating a

---

[134] Id.

[135] Id.

[136] See id at 1368–69.

[137] Id at 1369; see also *Youngstown Sheet & Tube Co. v Sawyer*, 343 US 579, 637 (1952) (Jackson, J, concurring) ("When the President takes measures incompatible with the expressed or implied will of Congress, his power is at its lowest ebb, for then he can rely only upon his own constitutional powers minus any constitutional powers of Congress over the matter.").

presumption in favor of self-execution. The Court did not mention any such presumption, and, in concluding that the treaties in question were non-self-executing, it did not require clear evidence of an intent to preclude domestic judicial enforcement. Instead, it carefully examined the text, structure, and ratification history of the treaties to discern whether they were self-executing. The Court also emphasized that "Congress is up to the task of implementing non-self-executing treaties,"[138] further suggesting that it did not have in mind a presumption in favor of self-execution.

Professor Vázquez argues that *Medellín* is consistent with a general presumption in favor of self-execution, but his claim depends upon an unlikely reading of the Court's reasoning. Professor Vázquez suggests that the Supreme Court interpreted Article 94 of the UN Charter as leaving parties to the Charter, including the United States, "some discretion not to comply" with ICJ decisions.[139] Instead of interpreting Article 94 as imposing a "hard" obligation on the United States to comply with *Avena*, he contends that the Court interpreted it as merely imposing a "soft" obligation to try to comply, or to use its best efforts to comply.[140] As a result, Professor Vázquez argues that the Court's non-self-execution analysis should be limited to treaty provisions that, *as a matter of international law*, convey nonjusticiable political discretion.

No party made this argument about Article 94, and, as far as I know, there is no support for it in international law (and Professor Vázquez himself notes that such an interpretation of Article 94 would almost certainly be wrong).[141] Instead, what the U.S. government had argued was that Article 94 constitutes "a commitment on the part of U.N. Members to take *future* action through their political branches to comply with an ICJ decision."[142] The Court quoted this language from the government's brief, and then immediately stated, "We agree with this construction of Article

---

[138] 128 S Ct at 1366.

[139] Vázquez, 122 Harv L Rev at 660 (cited in note 7).

[140] See id at 662.

[141] The ICJ has since confirmed that the *Avena* decision is unconditionally binding on the United States as a matter of international law. The ICJ noted that both the U.S. government and the U.S. Supreme Court accepted that proposition. See Judgment, *Request for Interpretation of the Judgment of 31 March 2004 in the Case Concerning Avena and Other Mexican Nationals (Mexico v United States of America)*, ¶¶ 28, 36, 44 (Jan 19, 2009), at http://www.icj-cij.org/docket/files/139/14939.pdf?PHPSESSID=d3b5b436b441b101118fb70dbc03dfaf.

[142] 128 S Ct at 1358.

94."[143] Neither the Court nor the parties suggested that Article 94 gave the United States some discretion not to comply with *Avena*. Indeed, the Court observed that, "No one disputes that the *Avena* decision—a decision that flows from the treaties through which the United States submitted to ICJ jurisdiction with respect to Vienna Convention disputes—constitutes an *international* law obligation on the part of the United States."[144] Instead of resisting or qualifying that proposition, the Court distinguished international obligations from the issue of self-execution, noting that "not all international law obligations automatically constitute binding federal law enforceable in United States courts."[145]

In support of his contrary reading of the decision, Professor Vázquez cites an observation by the Court that giving ICJ decisions immediate domestic effect would eliminate the "option of noncompliance" contemplated by the UN Charter's placement of enforcement authority with the Security Council. There is no suggestion in this observation, however, that the Court meant that the United States had the option *under international law* of not complying with an ICJ decision to which it was a party. Rather, the Court almost certainly meant that, given its veto power in the Council, the United States would as a practical matter have the ability to decide not to comply, and that the political branches were aware of that "option" when ratifying the relevant treaties. Indeed, the Court specifically noted that "the President and Senate were undoubtedly aware in subscribing to the U.N. Charter and Optional Protocol, [that] the United States retained the unqualified right to exercise its veto of any Security Council resolution."[146] The Court further made clear that the "noncompliance" it was referring to was "through exercise of the Security Council veto—always regarded as an option by the Executive and ratifying Senate during and after consideration of the [relevant treaties]."[147] By contrast, said the Court, direct enforcement of ICJ decisions by U.S. courts would "undermin[e] the ability of the political branches to determine whether and how to comply with an ICJ

---

[143] Id.

[144] Id at 1356.

[145] Id.

[146] Id at 1359.

[147] Id at 1360.

judgment."[148] In all these references, the Court is obviously referring to the *political* option of noncompliance, not one conferred
as a matter of law by the treaty.

Professor Vázquez contends that there is no way to explain the
Court's reliance on the phrase "undertakes to comply" in its self-
execution analysis other than through his reading of the decision.[149] In fact, as noted above, the Court (and Justice Stevens in
his concurrence) understood that phrase as suggesting a future
obligation to comply through political branch action. The Court
distinguished the phrase from more present-tense terms such as
"shall" and "must," and also noted that the phrase did not "indicate
that the Senate that ratified the U.N. Charter intended to vest
ICJ decisions with *immediate* legal effect in domestic courts."[150]
Regardless of whether this happens to be the best reading of the
phrase, the Court's approach is similar to that taken in *Foster* and
in a number of lower court decisions.[151] Indeed, Professor Vázquez
has himself noted in other writings that "[l]ater courts have interpreted *Foster* as establishing that 'words of futurity' indicate
that a treaty provision is not self-executing."[152] Professor Vázquez
argues that an intent-of-the-parties approach to self-execution
would not have shown that "undertakes to comply" was in fact
language of futurity, but, as I explain below, the Court was probably not following the intent-of-the-parties approach.

Despite all of this, *Medellín* need not be read as going to the
opposite end of the spectrum and requiring a presumption *against*
self-execution. Justice Breyer's dissent accused the majority of
adopting a clear statement requirement for self-execution, based
on the Court's comment in the presidential power portion of its
decision that, "[i]f the Executive determines that a treaty should
have domestic effect of its own force, that determination may be
implemented 'in mak[ing]' the treaty, by ensuring that it contains

---

[148] Id.

[149] Vázquez, 122 Harv L Rev at 661–62 (cited in note 7).

[150] 128 S Ct at 1358.

[151] See, for example, *Robertson v General Electric Co.*, 32 F2d 495, 500 (4th Cir 1929)
(citing "language of futurity" as evidence of non-self-execution); *Sei Fujii v California*, 242
P2d 617, 622 (Cal 1952) (finding UN Charter provisions to be non-self-executing because,
among other things, they were "framed as a promise of future action by the member
nations").

[152] Vázquez, 89 Am J Intl L at 703 n 40 (cited in note 6).

language plainly providing for domestic enforceability."[153] But the Court denied the charge, emphasizing that no "talismanic words" are required for self-execution.[154] The Court also made clear that self-execution should be determined on a treaty-by-treaty basis, stating, for example, that "under our established precedent, some treaties are self-executing and some are not, depending on the treaty."[155] In addition, the Court observed that prior decisions that have found treaties to be self-executing "stand only for the un-remarkable proposition that some international agreements are self-executing and others are not,"[156] and it reserved judgment on whether the relevant provision of the Vienna Convention on Con-sular Relations is self-executing, even though that provision does not contain a clear statement of self-execution.[157]

If the Court was suggesting any presumption in *Medellín*, it was probably just a presumption against giving direct effect to ICJ judgments. It was after all the enforceability of ICJ judgments, rather than the status of treaty obligations in general, that was the precise question before the Court. The Court recognized this, stating: "The question we confront here is whether the *Avena* judgment has automatic *domestic* legal effect such that the judg-ment of its own force applies in state and federal courts."[158] The Court subsequently noted that, "[g]iven that ICJ judgments may interfere with state procedural rules, one would expect the rati-fying parties to the relevant treaties to have clearly stated their intent to give those judgments domestic effect, if they had so intended."[159] A presumption against giving direct effect to ICJ judgments can easily be defended, however, without resort to any general presumption against treaty self-execution. ICJ judgments concern disputes between nations that will often be politically sensitive. As a result, there are good reasons to think that the political branches would want flexibility in deciding how to im-

[153] See 128 S Ct at 1369; id at 1380 (Breyer, J, dissenting).

[154] Id at 1366.

[155] Id at 1365.

[156] Id at 1364.

[157] See id at 1357 n 4.

[158] Id at 1356; see also id at 1357 n 4 ("The question is whether the *Avena* judgment has binding effect in domestic courts under the Optional Protocol, ICJ Statute, and U.N. Charter.").

[159] Id at 1363–64.

plement these judgments after they are issued. Direct judicial enforcement of these judgments might even raise constitutional concerns in some cases, relating, for example, to the Article III authority of the federal courts, or to the role of the states in the U.S. federal system.[160]

The Court's decision in *Medellín* will probably mean, as the dissenters asserted, that ICJ judgments issued pursuant to other ICJ clauses in treaties will also be deemed to be non-self-executing in the United States.[161] This issue will rarely arise, however, in view of the infrequency with which the ICJ issues judgments involving the United States. Moreover, few other nations (if any) give direct effect to ICJ judgments, so the United States will hardly be alone in failing to do so.[162] Nor does *Medellín* entail a significant change in U.S. practice: U.S. courts have never given direct effect to an ICJ judgment, and, in fact, the U.S. Court of Appeals for the District of Columbia Circuit held twenty years ago that such judgments were not enforceable in U.S. courts at the behest of private parties.[163]

The one possible deviation in *Medellín* from my treatment of the Supremacy Clause is the suggestion by the Court, in a variety of statements, that non-self-executing treaties do not have any status as domestic law.[164] My approach, by contrast, would distinguish between judicially enforceable treaty commitments and those that are not, while treating all of them as the supreme law of the land. Among other things, I believe my approach is easier to reconcile with the text of the Supremacy Clause, which states that "all" treaties ratified by the United States shall be the supreme

---

[160] See Curtis A. Bradley, *The Federal Judicial Power and the International Legal Order*, 2006 Supreme Court Review 59; Curtis A. Bradley, *International Delegations, the Structural Constitution, and Non-Self-Execution*, 55 Stan L Rev 1557 (2003).

[161] 128 S Ct at 1388 (Breyer, J, dissenting).

[162] See id at 1363 (observing that "neither Medellín nor his *amici* have identified a single nation that treats ICJ judgments as binding in domestic courts"); see also A. Mark Weisburd, *International Courts and American Courts*, 21 Mich J Intl L 877, 886–87 (2000) (finding little support in other countries for giving ICJ decisions binding force in domestic courts).

[163] See *Committee of U.S. Citizens Living in Nicaragua v Reagan*, 859 F2d 929, 937–38 (DC Cir 1988).

[164] See, for example, 128 S Ct at 1356 ("This Court has long recognized the distinction between treaties that automatically have effect as domestic law, and those that—while they constitute international law commitments—do not by themselves function as binding federal law.").

law of the land (and here Professor Vázquez and I are in agreement).[165]

There is in any event some ambiguity in the opinion about whether the Court really meant to say that non-self-executing treaties were not part of the supreme law of the land. The Court never actually phrases it that way, and, in an opinion otherwise highly focused on textual materials, it never seeks to explain how its statements about non-self-executing treaties accord with the text of the Supremacy Clause.[166] In addition, in a number of places in the opinion the Court appears to equate the self-execution issue with judicial enforceability.[167] The Court's general test for self-execution also focuses on whether the treaty is a "directive to domestic courts,"[168] not on whether the treaty is domestic law. Moreover, a number of the Court's references to lack of domestic law status were focused on the *Avena* judgment rather than on the underlying treaties.[169] Even the Texas Solicitor General, who successfully argued the case for Texas, has made clear that he views non-self-executing treaties as part of the supreme law of the land, despite the fact that his brief used phrasing similar to that used by the Supreme Court.[170]

The Court's position on this issue continued to be ambiguous

---

[165] See also Henkin, *Foreign Affairs and the United States Constitution* at 203–04 (cited in note 8) ("Whether [a treaty] is self-executing or not, it is supreme law of the land.").

[166] For an effort to reconcile the proposition that non-self-executing treaties lack the status of domestic law with the Supremacy Clause, see the postings by Nick Rosenkranz in the *Federalist Society Online Debate* (cited in note 27).

[167] See, for example, 128 S Ct at 1356 ("[N]ot all international law obligations automatically constitute binding federal law *enforceable in United States courts*.") (emphasis added); id ("The question we confront here is whether the *Avena* judgment has automatic *domestic* legal effect *such that the judgment of its own force applies in state and federal courts*.") (second emphasis added); id at 1361 ("The pertinent international agreements, therefore, do not provide for implementation of ICJ judgments *through direct enforcement in domestic courts* . . .") (emphasis added).

[168] Id at 1358.

[169] See, for example, id at 1357 ("[W]e conclude that the *Avena* judgment is not automatically binding domestic law."); id at 1372 ("For the reasons we have stated, the *Avena* judgment is not domestic law."). These statements are much easier to reconcile with the text of the Supremacy Clause, since, unlike treaties, ICJ judgments are not listed in the Supremacy Clause as part of the supreme law of the land.

[170] See Ted Cruz, Remarks, *Federalist Society Online Debate* (cited in note 27) ("Of course, all three treaties at issue (including Article 94 of the UN Charter) are 'federal law,' because all treaties are 'federal law.' That wasn't the question before the Court. The question was whether the treaties were 'self-executing,' by which the Court meant judicially enforceable in U.S. courts."). Cf. Brief for Respondent, *Medellín v Texas* at 14 (No 06-984) ("[U]nless the treaty reflects an agreement between the President and the Senate to create domestic law, no such law is made.").

in a subsequent order by the Court denying Medellín a stay of execution. In declining to issue the stay, the Court stated that "[i]t is up to Congress whether to implement obligations undertaken under a treaty which (like this one) does not itself have the force and effect of domestic law *sufficient to set aside the judgment or the ensuing sentence.*"[171] The italicized language would appear to be superfluous if the Court believes that non-self-executing treaties lack any domestic law status. For what it is worth, the Senate Foreign Relations Committee has expressed the view after *Medellín* that non-self-executing treaties are part of the supreme law of the land.[172]

While not particularly material to the analysis in this article, the issue of whether non-self-executing treaties have some domestic law status might matter in some contexts. It might matter, for example, in debates within the Executive Branch over whether the President is obligated to comply with a non-self-executing treaty.[173] It might also affect the Executive Branch's ability to take action voluntarily to enforce a non-self-executing treaty.[174] In *Medellín*, the Court reasoned that "the non-self-executing character of a treaty constrains the President's ability to comply with treaty commitments by unilaterally making the treaty binding on domestic courts."[175] At the same time, the Court disavowed any suggestion that a non-self-executing treaty, without implementing legislation, "preclude[d] the President from acting to comply with an international treaty obligation," and indicated that "[t]he President may comply with the treaty's obligations by some other

---

[171] *Medellín v Texas*, 129 S Ct 360, 361 (2008) (emphasis added).

[172] See, for example, Exec Rept 110–12, 110th Cong, 2d Sess, *Extradition Treaties with the European Union* (Sept 11, 2008) at 10 ("In accordance with the Constitution, all treaties—whether self-executing or not—are the supreme law of the land, and the President shall take care that they be faithfully executed."), at http://frwebgate.access.gpo.gov/cgi-bin/getdoc.cgi?dbname = 110_cong_reports&docid = f:er012.110.pdf.

[173] Cf. Derek Jinks and David Sloss, *Is the President Bound by the Geneva Conventions?* 90 Cornell L Rev 97, 158 (2004) (arguing that "the President's duty under the Take Care Clause includes a duty to execute treaties that are the law of the land"). The Take Care Clause of the Constitution provides that the President is obligated to take care that the "Laws" are faithfully executed. The government did not rely on that Clause as a source of authority in *Medellín*, and the Court briefly dismissed the Clause's relevance at the end of its opinion, on the ground that the Clause "allows the President to execute the laws, not make them," and that "the *Avena* judgment is not domestic law." 128 S Ct at 1372. The Court did not say there that non-self-executing treaties do not constitute "Laws" for purposes of the Take Care Clause.

[174] See generally Edward T. Swaine, *Taking Care of Treaties*, 108 Colum L Rev 331 (2008).

[175] 128 S Ct at 1371.

means, so long as they are consistent with the Constitution."[176]
The distinction between lack of judicial enforceability and lack of
domestic law status also mattered to Justice Stevens's concurrence:
because Justice Stevens regarded the treaty obligation in question
to be part of the supreme law of the land, even though not self-
executing, he suggested (somewhat cryptically, to be sure) that the
states had an obligation to comply with it, even though they would
not be forced to do so by the federal courts.[177]

B. RELEVANT INTENT

The *Medellín* decision is also generally consistent with my second claim, which is that the relevant intent for self-execution is
that of the U.S. treaty-makers. The Court stated that "[o]ur cases
simply require courts to decide whether a treaty's terms reflect a
determination *by the President who negotiated it and the Senate that
confirmed it* that the treaty has domestic effect."[178] The Court also
noted that "we have held treaties to be self-executing when the
textual provisions indicate that *the President and Senate* intended
for the agreement to have domestic effect."[179] And, in summarizing
its finding of non-self-execution, the Court explained that
"[n]othing in the text, background, negotiating and drafting history, or practice among signatory nations suggests that the *President or Senate* intended the improbable result of giving the judgments of an international tribunal a higher status than that enjoyed
by 'many of our most fundamental constitutional protections.'"[180]
The Court's rejection of the dissent's proposed multifactor approach to self-execution was also premised on an intent-of-the-
U.S. approach. The Court stated: "The dissent's contrary approach would assign to the courts—not *the political branches*—the
primary role in deciding when and how international agreements
will be enforced."[181]

There are, to be fair, a few indications in the opinion going the

---

[176] Id.

[177] See id at 1374 (Stevens, J, concurring).

[178] 128 S Ct at 1366 (emphasis added).

[179] Id at 1364 (emphasis added).

[180] Id at 1367 (emphasis added) (quoting *Sanchez-Llamas v Oregon*, 126 S Ct 2669, 2687 (2006)).

[181] Id at 1363 (emphasis added); see also id at 1360 (observing that "there is no reason to believe that the President and Senate signed up" for giving direct effect to ICJ decisions).

other way, which may suggest some confusion on the Court about the issue. The Court began its self-execution analysis by referring to Supreme Court decisions that have looked to the intent of the parties in interpreting substantive treaty terms.[182] It also asserted that its finding of non-self-execution was confirmed by the post-ratification understandings of the treaty parties, something that would not be particularly relevant under an intent-of-the-U.S. approach.[183] The Court even considered in a footnote whether the ICJ had views on the self-execution issue, while (properly) expressing some doubt about whether such views would be relevant.[184]

On balance, though, the Court's decision is best interpreted as endorsing an intent-of-the-U.S. approach. In addition to the many direct statements to this effect quoted above, the Court relied on the U.S. ratification history for the UN Charter rather than on the collective negotiating history. More generally, the Court did not attempt to ascertain how the relevant treaty language, such as "undertakes to comply," would be understood by other treaty parties. Furthermore, in the presidential power portion of its decision, the Court expressed the view that if the Executive Branch could make a non-self-executing treaty binding on domestic courts, it would be acting "in conflict with the implicit understanding of the ratifying Senate."[185] That assertion may or may not be persuasive with respect to the treaties at issue in *Medellín*, but the key point is that the Court focused here and elsewhere on the Senate's and the President's intent.

Professor Vázquez claims that, despite the overwhelming number of references in the opinion to senatorial and presidential intent, the Court could not have been considering that intent because it paid close attention to the treaty text. Such text, Professor Vázquez asserts, "reflects the intent of the parties, not the unilateral views of the U.S. treatymakers."[186] Professor Vázquez fails to recognize that, as discussed in Part III, the text could be relevant to *both* inquiries. Treaty text is of course relevant in ascertaining the collective intent of the parties, but it is also relevant

---

[182] See id at 1357–58.

[183] See id at 1363.

[184] See id at 1361 n 9.

[185] Id at 1369.

[186] Vázquez, 122 Harv L Rev at 659 (cited in note 7).

in ascertaining the unilateral intent of the U.S. treaty-makers, which is the only intent there is likely to be with respect to the issue of self-execution. Thus, as the Court explained, "we have held treaties to be self-executing when the textual provisions *indicate that the President and Senate intended* for the agreement to have domestic effect."[187] The Court also specifically defended its emphasis on treaty text by noting: "That is after all what the *Senate* looks to in deciding whether to approve the treaty."[188] Like Professor Vázquez, Justice Breyer's dissent in *Medellín* misses this point. Justice Breyer contends that looking at the treaty text for evidence concerning self-execution is, at best, "hunting the snark," because it is unlikely that the parties will have reached an agreement on the issue that would be incorporated into the text.[189] In fact, only an intent-of-the parties approach to self-execution would end up constituting a snark hunt.

To be sure, absent a specific declaration by the Senate, it is not clear that text by itself will provide *sufficient* evidence of the U.S. treaty-makers' intent concerning whether a particular treaty provision is self-executing. If the text does not, it may be unrealistic to think that the Court can avoid the indeterminacy and judicial discretion associated with the dissent's proposed approach. Despite its criticism of the dissent, however, the Court was probably not insisting that text is the only relevant consideration in discerning such intent. Indeed, as noted above, the Court looked to statements made in the ratification history to aid its understanding of this intent.[190] The subject matter of the treaties in question— international dispute resolution between nations—also appears to have been relevant to the Court's assessment of likely intent.[191] The Court even invoked functional considerations to support its analysis.[192] In rejecting the multifactor approach proposed in dissent by Justice Breyer, the Court appears principally to have been objecting to the idea that a treaty provision could be self-executing in some cases but not in others. A contextual approach could be

[187] 128 S Ct at 1364 (emphasis added).

[188] Id at 1362 (emphasis added).

[189] Id at 1381 (Breyer, J, dissenting). See also Vázquez, 122 Harv L Rev at 629, 636–37 (cited in note 7) (endorsing Justice Breyer's "snark" comment).

[190] See text accompanying note 126.

[191] See text accompanying note 128.

[192] See text accompanying note 129.

applied, however, in a more categorical way, such that a treaty provision would be either self-executing or not in all cases, avoiding the Court's concern.[193]

It is true, as Professor Vázquez points out,[194] that the presidential power portion of the Court's decision reflects a formalistic conception of lawmaking. The Court reasoned there that "the terms of a non-self-executing treaty can become domestic law only in the same way as any other law—through passage of legislation by both Houses of Congress, combined with either the President's signature or a congressional override of a Presidential veto."[195] One might infer from that discussion, as Professor Vázquez does, that the Court would resist the idea that the U.S. treaty-makers have an adjunct or lesser-included lawmaking power over self-execution. But this inference is far from clear, since the exercise of such a power still requires the use of the treaty process, that is, two-thirds Senate consent and presidential approval. The Court's concern in *Medellín*, by contrast, was with unilateral presidential control over the issue, especially when that control contradicted a decision made earlier by the U.S. treaty-makers. The Court noted, for example, that "[w]hen the President asserts the power to 'enforce' a non-self-executing treaty by unilaterally creating domestic law, he acts in conflict with the implicit understanding of the ratifying Senate."[196] Moreover, the Court's presidential power analysis actually appears to assume that the U.S. treaty-makers have exercised some domestic lawmaking power when deciding that a treaty shall not be self-executing, since this was the basis on which the Court concluded that President Bush was operating within the lowest category of Justice Jackson's *Youngstown* framework.[197]

---

[193] Cf. *F. Hoffmann-La Roche Ltd. v Empagran S.A.*, 542 US 155, 168–69 (2004) (rejecting case-by-case approach to determining whether comity factors supported the application of U.S. antitrust law to independent foreign injury in favor of categorical approach).

[194] See Vázquez, 122 Harv L Rev at 659 (cited in note 7).

[195] 128 S Ct at 1369.

[196] Id.

[197] See id at 1369 ("[T]he non-self-executing character of the relevant treaties not only refutes the notion that the ratifying parties vested the President with the authority to unilaterally make treaty obligations binding on domestic courts, but also implicitly prohibits him from doing so."). I am merely describing the Court's reasoning here, not endorsing it. The fact that the U.S. treaty-makers did not intend for ICJ decisions to be directly enforceable in U.S. courts would not necessarily mean that they wanted to preclude the President from implementing such decisions if he or she chose to do so. More generally,

C. STATUTES AND TREATIES

Consistent with my third claim, the Court also took account of the distinct nature of treaties in its self-execution analysis. Quoting the *Head Money Cases*, the Court noted at the outset that a treaty is "'primarily a compact between independent nations' that ordinarily 'depends for the enforcement of its provisions on the interest and the honor of the governments which are parties to it.'"[198] While the Court of course recognized that some treaties are also domestically enforceable in U.S. courts, this is only true, said the Court, "when the textual provisions indicate that the President and Senate intended for the agreement to have domestic effect."[199]

In finding that there was no such self-executing intent, the Court took account of the treaty context. Among other things, the Court observed that the requirement of compliance with ICJ decisions was situated within an international legal system that emphasized political rather than judicial enforcement—in particular, enforcement through the Security Council, where the United States holds a veto. The Court also expressed concern about transferring "sensitive foreign policy decisions" to the state and federal courts, given that "'[t]he conduct of the foreign relations of our Government is committed by the Constitution to the Executive and Legislative—"the political"—Departments.'"[200]

In addition, the Court also observed in a footnote that even when treaties are self-executing, "the background presumption is that '[i]nternational agreements, even those directly benefiting private persons, generally do not create private rights or provide for a private cause of action in domestic courts.'"[201] For this proposition, the Court quoted from the Restatement (Third) of Foreign Relations, which appears to be making an empirical claim about the nature of treaties. Professor Vázquez dismisses the Restatement's observation on the ground that "the Supremacy Clause generally makes treaties enforceable in our courts in the same circumstances as statutory and

---

the Court may have passed over too quickly the possibility that treaties, like some statutes, could delegate enforcement authority to the Executive Branch.

[198] Id at 1357.

[199] Id at 1364.

[200] Id at 1360 (quoting *Oetjen v Central Leather Co.*, 246 US 297, 302 (1918)).

[201] Id at 1357 n 3 (quoting Restatement (Third) of the Foreign Relations Law of the United States, § 907, cmt. a (cited in note 14)).

constitutional provisions of like content,"[202] but, for reasons already discussed, that is an overly broad reading of the Clause.

The Court's institutional process concerns associated with giving direct effect to ICJ judgments were also related specifically to the international context of the case. As noted above, the Court stated that the consequences of the argument that ICJ decisions have direct effect in the U.S. legal system "give pause," because the argument would mean that an ICJ judgment "is not only binding domestic law but is also unassailable" such that even erroneous ICJ rulings would override state and possibly even federal law. While it is common for domestic courts to exercise this sort of authority, the Court was obviously troubled by the idea that such authority had been delegated to actors outside of the U.S. legal system. In this respect, the decision was foreshadowed by the Court's earlier decision in *Sanchez-Llamas*, in which the Court resisted the idea that U.S. federal courts should be bound by the ICJ's interpretation of a treaty.[203] These concerns, which relate to democratic process and sovereignty, are not typically implicated by domestic statutes.

Finally, the Court's discussion of the "option of noncompliance" demonstrated its recognition of the dual law-and-politics nature of treaty commitments. The Court was not advocating the breach of U.S. treaty obligations, but it was recognizing that decisions about whether and how to comply with such obligations are not purely legal decisions but also involve questions of international politics. As discussed above, the duality of treaties suggests that the role of the courts in enforcing them may be somewhat more limited than with respect to statutes, especially when such enforcement poses a risk of undermining political branch management of foreign relations, a proposition evident at least since *Foster*. The long-standing doctrine of deference to Executive Branch treaty constructions, invoked by the Court in *Medellín*, also takes account of this proposition.

---

[202] Vázquez, 122 Harv L Rev at 627 n 131 (cited in note 7).

[203] See *Sanchez-Llamas v Oregon*, 126 S Ct 2669, 2684 (2006) ("If treaties are to be given effect as federal law under our legal system, determining their meaning as a matter of federal law 'is emphatically the province and duty of the judicial department,' headed by the 'one supreme Court' established by the Constitution.") (quoting *Marbury v Madison*, 5 US (1 Cranch) 137, 177 (1803)). The Court in *Medellín* made clear, however, that it was "not suggest[ing] that treaties can never afford binding domestic effect to international tribunal judgments." 128 S Ct at 1364–65.

VI. Conclusion

The Supreme Court's decision in *Medellín* is unlikely to result in a significant change in the extent of U.S. judicial enforcement of treaties, but it may make it less likely that certain academic ambitions about such enforcement will be achieved. As the Court appears to have recognized, treaties have a dual nature in that they are situated in the domain of international politics as well as in the domain of law, and this duality is relevant to their judicial enforceability. Their dual nature means that their domestic judicial enforceability is in part a political decision, not some automatic rule of the Supremacy Clause. The relevant intent in discerning whether treaties are subject to such domestic judicial enforceability is in turn the intent of the national political branches. Finally, the international political dimension of treaties means that, as a class, they are less likely than statutes to be subject to domestic judicial enforcement, especially in the modern era.

Although judicial practice may not change substantially after *Medellín*, we are likely to see increased use by the Senate of declarations of self-execution and non-self-execution. Assuming such declarations are valid, as this article has maintained, the Senate practice should simplify the issue of self-execution over time. The widespread and continuing use of congressional-executive agreements may have a similar effect. In other situations it may be appropriate to give deference to the current views of the Executive Branch about the treaty's domestic enforceability. There will of course continue to be circumstances in which there will be no clear guidance from the political branches, and in those cases courts are likely to make contextual judgments that take account of the text, structure, and subject matter of the treaty, lines of precedent and other historical practice, the congressional backdrop, and the functional consequences of direct judicial enforceability. The doctrine of treaty self-execution thus entails a degree of judicial discretion, but it is a type of discretion that is ultimately subject to political branch control.

SAMUEL ISSACHAROFF

PRIVATE CLAIMS, AGGREGATE RIGHTS

When you got nothing, you got nothing to lose. (Bob Dylan, as
told to Chief Justice John Roberts)[1]

The big constitutional cases just seem to announce themselves.
Mention segregation, abortion, or affirmative action, or Guantánamo, or even a crèche, and the blogs go all aflutter. These are the
cases that mark the Warren Court era, then the Burger Court, the
Rehnquist Court, and now the Roberts Court, though still a work
in progress. Will it be 5–4? Will Kennedy be the new O'Connor?
And what of stare decisis, of judicial restraint, of textualism and
originalism?

By contrast, the Court's procedural cases seem an afterthought.
Often they arise from what can fairly be described as trivial disputes.
When cert is granted, the likeliest response from the cognoscenti
Court watchers is, "they took cert on *that*?" After a quick search
to make sure there was indeed a circuit conflict, there is then the
sage response about how the Court is devoting its dwindling docket

Samuel Issacharoff is Reiss Professor of Constitutional Law, New York University School
of Law.

Author's note: My thanks to John Leubsdorf, Arthur Miller, Richard Nagareda, and
David Shapiro for discussion of the issues presented here. Andrew Furlow, Laura Miller,
and Colin Reardon provided research assistance for this article. This article benefited from
faculty workshop comments at Harvard Law School and Boston University School of Law.

[1] *Sprint Communications Co., L.P. v APCC Services, Inc.*, 128 S Ct 2531, 2550 (2008)
(Roberts, CJ, dissenting) (quoting "Like a Rolling Stone," on Highway 61 Revisited (Columbia Records 1965)). Aficionados would claim that, notwithstanding the songbook, the
song is classically sung as, "when you *ain't* got nothing, you got nothing to lose."

to one more outlier opinion from the Ninth Circuit. But even the truest of the Court's repeat players cannot help but wonder, "So what?"

And so it was with a trio of cases decided at the end of the last Term concerning some of the real dregs of the procedural brew. The first, *Sprint Communications Co., L.P. v APCC Services, Inc.*, concerned whether a bill collector was capable of filing suit in its own name in trying to enforce debts owed to operators of pay phones (remember those?),[2] an issue that long ago prompted one court to call the Rule 17 discussion of a real party in interest the "barnacle" of the Federal Rules.[3] Another, *Republic of the Philippines v Pimentel*, asked the timeless question of the proper relation between the underutilized federal interpleader rule and the impossible to comprehend "indispensable party" and "necessary party" requirements of Rule 19 of the Federal Rules[4]—which are now cleverly restyled since 2007 under the catchall, "required party." Perhaps this was finally the chance for the Court to clear up the "verbal anomaly"[5] of a rule that allows a party to be indispensable yet not necessary, or perhaps not. Closing out the trio came *Taylor v Sturgell*, a case presenting the ever-burning question of the role of virtual representation in setting the parameters for nonmutual offensive collateral estoppel, or more simply can one World War II–era vintage plane enthusiast be precluded from demanding FAA documents under the Freedom of Information Act simply because his fellow flight club buddy had already been told they were not available under FOIA.[6]

Standing alone, these three cases are of little moment, at best resolving technical issues of pleading or standing that in most instances can be easily accommodated by litigants in subsequent cases. Only *Pimentel*, concerning claims by a class of human rights victims against the estate of Ferdinand Marcos, had any underlying significance apart from the technical issue presented to the Court.

Taken together, however, the cases form a triptych illuminating

---

[2] *Sprint*, 128 S Ct 2531.

[3] *Virginia Elec. & Power Co. v Westinghouse Elec. Corp.*, 485 F2d 78, 83 (4th Cir 1973) ("'Rule 17(a) is a barnacle on the federal practice ship. It ought to be scraped away.'") (quoting John E. Kennedy, *Federal Rule 17(a): Will the Real Party in Interest Please Stand?* 51 Minn L Rev 675, 724 (1967)).

[4] *Republic of the Philippines v Pimentel*, 128 S Ct 2180 (2008).

[5] *Provident Tradesmens Bank & Trust Co. v Patterson*, 390 US 102, 117 n 12 (1968).

[6] *Taylor v Sturgell*, 128 S Ct 2161 (2008).

a deeper set of issues on the tension between our inherited system of civil procedure and claims that are fundamentally defined by their aggregative or public nature. Each case presents claims held by individuals (or individual firms) that are private in terms of the relief sought, but which are defined by their relation to comparable claims of similarly situated individuals. In essence they raise the problems that have challenged courts in trying to define the boundaries of class actions. But, as Justice Breyer noted in *Sprint,* "class actions constitute but one of several methods for bringing about aggregation of claims, i.e., they are but one of several methods by which multiple similarly situated parties get similar claims resolved at one time and in one federal forum."[7]

In this article, I will take up the problem of non-class aggregations. In particular, my focus is on the mismatch between rules that define party status in terms of the private nature of the rights asserted and a set of underlying substantive claims which, either formally or as a practical matter, do not fit within the framework of identifiably individual claims.

I. Procedure as the Handmaiden of . . . Procedure

The problem of the tension between the individual-claim premises of our procedural system and the pressures of mass society is not new. It is possible to trace the problem back to the medieval origins of the class action and the issues attendant to achieving a bill of peace where claimants are many and precise stakeholdings are diffuse.[8] For present purposes, however, I want to go back only forty years to the Supreme Court's first confrontation with the mass version of the most ordinary of common law claims in *State Farm v Tashire.*[9]

Tashire arose from a California road accident, certainly not a challenging concept for modern courts. The problem, however, was that the accident involved a Greyhound bus, leaving many passengers injured and two dead. The central issue in the case was who was at fault, Greyhound or the driver of the oncoming pickup truck.

---

[7] 128 S Ct at 2545.

[8] The best contemporary treatment is Stephen Yeazell, *From Medieval Group Litigation to the Modern Class Action* (1987). See also Robert G. Bone, *Personal and Impersonal Litigative Forms: Reconceiving the History of Adjudicative Representation,* 70 BU L Rev 213 (1990) (reviewing Yeazell, *From Medieval Group Litigation to the Modern Class Action*).

[9] 386 US 523 (1967).

The driver of the other vehicle had no assets to satisfy claims, save for an insurance policy worth $20,000, an amount clearly insufficient to satisfy the total claims should the driver indeed be culpable. Were the litigation limited to Greyhound and the oncoming driver, this would have been the most ordinary of tort suits. Liability would fall on one side or the other, or would be apportioned if that outcome were available under controlling state law.

In practical effect, whether Greyhound or the other driver was at fault would also control the outcome for all the passengers bringing claims because the question whether Greyhound bore liability would determine whether there would be any meaningful recovery. What the common law tort system could not provide was an organizing procedure to handle this question in the context of multiple claims, rather than a showdown between two parties. The procedural issue was joined when, seeking to limit its costs of defense, the driver's insurer, State Farm, deposited the $20,000 with a court in Oregon and sought to compel all claimants to seek an equitable distribution without a rush to the bank—precisely the role anticipated under interpleader. That proved relatively unproblematic since $20,000 would not go far if the insured were indeed liable and the liability of the insured was a common question for all potential claimants. The hard issue for the Court arose when Greyhound sought to achieve similar efficiencies by corralling all claims into the same forum—which would also have allowed for similar treatment of similarly situated passengers.

At some level of generalization, interpleader was perhaps the most suitable common law rule to use as a transition to mass claims. The premise of interpleader is that there are rivalrous claims to a fixed res and that a legally binding declaration of rights cannot be obtained without the participation of all possible claimants.[10] Interpleader allows the stakeholder to file suit against all potential claimants and compel a once-and-for-all declaration of rights as against the entire universe. While Greyhound was not operating with a fixed res, it would not have taken an extraordinary step to conceptualize the question of its liability *vel non* to be a common threshold that was collectively held by all the injured passengers, independent of the amount that any one passenger might be awarded if negli-

---

[10] The Court revisits the foundations of interpleader in *Ortiz v Fibreboard Corp.*, 527 US 815 (1999), in the context of a 23(b)(1) limited fund class action, what is in effect the plaintiffs' version of interpleader.

gence were proven. Put another way, either Greyhound was negligent or it was not. Nothing in the individual circumstances of
particular passengers or the particularized nature of the injuries they
suffered had any bearing on the liability determination. In turn,
that unifying question cried out for a consistent and dispositive
resolution.

But the Court could not find a mechanism to allow interpleader
without clear proof that there was a finite fund and that the sat-
isfaction of one claim necessarily compromised the claims of others.
In this early confrontation with mass harms, the Court recognized
both the need for procedural mechanisms to achieve finality and
the limitations of the procedures in the Court's toolbox:

> We recognize, of course, that our view of interpleader means
> that it cannot be used to solve all the vexing problems of mul-
> tiparty litigation arising out of a mass tort. But interpleader was
> never intended to perform such a function, to be an all-purpose
> "bill of peace." Had it been so intended, careful provision would
> necessarily have been made to insure that a party with little or
> no interest in the outcome of a complex controversy should not
> strip truly interested parties of substantial rights—such as the
> right to choose the forum in which to establish their claims,
> subject to generally applicable rules of jurisdiction, venue, service
> of process, removal, and change of venue.[11]

My initial claim is that the recent procedure cases are a reprise
of the central dilemma in *Tashire*. In order to recast the cases as
exemplars of the tension between collective claims and the indi-
vidualist presumptions of procedural rules, some attention is required to the exact issues presented in this Term's cases.

A. A REAL PARTY IN INTEREST

We begin with *Sprint*, a slight case that generated loud rum-
blings in a 5–4 split along the Court's familiar fissures. The underlying controversy arose from the requirement under the Telecommunications Act that long-distance phone carriers (the large
players in the field) compensate those who install and maintain
pay phones for the use of their equipment by consumers making
charge card calls or using 1-800 numbers.[12] Under federal law, the

---

[11] *Tashire*, 386 US at 535–36.
[12] See 47 USC § 226 (2000).

pay phone operators are supposed to be paid a fixed amount of less than $.50 for each such call,[13] at least in theory. But disputes frequently arise over these "dial-around" calls, and although the operators have a statutory right to sue for damages,[14] the reality is otherwise:

> Because litigation is expensive, because the evidentiary demands of a single suit are often great, and because the resulting monetary recovery is often small, many payphone operators assign their dial-around claims to billing and collection firms called "aggregators" so that, in effect, these aggregators can bring suit on their behalf.[15]

The collection firms described by the Court serve as agents for the pay phone operators, allowing them to spread the costs of enforcement over the entire group.[16] The aggregators bring suit in their own name seeking to recover the claims assigned to them, and charge a set fee for their services. When successful, the proceeds are then "reassigned" back to the operators. APCC Services is the market leader in this field, and the particular controversy that reached the Court concerned 1,400 different pay phone op-

---

[13] Telecommunications Act of 1996, Pub L No 104-104, 110 Stat 56 (1996). Congress directed the FCC to create a per call compensation plan for pay phone operators. From 1999 through 2004, the FCC set the rate at $.24 per call. Effective September 27, 2004, the FCC increased the rate to $.494, which is still in effect today. 47 CFR 64.1300(d) (1999). For the 2004 increase in rates, see 71 Fed Reg 3014 (Jan 19, 2006).

[14] *Global Crossing Telecommunications, Inc. v Metrophones Telecommunications, Inc.*, 127 S Ct 1513 (2007) (reaffirming the private right of action under the Communications Act of 1934).

[15] 128 S Ct at 2534.

[16] Among the original plaintiffs in the case, APCC Services is the largest aggregation service for collecting dial-around compensation for what are known in the trade as independent pay phone service providers (PSPs). Companies like APCC Services seek payment for PSPs from exchange carriers that connect calls made from pay phones. Complaint at 2–7, *Sprint*, 128 S Ct 2531 (2008) (No 1:99-CV-00696-ESH). The aggregators send claims to between 500 and 800 exchange carriers every quarter on behalf of the PSPs. Due to the large number of potential exchange carriers, the PSPs would be effectively prevented from collecting from any but the largest carriers due to the costs of sending and monitoring such a large number of invoices. For their service, the aggregators are paid a fee based on the number of pay phones and telephone lines operated by a given PSP. This general payment framework extends to situations in which the aggregator is forced to litigate repayment from the carriers. As part of the contractual services, all PSPs are required to make regular payments to a litigation fund should any one of them be forced to take their claims to court—in effect, a form of common pool litigation insurance. Telephone interview by Laura Miller with Ruth Jaeger, President and General Manager, APCC Services (Aug 27, 2008). As part of the assignment agreement between the aggregators and PSPs, all recovered damages (both litigated and nonlitigated) from the exchange carriers are turned directly over to the PSPs. 128 S Ct at 2535.

erators who had assigned their interests to APCC Services for joint collection.

The technical issue dividing the Court is well recognized as flowing from the need for an actual case or controversy: "a plaintiff's alleged injury must be an invasion of a concrete and particularized legally protected interest."[17] This is the constitutional reiteration of the long-standing prohibition on asserting claims of others, known as the prohibition on *jus tertii* claims.[18] The question was whether the assignment of rights with the complete reverter of proceeds would satisfy the legal interest required for standing on the part of the aggregators. Could a party whose only interest is the assignment of a chose in action bring suit in its own name, or would the American courts, following Blackstone, overlook the distinction between assignor and assignee as a "nicety . . . now disregarded"?[19]

At one level, the entire dispute turns on an extremely formal account of the history of assignment of claims. The Court divided on how the English and American common law treated such assignments for purposes of creating a triable controversy. (The Court also divided, stunningly, on the correct interpretation of a forty-year-old student law review comment's account of that history,[20] suggesting that something was askew with the Court's jurisprudential compass.) For the majority, there was no harm in allowing the assignee to pursue the collective claims because they were well grounded in established law and the defendant could not claim prejudice. Although such claims could have been brought as a class action, as Sprint advocated, the Court reasoned that the pay phone operators should not "be denied standing simply because they chose one aggregation method over another."[21] By contrast, the dissenters saw the severability of the right to sue

[17] *McConnell v FEC*, 540 US 93, 227 (2003).

[18] *Warth v Seldin*, 422 US 490, 499 (1975) (party "must assert his own legal rights and interests, and cannot rest his claim to relief on the legal rights or interests of third parties").

[19] *Sprint*, 128 S Ct at 2537, quoting William M. Blackstone, 2 *Commentaries* *442.

[20] Compare 128 S Ct at 2540 (Justice Breyer for the majority reading the Comment to provide for the assignability of the right to sue) with id at 2556 (Chief Justice Roberts invoking Comment for uncertainty over same issue). The dispute is over whether a majority or minority of jurisdictions in the United States allowed such assignees to file suit in 1967, as discussed in Michael Ferguson, Comment, *The Real Party in Interest Rule Revitalized: Recognizing Defendant's Interest in the Determination of Proper Parties Plaintiff*, 55 Cal L Rev 1452, 1475 (1967).

[21] 128 S Ct at 2545.

from the ultimate recovery as creating a sort of derivatives market for legal claims unmoored from traditional standing requirements.[22]

Buried in this dispute is the unexplored legacy of formal constraints on the legal market that compel such awkward assignments then reassignments. The relation between the pay phone operators and APCC Services is a classic principal-agent relation, with all the complex incentives at play that normally characterize such relations. In dissent, Chief Justice Roberts appeared to invite a simple solution to the agent standing question—at least on a going-forward basis. Were APCC Services simply to reserve a contingent interest in the outcome of the case, the real party in interest problem would be solved. Perhaps more interesting than the formalism of the legal resolution is the question whether such an arrangement would not also better align the principal-agent incentives that are at stake. Any assignment of interest to a claims collector who will get paid regardless whether the ultimate collections are successful or only partially successful, or not successful at all, is an invitation for an agent not to take the interests of the principal fully to heart.

Here again it is the formalism of the legal system that may be compelling this apparently suboptimal result. In order to be eligible for assignment of a contingent interest, a firm such as APCC Services would have to be a *law firm*. Otherwise, a private firm funding someone else's litigation and reserving an interest in the outcome could run afoul of traditional common law prohibitions on maintenance and champerty,[23] which bar nonlitigants from funding litigation in exchange for an equity stake in the outcome.[24]

---

[22] Id at 2551 (Roberts, CJ, dissenting).

[23] APCC Services is headquartered and incorporated in Virginia. The Virginia Supreme Court has defined champerty as "a bargain with the plaintiff or defendant in a suit for a portion of the land or other matter sued for in case of a successful termination of the suit, which the champertor undertakes to carry on at his own expense." *Ventro v Clinchfield Coal Corp.*, 199 Va 943, 953 (1958). There are very few exceptions to this rule, the one notable one being the representation of indigent parties. *NAACP v Harrison*, 202 Va 142, 162 (1960) ("The law has always recognized the right of one to assist the poor in commencing or further prosecuting legal proceedings. To deny this right would be oppressive and enable the other party, if his means so permits, an advantage over one with little means. Aiding the indigent is one of the generally recognized exceptions to the law of maintenance.").

[24] For a thoughtful discussion of the market-constricting effects of these rules, see Jonathan T. Molot, *A Market in Litigation Claims: A Market Alternative to Judicial Settlement Efforts* (draft on file with author).

Conceivably, a firm such as APCC Services could have a working relationship with a law firm able to undertake contingent representation, but at a cost to its business model. Even having a lawyer handle the exchange would be insufficient if any nonlawyers were stakeholders in APCC Services; sharing fees with nonlawyers would likely violate yet another of the market-constricting rules of the legal profession.[25] Finally, were APCC Services to try formally to file suit in the name of each claimant, there would be high transaction cost barriers in the form of either having to pay a filing fee for each claim or having to subject the suit to the procedural rigors of class certification. Bob Dylan is entirely correct, as per Chief Justice Roberts, about having nothing to lose—but it was the pay phone operators, whose rights were worthless on their own, who had nothing absent some collective enterprise.

Viewed in this light, the contractual arrangement devised by APCC Services is a privately structured way of overcoming the barriers to prosecuting small-value claims that independently do not justify the cost of litigation. In this sense, Sprint was entirely correct that the APCC Services arrangement was structured in rejection of—or at least as a substitute for—the formal aggregative procedures available under the Federal Rules.[26] This, however, begs the question why we should prefer what is in effect a public subsidy of aggregation, the class action,[27] to a mechanism that the market creates. In the context of repeat players, such as the com-

---

[25] Model Rules of Professional Conduct, Rule 5.4.

[26] There is more than a touch of irony in Sprint expressing its profound attachment to the protections afforded (to others, no less) by formal class action rules. Sprint's standard-form consumer contract for its long-distance services provides that its customers must agree to the following: "To the extent allowed by law, we each waive any right to pursue disputes on a classwide basis; that is, to either join a claim with the claim of any other person or entity, or assert a claim in a representative capacity on behalf of anyone else in any lawsuit, arbitration or other proceeding." Reproduced at http://www.negotiationlawblog.com/2007/07/articles/arbitration/then-fine-print-sprints-arbitration-clause/. This is part of the standard-form arbitration agreements designed to make many types of claims unenforceable. For a discussion of the controversies over the enforceability of these contracts in the consumer context, see Samuel Issacharoff and Erin F. Delaney, *Credit Card Accountability*, 73 U Chi L Rev 157, 170–77 (2006). For discussion of similar issues in the employment context, see Cynthia L. Estlund, *Between Rights and Contract: Arbitration Agreements and Non-Compete Covenants as a Hybrid Form of Employment Law*, 155 U Pa L Rev 379, 426–30 (2006).

[27] See generally Judith Resnik, *Money Matters: Judicial Market Interventions Creating Subsidies and Awarding Fees and Costs in Individual and Aggregate Litigation*, 148 U Pa L Rev 2119, 2144–59 (2000) (arguing that rulemakers liberalized the class action rule in order to enable disadvantaged litigants to pool resources).

mercial interests[28] whose claims are at stake here, there should be a presumption in favor of private ordering.[29] The exacting safeguards of the class action, a form of representation bereft of agreed-upon contractual relation between principals and agent, is neither required nor desirable in the context of informed relations between market actors.

The dissent's formalism would have frustrated a consensual market response to the emergence of commonly held interests among a group of private claimants. Without a mechanism to overcome the transactional barriers to individual suit, the assertion of rights (including the express statutory conferral of rights in the Cable Act) is really no more than just, well, blowing in the wind—to turn one last time to the persuasive authority of Bob Dylan.

B. REQUIRED PARTIES

Sprint presents only one of the reasons for which litigation might be incomplete without the inclusion of others. For the pay phone operators, the inability to jointly administer and prosecute their claims would have meant the inability to overcome the transactional bars to being able to recover contested funds. The insufficiency of the stakes is one of the obstacles that multiple litigants might face in presenting legally recognized claims. *Republic of the Philippines v Pimentel* involved another obstacle: the need for complete adjudication of the interests of other litigants in order to perfect a claim.

At issue in *Pimentel* was a judgment obtained by a class made up of thousands of human rights victims of the Marcos regime in the Philippines. In one of the more far-reaching uses of aggregate procedures, a federal district court in Hawaii had allowed 9,539 Philippine victims in the United States to present their claims to a jury through a statistical sampling of abuses, try the sample cases, then extrapolate the judgments to the class as a whole.[30] Obtaining

---

[28] For a defense of the presumption that contracts among repeat-play commercial actors should be entitled to great deference, see Alan Schwartz and Robert E. Scott, *Contract Theory and the Limits of Contract Law*, 113 Yale L J 541 (2003).

[29] For a related discussion of the relation between formal and informal methods of aggregations, see Richard A. Nagareda, *Class Actions in the Administrative State: Kalven and Rosenfield Revisited*, 75 U Chi L Rev 603, 631 (2008).

[30] The underlying *Pimentel* class action remains the only extrapolated judgment upheld on appeal. See *Hilao v Estate of Marcos*, 103 F3d 767 (9th Cir 1996). *Hilao* was a suit filed under the Alien Tort Statute, which provides aliens with a federal cause of action for torts

a judgment was one matter; finding the Marcos assets and collecting was another. There was, however, a brokerage account at Merrill Lynch in the United States, with funds belonging to Arelma, S.A., a Panamanian company incorporated by President Marcos in 1972. The $35 million in the account could be attached to compensate the class of human rights victims—assuming ownership by the Marcos estate could be established.[31]

Unfortunately for the class, the Marcos holdings were subject to competing claims. When Marcos finally fled the Philippines in 1986, a commission was established to recover property looted from the state by the former president.[32] That commission in 1991 sought a declaration from the Sandiganbayan, a special public corruption court in the Philippines, that all Marcos assets were the product of theft and should default to the state; that litigation remains unresolved in the Philippines. As part of the effort to recover looted assets, the commission and the Republic of the Philippines sought to have Merrill Lynch transfer the Arelma assets to an escrow account in the Philippines for final disposition. Merrill Lynch refused and sought guidance from the federal court with jurisdiction over the class action as to what to do with the competing claims to the assets.

The district court instructed Merrill Lynch to file an interpleader action, in effect forcing all parties to litigate their entitlement to the disputed assets in the District of Hawaii. As a practical matter, this meant that the district court took it upon itself to resolve the claims of the Philippine government and the Philippine commission for the return of the Marcos plunder.[33]

---

committed in violation of customary international law. *Hilao*, 103 F3d at 772; see also *Sosa v Alvarez-Machain*, 542 US 692, 724 (2004). The degree of judicial creativity available in ATS suits, see id at 738 (citing "residual common law discretion"), may have facilitated the use of innovative sampling techniques, avoiding the objection that such techniques alter the underlying substantive state tort law. See *Cimino v Raymark Industries, Inc.*, 151 F3d 297, 319 (5th Cir 1998).

[31] 128 S Ct at 2185.

[32] A recurring question in alien tort claims actions has been whether a remedy offered by the foreign nation at issue should preclude a federal suit in the United States from going forward. See *Khulumani v Barclay Nat'l Bank Ltd.*, 504 F3d 254, 259 (2d Cir 2007); id at 295–301 (opinion of Korman, J).

[33] The judge in question, Judge Manuel Real of the Central District of California who was sitting by designation in Hawaii, is not a stranger to accusations of exceeding his authority. His trial manner has drawn a significant amount of critical commentary. See, for example, *U.S. v Hall*, 271 Fed Appx 559 (9th Cir 2008) ("the catalog of inappropriate behavior by the trial court is long, so we merely summarize it here"). Most noteworthy, the Ninth Circuit has ordered plenary review of dozens of his old cases for evidence of

That in turn prompted the Philippine governmental interests to assert sovereign immunity, because under the rules of interpleader they would be an involuntary defendant in an American proceeding. Undeterred, the trial court decided that the action could proceed nonetheless as a claim by the Pimentel class because, according to the court, the Philippine claims against the estate were marginal and the Merrill Lynch assets were unaffected by any foreign state claims. As against the argument that the Philippine government entities were indispensable participants over whom the district court could not assert jurisdiction, the court found that there was no risk of harm because there were no valid claims to the funds that would be compromised.

As a result, the peculiar combination of interpleader and sovereign immunity implicated Rule 19, an oddly constructed rule that gives federal courts the power to dismiss or equitably limit the range of lawsuits because of their practical effects on either parties (realistically, the defendant) or—more significantly—those outside the litigation altogether. Together with Rule 24 (governing intervention by nonparties), Rule 19 marks a significant departure from the common law premise that litigation is a contained world of dispute resolution between two private individuals.[34] Both Rules 19 and 24 speak of interests that are implicated by a case, even though the formal categories of finality and preclusion normally would not extend beyond the actual parties to a case. Intervention permits outsiders to a dispute to demand a seat at the table, even over the objection of the parties to the case. Rule 19 goes further and provides a mechanism for courts to refuse to adjudicate a well-

---

outcome-determinative judicial misconduct. Terry Carter, *Real Trouble*, ABA J (Sept 2008), available at http://www.abajournal.com/magazine/real_trouble/.

[34] In an important article to which I shall return, Professor Abram Chayes well captures the essence of the common law dispute-resolution model:

  (a) The lawsuit is bipolar—it concerns two separate and easily identifiable parties;
  (b) The lawsuit is retrospective—it addresses completed events;
  (c) The right asserted and the remedy sought are interdependent—the latter flows from the former;
  (d) The lawsuit concerns a self-contained episode—the impact of the judgment is confined to the parties to the litigation; and
  (e) The process is party-initiated and party-controlled—the issues and facts in the case are developed by the parties and presented by them or their attorneys to the final arbiter.

Abram Chayes, *The Role of the Judge in Public Law Litigation*, 89 Harv L Rev 1281, 1282–83 (1976).

pleaded dispute because of the unsustainability of the boundaries defined by the case.

So far, so good. Unfortunately, Rule 19's attempt to bring common law concepts of interested parties into alignment with the demands of modern litigation quickly runs into difficulty, beginning with its odd structure and clumsy language. Rule 19(a) identifies persons to be joined if feasible, characterizing them as necessary if either complete relief cannot be granted in their absence or if the practical effect of an adjudication would be to implicate their rights or interests. Rule 19(a) identifies some, but not all, of the situations in which the reach of a case goes beyond the formal parties.

Thus, for example, Rule 19(a)(1)(A) provides that a party would be required if "in that person's absence, a court cannot accord complete relief among existing parties . . . ." This definition of a required party would not allow the expansion of any suit for money damages against a solvent defendant. Even if there would be tremendous efficiencies in resolving related claims once and for all, it is difficult to claim that complete relief within the suit as presented may not be afforded among the existing parties. Similarly, Rule 19(a)(1)(B)(ii) speaks of the risk of inconsistent obligations as requiring that additional parties be added. But multiple trials over the same events do not produce inconsistent obligations even if the jury determinations diverge, unless the defendant is obligated to comply with an impossible-to-meet uniform course of conduct. In any action for damages, a defendant could pay a winning plaintiff while avoiding payment to a losing plaintiff and incur no obligations that could not be met simultaneously. To return to the example of the bus accident from *Tashire*, complete relief may be afforded to all parties in any one-on-one part of the litigation, even if repeat adjudications found Greyhound sometimes negligent and sometimes not negligent for the exact same conduct. Indeed, except in cases of indivisible remedies like the classic sorts of injunctions—cases that might well trigger mandatory class-action treatment—the impracticability of complete relief or the compromise of the rights of nonparties is rarely triggered.

As a result, the Rule 19 inquiry usually ends without any impact on the case because only if the Rule 19(a) hurdle is crossed are the operational consequences of the Rule engaged. This takes the form of Rule 19(b), which allows a defendant to seek dismissal when a court is unable to join a needed party, as, for example, when the court would not have jurisdiction over the additional party. Rule 19(b) reads as a familiar balancing test that asks about the amount of prejudice to all parties if the case does or does not go forward, the systemic interests in ensuring that some forum is available to provide a remedy, and the equitable tools that the court might use to protect the interests of all affected parties.

The structure of the Rule puts courts in the unfamiliar posture of having to abide by a highly formal assessment of the parties whose joinder might be necessary, rather than proceeding immediately to a more conventional balancing of interests to manage equitably the litigation process.[35] The Supreme Court captured the difficulty of the inquiry: "To say that a court 'must' dismiss in the absence of an indispensable party and that it 'cannot proceed' without him puts the matter the wrong way around: a court does not know whether a particular person is 'indispensable' until it had examined the situation to determine whether it can proceed without him."[36] That difficulty is in turn compounded by the language of the Rule itself. Although Rule 19(a) referred to "necessary" parties, Rule 19(b) concerned "indispensible" parties, yielding the result that "the decision to proceed is a decision that the absent person is merely 'necessary' while the decision to dismiss is a decision that he is 'indispensable.'"[37] Little changed with the 2007 "stylistic" revisions to the Federal Rules, which tried to paper over the problem by substituting the uniform term "required." Now the Rule allows that persons "required" for purposes of Rule 19(a) "may turn out not to be required for the action to proceed after all" under Rule 19(b).[38]

Because Rule 19 neither expands the jurisdictional reach of courts nor gives parties potentially affected by litigation a right

---

[35] This is not a uniformly held assessment of the Rule. Wright and Miller, for example, are much more impressed with the post-1966 reforms that allowed a more "orderly procedure" by which courts can make a more limited initial inquiry under Rule 19(a). Charles Alan Wright, Arthur R. Miller, and Mary Kay Kane, 7 *Federal Practice and Procedure* § 1604 (2001). For the common law background of Rule 19, see Geoffrey C. Hazard, Jr., *Indispensable Party: The Historical Origin of a Procedural Phantom*, 61 Colum L Rev 1254, 1271 (1961) (tracing rules in equity that parties with an interest be joined if possible).

[36] *Provident Bank*, 390 US 102, 119 (1968).

[37] Id at 118.

[38] *Pimentel*, 128 S Ct at 2189.

to restructure the case, it does not realize its ambition of ensuring that the full range of disputed rights are adjudicated. As reflected in *Pimentel*, Rule 19 cannot provide the organizational mechanism to achieve "optimal aggregation,"[39] leaving its use in the hands of parties who strategically wish to force a suit to be dismissed rather than efficiently join all necessary parties.[40] The result is that there is limited force to this innovative procedure, despite Rule 19(b)'s grant of broad equitable power to courts to shape cases to align all necessary parties, or even to dismiss if the case could better be handled in another court. Even these equitable powers are triggered by the constricted ability to get to Rule 19(b) through the required parties provision of 19(a).

Pimentel presented the relatively unusual circumstance where the Rule 19(a) threshold could be met. The district court in Hawaii was set to decide competing claims to a limited fund which could have practical consequences for the Philippine entities that could not be made parties to the suit. This enabled the Supreme Court to find that the district court had been insufficiently attentive to the importance of the sovereign interest of the Philippines in not having its claimed governmental assets disposed of by an American proceeding.[41] Because of the narrow circumstance of sovereign immunity presented, Rule 19 could be held to dictate dismissal for failure to join a required party.

Of more concern here, however, is the inability of Rule 19, or any other existing procedure, to resolve the claim of the Pimentel class to the Merrill Lynch assets. The Supreme Court reversed the courts below for conceiving the litigation as an effort to satisfy the claims of the Pimentel class, rather than viewing the object of Rule 19 as "the public stake in settling disputes by wholes, whenever possible."[42] This use of Rule 19 allows only the termination of well-pleaded cases because of third-party effects. Because neither interpleader nor Rule 19 could provide the organizing basis for complete resolution of all the disputed claims

---

[39] Jay Tidmarsh and Roger H. Transgrud, *Complex Litigation: Problems in Advanced Civil Procedure* 95 (2002).

[40] Id.

[41] "The Republic and the Commission have a unique interest in resolving the ownership of or claims to the Arelma assets and in determining if, and how, the assets should be used to compensate those persons who suffered grievous injury under Marcos." 128 S Ct at 2190.

[42] Id at 2193, quoting *Provident Bank*, 390 US at 111.

against the Marcos estate, the alternative was dismissal of the entire action. At best, the class is left to wait until sufficient time has passed for an American court to determine that the Philippine interest in the Arelma assets had been abandoned. Given that the Sandiganbayan had already sat on the claims for seventeen years, the prospect of relief does not seem imminent.

C. WHO'S YOUR WINGMAN?

Despite the easy unanimity of the Court's decision, *Taylor v Sturgell* may well be the most troubling of these cases. The underlying facts involve the plans for an F-45 airplane, a model apparently sought out by some vintage airplane enthusiasts. Although the plans were held by the FAA, the agency refused to release them pursuant to an exemption in FOIA for trade secrets. For some undisclosed reason, the manufacturer, Fairchild, sought to protect its ongoing interests in this long-retired, fixed-wing, single-engine plane. That prompted suit by Greg Herrick, a member of the Antique Aircraft Association (AAA), who wanted to restore his private F-45 to its original condition. Herrick lost in the Tenth Circuit, which upheld the application of the trade secrets exemption under FOIA.[43]

Shortly after Herrick lost his case on appeal, his friend Brent Taylor retained the same lawyer to file the same request, only this time in District Court in D.C. Not only was the case filed by the same lawyer, using documents obtained by Herrick in discovery in his case, but Taylor and Herrick were planning to work on an F-45 restoration together. Moreover, Taylor was the executive director of the AAA, although there was no evidence that he had directly participated in Herrick's litigation. In short, Taylor sought to press the exact same claim for the same information based on the same legal theory pursued by the same lawyer in order to restore what may have been the same aircraft.

For the D.C. Circuit, this view of FOIA as a chance to ply the different courts of appeals looking for a favorable ruling was too much of a good thing. In a provocative opinion by Judge Douglas Ginsburg, the court found that Taylor could be bound by his "virtual representation" by Herrick in the prior litigation, even if Herrick had evinced no desire to represent anyone but himself.

---

[43] *Herrick v Garvey*, 298 F3d 1184 (10th Cir 2002).

By contrast to *Sprint*, the effect of the Ginsburg opinion would have been to impose a class-wide obligation upon the first party to file suit over a particular claim or issue, without any of the corresponding protections found in the formal processes of class certification.

Despite the "deep-rooted historic tradition that everyone should have his own day in court" and the prohibition on binding non-parties to a judgment in which they did not participate,[44] the D.C. Circuit found that under exceptional circumstances that tradition could yield to other considerations. Ginsburg explained that courts also have an obligation to promote judicial efficiency, protect defendants from repetitive litigation, and ensure consistency of results across similar cases.[45] So long as there was identity of interests across the cases and so long as the first litigant provided adequate representation, there was no reason to relitigate the claims if one of three additional factors were met: (*a*) a close relationship between the parties, (*b*) substantial participation by one party in the other's case, or (*c*) tactical maneuvering to avoid being bound by the first decision.[46] These factors had previously enabled courts to expand the range of preclusion from its narrow common law legacy,[47] but Ginsburg took this logic over the divide to adversely bind nonparties to the outcome of a judgment obtained in their absence. In Ginsburg's view, the close relationship between Taylor and Herrick was in itself sufficient to bind Taylor to the outcome of the adverse ruling by the Tenth Circuit.

The loose test devised by the D.C. Circuit could not stand.[48] The effect would have been to transform Herrick post facto into the representative for a class of potential claimants, each bound to the outcome of his litigation without notice or the ability to participate. Ginsburg's inquiry into the identity of interests and the adequacy of representation represent an informal attempt to recreate the pre-

---

[44] *Richards v Jefferson County*, 517 US 793, 798 (1996). See also *Martin v Wilks*, 490 US 755, 761 (1989).

[45] *Taylor v Blakey*, 490 F3d 965, 971–72 (DC Cir 2007).

[46] Id.

[47] Most notably, these were some of the same considerations that allowed the use of nonmutual issue preclusion. See *Blonder-Tongue Laboratories, Inc. v University of Illinois Foundation*, 402 US 313, 320–27 (1971); *Parklane Hosiery Co. v Shore*, 439 US 322, 335–37 (1979).

[48] Although I find the case intriguing, I joined an amicus brief of civil procedure and complex litigation professors urging reversal.

conditions for class certification under Rule 23(a). Similarly, turning preclusion on the "close relationship" between the parties is a poor substitute for the specifications on the relationship among class members under the three provisions of Rule 23(b). Most critically, however, the history of modern class action law, from *Hansberry v Lee*[49] forward, is one of greater procedural protections before rights may be terminated without direct participation. A loose standard of creating a representative action after the conclusion of litigation appeared a rash act of judicial frustration, confirming the insight from the leading treatise on procedure: "Impatience with repetitive litigation of common issues . . . has enticed some courts to rely on virtual representation in circumstances that go beyond anything that is easily justified. . . ."[50]

For the Supreme Court, the relaxed transformation of individual suits into representative actions violated core principles of litigant autonomy. Relying on an important decision by Judge Diane Wood of the Seventh Circuit, the Court ruled that "[a]n expansive doctrine of virtual representation . . . would 'recogniz[e], in effect, a common law kind of class action.'"[51] Justice Ruth Bader Ginsburg invoked two cases, *South Central Bell Telephone Co. v Alabama*[52] and *Richards v Jefferson County*,[53] in which the Court had rejected attempts by Alabama state courts to hold one group of taxpayers to the litigated position of another group of unsuccessful tax litigants, again in the absence of a formally certified class action. Further, as the Court established in *Martin v Wilks*,[54] a case involving the third-party effects of a settlement of employment discrimination claims by black firefighters against the City of Birmingham, even a class action will not have preclusive effects beyond the actual members of the class.[55] The easy holding in *Taylor* followed:

[V]irtual representation would authorize preclusion based on

---

[49] 311 US 32 (1940).

[50] 18A, Wright, Miller, and [Cooper], *Federal Practice and Procedure* 512–13 (2d ed 2002).

[51] 128 S Ct at 2176, quoting *Tice v American Airlines, Inc.*, 162 F3d 966, 972 (7th Cir 1998).

[52] 526 US 160 (1999).

[53] 517 US 793 (1996).

[54] 490 US 755 (1989).

[55] For an early defense of the outcome in *Martin*, see Samuel Issacharoff, *When Substance Mandates Procedure: Martin v Wilks and the Rights of Vested Incumbents in Civil Rights Consent Decrees*, 77 Cornell L Rev 189 (1992).

identity of interest and some kind of relationship between parties and nonparties, shorn of the procedural protections prescribed in *Hansberry, Richards,* and Rule 23. These protections, grounded in due process, could be circumvented were we to approve a virtual representation doctrine that allowed courts to "create *de facto* class actions at will."[56]

For all the lack of suspense in the result, the core problem in *Taylor* remains unresolved. At the end of the day, Taylor and Herrick were pressing the exact same claim, one that turned on the authority of the FAA and Fairchild to invoke a trade secrets exception to a statute, and not on any particularized inquiry about who the plaintiff happened to be. In *Martin v Wilks,* for example, the asserted injury to the white firefighters challenging a civil rights consent decree was a presumptive claim to the jobs in question. Similarly, if we go back to *Hansberry v Lee,* a case challenging racially restrictive housing covenants in Chicago, the black plaintiffs were seeking to move into a specific home and the issue was whether they were foreclosed from challenging the covenants by virtue of a prior lawsuit to which they were not a party.

What sets apart the earlier cases is not that there were similar claims raised by others, but that the right being asserted against the FAA by Herrick and Taylor was vested in undifferentiated fashion to the entire citizenry by a federal commitment to freedom of information. Taylor and Herrick could make no argument about an individual entitlement, and could not claim they were denied something in their personal capacity. Viewed this way, Taylor and Herrick have generalized grievances that put them perilously close to the taxpayers who repeatedly find themselves without standing when seeking to challenge government conduct.[57] While the private right of action in FOIA removes the standing challenge, it does not to address the undifferentiated nature of the claim. As the FAA argued, because "the duty to disclose under FOIA is owed to the public generally," a broader conception of preclusion should be available in public law cases.[58] Or, put another way, Taylor and Herrick were already in effect litigating for the entire public—but only if either of them won. Once one of them prevailed, the plans

---

[56] 128 S Ct at 2176, quoting *Tice,* 162 F3d at 973.

[57] For the most recent discussion of the taxpayer standing cases, see *Hein v Freedom from Religion Foundation, Inc.,* 127 S Ct 2553, 2563 (2007).

[58] Quoted at 128 S Ct at 2177.

would be in the public domain,[59] and available to all. The question is whether there is any mechanism by which estoppel could run in both directions, resolving the matter regardless of who prevailed.

Rather than reaffirm the application of settled rules of procedure, *Taylor* again exposed the inability of modern procedure to capture litigation over claims that exist only in the aggregate. *Herrick* could have been filed as a class action for binding class-wide relief under Rule 23(b)(2), but as I shall argue in the next section, there was no incentive to do so. Either Herrick individually was going to get the plans or he was not; he had no incentive to expand the scope of his litigation, assume obligations to others, and increase the cost of prosecuting the claim by bringing a class action that would get him no more return on his investment. Perhaps, as in *Pimentel*, more use could have been made of an interpleader action by the FAA, arguing in effect that the claims for the F-45 plans were a common res needing unitary adjudication. But, here again, the potential interpleader defendants would have been the entire American population, requiring notice and service across the country—a clearly ludicrous undertaking. At the end of the day, as against the specter of limitless claims holders, the Court could only quote from David Shapiro to the effect that "the human tendency not to waste money will deter the bringing of suits based on claims or issues that have already been adversely determined against others."[60] Maybe, maybe not.

Indeed, perhaps because the role of law is often to restrain "the human tendency," the Court did allow an alternative way of binding Herrick. Turning to the law of agency, the Court remanded for further examination of the question whether Taylor was acting as Herrick's de facto agent. Without a clear doctrine to determine the preclusive boundaries of public law claims, the Court licensed an inquiry into the relationship between Herrick and Taylor, allowing the FAA to defend against subsequent lawsuits on the basis of the

---

[59] The Court rejected the force of this point, in what appears to me a disingenuous distinction: "a successful FOIA action results in a grant of relief to the individual plaintiff, not a decree benefiting the public at large." 128 S Ct at 2177. As a formal matter, the Court is right. The government is not bound by issue preclusion and not even a determination in one Circuit binds the government in other courts outside that Circuit. *U.S. v Mendoza*, 464 U S 154 (1984). Nonetheless, once released through FOIA, neither the government nor Fairchild would any longer have exclusive control of the F-45 design specifications.

[60] 128 S Ct at 2178, quoting David Shapiro, *Civil Procedure: Preclusion in Civil Actions* 97 (2001).

personal contacts between successive litigants. The boundaries of this imprecise inquiry into the relationship of the litigants (how many meetings? dinner? drinks? discuss F-45s or airplane plans?) are potentially as unseemly as they are irrelevant to the underlying issue. Preclusion on the basis of who your friends are cannot be sound doctrine.

II. THE COSTS OF PROCEDURE

Some thirty years ago, Professor Abram Chayes set out to define a domain of public law litigation.[61] Chayes tried to delineate the role of courts in structural challenges to the administration of government by contrasting public law claims to the presumptions of a legal system founded primarily on common law disputes. For Chayes, the critical feature of a common law litigation was that it emerged from the autonomous conduct of the parties to the dispute. This was reflected both in the fact that the decision to litigate or settle was party initiated and party controlled, and that the boundaries of the dispute were self-contained. This last insight was critical because it meant that the impact of any judgment was confined to the parties themselves. As a descriptive matter, it is unclear that the presumed lack of effects of a judgment beyond the actual litigants can truly be the case in any system based on the precedential value of an evolving common law. Nonetheless, the general contours of private versus public law were well set out.

The emergence of a defined universe of public law litigation laid the foundation for the alteration of constitutional procedure that began with the Warren Court and has continued to this day. Judicial scrutiny of administrative practices led to the reemergence of a discrete procedural due process case law. In its initial incarnation in the cases leading up to *Goldberg v Kelly*,[62] the process constraints of notice and a hearing and the right to counsel were invoked to structure the conduct of the state in a way that made it amenable to judicial oversight. Subsequent cases, most notably *Mathews v Eldridge*,[63] refined the categorical commands of the early process cases to apportion procedural protections according to the impor-

---

[61] Chayes, 89 Harv L Rev 1281 (cited in note 34).

[62] 397 US 254 (1970).

[63] 424 US 319 (1976). As cogently expressed by Judge Posner, "[t]he less that is at stake, . . . the less process is due." *Van Harken v City of Chicago*, 103 F3d 1346, 1353 (1997).

tance of the claimed rights at stake. Further procedural refinements relaxed barriers to intervention[64] or even standing[65] in such cases, and seemed to welcome the multifaceted role that courts had to play in cases involving institutional conditions, constitutional rights, or voting arrangements—to give just a brief account of the deeper reaches of judicial superintendence of core structural arrangements of our society.[66]

As mass harm cases have come to assume a more central role in the modern litigation landscape, some of the bright-line divisions between the role of courts in private and public law have been eroded. The emergence of multidistrict coordination and the general rise of "managerial judging"[67] have forced courts increasingly to view even common law claims through the prism of their potential multiparty effects. In turn, the question was joined whether mass torts could be fitted within Chayes's model of public law disputes, and whether the individual, autonomous claims of the common law could survive translation to mass society.[68] If the defining feature of public law was its "polycentric" quality, reaching well beyond the particular litigants who happened to appear in court, then mass harms even as simple as the Greyhound bus accident in *Tashire* seemed to present a similar reach beyond the presumed bipolarity of the common law.

---

[64] See Carl Tobias, *Standing to Intervene*, 1991 Wis L Rev 415.

[65] *Northeastern Fla. Chapter, Associated Gen. Contractors of America v Jacksonville*, 508 US 656 (1993).

[66] For the emergence of the jurisprudence of the administrative state, see Richard B. Stewart, *The Reformation of American Administrative Law*, 88 Harv L Rev 1669 (1975).

[67] Judith Resnik, *Managerial Judges*, 96 Harv L Rev 374 (1982). The move to administration and settlement of disputes rather than the presumption of trials is confirmed in the 1983 amendments to the Federal Rules of Civil Procedure, Arthur R. Miller, *The August 1983 Amendments to the Federal Rules of Civil Procedure* 21 (Federal Judicial Center, 1984), and the subsequent marked decline in civil trials. Arthur R. Miller, *The Pretrial Rush to Judgment: Are the "Litigation Explosion," "Liability Crisis," and Efficiency Cliches Eroding Our Day in Court and Jury Trial Commitments?* 78 NYU L Rev 982 (2003). For an overview of the increased managerial conception of the role of courts, see Samuel Issacharoff, *Civil Procedure* (2d ed 2008), chap 8.

[68] See David Rosenberg, *The Causal Connection in Mass Exposure Cases: A "Public Law" Vision of the Tort System*, 97 Harv L Rev 851 (1984); Jack B. Weinstein, *Individual Justice in Mass Tort Litigation: The Effect of Class Actions, Consolidations, and Other Multiparty Devices* 41 (1995); Howard M. Erichson, *Mass Tort Litigation and Inquisitorial Justice*, 87 Georgetown L J 1983, 1985 (1999); Peter Schuck, *Mass Torts: An Institutional Evolutionist Perspective*, 80 Cornell L Rev 941 (1995). For a recasting of this debate to focus on the role of private counsel as private attorney general, see William B. Rubenstein, *On What a "Private Attorney General" Is—and Why It Matters*, 57 Vand L Rev 2129 (2004). For a synthetic overview of this field, see Richard Nagareda, *Mass Torts in a World of Settlement* (2007).

Easy recourse to labels and categories can obscure the core insight that originally led to the analogy. Following Chayes, there was a temptation to dispute how well the analogy to public law really worked and what happened when private stakeholders rather than the state were the object of scrutiny.[69] Notwithstanding the definitional disputes, the issue is not really whether diffuse common law disputes are fully a form of public law, but rather what do to about the manifestly public dimension of such private law disputes. Undoubtedly, a case like *Taylor* loses the characteristic feel of private law because the rights at stake are an artifact of a statutory commitment to governmental accountability to the citizenry at large. But in most mass harm cases, it is not so much that the underlying claims are public, but rather that the defining private law conditions of autonomy and self-containment cannot be met. Instead, cases such as *Sprint* and *Pimentel* assume the form of classic private law contract or tort claims under the conditions of mass society, even allowing for the extraordinary international dimension of the claims at issue in *Pimentel*.

Viewed from this perspective, two final observations emerge. The first is the striking parallel between the actual form of the disputes in the three Supreme Court cases from this past Term and the modern tripartite division of the class action device. The second is a return to the critical divide in *Sprint* to examine core relations between public and private ordering in the disposition of aggregated claims. I will address each of these in turn.

A. CLASS ACTION FORMALISM

Following the decisive amendments in 1966, contemporary class action practice employs different procedures, depending primarily on the relief being sought. As set out in the three provisions of Rule 23(b), class actions are formed by interlocking claims on a limited potential source of recovery (Rule 23(b)(1)(B)),[70] by the demand for common injunctive relief against a defendant (Rule

---

[69] See Jonathan T. Molot, *An Old Judicial Role for a New Litigation Era*, 113 Yale L J 27, 35–36 (2003).

[70] Although phrased more broadly, the only real use of Rule 23(b)(1) is through subsection (b) to create what is termed a limited fund class action. In effect, this is the procedural vehicle for plaintiffs to file an interpleader action protecting an equitable distribution of the proceeds and stopping a run on the bank. This is discussed in Samuel Issacharoff, *Governance and the Law of Class Actions*, 1999 Supreme Court Review 337.

23(b)(2)), or by the efficiency of common resolution of a common demand for damages (Rule 23(b)(3)). The class action rules try to draw a bright line between those claims that are inseparable from which individuals cannot opt out, and those in which some limited form of litigant autonomy is preserved. As conceptualized in the ALI's Aggregate Litigation approach,[71] the distinction is between claims for divisible versus indivisible remedies, with the former requiring more limited protections for those individuals who will be bound to the collective resolution of the claims.[72]

Each of the class action provisions has proven to be a contested battleground. The limited fund class action, like the interpleader action in *Tashire*, is narrowly construed to require both a fixed res that marks the outer bounds of the controversy and a set of claims against that fixed res whose excessive valuation is not determined by litigation or settlement—in other words, something that looks like the multiple personal injury claims against State Farm's paltry $20,000 indemnification obligation in *Tashire*.[73] Courts have similarly restricted efforts to expand the reach of injunctive class actions to capture even commonly created damages claims.[74] Finally, claims for collective prosecution of damages have engendered constant skirmishes over the exacting if imprecise requirements of "adequacy of representation" under Rule 23(a) and of "predominance" and "manageability" in Rule 23(b)(3).[75]

---

[71] American Law Institute, Principles of the Law of Aggregate Litigation (Tentative Draft No 1, Apr 7, 2008), at § 2.04. I serve as reporter on this project.

[72] See *Phillips Petroleum Co. v Shutts*, 472 US 797, 821–22 (1985).

[73] This is, for practical purposes, the holding of *Ortiz v Fibreboard*, 527 US 815 (1999).

[74] There is an active division in the Courts of Appeals on whether incidental claims for damages can form part of a (b)(2) class, and on what exactly is an incidental claim for damages. The polar positions are found in *Allison v Citgo Petroleum Corp.*, 151 F3d 402, 425 (5th Cir 1998) (permitting inclusion of equitable back-pay claims in a (b)(2) class but not permitting additional claims for legal damages), and *Robinson v Metro-North Commuter Railroad Co.*, 267 F3d 147, 164 (2d Cir 2001) (using "ad hoc balancing" to define what are incidental claims for monetary relief in a (b)(2) class). For a contrast of the approaches, see Lesley Frieder Wolf, Note, *Evading Friendly Fire: Achieving Class Certification After the Civil Rights Act of 1991*, 100 Colum L Rev 1847 (2000). The third leading approach is the use of hybrids with elements of both (b)(2) and (b)(3) protections in place. See *Allen v Int'l Truck and Engine Corp.*, 358 F3d 469, 470–72 (7th Cir 2004).

[75] The Supreme Court has demanded a "rigorous" examination of the requirements of Rule, *Gen. Tel. Co. of the S.W. v Falcon*, 457 US 147, 161 (1982), including a "demanding" examination of Rule 23(b)(3) in the settlement context. *Amchem Products, Inc. v Windsor*, 521 US 591, 624 (1997). As formulated by the ALI, the resulting doctrinal battles lead "advocates of class certification . . . to frame legal and factual issues at high levels of generality so as to argue for their commonality, whereas opponents of class certification have an incentive to catalogue in microscopic detail each legal or factual variation suggesting the existence of individual questions." § 2.02, Reporters' Notes, Comment a.

The three procedural decisions from last Term follow the basic contours of Rule 23, but each avoids the burdens that could defeat or at least frustrate efforts at class certification. *Pimentel* is the most directly analogous to a class action because the underlying claims had already emerged from a class suit against the Marcos estate. The critical problem was that the disposition of the assets required a final declaration of rights against the Marcos holdings on behalf of all possible claimants. Even without the complicating factor of sovereign immunity, the class mechanism could not integrate the disparate potential claims needed for a final disposition of assets. In order to achieve closure, such a final accounting had to include other potential claimants who shared no interest with the class of human rights claimants (indeed, were likely rivals for the same assets) and could not possibly be fitted within any of the Rule 23(a) prerequisites (e.g., typicality, commonality) that are necessary for the certification of a class. As a result, the class mechanism for addressing the limited recovery, certification under 23(b)(1), could not be invoked to achieve closure.

Similarly, *Taylor* presented a classic case for the creation of a (b)(2) class that would also not come into being. There was absolute commonality in the circumstances of all individuals—what is often termed the cohesiveness of the class for (b)(2) purposes— who might want to obtain airplane specifications from the FAA. Unitary adjudication of the demand for the plane specifications would satisfy concerns of both equity and efficiency in resolving the matter once and for all, and the same for all the similarly situated claimants. The problem was that there was no incentive for any claimant, or any claimant's counsel, to seek to certify a class. No individual claimant could possibly get more from leading a class action (either one gets the airplane specifications or one does not), and there was no incentive to undertake the additional litigation burdens of seeking to certify a class. Under FOIA, the only relief available is a governmental obligation to disclose the requested information, so whether the action is brought in the name of one or many does not increase what may be obtained. Further, because no damages are available, the only source of compensation for a prevailing attorney is statutory attorneys' fees which are computed on an hours-worked lodestar basis. This in turn means that an attorney has no incentive to expand the scope of the dispute since it benefits neither the client nor the attorney herself. In short, a case that called out for class-wide resolution on behalf of all vintage plane enthusiasts was doomed to fly solo.

Finally, *Sprint* was the one of these cases where the class action seemed tailor made for just this kind of small claim aggregation. To invoke the class action, however, would have mired the claimants in a drawn-out procedural bog. First, a class certification procedure would have been an opportunity for rival firms—including those who had not done the preparatory work—to claim that they should be class counsel.[76] Even if APCC Services (or its attorneys) emerged as class counsel, any proposed certification would have to withstand challenge as to the predominance and manageability of joint prosecution,[77] and any decision on certification would then be subject to the potential delays of interlocutory appeal under Rule 23(f). As discussed previously, the fact that the pay phone operators were repeat-player claimants against the long-distance carriers meant that private contract was a cheaper way to proceed than the cumbersome class action device.

The disutility of the class action for many forms of aggregate claims is not limited to smaller cases such as the ones from last Term. The most significant class action cases of the last decade were *Amchem Products v Windsor* and *Ortiz v Fibreboard*, the two attempts to use class action settlement procedures to close out asbestos liabilities for not only current claimants but future ones as well. While there are many reasons to be skeptical of the way these work-out deals were structured and negotiated, the Court's response was to ratchet up the formalism of the rules to curtail what it termed the "adventuresome" use of the class device.[78] As a result, class actions seemed to drop out of the available set of tools for attempting to settle most mass torts,[79] absent some extraordinary willingness of a settling defendant to allow some form of future claims to return to the tort system.[80]

---

[76] See Geoffrey P. Miller, *Competing Bids in Class Action Settlements*, 31 Hofstra L Rev 633, 633 (2003).

[77] For a critique of the misguided nature of the Rule 23(b)(3) categories, see Allan Erbsen, *From "Predominance" to "Resolvability": A New Approach to Regulating Class Actions*, 58 Vand L Rev 995, 1005–6 (2005).

[78] *Amchem*, 521 US at 617.

[79] See Howard M. Erichson, *A Typology of Aggregate Settlements*, 80 Notre Dame L Rev 1769, 1776 (2005) (describing the settlement class action as "precisely the tool that *Amchem* and *Ortiz* render nearly unusable for global resolutions of personal injury mass torts").

[80] This was the form taken in the sweeping settlement of personal injury claims for

Perhaps naively, the Court in the asbestos cases may have thought that it was restoring the primacy of what Justice Souter in *Ortiz* would term the "day-in-court ideal" of individual claimants represented by individual attorneys proceeding to trial.[81] That account cannot withstand the realities of plummeting rates of cases actually being tried to judgment,[82] nor the emergence of a raft of alternative mechanisms outside Article III courts that bundle claims in efforts to achieve closure.[83] While most of the responses are private aggregations of claims portfolios through the plaintiffs' bar,[84] other pathways have developed. In asbestos, a statutory option has emerged, offering an alternative to the perceived disutility of the class action device in contested mass torts.[85]

Thus it is noteworthy that the most important post-*Amchem* judicial developments on the proper considerations for the resolution of mass harms come not through the processes of litigation in Article III courts, but through a specific exception for asbestos bankruptcies under Section 524(g) of the Bankruptcy Code.[86] Rather than the formalized processes of class actions, Section 524(g) places a premium on private work-outs of mass torts—a

---

exposure to the diet drug fen-phen. For one of the many appellate treatments of this settlement, see *In re Diet Drugs (Phentermine/Fenfluramine/Dexfenfluramine) Products Liability Litigation*, 369 F3d 293 (3d Cir 2004). Under the fen-phen settlement, individuals whose claims matured after the settlement were allowed to receive payments on a fixed matrix formula or allowed to opt out at the time their injury presented itself and bring individual claims in the tort system, absent any claim for punitive damages. For an affirmative assessment of this settlement as properly balancing the individual interests of future claimants against the need for finality, see Richard A. Nagareda, *Autonomy, Peace, and Put Options in the Mass Tort Class Action*, 115 Harv L Rev 747 (2002); for a critical assessment arguing in favor of compelled aggregation, see David Rosenberg, *Mandatory-Litigation Class Action: The Only Option for Mass Tort Cases*," 115 Harv L Rev 831 (2002).

[81] 527 US at 846.

[82] The best empirical accounts are compiled in Symposium, *The Vanishing Trial*, 1 J Empir Legal Stud 459 (2004).

[83] The historic emergence of private responses to the need for efficient aggregation of mass claims is discussed in Samuel Issacharoff and John Fabian Witt, *The Inevitability of Aggregate Settlement: An Institutional Account of American Tort Law*, 57 Vand L Rev 1571 (2004). Richard Nagareda provides the most comprehensive account of the development of new institutional and legal responses in Richard A. Nagareda, *Mass Torts in a World of Settlement* (2007).

[84] This is discussed in Samuel Issacharoff, *"Shocked": Mass Torts and Aggregate Asbestos Litigation after Amchem and Ortiz*, 80 Tex L Rev 1925 (2002).

[85] See Elizabeth J. Cabraser, *The Class Action Counterreformation*, 57 Stan L Rev 1475, 1476 (2005).

[86] See Francis E. McGovern, *Asbestos Litigation II: Section 524(g) Without Bankruptcy*, 31 Pepperdine L Rev 233, 241 (2003); Issacharoff, 80 Tex L Rev at 1939 ("These prepackaged bankruptcies dramatically lower the transaction costs associated with conventional bankruptcies . . . .") (cited in note 84).

topic I return to in the next section—and offers the finality of bankruptcy protection for properly consummated private settlements. A debtor seeking bankruptcy protection for asbestos liabilities may proceed through a "pre-packaged" bankruptcy (known in the trade as "pre-packs") by showing that the plan is supported by a majority of the affected claimants, representing two-thirds of the amounts claimed against the debtor.[87] The real work is done by the requirement that the reorganization be supported by 75 percent of the debtor's asbestos claimants in order for the debtor to be able to get a "channeling injunction"—the bankruptcy procedure that forecloses any claim against the debtor not obtained ("channeled through") the bankruptcy court.[88] The channeling injunction is critical because it provides protection against claims made not only by present claimants (including the minority who might oppose the reorganization), but by future claimants as well.

To the untutored eye, the 524(g) workout looks strikingly similar to the efforts to obtain a judicial imprimatur for work-outs of present and future claims, as were struck down in *Amchem* and *Ortiz*. For good reason, as it appears that way to the tutored eye as well. The practical effect is that an agreement broadly supported by present claimants can be used to cram down the claims not only of dissenting plaintiffs, but of future claimants as well. The bankruptcy work-out includes a Future Claimants Representative who assumes a fiduciary responsibility.[89] But the major difference is that the statutory scheme substitutes an Article I judge for an Article III judge, hardly a stirring form of enhanced protection for the due process interests that are at stake.

Because Section 524(g) provided a more welcoming port for judicially supervised and judicially enforced private settlement, the locus of asbestos work-outs shifted there following *Amchem* and *Ortiz*. Perhaps not surprisingly, the most significant mass tort "class action" case following *Amchem* and *Ortiz* emerges not from the overly formalized class action context but from the more flexible procedures of bankruptcy. In *In re Combustion Engineering*,[90] Chief Judge Scirica of the Third Circuit had to apply to a complicated pre-pack what the *Amchem* Court defined as the "struc-

---

[87] 11 USC § 1126(c).

[88] See 11 USC § 524(g)(2)(B)(ii)(IV)(bb).

[89] 11 USC § 524(g)(4)(B)(I).

[90] 391 F3d 190 (3d Cir 2004).

tural assurance of fair and adequate representation for the diverse groups and individuals affected."[91] At immediate issue in *Combustion Engineering* was a multitiered payment scheme that created a private pre-petition trust for the bulk of the payout to present claimants and what was in effect a diminished corpus to serve as the bankruptcy estate for satisfying future claimants.[92] The two were linked because the approval of the bankruptcy trust was the predicate for the realization of the pre-petition trust and, accordingly, present claimants had a strong incentive to vote for the plan in order to get the benefits of the second trust.[93]

Examining the disputed reorganization as a bankruptcy case, Judge Scirica was able to recapture the essential equitable inquiry that was obscured by the procedural formalism of *Amchem* and *Ortiz*. As the Supreme Court has insisted, "[e]quality of distribution among creditors is a central policy of the Bankruptcy Code."[94] The Court looked to the class action asbestos cases for the controlling principles of equity and concluded, "[t]hough *Ortiz* was decided under [Rule] 23(b)(1)(B), the Court's requirement of fair treatment for all claimants—a principle at the core of equity— also applies in the context of this case."[95] As applied to the case, the proposed resolution failed, not because of any formal requirements of Rule 23 or any hypothesized need to return to the premise of the "day-in-court" ideal, but because the concerns of equity were sufficient to strike down a plan that gave preferential treatment to a group of voting claimants at the expense of those neither present nor voting.

---

[91] 521 US at 627.

[92] As described by the Third Circuit, "Combustion Engineering contributed half of its assets to a pre-petition trust (the 'CE Settlement Trust') to pay asbestos claimants with pending lawsuits for part, but not the entire amount, of their claims. The remaining, unpaid portion of these claims, known as 'stub claims,' provided prepetition trust participants with creditor status under the Bankruptcy Code." 391 F 3d at 201. The result was twofold. First, the "stub claimants" would remain as creditors able to vote on the plan of reorganization. Second, the actual bankruptcy trust (what remained after the creation of the CE Settlement Trust) could treat present and future claimants equally, even though present claimants would get the benefits of the pre-petition trust that were unavailable to any future claimant.

[93] 391 F3d at 242 n 56.

[94] Id at 239, quoting *Begier v IRS*, 496 US 53, 58 (1990).

[95] 391 F3d at 242 n 57.

B. PRIVATE AGGREGATION AND THE EMERGENCE OF INFORMAL
   REGULATION.

In its confrontation with the sweeping asbestos cases a decade
ago, the Supreme Court recognized the fundamental question for
all aggregation of claims: the indispensable role of an agent able
to solve the coordination problem among similarly situated claimants. Quoting the Seventh Circuit, the Court observed, "The policy at the very core of the class action mechanism is to overcome
the problem that small recoveries do not provide the incentive for
any individual to bring a solo action prosecuting his or her rights.
A class action solves this problem by aggregating the relatively
paltry potential recoveries into something worth someone's (usually an attorney's) labor."[96]
   On this view, the class action is a corrective to the inability of
the private market to overcome the transactional barrier to the
prosecution of private claims. The class action is a trade-off. In
exchange for greater judicial supervision and exacting standards
of noncontractual aggregation, the entrepreneurial agent (i.e., class
counsel) is provided a low-cost means of creating a litigation "entity."[97] The corollary, however, should be a recognition that where
private mechanisms emerge that similarly overcome collective action barriers, they should not only not be condemned, they should
be protected. Indeed, when dealing with the sorts of claims that
have historically been recognized by the common law, there is no
obvious reason to prefer public ordering to private ordering.[98] It
is possible to read a preference for privately managed aggregation
into the requirement in Rule 23 that the decision to certify a class
should compare the costs and benefits of the available joinder
devices.
   Privately ordered aggregation has certain characteristic features.
As with the class action, intermediaries are needed to bring these
claims into a form that overcomes the transaction costs barriers.

---

[96] *Amchem Products, Inc. v Windsor*, 521 US 591, 617 (1997), quoting *Mace v Van Ru Credit Corp.*, 109 F3d 338, 344 (7th Cir 1997).

[97] David L. Shapiro, *Class Actions: The Class as Party and Client*, 73 Notre Dame L Rev 913, 917–18 (1998) ("[T]he notion of the class as entity should prevail over more indi-vidually oriented notions of aggregate litigation.").

[98] This is the core of the legal process approach to the relation between law and private arrangements. See Henry M. Hart, Jr., and Albert M. Sacks, *The Legal Process: Basic Problems in the Making and Application of Law* 159–61 (William N. Eskridge, Jr., and Philip P. Frickey, eds, 1994) (describing private ordering as the "primary process of social adjustment").

These intermediaries are typically lawyers who are capable of bundling the claims informally through market aggregations. The viability of the claims then turns on the ability to lower transactional barriers, which includes the ability to amortize costs from the few cases that might need to be tried, and the calculation of damages payouts through a simple matrix formula.[99] As presented in *Sprint*, the question is whether there is anything sinister about this. For any one of these cases, the costs of actually prosecuting the claim would exceed its likely value. But no one with feet on earth believes that any one of these claims stands alone. It is hard to find a normative justification for driving out of the system claims of legal merit whose enforcement is compromised by the high transactions costs of our system. In most markets, the impulse is to find ways to lower transactions costs in order to preserve value, not to drive up the deadweight cost of doing business.

In some private aggregations the obstacle to effective litigation is not the small payout available for any given plaintiff, but the high fixed costs or the risks of loss in particular cases. A low expected return from a case can be the product of the low level of anticipated damages, or the high cost of prosecuting the claim, or the high risk of failure. As in cases where aggregation is necessitated by the small value of an individual claim, cases of high risk or high fixed costs require the ability to pool risk for those cases that do go to trial or to spread the fixed costs among similar cases.[100] Thus, the problem of efficient aggregation goes beyond the types of claims in *Sprint* to reach cases whose necessary aggregation is compelled by something other than the low value of a claim. Here, again, *Sprint* is instructive because the Court came close to burdening private aggregation with the imprecisions of formal procedural law.

But the burdens of procedure should not lead to an overstatement of what may be accomplished through private ordering. Our attention thus far has been directed to the failings of public ordering through the formal procedural system to address the chal-

---

[99] This is the crux of the argument developed in Issacharoff and Witt, 57 Vand L Rev 1571 (cited in note 83).

[100] This is an application of the basic economic model of litigation and settlement to the problem of efficient coordination of related cases. For the basic economic model, see Richard A. Posner, *Economic Analysis of Law* 597 (7th ed 2007); Steven Shavell, *Suit, Settlement, and Trial: A Theoretical Analysis Under Alternative Methods for the Allocation of Legal Costs*, 11 J Legal Stud 55, 56–57 (1982).

lenge of aggregation. The prospect of private ordering through market-based mechanisms, as presented in *Sprint*, appears in this context as a healthy tonic for the overly burdened demands for formal aggregations. As with all partially regulated areas of behavior, we might expect a "hydraulic" effect whereby sophisticated market actors will seek to evade regulation by searching out less regulated byways that might offer similar results. In a radically different domain, for example, the limitations imposed by our campaign finance system on candidates and parties raising and spending money directly may lead interest groups to find other institutional actors capable of leveraging financial resources into enhanced electoral prospects.[101]

Private ordering is a welcome addition to ordering through the public domain, but it is inherently limited. The ability to aggregate the low-value claims of the pay phone operators, for example, turned on the unique nature of the business at issue. In *Sprint*, both the long-distance carriers and the pay phone operators were repeat players in the long-distance calling market. Despite the low value of any particular transaction, there were still incentives to contract for the representation of the pay phone operators, even if no single transaction was worth prosecuting on its own. By contrast, in the typical consumer fraud case, only the seller is a repeat player, and any successful action for fraud would require the ability to aggregate many small-value claims without the need to contract with each individual consumer. For most low-value claims, therefore, private ordering cannot overcome the transactional bar to pursuing even meritorious actions. For such claims, the class action mechanism is indispensable, even if the requirements are burdensome.

Even where the stakes are sufficiently great to justify an individual action, private ordering may be insufficient to bring a necessary element of closure or protection of the settling parties from collateral challenge. In such cases, courts have turned to the concept of a "quasi-class action," inherited from cases under the Fair Labor Standards Act, to bridge the gap between public and private ordering. Almost alone in American law, the FLSA requires "opt-in" measures for class action, enabling private parties to contract into a system of collective representation, including the capacity

---

[101] This is an argument developed in Samuel Issacharoff and Pamela S. Karlan, *The Hydraulics of Campaign Finance Reform*, 77 Tex L Rev 1705 (1999).

to be bound by aggregated proceedings. The term "quasi-class" refers to the uncertain period during which an FLSA class has been asserted, but the structure has not yet been approved by the court and the putative class members have not yet decided to join in. As applied to mass harm cases by the indefatigable Judge Jack Weinstein, the term refers to a coordinated group of related cases whose joint supervision and aggregate resolution are subject to direct oversight and implementation by a court, usually an MDL court.[102]

The quasi-class occupies an interesting midpoint between public and private ordering, one that draws heavily on the equitable powers of courts in an area bereft of formal rules of procedure. In such hybrids, courts provide a guarantee of transparency and intragroup equity among the represented claimants, but exact a loss of litigant autonomy as courts also assume supervision of attorneys' fees and other matters that would be purely a matter of contract were the disputes to be resolved purely privately.

Take for example the controversies surrounding the current mass settlement of claims against Merck[103] for heart attacks and strokes caused by use of the painkiller Vioxx.[104] The litigation

---

[102] As initially formulated by Judge Weinstein, the salient features of the quasi-class were, "[t]he large number of plaintiffs subject to the same settlement matrix approved by the court; the utilization of special masters appointed by the court to control discovery and to assist in reaching and administering a settlement; the court's order for a huge escrow fund; and other interventions by the court." As a result, Judge Weinstein found that any settlement that ensued was subject to the court's "imposition of fiduciary standards to ensure fair treatment to all parties and counsel regarding fees and expenses." *In re Zyprexa Prods. Liab. Litig.*, 424 F Supp 2d 488, 491 (ED NY 2006). *See also In re Guidant Corp. Implantable Defibrillators Prods. Liab. Litig.*, MDL No 05-1708, 2008 WL 682174, at *18 (D Minn, March 7, 2008) (characterizing a mass tort proceeding as a quasi-class action and subjecting the global settlement to the court's equitable authority); *In re Vioxx Products Liability Litigation*, 574 F Supp 606 (ED La 2008).

[103] The settlement is set out at http://www.merck.com/newsroom/vioxx/pdf/Settlement_Agreement.pdf. I should disclose that I am counsel to the attorneys that negotiated this settlement agreement on behalf of plaintiffs.

[104] As I will discuss, the most controversial feature of the settlement was the requirement that each plaintiffs' lawyer settle her entire portfolio of claims, thereby precluding any adverse selection of which cases to settle and which to prosecute. For commentary on the controversies regarding the relation between this novel provision and the rules of ethics, see, for example, Adam Liptak, *In Vioxx Settlement, Testing a Legal Ideal: A Lawyer's Loyalty*, NY Times (Jan 22, 2008), at A12; Alex Berenson, *Some Lawyers Seek Changes in Vioxx Settlement*, NY Times (Dec 21, 2007), at C4; Nathan Koppel, *Vioxx Plaintiffs' Choice: Settle or Lose Their Lawyer*, Wall St J (Nov 16, 2007), at B1. Probably the most far-reaching condemnation came from University of Virginia law professor George Cohen who, in addition to claiming the settlement violated various ethical strictures, sent a complaint to the Federal Trade Commission. With the salutation "Dear FTC," Cohen charged that the settlement "is a per se illegal group boycott (concerted refusal to deal)" and should

history of Vioxx raises complicated issues of aggregation in terms of both substance and procedure, even in the streamlined version that follows. The critical issue—basically not disputed—was that Vioxx exposure over a prolonged period resulted in some increased number of heart attacks and strokes among the exposed population. The problem is that neither cardiac event is a signature injury, one that can be traced with any certainty to Vioxx consumption as opposed to a host of other genetic or environmental causes. Put another way, the only proof of harm from Vioxx was epidemiological, which meant that even a threshold determination of liability in any individual case could only be established probabilistically by reference to the entire exposed population. Moreover, because of the extensive reliance on contested expert testimony, these cases were likely to be expensive to prosecute.

Under the customary working of our tort system, these cases should have been tried on a one-at-a-time basis and one would have expected discordant results. In theory, all plaintiffs could have lost their claims because even the elevated levels of cardiac risk following Vioxx exposure could not make causation more likely than not, presumably the standard necessary to survive summary judgment. In reality, however, an otherwise healthy athlete who has an unexplained heart attack after taking Vioxx is likely to get to the jury in many if not most jurisdictions. As cases began to trickle through the litigation pipeline, a total of eighteen were tried to judgment prior to the national settlement. Of these, Merck won thirteen and plaintiffs won five, though some were later reversed on appeal. In those cases that Merck lost, juries awarded large compensatory damages and sweeping punitive damages. The most salient result was that despite relying on common epidemiological evidence, some plaintiffs received nothing, while others were awarded millions.

The eighteen cases that went to trial established the hurdles confronting other plaintiffs and the damages prospects facing Merck. This was an excellent basis for an informed settlement that would discount the risks faced by all sides and provide for comparable treatment of comparably situated plaintiffs. Indeed, that understanding laid the foundation for a settlement of $4.85 billion

---

be prosecuted as such; no FTC action ensued. See Ted Frank, PointofLaw.com, George Cohen's Letter to the FTC Re the Vioxx Settlement, http://www.pointoflaw.com/archives/004680.php#4680.

to be distributed among plaintiffs who had filed suit before the statute of limitations had run and who could prove certain elements of exposure and harm. The difficult issue was how to create an effective bill of peace that would bring a reasonable (and reasonably certain) end to the litigation, enabling the plaintiffs to be compensated and Merck to obtain closure. A publicly ordered settlement through the use of a class action was too unwieldy because of the elevated burdens on organizing a class after *Amchem* and *Ortiz*, as well as the inability to confine the dispute to those individuals who had filed suit in a timely manner before the statute of limitations had run.[105] For all practical purposes, no individual lawsuit could serve as the vehicle for a comprehensive settlement without having a mechanism to coordinate with all potential claimants. The Vioxx claimants found themselves in the same position as the plaintiff class in *Pimentel*.

As in *Pimentel*, one option might have been to wait many years for all claims to work their way through the legal system, a prospect as likely to bring closure as the Philippine appellate procedures. Fortunately in Vioxx, a novel solution could be crafted through private ordering that—like the bankruptcy work-outs under Section 524(g)—would combine private settlement with judicial oversight. The settlement turned centrally on the economic realities of the litigation marketplace for complicated liability claims in mass-harm cases. Cases that involve systemic harms, high fixed costs, and uncertain prospects of recovery, such as Vioxx, simply cannot be handled on a one-off basis under arrangements approximating Justice Souter's ideal of individuals represented privately anticipating their day in court. Rather, the economics of risky pharmaceutical claims meant that even lawyers who were retained by an individual client had to refer the claim up the litigation ladder to firms that could amortize the cost of litigation across a portfolio of cases—in effect, creating cross-subsidies for the prosecution of those claims that might actually reach trial. In the absence of such concentration of claims, plaintiffs could offer

---

[105] Numerous class actions had been filed over Vioxx exposure, though none was being seriously prosecuted for personal injury claims. One unintended consequence of class action law was that were the case to be resolved as a class action, the statute of limitations would be tolled for all putative class members, in effect reopening the litigation to a new crop of potential claimants. This is the effect of class-wide tolling under *American Pipe & Constr. Co. v Utah*, 414 US 538 (1974).

no credible threat to litigate and, by extension, could not reasonably hope to secure settlements.

In Vioxx, plaintiffs' firms who consolidated large numbers of cases took a small number of cases to trial, allowing these to serve as the bellwethers for assessing the likely litigation fortunes of thousands more claims in the pipeline. Following the eighteen cases that were tried to judgment, a settlement was constructed that was structured as an offer from Merck, the manufacturer of Vioxx. Before such an offer was extended, however, the terms had been negotiated with a leading group of plaintiffs' counsel, with the litigated cases serving as the benchmark values for the broad work-out. Having the backing of several of the major representatives of Vioxx plaintiffs, Merck then presented for acceptance or rejection by individual plaintiffs, rather than for court implementation as with a class action. The novel feature of the settlement was that while the offer was made to each Vioxx plaintiff individually, the offer was only valid if accepted by all the clients represented by any particular attorney or law firm. In order to provide closure, however—and to substitute for the inability to use effectively the class action device, as Sprint had asserted in *Sprint*—the offer required any participating lawyer to certify that all his or her clients had agreed to the terms. In broad outlines, the offer provided closure with each firm independently (subject to an overall 85 percent acceptance rate to be effective) or it would not become effective. Individual claimants remained free to reject the proposed deal but, assuming court approval and barring exigent circumstances, would have to find other counsel to handle their claims. Participating lawyers or law firms could receive no referral fee nor have any ongoing interest in any case that remained in litigation. The terms of the offer and oversight over withdrawals from nonsettling cases were placed in the hands of the federal and state court judges in whose courts the individual cases had been consolidated.

In effect, the settlement tried to use the forces of market aggregation to realize the sort of consensual closure that the formal rules of procedure could not provide. The settlement then created an ad hoc form of judicial oversight over everything from withdrawal from representation to fees permitted. What Vioxx offered, if accepted, was a novel means of using private ordering to bring sensible closure to common claims, with court supervision, but outside the boundaries of formal procedural law.

Predictably, the Vioxx settlement provoked significant controversy, in large part as a result of the apparent tension between the consolidated nature of the settlement offers and the individual-representation premises of traditional litigation. In this instance it was not the Federal Rules of Civil Procedure that were the issue so much as ethical rules governing representation on matters such as client authority over acceptance of a settlement,[106] the conditions for attorney withdrawal from representation,[107] the duty owed by a lawyer to each client,[108] and even the prohibitions on lawyers entering into agreements restricting future representations.[109] Most of these criticisms have faded in light of the overwhelmingly positive response by plaintiffs (who collectively had not recovered a cent prior to the settlement) to the terms of the offer. But I do not seek here to defend the structure of the settlement against these criticisms and concerns, something I have done in other settings. My argument here is simply that the Vioxx settlement, in order to provide closure to claims premised on the epidemiological risk faced across the cohort of users of the drug, had to devise a private arrangement to overcome the disfunctionality of the formal procedural system. Independent of any considerations of the structure or the ultimate fairness of the settlement terms, the fact remains that there was no way to achieve closure within any of the established pathways of the formal joinder devices available in aggregate litigation.

It is of course possible to reject my premise that the legal system should be attentive to the coordinated resolution of mass claims. Certainly, there are other values besides orderly resolution of claims that animate our legal system.[110] Certainly, we could return to the Kantian commitment to the integrity of the individual and

---

[106] *Model Rules of Prof'l Conduct R*, 1.2(a) (2002) ("[a] lawyer shall abide by a client's decision whether to settle a matter").

[107] *Model Rules of Prof'l Conduct R*, 1.16(b)(1) (2002) (allowing withdrawal only if it "can be accomplished without material adverse effect on the interests of the client").

[108] *Model Rules of Prof'l Conduct R*, 2.1 (2002) (requiring lawyer to "exercise independent professional judgment and render candid advice").

[109] *Model Rules of Prof'l Conduct R*, 5.6(b) (2002) (prohibiting any agreement in which a restriction on the lawyer's right to practice is part of the settlement of a client controversy").

[110] The inescapable citation here is to Owen Fiss, *Against Settlement*, 93 Yale L J 1073 (1984).

ask whether the focus on the collective quality of claims does violence to the foundational assumptions of our legal system.[111] But even if such individualism were the cornerstone of our legal system, the question remains what to do when these Kantian individuals live cheek-by-jowl and interact en masse.

III. Conclusion

Efforts to aggregate cases must confront two obvious pitfalls: too much aggregation and too little aggregation. Lumping claims together is intended to and does alter the litigation dynamics, particularly in small-value cases. But an excess can produce its own distortions, as illustrated by Judge Richard Posner's concern that the excessive stakes in any particular class action might coerce settlement through a forced bet-the-ranch sweepstakes.[112] Alternatively, in a recent case involving the propensity of Ford Explorers to suffer tire damage and roll-over, Judge Frank Easterbrook cautioned about the "central planner" mentality that would not allow claims to accrue and the courts to learn from the experience of trials.[113]

On the other hand, even legally valid claims that fail to justify their full cost of prosecution will be stillborn without some procedural device that promotes efficiency. To go back to *Tashire*, it is noteworthy that it was litigated at the same time as the sweeping 1966 amendments to Rule 23 were coming into effect. Though no one thought that the newly crafted class action device would reach all manner of mass harms, the subsequent development of class action law offered some hope that efficient and fair resolution of large-scale disputes was at hand. The three cases from last Term not only show that the class action device remains limited, but also that other formal procedural mechanisms for handling mass

---

[111] For a rather stark attack on David Shapiro and me for even contemplating that a certified class might be an "entity" distinct form the mere agglomeration of its members, see Martin H. Redish and Nathan D. Larsen, *Class Actions, Litigant Autonomy, and the Foundations of Procedural Due Process*, 95 Calif L Rev 1587–1600 (2007).

[112] The extent of the extortion or blackmail effect is, not surprisingly, a subject of dispute. See *In re Rhone-Poulenc Rorer, Inc.*, 51 F3d 1293, 1298 (7th Cir 1995) ("[Faced with a class action, defendants] may not wish to roll these dice. That is putting it mildly. They will be under intense pressure to settle."); Charles Silver, *We're Scared to Death: Class Certification and Blackmail*, 78 NYU L Rev 1357 (2003) (challenging the coercive power of the class action); Bruce Hay and David Rosenberg, *"Sweetheart" and "Blackmail" Settlements in Class Actions: Reality and Remedy*, 75 Notre Dame L Rev 1377 (2000).

[113] *In re Bridgestone/Firestone, Inc.*, 288 F3d 1012, 1020 (7th Cir 2002).

actions or the resolution of claims not defined by autonomous rights holders are similarly inadequate.

Viewed from this perspective, the question is what to do about the limitations of our procedural devices. One approach, unfortunately reflected in the *Sprint* dissent, is to draw the line around inherited formal procedural devices. In my view, a better approach is to recognize the limitations of what formal procedural law may offer and to look favorably upon market mechanisms that may provide alternative means of organizing and resolving common claims. A market in privately ordered procedural alternatives not only takes away some of the central planner concerns raised by Judge Easterbrook, but also eases the pressure on the limited procedural tools already at hand. Notwithstanding the complications of mass society, there should be an allure to private ordering of privately held individual claims, even when they are presented by the bushel basket.

ANN WOOLHANDLER

DELEGATION AND DUE PROCESS: THE HISTORICAL CONNECTION

I. Introduction

In *Whitman v American Trucking Associations*, the Supreme Court reiterated the established modern doctrine that Congress may not delegate power to an executive agency unless Congress has supplied "an intelligible principle" to guide the agency's actions.[1] Judge Harold Leventhal of the D.C. Circuit had urged, in a well-known opinion, that an apparent congressional "blank check" might be remedied by procedural constraints on the agency,[2] together with the agency's supplying its own substantive standards.[3] Scholars sim-

Ann Woolhandler is William Minor Lile Professor of Law, University of Virginia.

Author's note: Thanks to Michael Collins, Barry Cushman, Liz Magill, Jerry Mashaw, Caleb Nelson, Ryan Rakness, George Rutherglen, Rich Schragger, and James Stern.

[1] *Whitman v American Trucking Ass'ns*, 531 US 457, 472 (2001), citing *J. W. Hampton, Jr. & Co. v United States*, 276 US 394, 409 (1928) (Scalia).

[2] *Amalgamated Meat Cutters v Connally*, 337 F Supp 737, 759 (DDC 1971) (three-judge court) ("The claim of undue delegation of legislative power broadly raises the challenge of undue power in the Executive and thus naturally involves consideration of the inter-related questions of the availability of appropriate restraints through provisions for administrative procedures and judicial review.").

[3] Id at 758 ("Another feature that blunts the 'blank check' rhetoric is the requirement that any action taken by the Executive under the law . . . must be in accordance with further standards as developed by the Executive."). The idea that agency-supplied standards may make up for a lack of congressional specificity is also associated with the work of Kenneth Culp Davis and Lisa Bressman. See, for example, Kenneth Culp Davis, *Discretionary Justice: A Preliminary Inquiry* 55–56 (LSU, 1969) (recommending administrators' development of standards, particularly through rulemaking, to limit their discretion, given that Congress cannot be expected to provide needed clarification); Lisa Shultz Bressman, *Schecter Poultry at the Millennium: A Delegation Doctrine for the Administrative State*, 109

ilarly have noted that in the few instances in which the Supreme
Court struck down a statute for excessive delegation, the agencies
lacked procedural safeguards.[4] But *Whitman* rejected at least part
of Judge Leventhal's approach, holding that the agency's supplying
intelligible principles post-delegation could not make up for Congress's prior failure to supply them.[5] *Whitman*'s insistence on con-
gressionally-supplied substantive standards also implies that procedural strictures on the agency's administration of a statute
(whether generated by courts, the legislature, or the agency itself)
should generally be irrelevant to the nondelegation issue.

   At first glance, the logic of *Whitman* seems sound: due process
and delegation seem to present analytically independent questions.
Separation of powers requires substantive congressional directives;
procedural due process is a free-standing constitutional requirement.[6] The distinction between delegation and due process seems
all the more obvious when one considers that due process requirements apply to states as well as to the federal government, whereas
federal constitutional nondelegation doctrine applies primarily to

---

Yale L J 1399, 1402 (2000) (arguing that nondelegation doctrine should focus less on who
should make law and more on how the agency exercises delegated lawmaking authority);
id at 1415 (recommending a new delegation doctrine requiring agencies to issue rules that
limit their discretion); Lisa Shultz Bressman, *Disciplining Delegation after Whitman v American Trucking Ass'ns*, 87 Cornell L Rev 452 (2002) (recommending that the courts use
administrative rather than constitutional law to force the agencies to develop standards
to limit their discretion).

   [4] See Kenneth Culp Davis, *Administrative Law* § 2.01, at 76 (West, 1958) ("In only two
cases in all American history have congressional delegations to public authorities been
held invalid. Neither delegation was to a regularly constituted administrative agency which
followed an established procedure designed to afford the customary safeguards to affected
parties." (footnote omitted)); Richard J. Pierce, Jr., Sidney A. Shapiro, and Paul R. Verkuil,
Administrative Law and Process § 3.4.2 (Foundation, 4th ed 2004) (describing case law as
indicating that "[v]ague delegations that otherwise might be excessive would pass muster
if the scope of power was narrower, or if those subject to the agency's regulatory efforts
were afforded sufficient procedural protections.").

   [5] 531 US at 472, rev'ing in part *American Trucking Ass'ns v EPA*, 175 F3d 1027, 1034–38
(DC Cir), modified in part and reh'g en banc denied, 195 F3d 4 (DC Cir 1999).

   [6] See Sotirios A. Barber, *The Constitution and the Delegation of Congressional Power* 32 (U
Chicago, 1975) ("If the principal matter at issue in the due process claim involves the
distinction between governing individual conduct by discretion and by rule, the simple
answer is that rules formulated by administrators may be at least as good, *qua rules*, as
those drafted by legislators. The rule of nondelegation is linked with due process through
the norm that individual conduct ought to be governed by rules only if the legislature
alone is adequate to the task of making rules."); id at 13 (rejecting various theoretical
foundations for nondelegation doctrine, including due process, in favor of the concept of
constitutional supremacy); Lawrence Alexander, *The Relationship Between Procedural Due
Process and Substantive Constitutional Rights*, 39 U Fla L Rev 323, 340 (1987) (arguing that
separation of powers is a separate concern from procedural due process, and pointing out
that agencies would need to supply process to implement even agency-generated rules).

congressional legislation.[7] And while some have argued that both due process and nondelegation have the same ultimate aims to protect individual rights,[8] others argue that if nondelegation were primarily about protecting individual rights, then even an extreme delegation would be constitutional absent a threat to such rights.[9]

But during the formative era of the modern regulatory state, the link between delegation and due process was much closer than the modern understanding, reflected in *Whitman*, suggests. This article explores how legislative delegation influenced the growth of procedural due process from the promulgation of the Fourteenth Amendment in 1868[10] until the end of the *Lochner* era in 1937. Scholarship about that period has focused more on substantive than procedural due process,[11] but even the famous (or infamous) developments in substantive due process during that period were, to some extent, an outgrowth of the interaction between delegation and procedural due process.

---

[7] See Alexander, 39 U Fla L Rev at 340–41 (cited in note 6) (pointing to the fact that procedural due process applies to states as well as the federal government to show that procedural due process is distinct from separation of powers).

[8] See Rebecca L. Brown, *Separated Powers and Ordered Liberty*, 139 U Pa L Rev 1513, 1514, 1516 (1991) (arguing against treating separation of powers as separate from its goal of promoting the protection of individual rights); id at 1535 (noting that Montesquieu associated separation of powers with protections of life and liberty from arbitrary control, concerns associated with due process); id at 1557–58 (indicating that the separation-of-powers inquiry should be whether the "challenged action tends to foster unaccountable, biased, or otherwise arbitrary government decisionmaking and, if so, whether the impairment of government process will affect individuals," but also indicating that due process analysis should remain separate from the separation-of-powers inquiry).

[9] See Barber, *The Constitution and the Delegation of Congressional Power* at 33 (cited in note 6) ("If substantive due process were the sole foundation of the rule of nondelegation, no delegation could be unconstitutional, however extreme, in the absence of injury to protected rights.").

[10] Ideas associated with *Lochner v New York*, 198 US 45 (1905), were already evident at the beginning of this period, and began to see their way into majority Fourteenth Amendment decisions in the 1890s. See generally Charles W. McCurdy, *Justice Field and the Jurisprudence of Government-Business Relations: Some Parameters of Laissez Faire Constitutionalism, 1863–1897*, 61 J Am Hist 970 (1975) (showing the consistency of the antimonopoly and antiregulatory strands of Field's jurisprudence).

[11] This is not to say that there has been no attention to procedures during this period. See, for example, Richard Stewart, *The Reformation of American Administrative Law*, 88 Harv L Rev 1667, 1672–74 (1975) (describing a traditional model of administrative law that developed between 1880 and 1960, that required legislative rules to limit the agency, decisional procedures to assure compliance with those rules and to promote judicial review, and judicial review to assure the foregoing). In addition, administrative law casebooks contrast *Londoner v Denver*, 210 US 373 (1908), with *Bi-Metallic Investment Co. v State Board of Equalization*, 239 US 441 (1915), to show the differential application of procedural due process to particularized versus generalized determinations. See, for example, Peter L. Strauss et al, *Gellhorn and Byse's Administrative Law* 238–41 (Foundation, 10th ed 2003).

The article particularly looks at tax assessment cases, with occasional comparison to developments in railroad regulation. Courts during this period presumed that decisions made by the legislature had factual support, as courts do today, and, notably, this presumption applied not only to statutes making general rules but also to statutes making individualized exactions in areas of "public rights" such as taxation. The Supreme Court eventually held, though, that this presumption did not apply when the power was exercised by delegees. To assure that delegees' determinations had factual support, the Court required that the delegees follow certain procedures. That is how the connection between delegation and procedural due process was established. The Court later supplemented, or in some cases replaced, the requirement of process with a requirement—enforced by judicial review—that the delegee's action not be substantively arbitrary, as an alternative way to assure factual support for the delegee's decision.

The substantive and procedural requirements for delegees, however, eventually came to restrict the legislature. The Court extended review for substantive arbitrariness to enactments of the legislature itself. What is more, the procedural requirements that the Court applied when delegees made individualized exaction decisions made it less acceptable for legislatures, which operated without such procedures, to make such decisions. As heightened procedural and substantive requirements reverberated up the delegation chain to restrict the legislature as well as its delegees, the connection between delegation and due process weakened.

Part II of this article discusses the Court's assumption at the beginning of the Fourteenth Amendment era that legislatures could validly make particularized exaction decisions in the area of taxation and railroad regulation, without judicially prescribed procedures. The assumption of legislative competence was an outgrowth of the Court's characterization of these areas as ones involving "public rights"—areas of plenary legislative power. The assumption, however, runs counter to modern separation-of-powers notions that legislatures must only act generally when imposing exactions. Part III addresses the Court's sometimes-expressed assumption that the legislature's delegees, such as municipalities and railroad commissions, could operate with a similar lack of process as the legislature. Part IV describes how legislative delegation came to require more processes in the area of tax assessment, based on the reasoning that presumptions of factual support attending legislative action would not attend delegee determinations. Part V discusses how the Court retreated from requiring additional agency procedures for certain types of tax determinations, substituting substantive arbitrariness review. Arbitrariness review helped assure factual support for governmental decisions; procedural and substantive due process were thus closely tied. Part VI shows how this substantive arbitrariness review, first applied to delegees, later came to be applied to legislative determinations. Finally, Part VII suggests that this account provides a corrective to top-down views whereby constitutional constraints apply first to legislatures and only by extension to their delegees, with procedures being a way to translate constitutional constraints on general legislation to the particularized applications of the executive.[12] History suggests that we may have arrived at such top-down insights from the bottom up—that is, by the Court's imposing procedural and substantive due process requirements on delegees that looped back to limit the legislature's ability to adjudicate and its ability to act arbitrarily.

II. Legislatures' Particularized Public Rights Decisions

A. BACKGROUND: ANTEBELLUM AGENCY PROCEDURAL DUE PROCESS

In the antebellum era, as illuminated in articles by Professor Jerry Mashaw, Congress placed important powers over allocation of public lands, pensions, and disbursements in federal executive officers.[13] What is more, Congress sometimes itself made specific determinations, such as confirming title to lands originally acquired from foreign governments, following an initial commission determination.[14] Nevertheless, as Mashaw concludes, "there seems

---

[12] Compare Richard H. Fallon, Jr., *Some Confusions About Due Process, Judicial Review, and Constitutional Remedies*, 93 Colum L Rev 309, 326–27 (1993) (discussing greater ease of substantive due process challenges to legislation and rules than to isolated official action, which makes sense given that due process increasingly seeks to maintain structures that keep government lawbreaking within tolerable limits).

[13] Jerry L. Mashaw, *Recovering American Administrative Law: Federalist Foundations, 1787–1801*, 115 Yale L J 1256, 1277 (2006) (*Federalist Foundations*) (referring to disputes over pensions, tax collection, and land patents as early harbingers of mass administration).

[14] See Jerry L. Mashaw, *Reluctant Nationalists: Federal Administrative Law in the Republican Era*, 116 Yale L J 1636, 1713, 1726 (2007) (*Reluctant Nationalists*) (noting the practice of at least nominal congressional confirmation of commission determinations of land title in the territories); id at 1731–33 (suggesting that the acceptance of administrative adjudication of land claims resulted in part from the involvement of Congress in claims administration). See generally Jerry L. Mashaw, *Administration and "The Democracy": Administrative Law*

to have been little legislative, and no judicial, attention to the processes by which rules were promulgated and cases decided."[15] This is not to say that the agencies acted without internal process or judicial oversight. The departments themselves often adopted regularized procedures to control their bureaucracies,[16] and common law actions were available against officers to contest some official acts.[17]

One might have thought the Fifth Amendment would be a source of requirements for process in federal agencies. But when the Court squarely addressed a Fifth Amendment challenge to agency procedure in 1856, in *Murray's Lessee v Hoboken Land and Improvement Company*, the Court was more focused on whether Article III courts must be involved than on the processes due when they were not.[18] *Murray's Lessee* held that the Treasury's summary process for seizing lands of an embezzling customs collector did not require judicial process. The basis of the holding was the Court's distinction between "public rights," whose final determination might be placed outside the regular judiciary, and private rights whose determination required judicial participation.[19]

During the nineteenth century, public rights included, inter alia, interests in government lands, interests in holding public office,

---

from Jackson to Lincoln, 117 Yale L J 1568 (2008) (detailing a nineteenth-century model of administrative accountability relying on political oversight and internal hierarchical control).

[15] Mashaw, *Federalist Foundations*, 115 Yale L J at 1341 (cited in note 13); see also Mashaw, *Reluctant Nationalists*, 116 Yale L J at 1646 (cited in note 14) (noting lack of systematic procedures for both rulemaking and adjudication); see also Ann Woolhandler, *Judicial Deference to Administrative Action—a Revisionist History*, 43 Admin L Rev 197, 211 (1991) (indicating that under the deferential "res judicata" model that the courts applied to many federal administrative determinations during the nineteenth century, the courts showed little concern for the adequacy of agency process).

[16] Mashaw, *Reluctant Nationalists*, 116 Yale L J at 1657 (cited in note 14); see also id at 1667 (discussing development of systems of internal controls by Treasury).

[17] See id at 1646; Woolhandler, *Judicial Deference*, 43 Admin L Rev at 201–02 (cited in note 15) (discussing availability of common law actions).

[18] 59 US (18 How) 272, 275 (1856), discussed in Mashaw, *Reluctant Nationalists*, 116 Yale L J at 1733 (cited in note 14) (noting that the Court treated the due process and Article III issues as the same—that is, whether the Constitution required judicial process); id at 1734 (stating that *Murray's Lessee* reveals a lack of the category of administrative due process: "The question was simply one of which process applied: administrative, judicial, or perhaps legislative."). The parties contesting the validity of the distress warrant would necessarily be trying to show it was void. 59 US at 275 (indicating that if the warrant was an exercise of judicial power it would be void).

[19] 59 US (18 How) at 284.

and purely statutory rights of individuals.[20] Private rights included traditional interests in property and bodily security. In contexts such as imposing fault-based liability for torts or crimes, divestiture of private rights required regular court process; the legislature effectively was required to entrust individualized exaction determinations to the judiciary.[21] Nevertheless, there were contexts in which divestiture of traditional property interests was treated as involving public rights that could be divested without the regular courts.[22] *Murray's Lessee* signally included tax assessment as a public right not requiring judicial process, noting that "probably there are few governments which do or can permit their claims for public taxes, either on the citizen or the officer employed for their collection or disbursement, to become subjects of judicial controversy."[23]

B. LEGISLATIVE PARTICULARITY AND THE PRESUMPTION OF FACTUAL SUPPORT AFTER THE CIVIL WAR

Even after the Civil War, the assumption still prevailed that legislatures could place the determination of matters of public right outside of the regular court system. In his article addressing the exercise of federal adjudicatory power outside of Article III courts, Caleb Nelson observed that the underlying premises for allowing the elimination of Article III involvement as to matters

---

[20] See Ann Woolhandler, *Public Rights, Private Rights, and Statutory Retroactivity*, 94 Georgetown L J 1015, 1021 (2006).

[21] See John Harrison, *Substantive Due Process and the Constitutional Text*, 83 Va L Rev 493, 507 (1997) (discussing the nineteenth-century view that due process encompassed a principle of separation of powers, that is, that only the judiciary and not the legislature could divest private rights); Caleb Nelson, *Adjudication in the Political Branches*, 107 Colum L Rev 559, 593 (2007) (noting the nineteenth-century assumption that Congress could not give the political branches conclusive authority when the determination of adjudicative facts as to core private rights was at stake).

[22] See Nelson, 107 Colum L Rev at 597–98 (cited in note 21) (indicating that the Court saw rate regulation orders requiring the payment of money as involving private rights but saw prospective orders as different, although confiscatory rates eventually came to be seen as involving private rights). There may be a current tendency to divide the universe of due process protections into procedural requirements for traditional common law interests (which are generally taken for granted), and more recent protections for new property such as welfare benefits. The extension of procedural due process protections for new property has received extensive scholarly attention. See generally Cynthia Farina, *Conceiving Due Process*, 3 Yale J L & Feminism 189 (Spring 1991) (reviewing various strands of procedural due process scholarship). An intermediate step between protection for traditional interests and for new property, however, was the extension of protections to "public rights" that involved invasions of traditional common law interests.

[23] *Murray's Lessee*, 59 US (18 How) at 282.

of public right were (*a*) that the legislature might make particularized determinations of matters of public right itself, with little by way of judicial review; and (*b*) it followed that the legislature might delegate such matters to agents, who could make particularized decisions with a similar lack of regular court involvement.[24] For example, the Court assumed that Congress could order removal of a specific bridge or wharf as an obstruction of interstate commerce, and that Congress could delegate such decision making to an officer without involving the regular courts.[25]

The absence of judicial review as to matters of public right, moreover, might entail not only a lack of court-accorded process, but also the absence of judicial review of legislative and agency procedures. Thus, one may embroider onto Nelson's premises these further possible premises: (1) legislatures could make decisions about public rights without having to employ any judicially-prescribed procedures, from which it might follow that (2) legislative delegees could make public rights decisions without having to employ judicially-prescribed procedures. This section focuses on premise 1—that legislatures might make particularized decisions on matters of public rights without prescribed processes. The next section will look at premise 2.

Neither the nineteenth-century nor the modern Supreme Court has required judicial-style proceedings before legislatures pass general laws. And as to particularized decisions, the ongoing supposition has long been that if the legislature may properly make an individualized decision (e.g., to grant a benefit), it may do so without judicially-imposed process. Accordingly, nineteenth-century legislatures could make individualized public rights decisions, for example, to award a pension or federal lands. This legislative freedom parallels modern special bills and specific appropriations.

"Public rights" as understood in the nineteenth century, however, encompassed not only governmental benefits, but also certain exactions such as taxation. The Court at times seemed to assume that legislatures could make individualized decisions as to such public rights exactions, as in the case of special assessments.

Special assessments were taxes imposed on designated properties

---

[24] Nelson, 107 Colum L Rev at 596–97 (cited in note 21).

[25] Id.

to fund projects such as street paving or drainage.[26] Such assessments provided a significant source of funding for municipal capital improvements in the nineteenth century[27] and have modern parallels in development fees.[28] Because special assessments typically affected a subset of properties within a political subdivision (thus distinguishing them from general taxation), the Court assumed that such taxes could only be imposed on properties benefited by the improvement that the taxes were to pay for.[29] Special assessment cases often included at least two determinations: a determination of a benefits district, and the actual assessment on individual pieces of property. The latter determination of benefit

---

[26] See generally Stephen Diamond, *The Death and Transfiguration of Benefit Taxation: Special Assessments in Nineteenth Century America*, 12 J Legal Stud 201, 231, 239–40 (1983) (providing an insightful history of benefits taxation including state law developments, and concluding that such taxes did not become a basis for government's recouping private windfalls); Victor Rosewater, *Special Assessments: A Study in Municipal Finance* (Colum U, 2d ed 1898) (providing an overview of then-current law in the states); id at v–vi, 75–76, 79–81 (noting problems of extravagant improvements and excessive and abusive impositions, on the one hand, and obstruction of needed public works on the other); Robin L. Einhorn, *Property Rules: Political Economy in Chicago, 1833–1872*, 104–83 (U Chi, paperback ed 2001) (studying special assessment system in Chicago); Saul Levmore, *Just Compensation and Just Politics*, 22 Conn L Rev 285, 294, 303, 307 (1990) (addressing puzzle of why special assessments are not a more common form of taxation, and proposing that political bargaining works fairly well in many contexts, but that political markets function less well when individuals are specially affected).

[27] See Diamond, 12 J Legal Stud at 202 (cited in note 26) (stating that special assessments "developed simultaneously with the general property tax as one of the twin financial pillars of state and local government.").

[28] See Vicki Been, *"Exit" as a Constraint on Land Use Exactions: Rethinking the Unconstitutional Conditions Doctrine*, 91 Colum L Rev 473, 473 (1991) (referring to older benefits assessment cases in discussing the advisability of modern limitations on development exactions); Richard Briffault, *A Government for Our Time? Business Improvement Districts and Urban Governance*, 99 Colum L Rev 365, 414–15 (1999) (tracing the origins of business improvement districts to special assessment districts, and describing benefits assessments as a cross between a tax and a user fee); R. Marlin Smith, *From Subdivision Improvement Requirements to Community Benefit Assessments and Linkage Payments: A Brief History of Land Development Exactions*, 50 L & Contemp Probs 5, 5–8 (1987) (indicating that municipalities were most successful at requiring construction of improvements as a condition of subdivision plat approval, but less successful at requiring mandatory off-site improvements). The Supreme Court has required a nexus between the conditions for development approval and the asserted harms caused by the development. See, for example, *Nollan v California Coastal Commission*, 483 US 825, 837 (1987) (holding that the commission could not condition a building permit on public access to the beach).

[29] See, for example, *Fallbrook Irrigation Dist. v Bradley*, 164 US 112, 176 (1896); *Norwood v Baker*, 172 US 269, 278–79 (1898); see also Rosewater, *Special Assessments* at 88–90 (cited in note 26) (noting that the principle of benefit distinguished special assessment from general taxes, but it is a forced exchange). But see Diamond, 12 J Legal Stud at 231 (cited in note 26) (suggesting that because the courts did not require a close connection between benefits and the assessment, special assessment came to resemble general taxes except when eminent domain was also involved).

might be made case by case, or by a mathematical formula, such as front footage for street improvements.

The Court allowed state-level legislatures to make not only the relatively more general determination of what properties to include in a benefits district but also the more particularized determinations of benefits to a small number of properties. In the 1888 case of *Spencer v Merchant*, for example, the New York Court of Appeals had set aside a prior local commission assessment for street improvements for lack of an agency hearing.[30] The city then obtained state legislation providing that the total of the unpaid assessments with expenses and interest be imposed on the "isolated parcels" whose owners had not yet paid, some of which did not have street frontage.[31] Although those property owners could be heard on the apportionment as among themselves,[32] it seems doubtful that the hearing would result in much change to the city's prior assessments given that the total to be apportioned among the properties would remain unchanged.[33] On direct review, the Supreme Court found no due process violation with the legislative imposition of the amount of benefits on these remaining properties, and treated the legislative determination of benefits as "conclusively settled."[34] Reflecting similar views, a late nineteenth-century treatise noted, "When an assessment for local improvement is irregular, the legislature may itself make, instead of authorize, a reassessment."[35] And later cases reiterated that legislative determination or confirmation of amounts due on particular parcels would foreclose many forms of review.[36]

Despite such cases, presumably legislatures typically passed more general tax laws and delegated assessments of particular properties to agents. There were only a handful of cases reaching

[30] See 125 US 345, 351 (1888). State law had provided for a hearing on laying out the street, but not as to an assessment for grading and other expenses. Id.

[31] Id.

[32] Id at 356–57 (indicating such a hearing was all that was constitutionally required).

[33] See id at 354 (quoting from the New York Court of Appeals, that the parties were complaining that they had never been heard as to the original apportionments, and find themselves practically bound by it as between their lots and those of the owners who paid).

[34] Id at 357.

[35] See Rosewater, *Special Assessments* at 107 & n 4 (cited in note 26).

[36] See *Road Improvement Dist. No. 1 v Missouri Pac. RR Co.*, 274 US 188, 191 (1927) (legislative confirmation of a particularized assessment "placed the assessment on the same plane as if it were made by the legislature," and would restrict review); notes 141–44 and accompanying text.

the Court where legislatures involved themselves in determining the amount due on particular parcels.[37] But these cases indicate that the Court was not speaking altogether figuratively when, in a property tax case, it referred to "the legislative function of making an assessment."[38]

C. JUDICIAL REVIEW AS A SUBSTITUTE FOR THE ABSENCE OF
LEGISLATIVE PROCEDURES?

The Court, then, did not require any special process in the legislature for making even relatively particularized decisions to assess a small number of properties. Did the Court make up for the lack of legislative process by requiring judicial process—that is, by requiring judicial review of the legislative decision? Judicial review would provide procedures while checking on the substantive determination of benefit to the properties assessed for the improvement. But in accordance with *Murray's Lessee*'s notion that a tax assessment required no judicial intervention, the answer in early Fourteenth Amendment decisions often seems to have been that no judicial review was required. The nineteenth-century Court acted on the presumption that the legislature's decision was based on sufficient facts, similar to the modern Court's rational basis scrutiny. But the nineteenth-century Court applied this presumption to adjudicative as well as to legislative facts.

This presumption justified not only the lack of process in the legislature, but also the lack of judicial review. In *Spencer v Merchant*, the Court quoted with approval the reasoning of the New York court below: "The question of special benefit and the property to which it extends is of necessity a question of fact, and, when the legislature determines it in a case within its general

[37] See text accompanying notes 139–45.

[38] *Security Trust & Safety Vault Co. v City of Lexington*, 203 US 323, 334 (1906) (stating that the state court in lowering an assessment "has not assumed the legislative function of making an assessment. It has merely reduced, after a full hearing, the amount of an assessment made by the assessor under color, at least, of legislative authority."); see also *State Railroad Tax Cases*, 92 US 575, 615 (1875) ("The levy of taxes is not a judicial function. Its exercise, by the constitutions of all States, and by the theory of our English origin, is entirely legislative."); compare *Londoner v Denver*, 210 US 373, 385–86 (1908) ("But where the legislature of a State, instead of fixing the tax itself, commits to some subordinate body the duty of determining whether, in what amount, and upon whom it shall be levied, and of making an assessment and apportionment, due process of law requires that at some stage of the proceedings before the tax becomes irrevocably fixed, the taxpayer shall have an opportunity to be heard, of which he must have notice, either personal, by publication, or by a law fixing the time and place.").

power, its decision must, of course, be final."[39] The Court stated that "objections that the sum raised was exorbitant, and that part of the property assessed was not benefited, presented no question under the Fourteenth Amendment to the Constitution, upon which this court could review the decision of the State court."[40]

Early Fourteenth Amendment challenges to state rate regulation for railroads and grain elevators paralleled the tax assessment cases. In *Munn v Illinois*, the Court treated grain elevators and railroads as affected with a public interest and thus subject to plenary legislative control of rate-making, effectively without any required process and without judicial review for reasonableness.[41] Given this legislative competence, the Court would assume that facts existed to support the legislation.[42] Judicial determination of reasonableness was uncalled for when the legislature had spoken.[43] Thus judicial process did not step in to make up for the absence of judicial-style process within the legislature.

III. Delegation as Not Requiring Additional Process

If legislative fact-finding whether of the general or particular variety called for no specific process (premise 1, above), did it follow that a legislative delegee was similarly free to make determinations without process and with a similar presumption of factual correctness (premise 2, above)? At times in the 1880s and into the 1890s, the Court spoke as if this were the case, as illustrated by cases in which delegees promulgated railroad rates or ordered railroads to eliminate grade crossings.

The Court at first gave state commissions a free hand in procedure for rate-making. In *Spring Valley Water Works v Schottler*, for example, the Court rejected an objection to a city's removing utility representatives from the rate-making board, and suggested that the legislature's delegation of power to municipal authorities

---

[39] 125 US at 353.

[40] Id at 356, describing with approval *Davidson v New Orleans*, 96 US 97, 100, 106 (1878).

[41] 94 US 113 (1877).

[42] 94 US at 132 (referring to whether the rate regulations were necessary to address abuses by virtual monopolies).

[43] *Peik v Chicago & North-Western Ry Co.*, 94 US 164, 178 (1877) (rejecting claim that the courts and not the legislature must decide what is reasonable); *Chicago, Burlington & Quincy RR Co. v Iowa*, 94 US 155, 161–62 (1877) (stating that courts would not decide reasonableness of rates if the legislature had set them); *Munn*, 94 US at 134 (stating that for protection against abuses by legislatures, the people must resort to the polls).

made no difference in *Munn*'s application.[44] Similarly, in a case where a city without hearing ordered railroads to build a viaduct and allocated costs among the railroads, the Court stated, "But if, as we have seen, it would have been competent for the legislature to have put the burden of these repairs upon one of the parties, or to have apportioned them among the parties, as it saw fit, so it may make a due apportionment through the instrumentality of the city council."[45] The Court cited with approval language from an opinion of Justice Peckham while sitting on the New York Court of Appeals holding that a landlord could be ordered by the Board of Health to provide running water to a tenement:

> The legislature has power, and has exercised it in countless instances, to enact general laws upon the subject of the public health or safety, without providing that the parties who are to be affected by those laws shall first be heard before they shall take effect in a particular case . . . The fact that the legislature has chosen to delegate a certain portion of its power to the board of health, . . . would not alter the principle, nor would it be necessary to provide that the board should give notice and afford a hearing to the owner before it made such order . . . .[46]

The idea that a delegee might operate with a similar lack of process as could the legislature may have been buttressed by the

---

[44] 110 US 348, 354 (1884) (stating that the board acting as a tribunal would be bound to exercise honest judgment and would not be presumed to act otherwise). The Court, however, termed the board's power to fix prices "judicial in nature." Id at 353; see also *State Railroad Comm'n Cases*, 116 US 307, 331, 335 (1886) (rejecting facial due process challenges, in addition to Commerce Clause and Contracts Clause challenges, to railroad commission's rate-making powers, although also noting that the states would lack power to fix rates that would take property); id at 333 (noting that the statute provided for due notice to the company and proper inquiry).

[45] *Chicago, B. & Q. R. Co. v Nebraska*, 170 US 57, 76 (1898) ("The latter was not directed to proceed judicially, but to exercise a legally delegated discretion"). The railroad was, however, given some opportunity to raise the invalidity of the ordinance and the reasonableness of the amount apportioned when it was sued by the state for not making the improvements, but the U.S. Supreme Court did not apparently review the reasonableness of the amount. See id at 77 ("The validity of the statute and of the ordinance having been passed upon and upheld by the courts of the State, it is not the function of this court, apart from the provisions of the Federal Constitution supposed to be involved, to declare state enactments void, because they seem doubtful in policy and may inflict hardships in particular instances."). The Court would later require agency hearings before agencies could require railroads to make significant expenditures for, e.g., connecting lines and grade improvements, at least where judicial review was restricted. See *Southern Ry Co. v Virginia*, 290 US 190, 199 (1933), and note 160 and accompanying text.

[46] *Chicago, B. & Q. R. Co. v Nebraska*, 170 US at 77 (original ellipses), quoting *Health Dept v Trinity Church*, 154 NY 32 (1895).

perception that officials in determining matters of public rights were not operating wholly outside the legislative branch.[47] Indeed, denominating a matter a public right implied that it was one of plenary legislative control; courts thus might see officers administering such rights as closely associated with the legislature. Some scholars of federal administration have noted that the Court sometimes distinguished "administrative" matters that were more under legislative control from those that were more squarely "executive."[48] They have also noted that it has only recently become widely accepted that all federal governmental powers are either legislative, executive, or judicial, and that agencies are necessarily under the executive.[49] Given the Court's sometimes expressed lack of interest in *state* separation of powers,[50] one might expect the Court to find a partly legislative characterization of state and local administrators that much easier.

IV. DELEGATION AS REQUIRING ADDITIONAL PROCESS

A. TAX DISTRICTING AND ASSESSMENTS BY MUNICIPALITIES AND OTHER DELEGEES

Although the Court made statements giving delegees the same procedural latitude as legislatures in the context of railroad reg-

[47] Compare *United States v George S. Bush & Co.*, 310 US 371, 380 (1940) (Douglas) (holding that the courts could not review the president's raising a tariff based on the Tariff Commission's comparison of prices using a particular conversion rate, stating that "it has long been held that where Congress has authorized a public officer to take some specified legislative action when in his judgment that action is necessary or appropriate to carry out the policy of Congress, the judgment of the officer as to the existence of facts calling for that action is not subject to review").

[48] See Lawrence Lessig and Cass R. Sunstein, *The President and the Administration*, 94 Colum L Rev 1, 46 (1994) (suggesting that nineteenth-century scholars saw federal agency powers as more divisible between executive functions and administrative functions, with executive functions deriving more directly from Article II and encompassing areas of political and unreviewable discretion of the president, while administrative functions derived from Article I legislation and were more controlled by law).

[49] See id at 5 (indicating that prior to the 1980s it was accepted that Congress could restrict the president's power to remove officers with quasi-judicial and quasi-legislative functions); Mashaw, *Federalist Foundations*, 115 Yale L J at 1286 (cited in note 13) (noting that Congress during the Federalist period saw the Treasury Department as more or less answerable to it); Peter P. Swire, Note, *Incorporation of Independent Agencies into the Executive Branch*, 94 Yale L J 1766 (1985) (arguing that it was time to reject the view of independent agencies as between the branches in favor of an executive characterization).

[50] See, for example, *Prentis v Atlantic Coast Line Co.*, 211 US 210, 225 (1908) (stating that there was no constitutional concern with the state court's combining legislative and judicial powers in their ability to revise railroad rates); see also *Crowell v Benson*, 285 US 22, 57 (1932) (adverting to state freedom to distribute state powers).

ulation, such statements were less evident in tax-assessment cases. One reason was then-prevalent practices; most states provided the opportunity to contest an assessment at least once either before a board or a regular court under their own statutes and constitutions.[51] Uncertainty may have existed for a time as to whether the federal constitution required an opportunity to contest an assessment; Justice Miller stated in 1877 that "the fact that most of the States now have boards of revisers of tax assessment does not prove that taxes levied without them are void."[52] But by the 1880s a consensus existed that the Fourteenth Amendment required notice and an opportunity to contest the amount of a particularized assessment at least once, whether in an agency or a court.[53]

In contrast to early rate-regulation cases, in tax-assessment cases the Court used the fact of delegation to mean that more process would be required of the delegee.[54] Some of the Court's pronouncements requiring agency process contrasted legislative decisions to those of lesser bodies. For example, in rejecting a procedural challenge to a legislatively-imposed special assessment for water works measured by street front footage, the Court noted:

> There is a wide difference between a tax or assessment prescribed by a legislative body, having full authority over the subject, and one imposed by a municipal corporation, acting

---

[51] See *Hagar v Reclamation Dist.*, 111 US 701 (1884) (in a benefits taxation case, discussing that most states either had boards of equalization to correct errors in valuation or allowed a court proceeding); *Stanley v Supervisors of Albany*, 121 US 535, 550 (1887) (observing that probably all states made provision for corrections of error and irregularities of assessors, generally through boards but sometimes by a right to appeal to the courts); *Lent v Tillson*, 140 US 316, 329 (1891) (discussing California Supreme Court's decision, which noted that a state special assessment statute provided for a hearing to meet constitutional hearing requirements); see also *Auffmordt v Hedden*, 137 US 310, 324 (1890) (referring to the system of appeals of appraisal in the federal executive branch, and also the opportunity to go to court); Thomas M. Cooley, *Treatise on the Law of Taxation* 265–66 (Callaghan, 1876) (indicating that the statutes of perhaps all the states provided for hearings before assessments became final and it has been customary to provide notice and hearing "as a part of what is 'due process of law' for these cases").

[52] *McMillen v Anderson*, 95 US 37, 42 (1877) (rejecting a claim that the taxpayer was entitled to a hearing as to whether he was a retail liquor dealer, although indicating judicial remedies against the collector might be available).

[53] See, for example, *Hagar v Reclamation Dist.*, 111 US 701, 710–11 (1884) (indicating that federal due process required either an opportunity to be heard before a board or a court).

[54] Compare Diamond, 12 J Legal Stud at 234–35 (cited in note 26) (discussing delegation doctrine with its requirement of some judicial scrutiny as somewhat submerging the requirement of benefit, but reconciling the benefit requirement to legislative control of taxation).

under a limited and delegated authority. And the difference is
still wider between a legislative act making an assessment and
the action of mere functionaries, whose authority is derived
from municipal ordinances.[55]

As to inclusion of specific properties in an irrigation district, the
Court stated, "The legislature not having itself described the district, has not decided that any particular land would or could
possibly be benefited as described, and, therefore, it would be
necessary to give a hearing at some time to those interested upon
the question of fact whether or not the land of any owners which
was intended to be included would be benefited by the irrigation
proposed."[56]

Delegation arguments requiring more process of the delegee
(than of the legislature) began with the same first premise as delegation arguments requiring no additional process: the legislature
could have made the decision itself without any judicialized process. Indeed, the argument that delegation is a reason for additional process almost necessarily begins with the assumption that
the legislature could have made the decision itself—but in this
instance has directed an agent to make the decision. Had the
legislature made the decision, the Court would presume sufficient
facts supported the decision. The lesser political status of a delegee
undermined this presumption.[57] Absent the presumption, a hearing would help to assure factual support.[58]

---

[55] *Parsons v District of Columbia*, 170 US 45, 51–52 (1898) (rejecting a Fifth Amendment
challenge to a congressionally imposed assessment for the district); see also *Spencer v
Merchant*, 125 US 345, 356 (1888) ("When the determination of the lands to be benefited
is entrusted to commissioners, the owners may be entitled to notice and hearing upon the
question whether their lands are benefited and how much.").

[56] *Fallbrook Irrigation Dist. v Bradley*, 164 US 112, 167 (1896). Justice Brewer had in an
1893 opinion for the Court held no hearing was required for a municipality's decision to
include properties within a district, a position contrary to the earlier expressions of the
Court in *Spencer v Merchant*, 125 US 345 (1888), and later expressions in *Fallbrook*, 164
US 112 (1896). See *Paulson v Portland*, 149 US 30, 40 (1893). Brewer reasoned that a
municipality, at least one that operated by charter, ought to be treated as a "miniature
state, the council its legislature" for districting decisions, id at 37, a position that the
Court would more fully adopt later. See text accompanying notes 114–19.

[57] See, for example, *Southern Ry Co. v Virginia*, 290 US 190, 197 (1933) ("In theory, at
least, the legislature acts upon adequate knowledge after full consideration and through
members who represent the entire public.").

[58] See, for example, *Fallbrook*, 164 US at 174–75 (while indicating a hearing was required
for a locally designated district, stating, "The legislature, when it fixes the district itself,
is supposed to have made proper inquiry, and to have finally and conclusively determined
the fact of benefits to the land included in the district, and the citizen has no further

Assuming for the moment that a state legislature can make a determination and be entitled to deference, does it make sense as a matter of *federal* constitutional law to see municipalities and other agents as entitled to less deference than the state legislature? One might argue that by this subordinating treatment, the Court inappropriately edges into deciding issues of state separation of powers, which the Court treated as largely outside federal constitutional law even pre-*Erie*.[59]

One might respond, however, that state legislatures have federal constitutional status[60] that arguably entitles them to deference not necessarily enjoyed by other state governmental entities, and such heightened status maps onto the realities of the organization of state government. While the current Court in many contexts gives equal constitutional deference to lower-level state-governmental entities such as municipalities (e.g., in evaluating general legislation), it gives them less in others (e.g., in applying sovereign immunity doctrine).[61] And if the Court's differential constitutional deference as between state legislatures and their delegees makes constitutional sense, it is even easier to justify differential deference as between Congress and federal agencies—given that federal government separation of powers is incontestably a federal constitutional matter.

To the extent that hearings supply factual support, and factual support is a requirement of rationality,[62] the Court's requirements of agency processes suggested that substantive rationality might

---

constitutional right to any other or further hearing upon that question."); id at 175 ("Unless the legislature decide the question of benefits itself, the landowner has the right to be heard upon that question before his property can be taken").

[59] See note 50.

[60] See, for example, US Const, Art I, § 3 (amended 1913 by Amend XVII), § 4, § 8, cl 17; Art II, § 1, cl 2; Art IV, § 3, cl 1, § 4; Art V; Art VI, cl 3.

[61] See Rich Schragger, *Reclaiming the Canvassing Board: Bush v. Gore and the Political Economy of Local Government*, 50 Buff L Rev 393, 407–11 (2002) (describing a formal doctrine under which local governments are distrusted constitutional nonentities, and a shadow doctrine treating them as trusted sovereigns).

[62] Compare *ICC v Louisville & N. RR Co.*, 227 US 88, 91 (1913) (in rejecting the ICC's arguments for the conclusiveness of its findings as to reasonableness, stating, "A finding without evidence is arbitrary and baseless. And if the Government's contention is correct, it would mean that the Commission had a power possessed by no other officer, administrative body, or tribunal under our Government. It would mean that where rights depended upon facts, the Commission could disregard all rules of evidence, and capriciously make findings by administrative fiat. Such authority . . . comes under the Constitution's condemnation of all arbitrary exercise of power."), quoted with approval in *Southern Ry Co. v Virginia*, 290 US 190, 195 (1933).

also be a condition of delegation. Indeed, the Court adverted to nonarbitrariness as a condition of delegation in 1886, in *Yick Wo v Hopkins,* when it struck down an ordinance that gave city supervisors standardless discretion that they used to deny laundry permits to people of Chinese origin.[63] First noting state-court practices of review of certain types of legislation for reasonableness, the Court continued:

> The same principle has been more freely extended to the quasi-legislative acts of inferior municipal bodies, in respect to which it is an ancient jurisdiction of judicial tribunals to pronounce upon the reasonableness and consequent validity of their by-laws. In respect to these, it was the doctrine, that every by-law must be reasonable, not inconsistent with the charter of the corporation, nor with any statute of Parliament, nor with the general principles of the common law of the land, particularly those having relation to the liberty of the subject or the rights of private property.[64]

This statement accords with Professor Mary Sarah Bilder's recent tracing of the Founders' presumption of judicial review to the English courts' review of the acts and by-laws of corporate bodies—including municipal corporations—for repugnancy with their charters, the laws of Parliament, and the common law.[65] While the Court during the *Lochner* era would eventually use implied reasonableness limitations on government to strike down even legislatures' acts,[66] the concept of delegation suggested that the Court might more readily apply a reasonableness or nonarbitrar-

---

[63] 118 US 356, 369–70 (1886) ("When we consider the nature and theory of our institutions of government . . . we are constrained to conclude that they do not mean to leave room for the play and action of purely personal and arbitrary power. Sovereignty itself is, of course, not subject to law, for it is the author and source of law; but in our system, while sovereign powers are delegated to the agencies of government, sovereignty itself remains with the people . . . ."); see also id at 366 (finding the ordinance faulty in part for providing no standards).

[64] Id at 371.

[65] Mary Sarah Bilder, *The Corporate Origins of Judicial Review,* 116 Yale L J 502, 504, 518 (2006). Bilder rejects natural law and separation of powers as necessarily the fonts of such review. Id at 509, 511–12. The British government through Privy Council review imposed similar limitations on the delegated authority of colonial governments even when they did not act under charters, and state courts reviewed early state laws for repugnancy to written constitutions. Id at 537–38, 544. Bilder concludes that judicial review of legislation was a well-accepted practice by the time of the new Constitution, although—given Parliamentary supremacy—it was unclear that judicial decisions should necessarily trump congressional ones. Id at 542.

[66] See note 178; text accompanying notes 146–54.

iness constraint the further down the government actor was on the delegation chain.[67] And, indeed, as described in Part V below, the Court would apply an arbitrariness constraint to delegees' decisions in tax-assessment cases.

B. PROCESS REQUIRED IN THE AGENCY

The procedural requirements that the Court imposed on municipalities and boards for hearings on value and benefits were not demanding. The Court required notice, although statutory specification of dates when assessments would be made and open to contest generally sufficed.[68] The taxpayer by right must have at least one chance to contest an assessment by hearing, although the Court did not outline much by way of formalities for such hearings;[69] it required an opportunity for personal appearance and argument in the special assessment case of *Londoner v Denver*.[70] Judicial process could substitute for the required agency process; if the state provided a court hearing in which an assessment could be contested, then the absence of agency process would not constitute a due process violation.[71]

---

[67] See Cooley, *Law of Taxation* at 72 (cited in note 51) (in discussing why state power of taxation was broader than municipal, stating, "A municipal government is one of delegated and limited powers, whose authority is generally to receive a somewhat strict construction, and which must find the purposes for which it may tax clearly confided to its charge by the state."); James L. High, *Treatise on the Law of Injunctions* 208, § 369 (Callaghan, 1873) (stating that "the courts of equity have been inclined in the case of assessments by municipal corporations to relax somewhat the stringency of the rule of noninterference as applied to the collection of state taxes"); compare Mashaw, *Reluctant Nationalists*, 116 Yale L J at 142 (cited in note 14) (indicating that although the general principle was not established as of 1815, Marshall's separate opinion in *Otis v Watkins*, 13 US (9 Cranch) 339 (1815), manifests the view "that now forms the core of judicial review of administrative action: discretion is always conferred on administrators on the implicit assumption that it will be reasonably exercised.").

[68] See, for example, *Fallbrook Irrigation Dist. v Bradley*, 164 US 112, 171 (1896).

[69] Id at 171. The Court read the statute in question, by providing a hearing on the petition to form an irrigation district before the board of supervisors, as allowing those affected by the proposed project a right to appear and contest the facts on which the petition was based before the board, including the inclusion of any particular land in the district. Id.

[70] 210 US 373, 386 (1908); see also *Auffmordt v Hedden*, 137 US 310, 323 (1890) (rejecting a challenge to federal customs procedures that did not accord the importer the right to hear and cross-examine witnesses against him).

[71] See *Security Trust and Safety Vault Co. v City of Lexington*, 203 US 323, 333 (1906) (holding that although statutory notice and opportunity to be heard of right were required as to an assessment occurring outside of the ordinary assessment period, the state trial court's affording a full hearing as to the validity and amount of the assessment cured the deficiency).

While most state and local agencies did accord some assessment process, cases inevitably arose where it was lacking. In one case, the assessor had entered an assessment outside the ordinary time period such that the assessment did not appear on the regular rolls for review and potential contest by the taxpayer before the board of equalization. Justice Peckham stated, "Such assessment could not be enforced unless the taxpayer could thereafter at some time, and as a matter of right, be heard upon the question of the validity and amount of such tax."[72] In another case, the Court found an assessment invalid when local authorities disallowed any contest of an assessment for property omitted in good faith from a return.[73] Procedures for special assessments such as street improvements were perhaps less well established than those for ad valorem taxes,[74] but the Court easily extended procedures similar to those for contesting ad valorem assessments in settings where the assessors made individualized determinations of benefits.[75]

For the most part (with some short-lived exceptions discussed below), the Court required no hearing if a tax were assessed in a way that was formulaic or mathematical, such as by front footage on an improved street.[76] Rather, it was the softer determination of value or of benefit that required a chance for contest. The Court operated with a sense of the extent to which hearings would add to accuracy, at times foreshadowing *Mathews v Eldridge* balancing.[77] The Court accordingly required no hearing to impose a flat occupational tax,[78] and Justice Field noted that for poll and license taxes, as opposed to taxes involving individual assessments of value,

[72] Id at 332.

[73] *Central of Georgia Ry Co. v Wright*, 207 US 127, 141–42 (1907); see also *Turner v Wade*, 254 US 64, 70 (1920) (treating the statutorily directed entry of the original assessment upon arbitrators' disagreement as an absence of notice and hearing, when the arbitrators had agreed the original assessment was too high but disagreed as to amount).

[74] See Diamond, 12 J Legal Stud at 232 n 136 (cited in note 26) (indicating that the states were divided as to whether individual hearings on assessment were required).

[75] See, for example, *Paulsen v Portland*, 149 US 30, 40 (1893) (approving the particular provisions as interpreted by the state supreme court and as applied by the municipality as providing notice and a right to be heard as to the proportion of costs to be borne, although not requiring a hearing as to inclusion in the district).

[76] See notes 95–110 and accompanying text.

[77] 424 US 319 (1976); compare Thomas C. Grey, *Procedural Fairness and Substantive Rights*, in J. Roland Pennock and John W. Chapman, eds, XVIII *Nomos* 182, 184–85 (NYU, 1977) (stating that a balancing element is inevitable in procedural fairness).

[78] See *McMillen v Anderson*, 95 US 37, 42 (1877).

nothing would be added by according a hearing to a taxpayer.[79] Similarly, in the police power decision of *Lawton v Steele*, the Court approved a state statute allowing summary destruction of fishing nets found on or near the water, without prior hearing. The Court considered the low value of the nets, and the clog on enforcement that prior hearings would entail.[80]

C. SCOPE OF JUDICIAL REVIEW FOR AGENTS' PROCEDURES AND FOR
   SUBSTANCE

The procedural due process requirements on agencies entailed, of course, that the Court could review tax assessments for lack of appropriate procedures. But assuming that the state or local agency provided an adequate hearing, to what extent did *Murray's Lessee*'s suggestion that judicial process might be dispensed with remain true for other issues?

A claim of an overassessment of state or local taxes without more was not treated as a federal question nor was it an issue requiring judicial review.[81] This lack of review was true both as to actions originating in the state courts,[82] as well as in the federal

---

[79] *Hagar v Reclamation Dist.*, 111 US 701, 709–10 (1884).

[80] 152 US 133, 140–41 (1894). The likely accuracy of the summary determination probably also played a role. No nets were allowed at all on, or on the shores of, the particular waters. Id at 135.

[81] See *Hibben v Smith*, 191 US 310, 320, 321–22 (1903) (on direct review, holding that no federal constitutional question arose in a challenge to the factual determination of benefits by a board, and due process did not require judicial review of an assessment); compare *Auffmordt v Hedden*, 137 US 310 (1890) (indicating that federal customs determinations of value would be given finality); *Muser v Magone*, 155 US 240, 246–47 (1894) (discussing reviewable and unreviewable aspects of federal customs determinations; valuation in the absence of fraud was unreviewable). But see Nelson, 107 Colum L Rev at 580 (cited in note 21) (indicating that importation of goods was considered a privilege, allowing Congress discretion to make administrative determinations of value final). State and federal statutes and common law actions nevertheless might supply more complete review than the constitutional minimum. See, for example, *State Railroad Tax Cases*, 92 US 575, 613 (1876) (referring to system of corrective justice for federal taxes within the executive, and the possibility of suing the collector for taxes paid if the taxpayer were not satisfied). If a state court supplied judicial review of value, federal courts could as well in a case of proper jurisdiction. See, for example, *Road Dist. v St. Louis*, 257 US 547 (1922) (allowing removal and taking of evidence as the state court would do in a case of contest of a special assessment).

[82] See, for example, *Hibben*, 191 US at 320. On direct review, the Seventh Amendment limited Supreme Court review of jury-found facts (generally not at issue in tax-assessment cases); in addition, writ-of-error review encompassed only review of law. Compare *Chicago, Burlington & Quincy RR v Chicago*, 166 US 226, 245–46 (1897) (indicating that the Court was restricted in its review of a jury verdict of one dollar to the railroad when part of its land was condemned for a road, both by the Seventh Amendment and writ-of-error review,

courts.[83] On direct review of a case in which the taxpayer complained that city officials had assessed his farmland at urban values, the Court noted, "It is alleged, and probably with truth, that the estimate of the value of the land for taxation is very greatly in excess of its true value. Whether this be true or not we cannot here inquire."[84] And in a special assessment case the Court provided a catalogue of what would *not* constitute a due process violation:

> . . . neither the corporate agency by which the work is done, the excessive price which the statute allows therefore, nor the relative importance of the work to the value of the land assessed, nor the fact that the assessment is made before the work is done, nor that the assessment is unequal as regards the benefits conferred, nor that personal judgments are rendered for the amount assessed, are matters in which the state authorities are controlled by the Federal Constitution. . . . The remedy for abuse is in the state courts. . . .[85]

On the one hand, then, delegation required at least one chance for a hearing as to a particularized assessment decision because the presumption of factual regularity attending legislative determinations on matters of public right was no longer operative. On the

---

although giving full review of the instructions to the jury). Such restrictions, however, did not stop the Court from de novo review of rate reasonableness. See *Northern Pac. Ry Co. v North Dakota*, 236 US 585, 593 (1915) (on writ of error reviewing rates, stating, "This court will review the findings of facts by a state court (1) where a Federal right has been denied as the result of a finding shown by the record to be without evidence to support it, and (2) where a conclusion of law as to a Federal right and findings of fact are so intermingled as to make it necessary, in order to pass upon the Federal question, to analyze the facts." (citations omitted)). Nor did they stop the court from finding certain tax decisions arbitrary upon delving into the record. See text accompanying notes 126–28.

[83] See, for example, *Fallbrook Irrigation Dist. v Bradley*, 164 US 112, 168 (1896) (in case originating in lower federal courts, facts determined by the board of supervisors would be considered final; stating, "Unless this court is prepared to review all questions of fact of this nature decided by a state tribunal, where the claim is made that the judgment was without any evidence to support it or was against the evidence, then we must be concluded by the judgment on such a question of fact, and treat the legal question as based upon the facts as found by the state board."); *State Railroad Tax Cases*, 92 US 575, 614–15 (1876) (in appeals from a lower federal court, indicating that a court of equity would not interfere to address "mere errors or excess of valuation, or hardship or injustice of law, or any grievance which can be remedied by a suit at law").

[84] *Kelly v Pittsburgh*, 104 US 78, 80 (1881) (and citing additional cases); see also *Spencer v Merchant*, 125 US 345, 355 (1888) (reiterating this point from *Kelly*).

[85] *Walston v Nevin*, 128 US 578, 582 (1888) (on direct review; citations omitted). The assessment method by square feet in *Walston* was prescribed by state-level legislation. See also *Pittsburgh, Cincinnati, Chicago and St. Louis Ry Co. v Backus*, 154 US 421 (1894) (approving application of unit taxation prorated by in-state mileage, and assuming, because evidence was taken on the issue, that the board had taken into account the railroad's ownership of high-value out-of-state real estate).

other hand, if such a hearing were accorded, the decisions as to value and benefit could be treated as effectively final. This finality was partly based on the "legislative" nature of tax assessment. As the Court stated as to why federal equity relief would not readily be available to restrain taxes:

> One of the reasons why a court should not thus interfere, as it would in any transaction between individuals, is, that it has no power to apportion the tax or to make a new assessment, or to direct another to be made by the proper officers of the State. These officers, and the manner in which they shall exercise their functions, are wholly beyond the power of the court when so acting. The levy of taxes is not a judicial function. Its exercise, by the constitutions of all the States, and by the theory of our English origin, is exclusively legislative.[86]

The Court's disclaimer of a constitutional dimension to mere overassessment, however, could be trumped by allegations of over-assessment plus something more. Often this something more was a systemic problem. An allegation of an unconstitutional taxing statute or a tax on federally-exempt property would require judicial attention if properly raised—whether on direct review[87] or in a federal trial forum with jurisdiction.[88] So too would issues of im-

---

[86] *State Railroad Tax Cases*, 92 US 575, 614–15 (1875). The Court, however, indicated that actions at law could be available, and also actions in equity under appropriate circumstances. Id. The quotation supports Tom Merrill's observation that the Court sometimes seemed more concerned that nonjudicial business would contaminate the judiciary than that judicial business would escape the regular court system. Thomas W. Merrill, *The Origins of the Appellate Review Model of Administrative Law*, draft of Sept 26, 2008, at 44–45; compare *Upshur v Rich*, 135 US 467, 472–73 (1890) (stating that review of a tax assessment was not a judicial case that could be removed to federal court, although contests as to taxes could become judicial cases).

[87] See, for example, *Brennan v Titusville*, 153 US 289 (1894) (on direct review, invalidating a municipal fee on hawkers as a tax on interstate commerce when applied to agents sent by out-of-state manufacturers); *Ward v Love County*, 253 US 17 (1920) (on direct review, rejecting state court's determination that taxes were voluntarily paid, and finding a violation of a federal law prohibition on the taxation of the Indians' allotments).

[88] See, for example, *Pickard v Pullman's Car Co.*, 117 US 34 (1886) (affirming a lower federal court's determination that the taxpayer was entitled to a refund of a tax violating the Commerce Clause); *Allen v Pullman's Palace Car Co.*, 191 US 171 (1903) (granting recovery of taxes paid under protest that violated the Commerce Clause); compare *Chicago, Burlington and Quincy Ry Co. v Babcock*, 204 US 585, 597 (1907) (on review from a lower federal court, rejecting a challenge to an assessment, noting that no United States franchises were involved). Apart from requirements of a federal question or diversity, federal equity jurisdiction had additional requirements. Even when a taxpayer claimed that a taxing statute was unconstitutional, he could be required to pay and seek a refund at law. Compare *Raymond v Chicago Union Traction Co.*, 207 US 20, 40 (1907) (indicating that equity was justified because the case involved more than the unconstitutionality of the law under

proper methodologies or wrong principles even with respect to one taxpayer[89]—frequently at issue in cases alleging a failure to limit taxation of railroads to intrastate property as required by the Commerce Clause and due process.[90] Long-standing overassessments affecting many properties could evoke a federal equity forum,[91] and the Court was not always picky as to how long-standing or widespread the overassessment had to be.[92] Eventually, as discussed more fully below, the Court would soften its earlier refusal to look at factual errors in assessments, by recognizing that an extremely arbitrary overassessment would indeed state a Fourteenth Amendment violation.[93]

Overall, the Court's system of judicial review of taxation comported with Richard Fallon's description of due process as often

---

which the tax was levied). The Court later restricted the availability of refund actions in the federal court. See Ann Woolhandler, *The Common Law Origins of Constitutionally Compelled Remedies*, 107 Yale L J 77, 135–44 (1997).

[89] See, for example, *Pittsburgh, Cincinnati, Chicago & St. Louis Ry Co. v Backus*, 154 US 421 (1894) (on direct review, considering but rejecting challenge to unit taxation method, and giving a strong presumption in favor of the regularity of the assessment); *Fargo v Hart*, 193 US 490, 502 (1904) (stating that state's taking into account, for in-state taxation, bonds held out-of-state by the express company was "not a mere case of overvaluation, but is an assessment made upon unconstitutional [under the Commerce Clause] principles," and a resort to federal equity was proper); *Raymond*, 207 US at 26 (statement of the case), 37 (in an equity case from a lower federal court, finding state action and a constitutional violation in board of equalization's using a method starting with 100 percent of the value of the property of the complainants, while others' property was assessed starting with 65–75 percent); *Northern Pac. Ry Co. v Adams Co.*, 1 F Supp 163, 184, 185, 187, 190 (ED Wash 1932) (finding the ad valorem assessments of several railroads to have been made by improper methods or wrong principles). But see *Chicago, Burlington & Quincy Ry Co. v Babcock*, 204 US 585, 595–96 (1907) (Holmes) (providing a crabbed reading of when a taxpayer could challenge methodologies); see also *Raymond*, 207 US at 41 (Holmes dissenting) (opining that it should take something extraordinary to find a constitutional violation in a tax assessment).

[90] *Chicago, Burlington & Quincy Ry Co. v Babcock*, 204 US at 592 (on review from a lower federal court, noting that taxation of out-of-state property was first considered to be a Commerce Clause problem and later also a due process problem).

[91] See *Cummings v National Bank*, 101 US 153, 157 (1880) (stating that while state law allowed for injunctions against an illegal tax, federal equity even apart from state law would be available when a rule or system of valuation was designed to operate illegally and applied to a large class).

[92] See, for example, *Raymond*, 207 US at 37–38 (invalidating a tax that for one year was based on a higher percentage of value than for other taxpayers). Nor was the Court always clear as to whether these claims for equal treatment to other taxpayers raised state or Fourteenth Amendment issues. See *Cummings*, 101 US at 157–58 (stating that equity would be available when a system of valuation was "designed to operate unequally and to violate a fundamental principle of the Constitution," but proceeding to discuss equal taxation provisions of the Ohio constitution); see also Woolhandler, 107 Yale L J at 146 (cited in note 88) (discussing availability of federal equity to address state equal taxation claims).

[93] See text accompanying notes 122–33.

requiring systems that keep government reasonably in check, rather than case-by-case review.[94] The requirements were of hearing rights, coupled with review for arguably more systemic issues together (eventually) with claims of arbitrariness beyond mere error. The next section will take a closer look at the interaction of requirements of procedure and substantive arbitrariness review in the area of special assessments.

V. Rejection of Procedural Requirements for Agents in Favor of Substantive Arbitrariness Review

Toward the end of the nineteenth century, the Court's management through skeletal procedural requirements looked as if it would become more intense for special assessments. Benefit remained a constitutional requirement for localities' special assessments, but it was not at first clear whether the Court would impose a light or heavy version of due process for the determination of benefit. The light version, as to which the Court stood firm, required municipalities or other delegees to hold hearings to allow contests when assessors had made property-specific determinations of benefit not based on self-applying formulae like front feet on an improved street. The heavy version would have required a city or other delegee (1) to hold hearings if a taxpayer complained that a formulaic tax rule such as front foot resulted in taxes greatly in excess of benefits, and (2) to hold hearings in designating benefits districts or to allow an individual property owner to contest inclusion. While the Court would require neither of these, the rejection of such procedures may have encouraged the Court to undertake substantive review of assessments.

A. MATHEMATICAL RULES

The Court in 1898, in *Parsons v District of Columbia*, held that legislatively-set rules for assessing benefits by linear footage for waterworks were unassailable, and that no hearing in which a taxpayer might contest benefits was necessary. At the same time, the Court indicated that hearings might be required for assessments

---

[94] Fallon, 93 Colum L Rev at 311 (cited in note 12).

where a delegee rather than the legislature prescribed such a front-age rule.[95]

Shortly thereafter, *Norwood v Baker* tested this proposition.[96] The plaintiff presented an appealing case for a hearing to determine whether a front-foot rule resulted in a tax greatly exceeding benefits. A village extended a road through the middle of the plantiff's property, and she was awarded $2,000 in a condemnation proceeding. The village then assessed her property for the entire $2,000 plus the costs of the condemnation proceeding based on the village council's front-foot allocation of benefits.[97] Justice Harlan writing for the majority stated that "the exaction from the owner of private property of the cost of a public improvement in substantial excess of the special benefits accruing to him is, *to the extent of such excess,* a taking, under the guise of taxation, of private property for public use without compensation."[98] Perhaps to avoid the imputation that the Court was moving all the way to treating every overassessment of benefits as a constitutional question, Harlan characterized the problem as an unconstitutional *"rule or system of valuation"*;[99] "[t]he assessment was in itself an illegal one because it rested upon a basis that excluded any consideration of benefits."[100] *Norwood* effectively required the municipality to afford an opportunity to contest benefits even for mathematical assessment rules,[101] and suggested that the opportunity to show a lack of particular benefits might be necessary even if the rule were legislatively prescribed.[102]

---

[95] 170 US 45, 51–52 (1898), discussed in text accompanying note 55; see also id at 50 (treating the issue for review as one of the constitutionality of congressional legislation).

[96] 172 US 269 (1898).

[97] Id at 276. State law gave the municipality several other options including specific benefits determinations. Id at 272, 289–90. The council chose among those options in providing by ordinance for a front-foot measure of benefits in *Norwood.* See id at 274.

[98] Id at 279 (original italics).

[99] Id at 292 (original italics); see also id at 290 (stating that city proceeded on the theory that "the abutting property could be made to bear the whole cost of the improvements, whether such property was benefited or not to the extent of such cost").

[100] Id at 291.

[101] See *French v Barber Asphalt Paving Co.,* 181 US 324, 344 (1901) (describing *Norwood*).

[102] 172 US at 279; see also *Wight v Davidson,* 181 US 371, 386 (1901) (Harlan dissenting) (arguing that a congressional act directing that not less than half of damages for condemnation be assessed to abutting lands was contrary to *Norwood*'s holding). Brewer, dissenting in *Norwood,* argued that legislative determinations of benefits were sufficient, and that the city's common council exercised legislative power. 172 US at 298. This comported with his earlier opinion for the court in *Paulson v Portland,* 149 US 30, 37, 40 (1893), discussed in note 56.

The *Norwood* rule sufficiently conflicted with local practice to cause a raft of similar cases to come before the Court on direct review, perhaps spurring the Court to retreat from its hearing requirement.[103] Perhaps, too, mathematical rules for assessment may have seemed overall at least as fair as individual benefits determinations.[104] Thus in a group of turn-of-the-century decisions the Court held that localities using front-foot rules need not accord an opportunity to show the lack of benefit.[105] It distinguished *Norwood* on a grab bag of grounds.[106]

Included in the reasons for distinguishing *Norwood* was that the front-foot rule in *Norwood* had not been prescribed by the state-level legislature: "The legislature of the State had not defined or designated the abutting property as benefited by the improvement."[107] The Court proceeded to approve several cases where a front-foot rule was prescribed by state statute with no opportunity for hearing on specific benefit.[108] But provision in a city charter

---

[103] See Robert C. Ellickson, *Suburban Growth Controls: An Economic and Legal Analysis*, 86 Yale L J 385, 473 (1977) (indicating that *Norwood* led to a flood of litigation, leading the Court to backtrack, and that the "evolution of federal law of special assessments supports the wisdom of not applying federal law to localized growth control disputes"); Jed Rubenfeld, *Usings*, 102 Yale L J 1077, 1137 n 267 (1993) (using *Norwood*'s demise as an example of the rejection of the idea that taxes must produce equivalent-value benefits to the taxpayer).

[104] Compare Cooley, *Law of Taxation* at 451–52 (cited in note 51) (opining that front foot might be as good or better than other ways to estimate benefits in many cases); Diamond, 12 J Legal Stud at 219, 224–27 (cited in note 26) (with particular reference to New York practices, indicating that front-foot rules were developed to respond to abuse, but that special assessments remained an avenue for corruption under the Tweed Ring, and that New Jersey courts preferred individualized determinations).

[105] See, for example, *French v Barber Asphalt Paving Co.*, 181 US 324 (1901); compare Diamond, 12 J Legal Stud at 230–31 (cited in note 26) (interpreting the case law that developed after *Norwood* as treating special assessments like ordinary property tax assessments, except when they were tied to an exercise of eminent domain). But see Rosewater, *Special Assessments* at 102–06 (cited in note 26) (in 1898 treatise, discussing state cases requiring that general benefits not be specially assessed).

[106] See *French*, 181 US at 344.

[107] *Wight v Davidson*, 181 US 371, 384 (1901) (involving a congressional provision). But see *French*, 181 US at 370 (Harlan dissenting) (arguing that there was legislative sanction for the frontage rule in *Norwood*, such that it could not properly be distinguished on that ground).

[108] See *Towawanda v New York*, 181 US 389, 391 (1901) (approving town's use of front-foot rule provided by New York statute that did not provide for inquiry into benefits); *Webster v Fargo*, 181 US 394 (1901) (similar holding as to local action pursuant to North Dakota statute); *Detroit v Parker*, 181 US 399, 399 (1901) (similar holding where action was pursuant to statute that was also the city charter); *Louisville & N. R. R. Co. v Barber Asphalt Co.*, 197 US 430, 434–35 (1905) (Holmes) (rejecting railroad's challenge to a statutorily prescribed formula assessment for street improvements, indicating that if some properties might not receive any benefit, "that hardship must be borne as one of the

also sufficed.[109] In cases thereafter, the Court continued to speak as if the level of authority for formulaic assessments made a difference, but at the same time generally found the municipality's authority sufficiently plenary to count as legislative.[110]

B. DISTRICTING DECISIONS BY MUNICIPALITIES AND OTHER AGENTS

Related issues surfaced as to designations of benefits districts, particularly for drainage and levee taxation.[111] On several occasions in the 1880s and 1890s, the Court indicated that a hearing on districting would be required if the district were not legislatively determined.[112] Later cases indicated that no separate hearing on district formation was required so long as the property owner had the later opportunity to argue the lack of particular benefits. This made sense, because the benefits hearing at least theoretically could result in a finding of no benefit at all, effectively excluding the property from the district.[113]

---

imperfections of human things," and also stating that potential uses of the land for other than a roadbed might be considered).

[109] *French*, 181 US at 326 (noting that the rule was prescribed by the city charter); *Cass Farm Co. v Detroit*, 181 US 396, 397 (1901) (rejecting a contest to front-foot provisions of charter and paving ordinance).

[110] See, for example, *Withnell v Ruecking Construction Co.*, 249 US 63, 68–69 (1919) (stating that while the entitlement to a hearing "depends upon the authority under which the assessment is made," no hearing was required when the assessment was made in accordance with rules of the city charter, which had been adopted by the people's vote under state constitutional authority).

[111] Formula assessment rules would often obviate the need for a separate districting decision for street improvement.

[112] See *Fallbrook Irrigation Dist. v Bradley*, 164 US 112, 167, 171, 174 (1896) (indicating that a hearing on inclusion within the district was required, but finding sufficient the publication of notice of the board of supervisor's meeting where the petition to form the district would be heard); *Spencer v Merchant*, 125 US 345, 356 (1888) (indicating a hearing would be required for a commission determination of which lands were benefited, but not for the legislative determination at issue in the case); see also *Embree v Kansas City and Liberty Blvd Rd Dist.*, 240 US 242, 247, 250 (1916) (in a case where the Court rejected a challenge to a district established by an order of the county court, stating that a hearing as to inclusion in the district was required, "as the district was not established by the legislature, but by an exercise of delegated authority," but no hearing would be necessary as to different rates by zones prescribed by legislation). But see *Paulsen v Portland*, 149 US 30, 37, 40 (1893) (Brewer) (treating the city as a "miniature" state and not requiring a districting hearing, although notice and hearing were required as to the allocation of costs among properties).

[113] *Voigt v Detroit*, 184 US 115, 120, 122 (1902); *Goodrich v Detroit*, 184 US 432, 440 (1902) (holding that no hearing need be given as to initial inclusion within a benefits district, when later hearing for apportionment of the benefit would allow property owner to claim he was benefited less than the amount assessed or not benefited at all); compare *Londoner v Denver*, 210 US 373, 378 (1908) (not requiring a hearing as to the establishment of an assessment district, but requiring a later hearing as to the specific assessment).

But as was true in cases involving front-foot rules, the Court eventually began to treat municipalities and other delegees as if they exercised the authority of state-level legislatures in designating districts. For example, in a 1919 decision, the Court held that when the state had delegated all legislative power to form sewer districts to cities, no hearing on inclusion in the district was required.[114] In the particular case, moreover, the taxpayer would never receive a hearing on benefit, because state legislation provided for allocation in proportion to area[115] (which presumably the locality could have provided as well).[116] While the Court distinguished prior cases as ones in which state law had not conferred such plenary legislative power,[117] it seemed to treat most cases as involving sufficiently plenary legislative power to allow for the districting designation without a hearing.[118]

Thus the Court experimented with requiring hearings when taxpayers contested application of mathematical formulae for benefits or inclusion in a benefits district, but ultimately backed off. By allowing the use of mathematical formulae and the inclusion in districts without hearings, the Court indicated that the Con-

---

[114] *Hancock v Muskogee*, 250 US 454, 456 (1919) (relying on Oklahoma decisions that the entire legislative power on this issue had been delegated to the municipalities); compare *Houck v Little River Drainage Dist.*, 239 US 254, 264 (1915) (holding constitutional a statute that provided notice and a court hearing before creation of the district, and indicating that such a duly organized district "had the same footing as if it had been created by the legislature directly"); see also id at 262 (describing broad powers of state to designate tax districts and to delegate this power).

[115] Id at 458–59.

[116] See text accompanying notes 105–10.

[117] 250 US at 458.

[118] See *Goldsmith v George G. Prendergast Construction Co.*, 252 US 12, 17 (1920) (in case contesting the locality's exclusion of a park from the sewerage district for assessment, noting that the establishment of the sewer district was committed to local authorities by the St. Louis charter and had the force and effect of a state statute; also indicating that on direct review the Court would only interfere for arbitrariness or if the assessment were "wholly unequal in operation and effect"); *Ivey v Keeling*, 281 US 699 (1930) (on direct review, dismissing for want of a substantial federal question an objection to inclusion in a high school district designated by the county board of school trustees; the opinion below stated that statutes had conferred on that body authority to create such districts, 15 SW2d 1097–98 (Tex App 1929)); *Chesebro v Los Angeles County Flood Control Dist.*, 306 US 459, 465–66 (1939) (treating a large flood district's acquisition of drainage district in accordance with conditions prescribed by the state legislature as sufficiently legislative as not to require a hearing on benefits). Ellickson reported *Chesebro* as the last special assessment case he found in the Supreme Court. See Ellickson, 86 Yale L J at 473 n 265 (cited in note 103). In *Browning v Hooper*, 269 US 396, 404–06 (1926), the Court held creation of a district by petition and election invalid for want of a hearing, and distinguishing cases where the legislature or the municipality to which the state had granted full legislative powers over the subject had selected the territory.

stitution did not require too fine a correlation between special assessments and benefits.[119] These experiments provide context for Justice Holmes's decision in *Bi-Metallic Investment Company v State Board of Equalization* that delegees' adoption of more rule-like or generalized policies—as distinguished from individualized determinations of value or benefit—would not be subject to due process hearing requirements.[120] *Bi-Metallic* was, however, an easier case, given the generality of the State Board of Equalization's reassessment of the entire city of Denver, and given taxpayers' remaining opportunity to argue particular valuations.[121]

By indicating in tax-assessment cases that the constitutional guarantee of procedural due process did not restrain how agencies made rules (including even rules of only modest generality), the Court flattened the distinction between state-level legislatures and lower-level delegees for constitutional procedural due process review. Requiring no process of municipalities in creating benefits districts, for example, suggested that factual regularity might be presumed for municipal decisions as it was for state legislative decisions. This development would help to undermine the connection between delegation and due process.

C. ARBITRARINESS REVIEW AS A BACKUP

The retreat from requiring process for front-foot rules as well as for inclusion in districts, however, was accompanied by at least a small consolation prize. Extreme arbitrariness, even in assessments by a rule and in districting, would violate the Fourteenth Amendment. This was an advance on the Court's prior (sometimes qualified) statements that individual inequitable assessments did not rise to constitutional status.[122] Harlan's decision in *Norwood*

---

[119] See *Houck*, 239 US at 265; see also Diamond, 12 J Legal Stud at 240 (cited in note 26) (concluding that benefit taxation came to rest less on a theory of individual benefit from a particular project and more on a theory "that in aggregate, each individual received benefits from public expenditures roughly equivalent to his tax burdens").

[120] *Bi-Metallic Investment Co. v State Board of Equalization*, 239 US 441 (1915); see also *Pacific States Box & Basket Co. v White*, 296 US 176, 185 (1935) (Brandeis) (stating that the same presumption of facts to support legislation would attach to a state agency regulation, particularly one adopted after hearing).

[121] 239 US at 443–44.

[122] See text accompanying notes 81–85; see also *Fallbrook Irrigation Dist. v Bradley*, 164 US 112, 169–70 (1896) (stating that inclusion of lands that clearly could not benefit might be subject to review, although "A question of this kind would involve no constitutional element, and its solution would depend on the ordinary jurisdiction of courts of justice over this class of cases.").

had shied from relying on overassessment alone as a Fourteenth Amendment violation, indicating that the due process problem was the absence of the availability of a hearing to contest a rule-based assessment that grossly exceeded benefit.[123] But in abandoning *Norwood*'s hearing requirement in early twentieth-century cases, the Court effectively reinterpreted it as a substantive arbitrariness case—one deserving relief on its extreme facts, as a "confiscation" or "an abuse of law."[124] The Court assured that courts of equity would continue to afford a remedy "where there is an attempt, under the guise of legal proceedings, to deprive a person of his life, liberty, or property without due process of law," as "was the nature and effect of the proceedings in the case of *Norwood v. Baker.*"[125]

The promise of review for arbitrariness was not entirely empty; the Court occasionally found a districting decision or a particular assessment based on a mathematical rule to be arbitrary. For example, in the 1916 *Myles Salt Co. v Board of Commissioners*, the Court on direct review held that the plaintiff had stated a due process claim in alleging that a local government included in a drainage district an island whose erosion problem would be exacerbated by the drainage project.[126] In a different case from the same year, Justice Holmes found a Fourteenth Amendment violation when a complainant's property was assessed based on square footage 500 feet back from the improved street, while others were assessed only up to 240 feet, based on "mechanically" following "an ordinance that is a farrago of irrational irregularities throughout."[127] A later case struck down an individualized benefits deter-

---

[123] See text accompanying notes 99–100.

[124] *French v Barber Asphalt Paving Co.*, 181 US 324, 344 (1901).

[125] Id at 345; see also *Wight v Davidson*, 181 US 371, 385 (1901) (similar); compare *Hibben v Smith*, 191 US 310, 326 (1903) (indicating federal courts ought not to interfere in a question of the amount of an assessment unless there has been some course amounting to a confiscation of property or personal rights as in *Norwood*).

[126] 239 US 478, 482 (1916) (noting the allegation that the taxation was an effort to take the plaintiff's property without due process of law); id at 481 (posing the issue as whether the action fell within the "principle or its limitation" that state legislatures and local administrative bodies could designate drainage districts "and their action cannot be assailed under the Fourteenth Amendment unless it is palpably arbitrary and a plain abuse"); id at 485 (concluding that the power was "arbitrarily exerted, imposing a burden without compensating advantage of any kind").

[127] *Gast Realty and Investment Co. v Schneider Granite Co.*, 240 US 55, 59 (1916) (on direct review, finding the tax violative of the Fourteenth Amendment (not specific as to any clause)). The Court found the ordinance unconstitutional, but limited its decision "to

mination stating: "To say that 9.7 miles of railroad in a purely farming section, treated as an aliquot part of the whole system, will receive benefit amounting to $67,900.00 from the construction of 11.2 miles of gravel road seems wholly improbable, if not impossible."[128]

An interesting feature of the decisions is the Court's implicitly seeing substantive Fourteenth Amendment review for arbitrariness[129] as a cheaper and less intrusive substitute for additional procedures when local governments used formula benefits assessments or designated benefits districts.[130] This substitutability of mild substantive review for procedural requirements lends support

---

those, who like the plaintiff in error, have suffered from inequalities that have no justification in law." Id at 60; *Straight Creek Drainage Dist. No. 2 v Chicago, R.I. & P. Ry Co.*, 36 F2d 650, 652 (10th Cir 1929) (holding that the drainage district's assessing most of the drainage costs based on assessed value, leading to the railroad's paying for large part of improvements for which it would receive little benefit, was palpably arbitrary and discriminatory in violation of the Fourteenth Amendment (likely referring to equal protection)).

[128] *Kansas City Southern Ry Co. v Road Improvement Dist. No. 6 of Little River County, Ark.*, 256 US 658, 660–61 (1921) (holding the act under which the district was created unconstitutional as applied, and that assessors' use of more definite standards for individuals' property than for the railroad's was a discrimination "so palpably arbitrary as to amount to a denial of equal protection of the law"); see also *Great Northern Ry Co. v Weeks*, 297 US 135, 152 (1936) (on cert to a lower federal court, holding that the failure to reduce a valuation given great drop in values deprived the taxpayer of due process); see also id (stating that the "assessment being shown to have been arbitrarily made and grossly excessive," plaintiff did not need to show overassessments for other years); id at 153 (Stone dissenting, joined by Brandeis and Cardozo) (claiming that this was the first case in which the Court had set aside a tax as violating the Fourteenth Amendment on the ground that it was too high without a showing that the assessment was discriminatory or that the taxpayer was bearing an undue share of the tax burden imposed on all property owners in the state).

[129] As indicated in the parentheticals, the Court sometimes spoke generally of the Fourteenth Amendment, sometimes spoke of due process, and sometimes mentioned inequalities or equal protection. See notes 127–28. The nonarbitrariness norm partakes of both due process and equal protection. See Fallon, 93 Colum L Rev at 372 (cited in note 12) (indicating that the nonarbitrariness norm is one of equal protection as well as substantive due process).

[130] Compare *Miller & Lux v Sacramento & San Joaquin Drainage Dist.*, 256 US 129, 130–31 (1921) (on direct review, in rejecting a claim that an opportunity to show lack of benefit was necessary with respect to an assessment within a legislatively designated district, adverting to arbitrariness review under *Myles*, but finding the complaint's allegations of arbitrariness insufficient); *Southern Ry Co. v Virginia*, 290 US 190, 194 (1933) (indicating a hearing was required despite the state court's saying review for arbitrariness was available in the courts). Obviously procedural requirements and arbitrariness review (or more searching review) do not need to be substituted for one another, but may complement each other. See Stewart, 88 Harv L Rev at 1670, 1672–74 (cited in note 11) (describing a traditional model of administrative law that, inter alia, requires agencies to follow decisional procedures to promote accuracy, rationality, and reviewability); see also *Kansas City Southern*, 256 US at 660–61 (in a case involving an individual assessment (where an individual hearing would be required) engaging in arbitrariness review).

to Larry Alexander's observations that substance and procedure are part of a package manifesting a general constitutional prohibition on governmental arbitrariness.[131]

Substantive arbitrariness, moreover, was not inherently indeterminate in the tax context. Rather, it consisted in a gross lack of factual support for a determination of benefit or value.[132] Thus, just as the Court required delegees to accord procedures to assure at least minimal factual support to justify a deliberate government exaction, so too might it provide arbitrariness review with a similar end in view. In addition, arbitrariness review policed for gross inequality as among taxpayers.[133]

[131] Lawrence Alexander, *The Relationship Between Procedural Due Process and Substantive Constitutional Rights*, 39 U Fla L Rev 323, 332–34 (1987) (arguing that procedures and substance are part of one package, all substantive, and that substantive constitutional constraints are in the background of every award and denial of even optional benefits); Fallon, 93 Colum L Rev at 310 (cited in note 12) (identifying a pervasive substantive due process norm of nonarbitrariness, providing that government officials must act based on public-spirited rather than self-interested or invidious motivation, and that there must be a rational relationship between government ends and means); compare Michael J. Phillips, *How Many Times Was Lochner-Era Substantive Due Process Effective?* 48 Mercer L Rev 1049, 1063 (1997) (arguing that there has been overcounting of the number of laws that the Court struck down on substantive due process grounds, and noting some were procedural due process cases, which the Court at the time did not distinguish from substantive cases). But see Fallon, 93 Colum L Rev at 343 (cited in note 12) (noting that it is not proper to see all issues of substance as transferable to ones of procedure; for example, where procedures are not feasible, it makes more sense to look directly at whether the deprivation is substantively justified).

[132] Such factual support helped to assure conformity to public purposes that were relevant to a particular decision, and also helped to assure that a decision was not made for constitutionally reprobated reasons. See Cass Sunstein, *Naked Preferences and the Constitution*, 84 Colum L Rev 1689, 1696–97 (1984) (discussing a pervasive theme of various constitutional constraints that the distribution of resources should not go to one group rather than another based solely on raw political power, but rather that at least a minimal public purpose should support governmental activities).

[133] Arbitrariness review treated wealth redistribution through ad hoc assessment decisions as an impermissible end, and this prohibition subsists under current equal protection law. Compare *Allegheny Pittsburgh Coal Co. v County Comm'n*, 488 US 336 (1989) (requiring a remedy for taxpayers when the assessor based assessments on recent purchase prices but made only minor modifications if properties had not been recently sold, resulting in gross disparities in assessments violating due process) with *Nordlinger v Hahn*, 505 US 1 (1992) (approving a similar tax assessment scheme adopted by a statewide ballot initiative), discussed in Erin A. O'Hara and William R. Dougan, *Redistribution through Discriminatory Taxes: A Contracterian Explanation of the Role of the Courts*, 6 Geo Mason U L Rev 869 (1998) (providing a contracterian justification for the Court's effectively allowing redistribution based on ballot initiatives and legislation but not based on administrative decisions).

VI. Arbitrariness Review Applied to Legislative Determinations

A. LEGISLATIVELY-APPROVED SPECIAL ASSESSMENTS

As noted above, the Court at first purported to treat legislatively-approved assessments as final. Recall that in the late 1880s in *Spencer v Merchant*, where the New York legislature had confirmed a sum representing benefits to be assessed on a limited number of properties, the Court indicated that a claim that some properties were not benefited and the amounts were exorbitant did not raise a due process issue.[134] The Court quoted with approval the New York Court of Appeals decision below that a legislative confirmation of specific benefits "must of course be final," even if such a determination by a lower-level body standing alone might not be.[135] Accordingly, Court decisions finding particular assessments arbitrary began in the context of assessments by local assessors and other delegees.[136] And in limiting *Norwood*, the Court relied in part on the fact that the municipality and not the legislature had chosen the front-foot rule whose application was at issue in that case.[137]

The availability of arbitrariness review for municipal and other delegee assessments, however, would soon include state-level legislative assessments. While suggested as a possibility in earlier cases,[138] such arbitrariness review had tangible results in 1920s cases involving ongoing attempts by Arkansas officials to mulct railroads for local improvements and to insulate their decisions

---

[134] 125 US 345, 355–56 (1888), citing *Davidson v New Orleans*, 96 US 97 (1878).

[135] 125 US at 353; see also id at 356 (indicating that commissioner's determinations might require notice and hearing).

[136] See text accompanying notes 126–28.

[137] See text accompanying note 107.

[138] *Wagner v Baltimore*, 239 US 207, 218–20 (1915) (reaffirming that no hearing was required when the legislature imposed a small tax per front foot for past improvements, but also suggesting that a court of equity could grant relief for a flagrant abuse which was not here alleged or shown); *Branson v Bush*, 251 US 182, 189–90 (1919) (reiterating that legislative inclusion within a district would be conclusive, although also indicating that a flagrant abuse could be addressed); compare *Martin v District of Columbia*, 205 US 135, 139–40 (1907) (Holmes) (stating that constitutional rights were matters of degree, and interpreting a congressional statute that required a jury to apportion costs nevertheless to require that the assessment not exceed benefit, as it clearly did for the properties in question).

from review by seeking state legislative confirmation.[139] For example, in *Road Improvement District v Missouri Pacific Railroad*, the local district assessed a railroad for supposed benefits from a parallel road that the railroad sensibly claimed would compete with, rather than benefit, the railroad. While the railroad was contesting the assessment in federal court, the road district obtained state legislative confirmation of the particular assessment.[140]

The Court treated the legislative confirmation as significantly limiting judicial review.[141] The Court thus indicated that it would not review the allegation that the railroad had been assessed by different methodology from other property, as it would have if the assessment had not been legislatively confirmed:

> But this testimony must be put aside by reason of the legislative adoption of the assessments. The modes in which the assessors arrived at the amounts assessed were not shown on the assessment roll or communicated to the legislature; so the question of discrimination must be determined independently of the theories and processes of the assessors, as if the assessments were made directly by the legislature.[142]

But the Court also made clear it would review the legislative assessment for arbitrariness and delved into the factual record.[143] The Court held that the legislatively-confirmed assessment of $54,062 would violate due process if not reduced to $15,000 or

---

[139] Compare *Thomas v Kansas City Southern Ry Co.*, 261 US 481, 483–84 (1923) (although noting that the legislature's determination that lands will be benefited is ordinarily conclusive, affirming lower federal court's injunction against an Arkansas legislatively-authorized tax ad valorem within a legislatively-created drainage district, which resulted in 3.61 miles of railroad tracks being assessed for 57 percent of the cost of the improvements when the benefits would be primarily to lands that would become tillable).

[140] *Road Improvement Dist. No. 1 v Missouri Pac. RR Co.*, 274 US 188, 190 (1927).

[141] Id at 191 ("There can be no doubt that the legislative confirmation placed the assessment on the same plane as if it were made by the legislature, and thereby cured any mere irregularities on the part of the assessors" but could not prevent inquiry into constitutional limitations).

[142] Id at 192.

[143] Id at 192–94; see also *Kansas City Southern Ry Co. v Road Improvement Dist. No. 3*, 266 US 379, 383 (1924) (on direct review in another case in which the locality obtained legislative confirmation of a particularized benefits assessment during the pendency of court proceedings, reviewing record evidence but not finding arbitrariness); compare *Valley Farms Co. v Westchester County*, 261 US 155 (1923) (rejecting a challenge to a legislatively-set district and use of ad valorem assessment for a sewer district for lack of a sufficient showing of arbitrariness).

less.[144] In a later case, the Court similarly held that a road-improvement assessment on a pipeline was arbitrary, despite legislative ratification.[145] The presumption of factual support for individualized legislative tax determinations had clearly faded.

B. LEGISLATIVELY-APPROVED RATES

This application of substantive arbitrariness standards to delegees as a prelude to applying such standards to the legislature echoed what had occurred earlier for railroad rate regulation. As noted above, the Court in *Munn* indicated that due process did not require judicial review for legislatively-prescribed rates, and the Court at first seemed to indicate that agency-set rates would be similarly exempt.[146] In its 1890 decision in *Chicago, Milwaukee & St. Paul Railway Company v Minnesota*, however, the Court edged away from *Munn* by requiring judicial review of the substantive reasonableness of commission-set rates.[147] The Court noted the lack of agency procedures: "No hearing is provided for, no summons or notice to the company before the commission has found what it is to find and declared what it is to declare, no opportunity provided for the company to introduce witnesses before the commission, in fact, nothing which has the semblance of due process of law. . . ."[148] The state court had then treated the agency rate determination as final.[149] The Court's prescribed antidote for these shortcomings was to require regular courts to review agency rates

---

[144] 274 US at 195. The Court also found an equal protection violation in the railroad's being assessed on personalty when other properties were not. Id at 194.

[145] *Standard Pipe Line Co. v Miller County Hwy & Bridge Dist.*, 277 US 160, 161–62 (1928) (in another Arkansas case, reversing the federal Circuit Court which had read recent cases as suggesting narrow constitutional review, and finding the assessment "arbitrary and unreasonable in amount").

[146] See text accompanying notes 41–44.

[147] 134 US 418, 457–58 (1890); see also Paul R. Verkuil, *The Emerging Concept of Administrative Procedure*, 78 Colum L Rev 258, 261–63 & n 13 (1978) (discussing *Milwaukee Road* as manifesting a notion of per se procedural inadequacy of administrative as opposed to judicial process). See generally Stephen A. Siegel, *Understanding the Lochner Era: Lessons from the Controversy Over Railroad and Utility Rate Regulation*, 70 Va L Rev 187, 211–13 (1984) (discussing *Milwaukee Road* as moving toward value and not merely title and possession as part of the concept of constitutionally protected property).

[148] 134 US 418, 457 (1890).

[149] Id.

for substantive reasonableness, rather than requiring more agency process.[150]

For several years the Court treated the *Milwaukee Road* decision as applicable only to commission-set rates and not legislatively-set rates. In *Budd v New York*, the Court refused to review the reasonableness of a legislative rate, and distinguished *Milwaukee Road*: "That was a very different case from one under the statute of New York in question here, for in this instance the rate of charge is fixed directly by the legislature."[151] The Court cited as support *Spencer v Merchant*, a case discussed above in which the Court indicated that while legislative determinations of total benefits to be assessed against a small number of properties were conclusive, delegees' determinations might require notice and hearing.[152]

But as would prove true in the area of tax assessments, the line between legislative determinations and those made by delegees did not hold. Due process requirements of judicial review for delegees' determinations suggested similar requirements for legislative rates. By the late 1890s, the Court held judicial review of rate reasonableness was required whether the rates were commission- or legislatively-set. When the Court held in *Reagan v Farmers' Loan & Trust* that commission-set rates were subject to plenary federal equity review and struck down the rates as violative of the Fourteenth Amendment, it did not rest its holding on the fact that the rates at issue were commission-set.[153] And legislatively-set rates were at issue in *Smyth v Ames*, where the Court prescribed a constitutional standard of a fair return based on a current-value rate base.[154]

---

[150] Id at 457–58 (indicating that judicial review of reasonableness was required to prevent a deprivation of property without due process).

[151] 143 US 517, 546 (1893); see also *Brass v North Dakota*, 153 US 391 (1894) (following the holding in *Budd* in not reviewing the reasonableness of a legislatively-set rate for grain elevators); Verkuil, 78 Colum L Rev at 262 n 12 (cited in note 147) (citing *Munn* and *Budd* as examples of the Court's distinguishing between substantive control imposed by the legislature as opposed to an administrative body).

[152] 143 US at 546, citing *Spencer v Merchant*, 125 US 345, 356 (1888).

[153] *Reagan v Farmers' Loan and Trust*, 154 US 362, 394 (1894) (referring to the act that made commission rates conclusive in all actions between private individuals and the companies).

[154] *Smyth v Ames*, 169 US 466, 528 (1898) (referring to legislatively-set rates); id at 546 (stating that the rate should be based on "the fair value of the property being used for the convenience of the public"); see also Siegel, 70 Va L Rev at 224 (cited in note 147)

By characterizing unreasonable rates as confiscation in cases such as *Smyth*, the Court moved railroad regulation partly from the public rights camp into private rights territory, where full judicial process was required.[155] This mandatory regular-court review for confiscation took pressure off the Court to articulate requirements of agency process in rate regulation.[156] Emphasis on agency process grew in the early twentieth century as the Court increasingly allowed review on an agency record in ICC cases[157] and in state court cases that came to the Court on direct review.[158]

(indicating that *Smyth* announced the present value test that would remain for the next forty years).

[155] 169 US at 528 (describing the need for judicial involvement in rate reasonableness); see also *Milwaukee Road*, 134 US at 457–58 (same). The status of railroad rate regulation as involving private rights remained somewhat ambiguous, such that *Crowell v Benson*, 285 US 22 (1932), is generally treated as the first case explicitly to address whether private rights might be placed for initial adjudication in an agency. See note 170. This ambiguity may have been partly due to the fact that not all challenges to rates would state claims for confiscation. The Court allowed states to prescribe some cross-subsidization within an intrastate system; confiscation claims thus ordinarily involved a whole system of intrastate rates based on an intrastate rate base. See, for example, *Minnesota Rate Cases*, 230 US 352, 434, 466 (1913) (indicating that the intrastate rate base had to be determined and that for purposes of determining a fair return, the results of the entire intrastate business had to be taken into account). On the other hand, the Court indicated that it was possible, even within a generally remunerative system, that some rates could violate due process and equal protection strictures. See, for example, *Northern Pacific Ry Co. v North Dakota*, 236 US 585, 595–97, 599–600 (1915) (on direct review, holding that the state had violated the Fourteenth Amendment in providing an unremunerative rate for coal transportation, even if the Court would ordinarily not concern itself with the details of a rate schedule that overall provided remunerative intrastate rates).

[156] See *Home Tel. and Tel. Co. v City of Los Angeles*, 211 US 265, 278 (1908) (in declining specifically to delineate rate-making procedures, noting that state and federal courts were open to those who claimed their property was confiscated).

[157] See Merrill, draft at 28–32, 72–73 (cited in note 86) (discussing the Court's move, with the Hepburn Act of 1906, to a more appellate-style review model, which allowed the Court to move off micromanagement of the ICC while providing continuity with past practice). The Court indicated that in cases alleging confiscation, a railroad might not be totally debarred from introducing new evidence. See *Manufacturers' Ry Co. v United States*, 246 US 457, 488–89 (1918). But see *New York v United States*, 331 US 284, 334–36 (1947) (indicating that remand to the ICC ordinarily was appropriate where further evidence on the issue of confiscation was necessary).

[158] See *Washington v Fairchild*, 224 US 510, 525–27 (1912) (on direct review, finding no error in the state court's disallowing new evidence when there had been adequate opportunity for presentation of evidence before the commission which acted somewhat like a master in chancery), discussed in Merrill, draft at 32 (cited in note 86); see also 224 US at 525 (indicating that a hearing was required, but was provided here). The Court at the same time provided robust fact review. See id at 528 (reviewing record to determine if an order to build a connecting line was so unreasonable as to amount to confiscation, because what purports to be a question of fact can be so involved with issues of law as to be effectively the latter); id at 531 (finding evidence of necessity for the connecting line insufficient). Federal equity courts apparently continued to take new evidence in cases involving state rates and related orders, at least where constitutional issues of confiscation or the Commerce Clause were involved. See, for example, *Minnesota Rate Cases*, 230 US

The Court would eventually impose various hearing requirements for rate-making[159] as well as for agencies' imposition of out-
of-pocket expenditures such as in ordering grade improvements.[160]
The Court justified such procedures as preventing the grant of
power to a state or federal agency from "being a pure delegation
of legislative power"[161]—a pure delegation being one where the
agency was free to act arbitrarily due to lack of procedures and
rules.[162] Thus delegation—if at first a reason for the Court's not

---

352, 380 (1913) (adverting to the lower federal court's referring these issues to a special
master, who took evidence); *Wichita RR and Light Co. v Public Utilities Comm'n of Kansas*,
260 US 48, 55 (1922) (holding that the lower federal court should have accorded the
opportunity "to traverse the allegation of fact by the Kansas Company as to the basis for
the order of the Commission and also to maintain by evidence and argument the issue as
to due process of law and the equal protection of the law. The charge that the order made
a classification denying due process and the equal protection of the law was a mixed
question of law and fact, upon which the complainant had a right to be heard."). The
Court, however, would eventually hold that utilities had no right to relitigate facts merely
because a constitutional right was involved. See, for example, *Alabama Pub. Serv. Comm'n
v Southern Ry Co.*, 341 US 341, 348–49 (1951).

[159] See, for example, *ICC v Louisville & N. RR Co.*, 227 US 88, 92–93 (1912) (requiring
that evidence supporting the decision be in the record and rejecting the ICC's argument
that "having been given legislative power to make rates it can act, as could Congress, on
such information, and therefore its finding must be presumed to have been supported by
such information, even though not formally proved at the hearing."); *Wichita RR and Light
Co. v Public Utilities Comm'n of Kansas*, 260 US 48, 58–59 (1922) (relying on state statute,
requiring statement of reasons in electricity rate case); compare *Home Tel. and Tel.*, 211
US at 278 (although not specifying procedures, stating as to telephone rate-making, "It
may be that the authority to regulate rates, conferred upon the city council by § 31 of
the charter, is not an authority, arbitrarily, and without investigation, to fix rates of charges
and that if charges were fixed in that manner the act would be beyond the authority of
the council.").

[160] See, for example, *Fairchild*, 224 US at 525, 528, 531 (on direct review requiring a
hearing to determine if the railroad would be required to build a connecting line, and
while holding that procedures here were adequate, finding the evidence in the commission
record inadequate to show necessity); *Southern Ry Co. v Virginia*, 290 US 190, 195 (1933)
(stating that to require abolition of the established grade crossing and the construction
of an overhead would take the railroad's property and that without the establishment of
proper hearing requirements, violated the Fourteenth Amendment).

[161] *Wichita RR*, 260 US at 58–59.

[162] Id ("The maxim that a legislature may not delegate legislative power has some qualifications, as in the creation of municipalities, and also in the creation of administrative
boards to apply to the myriad details of rate schedules the regulatory police power of the
State. The latter qualification is made necessary in order that the legislative power may
be effectively exercised. In creating such an administrative agency the legislature, to prevent its being a pure delegation of legislative power, must enjoin upon it a certain course
of procedure and certain rules of decision in the performance of its function. It is a
wholesome and necessary principle that such an agency must pursue the procedure and
rules enjoined and show substantial compliance therewith to give validity to is action."),
quoted in *Mahler v Eby*, 264 US 29, 44–45 (1924) (in requiring the secretary of state to
make an explicit finding of undesirability for deportation) and in *Panama Refining Co. v
Ryan*, 293 US 388, 432 (1935) (in holding that even were it possible to derive from the
act prerequisites for the president's prohibiting transportation of oil, the Executive Order

prescribing procedures for railroad regulation as described in Part
III—spurred both reasonableness review in the courts and requirements of additional process in the agency, as it had in the
case of taxation.[163]

VII. Conclusion: Reflections on Current Understandings

From a modern perspective, one might view requirements
of procedures based on delegation in the area of taxation as merely
manifesting the usual legislative versus executive distinction—that
is, between making general laws, and bringing those laws to bear
on particular individuals. The legislature, particularly in prescribing exactions, enacts general laws for which no process is required.
But if an executive official makes an individualized determination
of benefit or value as part of implementing tax laws, then process
would be required.

From a modern perspective, one might also conclude that the
Court imposed procedures as a way to implement the same constitutional constraints that applied to the legislature to the legislature's delegee.[164] (In addition, procedures helped to assure fidelity to statutory mandates.) For example, a state legislature could
not properly legislate higher tax rates for out-of-staters or even
in-staters when their property was indistinguishable from property
that was otherwise universally taxed at a lower rate. And an assessor
is under similar constraints. But while the federal courts may easily
review legislation challenged as violating the Constitution, it
would be impossible to review every claim of overassessment.[165]

was defective for its failure to provide findings or a statement of grounds for the president's
action).

[163] In requiring hearings as to grade crossing improvements (decisions that the Court
had previously suggested a delegee might make without process, see text accompanying
note 45), the Court reasoned as it often had in tax cases that the presumption of factual
regularity attending legislative determinations would not be made for lesser bodies. *Southern Ry*, 290 US at 195.

[164] Compare Alexander, 39 U Fla L Rev at 335–36 (cited in note 131) (arguing that
there is "a general substantive constitutional value that proscribes arbitrariness in the
substance of rules and therefore in the procedures by which they are allocated"); Fallon,
93 Colum L Rev at 362 (cited in note 12) (noting that under modern due process law the
farthest reaching duty of care, making judicial review the easiest to obtain, is in cases
involving rules of general applicability, where systemic effects of a departure from constitutional norms are likely to be the greatest).

[165] Compare Grey, XVIII *Nomos* at 202 (cited in note 77) (concluding that some substantive
constitutional rights may be judicially enforced largely through procedural constraints, because
institutional constraints on judicial power prevent more direct enforcement).

The Court thus required agency procedures, together with judicial review addressing systemic or particularly egregious problems, to provide an acceptable level of compliance with constitutional and statutory constraints.[166]

It seems helpful and uncontroversial to suppose that (1) legislatures make general laws, and procedural requirements kick in when the executive branch brings general laws to bear on particular individuals, and (2) procedures help to impose substantive constitutional constraints on executive actors akin to those that apply to legislatures. From the historical perspective of this article, however, that account is too top-down; it assumes that constitutional constraints apply first to legislative action and only by extension of reasoning to their delegees—when perhaps the developments were bottom up.

A. FROM PROCEDURAL DUE PROCESS TO SEPARATION OF POWERS

First, the assumption that the legislature would impose exactions only through general laws is not entirely historically correct. Rather, as discussed above, the Court seemed to assume that legislatures might effectively impose certain kinds of particularized assessments and out-of-pocket expenditures in the area of public rights. Designating a matter as one of public right not only meant that courts could be largely excluded from review of specific exaction decisions, but also implied that the legislature could make such decisions itself.

Likely the growth of procedural due process for delegees helped to make legislatures' engaging in specific exaction determinations less acceptable. The Court first reasoned in taxation cases that if a delegee rather than the legislature made the exaction decision, the delegee must accord process. But if due process required the delegee to accord the opportunity to present evidence for individualized determinations of benefit or value, it seemed to follow that the legislature must supply process if it made its own decision, or not make such a particularized determination at all. The presumption that the legislature acted on sufficient facts—the presumption that had been used to distinguish legislative determi-

---

[166] See Fallon, 93 Colum L Rev at 336 (cited in note 12) (stating that it would be unworkable to require careful judicial review of administrative fact-finding in every case, but that the courts still acknowledge a duty to police fact-findings at a wholesale level).

nations from those of delegees—would become increasingly questionable for individual exaction cases, such as those in which the Arkansas legislature confirmed large assessments against a particular railroad or pipeline.[167] And given that the Court has never proved willing to impose judicialized procedures on legislatures, it would seem to follow that legislatures could not engage in tax assessment or other specific exactions.

In short, the legislature would be *required* to delegate individualized exactions in the area of public rights,[168] as was already true in the area of private rights exactions such as criminal or tort liability where regular courts made individualized determinations.[169] (Simultaneously, private rights were arguably being brought closer to public rights in cases such as *Crowell v Benson*.[170]) Delegation doctrine, generally thought to limit the extent and conditions under which legislatures could hand off decisions to a delegee, ultimately came to limit the extent to which legislatures could retain certain particularized decisions for their own determination. Delegation's requirements of procedural due process were thus translated into separation-of-powers limitations on legislatures' specific acts.

To be sure, it is somewhat difficult to pinpoint much in the Supreme Court's case law, ancient or modern, forbidding legislatures from making specific nonpunitive exactions in public rights cases.[171] The Court during the period under study continued to say, for example, that legislatures could confirm tax assessments and that such confirmations would be subject to less review than

---

[167] See notes 138–45 and accompanying text.

[168] Such delegation is not required for the legislature's grant of individualized benefits.

[169] See note 21.

[170] 285 US 22 (1932), discussed in Nelson, 107 Colum L Rev at 598–602 (cited in note 21) (describing how *Crowell* and labor cases paved the way for administrative agencies to act as fact-finding adjuncts to the federal courts for many statutory claims, including those for monetary relief); see also Richard H. Fallon, Jr., *Of Legislative Courts, Administrative Agencies, and Article III*, 101 Harv L Rev 915, 924 (1988) (discussing *Crowell* as going beyond prior cases in ratifying adjudication in non-Article III courts for private rights cases); see also id at 918, 966–67 (advocating an appellate review model that requires Article III review of administrative decisions largely without regard to the traditional public/private rights distinction). But see Merrill, draft at 42 (cited in note 86) (claiming that ICC cases after the 1906 Hepburn Act had already adopted a *Crowell*-like appellate review model, for determinations of monetary liability between shippers and carriers).

[171] See, for example, *Nixon v Administrator of the General Services Administration*, 433 US 425 (1977) (finding no bill of attainder problem with Congress's passing a law to remove custody of Nixon's documents from him to the government).

if the assessment had never been confirmed.[172] But it seems likely that the modern Court would find a legislative determination of value for tax assessment unacceptable.[173] The Court's later invalidation of legislation removing particular people from government employment on bill-of-attainder grounds[174] comported with a lessened sense of the propriety of particularized legislative exactions in public rights areas once thought subject to more plenary legislative control.[175]

B. ARBITRARINESS REVIEW: FROM DELEGEES TO LEGISLATURES

It also may be a mistake in terms of historical sequencing to say that there are general nonarbitrariness requirements on legislatures that also became applicable to delegees. This conclusion seems somewhat anomalous, because the nineteenth-century Court saw the Constitution as most typically invalidating legislation rather than specific acts of officers. Indeed, the Court sometimes felt it needed to explain how constitutional constraints on legislatures also applied to delegee decisions.[176] Accordingly, the

---

[172] See notes 141–42 and accompanying text. But see *Springer v Philippine Islands*, 277 US 189, 201–02 (1928) (holding that under the Philippine Organic Act and consistently with state and federal separation of powers, the Philippine legislature could not vote the stock of a corporation largely owned by the Philippine government).

[173] Compare *Monongahela Navigation Co. v United States*, 148 US 312, 327–28, 345 (1893) (holding that the question of compensation for expropriation of a lock was judicial, not legislative, such that the Court would ignore Congress's direction not to consider the value of the franchise to collect tolls).

[174] See *United States v Lovett*, 328 US 303, 315 (1946) (invalidating as an attainder an appropriation provision that specified individuals could not be paid). See generally Note, *The Bounds of Legislative Specification: A Suggested Approach to the Bill of Attainder Clause*, 72 Yale L J 330 (1962) (arguing for a broad reading of the attainder prohibitions to forbid trial by legislature).

[175] Compare *INS v Chadha*, 462 US 919 (1983) (striking down, for lack of bicameralism and presentment, the legislative veto of an executive grant of relief from deportation). One might see the whole proceeding in *Chadha* as part of Congress's providing a benefit of a suspension of deportation. Id at 926. The Court said it expressed no opinion on whether legislation requiring deportation would violate the Constitution. Id at 954 n 17; see also id at 959 (Powell concurring) (arguing that the legislative veto improperly allowed the legislature to perform a judicial function). The Court applied *Chadha* to invalidate legislative vetoes of agency rulemaking, thus indicating that the majority was not necessarily focused on particularized decisions. See *Process Gas Consumers Group v Consumer Energy Council of America*, 463 US 1216 (1983).

[176] See *Chicago, B. & Q. RR v Chicago*, 166 US 226, 233–37 (1897) (discussing how if the Fourteenth Amendment forbade legislative condemnation of property without compensation, the amendment must also forbid a judicial proceeding that effectively did the same); Ann Woolhandler, *Demodeling Habeas*, 45 Stan L Rev 575, 607 (1993) (discussing the nineteenth-century Court's tendency to view the issue of constitutionality as specific to statutes); see also Fallon, 93 Colum L Rev at 326–27, 362 (cited in note 12) (discussing

Court often tied its findings of arbitrariness by delegees to legislative acts that had granted the authority to make decisions.[177]

Nevertheless, the eventually articulated Fourteenth Amendment requirements for rationality and nonarbitrariness often seemed to get a boost from the Court's greater ease in applying these implied limitations to delegees than to state legislatures.[178] As noted above, English practices documented by Mary Sarah Bilder of judicial review for conformity to charters applied to municipal corporations, a practice to which the Court adverted in suggesting that it might more readily review delegees' actions than those of state legislatures.[179] In addition, Michael Collins has found that many substantive due process norms got their start as general constitutional law constraints applied in diversity, constraints that later crossed over to the Fourteenth Amendment.[180] In both the general common law and early crossover cases, municipal decisions were often at issue.[181] And Caleb Nelson has recently shown that the

that modern substantive due process review is harder to obtain for relatively isolated torts than for legislation and rules).

[177] See, for example, *Yick Wo v Hopkins*, 118 US 356, 374 (1886) (treating the ordinance under which the supervisors acted as invalid in allowing the arbitrary denial of permission to operate a laundry in a wooden building).

[178] To be sure, the Court in this era was also starting to invalidate state legislation based on substantive due process grounds, and one might characterize any such case as effectively resting on a finding of arbitrariness, or lack of a substantial relation to a permissible governmental end. See, for example, *Allgeyer v Louisiana*, 165 US 578 (1897) (striking down a state law forbidding transactions with out-of-state insurers that had not complied with state registration requirements, and adverting to concerns for extraterritoriality and liberty of contract). Some scholars consider *Allgeyer* to be the original substantive due process case, although some consider that honor to belong to *Chicago, Milwaukee & St. Paul Ry v Minnesota*, 134 US 418 (1890). See Michael G. Collins, *October Term, 1896—Embracing Due Process*, 45 Am J Legal Hist 71, 71 n 4 (2001) (citing authorities that take these positions).

[179] *Yick Wo*, 118 US at 371; see also id at 371–73 (discussing state cases finding municipal regulations unreasonable, including one involving gas rates set by a city); compare *Garfield v Goldsby*, 211 US 249, 262 (1908) (granting mandamus to require the secretary of interior to restore Goldsby to the citizenship rolls of the Chickasaw nation, after the secretary's predecessor had struck Goldsby's name without notice and a hearing, and in responding to arguments that the secretary's decisions were to be conclusive stating that "there is no place in our constitutional system for the exercise of arbitrary power, and if the Secretary has exceeded the authority conferred upon him by law, then there is power in the courts to restore the status of the parties aggrieved by such unwarranted action").

[180] Michael G. Collins, *Before Lochner—Diversity Jurisdiction and the Development of General Constitutional Law*, 74 Tulane L Rev 1263, 1267–68 (2000).

[181] Id at 1274 (discussing *Township of Pine Grove v Talcott*, 68 US (19 Wall) 666 (1874)); id at 1311 (discussing *Chicago, B. & Q. RR v Chicago*, 166 US 226 (1897)). While focus on municipalities was no doubt partly due to municipalities' being more readily suable in federal court than states, this is not a complete response given the availability of suits against individual state officers, and also given the Court's explicitly distinguishing its review of legislatures and lower-level delegees. See text accompanying notes 54–58.

Court was willing to inquire into administrative motivation well before it was prepared to engage in similar inquiries of legislative motivation.[182]

This article's discussion of taxation and rate regulation shows a similar pattern with respect to a general rationality norm. In several decisions, the Court found these strictures applicable to the delegee while seeming to indicate that a decision by the legislature on the same topic would not be subject to similar review.[183] The Court would later apply such strictures to the people's initial delegee—the legislature.

---

[182] See Caleb Nelson, *Judicial Review of Legislative Purpose*, 83 NYU L Rev 1784, 1808 & n 95, 1809 & n 98 (2008).

[183] See text accompanying notes 54–56, 146–52; compare *Dobbins v Los Angeles*, 195 US 223, 236 (1904) (stating that "it is now thoroughly well settled by decisions of this court that municipal by-laws and ordinances, and even legislative enactments undertaking to regulate useful business enterprises, are subject to investigation in the courts with a view to determining whether the law or ordinance is a lawful exercise of police power . . .").

CASS R. SUNSTEIN

JUDGING NATIONAL SECURITY POST-9/11: AN EMPIRICAL INVESTIGATION

In the aftermath of the attacks of September 11, 2001, Congress
and the executive branch have embarked on a number of new initiatives, raising a series of fresh legal questions.[1] Many of those
questions involve the relationship between national security and
some kind of individual right. Does the president have the authority
to detain people without trial?[2] Do existing provisions of law allow
the use of military commissions?[3] Can certain information be with-
held from the public?[4] When, exactly, does the government need
a search warrant to obtain access to previously private information?[5]
May the executive engage in wiretapping?[6]

It is easy to find two sets of recommendations for how courts
should approach such questions. On a widely held view, judicial

Cass R. Sunstein is Felix Frankfurter Professor of Law, Harvard Law School.

AUTHOR'S NOTE: I am grateful to the Program on Risk Regulation for valuable support;
to Elisabeth Theodore, Emily Ullman, Beth Bell, and Jason Yen for indispensable research
assistance; and to Cassandra Wolos for the statistical analysis, which saved me from many
errors. Martha Nussbaum, Geoffrey Stone, David Strauss, and Adrian Vermeule provided
valuable comments on a previous draft. Special thanks to Vermeule for discussions that
inspired this project; those discussions produced the hypotheses that are tested here.

[1] The literature is voluminous. For one account, see David Cole and Jules Lobel, *Less
Safe, Less Free: Why America Is Losing the War on Terror* (2007).

[2] See *Hamdi v Rumsfeld*, 542 US 407 (2004).

[3] See *Hamdan v Rumsfeld*, 548 US 557 (2006).

[4] See *ACLU v Dept. of Def.*, 2008 WL 4287823 (2d Cir).

[5] See, e.g., *U.S. v bin Laden*, 126 F Supp 2d 264 (SDNY 2000).

[6] See *ACLU v NSA*, 493 F3d 644 (6th Cir 2006).

deference is the appropriate presumption or even rule.[7] Courts lack information about the potentially serious consequences of their judgments, and the elected branches are in the best position to balance the competing considerations. If courts should generally be reluctant to invalidate the decisions of the executive and legislative branches,[8] then their reluctance should be increased when national security is at stake.

On a competing view, also widely held, the argument for a strong judicial role is not at all weakened when a national security threat leads the elected branches to test the legal boundaries.[9] In "perilous times,"[10] it might be thought, those branches are especially prone to a serious form of lawlessness, perhaps because of a kind of public panic, and it becomes all the more important for courts to insist on compliance with the rule of law. On this view, the system of checks and balances, including an independent judiciary, is no less dispensable when the stakes are high and damaging intrusions on liberty are likely.[11] Defenders of this position contend that history is on their side: Intrusions on civil liberties, popular at the time but indefensible in retrospect, have occurred at many periods in American history.[12]

While the competing normative positions have been defended in great detail, we know much less about what courts actually do. The literature on that question is sparse.[13] In the post-9/11 era, it is essentially nonexistent. Of course the decisions of the Supreme Court are the most important ones, but in order to undertake a statistical analysis, it is necessary to examine lower court decisions, which are sufficiently numerous to test various hypotheses. In this essay, I describe the results of an effort to compile and analyze all relevant courts of appeals decisions between 9/11 and September 2008. The compilation consists of nearly all cases decided during

---

[7] See Richard A. Posner, *Not a Suicide Pact* (2007); Eric Posner and Adrian Vermeule, *Terror in the Balance* (2007).

[8] See Adrian Vermeule, *Judging Under Uncertainty* (2006).

[9] See Cole and Lobel, *Less Safe, Less Free* (cited in note 1).

[10] See Geoffrey Stone, *Perilous Times* (2004).

[11] See William Rehnquist, *All the Laws But One* (1997), for a qualified endorsement of this view.

[12] See id.

[13] The best discussion is Lee Epstein et al, *The Supreme Court During Crisis*, 80 NYU L Rev 1 (2005).

the administration of George W. Bush. The principal findings are as follows:

1. The overall rate of invalidation is low. The government loses only 15% of the litigated cases—a lower figure than in almost all other domains of federal law.
2. There is a significant difference between the voting patterns of Republican appointees and those of Democratic appointees. The Republican invalidation rate is 12%; the Democratic invalidation rate is 23%. Because the latter invalidation rate is almost double the former, the fate of government action might well depend on the composition of the panel.
3. Notwithstanding the different voting patterns of Republican and Democratic appointees, the standard panel effects are not found. The invalidation rates of Republican appointees do not differ if they are sitting with zero, one, or two Republican appointees. The invalidation rates of Democratic appointees are not affected by whether they are sitting with zero, one, or two Democratic appointees. This is a highly unusual finding; in the vast majority of domains of federal law, judicial votes are greatly affected by panel composition.[14]
4. Invalidation rates have not changed over time. Contrary to what might well be expected, the invalidation rate was the same in the first three years after the attacks of 9/11 as in the following four years.

My goal here is to elaborate these results and to offer some comments and explanations. In the process, I aim not only to explore the national security cases post-9/11, but also to provide some more general remarks on the analysis of judicial voting patterns, and about what can and cannot be learned from quantitative studies of this sort. A central point here involves *selection effects*: Because litigants are responsive to the likelihood of victory, it is important to be careful in drawing lessons from any particular invalidation rate. Nonetheless,

---

[14] See, e.g., Frank Cross, *Decision Making in the U.S. Courts of Appeals* (2006); James Brudney et al, *Judicial Hostility Toward Labor Unions? Applying the Social Background Model to a Celebrated Concern*, 60 Ohio L J 1675 (1999); Richard Revesz, *Environmental Regulation, Ideology, and the D.C. Circuit*, 83 Va L Rev 1717 (1983); William M. Landes and Richard A. Posner, *Rational Judicial Behavior: A Statistical Study*, J Legal Analysis (forthcoming 2009); Cass R. Sunstein et al, *Are Judges Political? An Empirical Analysis of the Federal Judiciary* (2006).

the four general findings are inconsistent with some plausible intuitive judgments about likely judicial behavior post-9/11.

The remainder of the essay is organized as follows. Part I offers a discussion of background and method; it also outlines the central findings. Part II attempts to explain them, with particular emphasis on ideological voting and on the largest puzzle, which is the absence of the standard panel effects. Part II explores why judicial votes, in ideologically contested cases, are typically affected by the votes of other judges on the panel. In the process, it offers an account of why the typical pattern is not observed in national security cases, and of when and why we should expect to see judges (and perhaps others) strongly affected by the views of their colleagues. Part II also offers some brief speculations about what might be expected in the future.

I. Background, Method, Results

A. IDEOLOGICAL DIFFERENCES AND PANEL EFFECTS

To understand the current study, it is important to have a general sense of other studies of judicial behavior, which have revealed three pervasive phenomena. The first is *ideological voting*. In numerous areas, Republican and Democratic appointees show significant differences in liberal voting rates.[15] This finding is based on conventional measures of ideological differences, by counting, as a "liberal vote," a judgment in favor of (for example) affirmative action programs, campaign finance regulation, plaintiffs in sex discrimination cases, the right to choose abortion, or labor unions in cases involving the National Labor Relations Act. The difference between Republican and Democratic appointees varies by case category, but in many areas, it is significant; in a large data set, the liberal voting rate of Republican appointees is 40% and that of Democratic appointees is 52%, for an overall difference of 12%.[16]

Of course it would be a mistake to conclude, from this difference, that judicial voting can be reduced to ideological predispositions. Even in the most ideologically contested domains, most

[15] Landes and Posner, *Rational Judicial Behavior* (cited in note 14); Sunstein et al, *Are Judges Political? An Empirical Analysis of the Federal Judiciary* at 20–21 (cited in note 14); Cross, *Decision Making in the U.S. Courts of Appeals* (cited in note 14).

[16] Sunstein et al, *Are Judges Political?* at 20–21 (cited in note 14).

decisions are unanimous, and judges thus agree across party lines. Nonetheless, Republican and Democratic appointees show significant differences in liberal voting rates. Those differences mean that the outcome of many disputes is determined by the random assignment of judges to panels.[17]

The second phenomenon is *ideological dampening*. When they are in the minority on three-judge panels, both Republican and Democratic appointees show significantly more moderate voting patterns than when they are in the majority.[18] Apparently both sets of appointees are willing to offer *collegial concurrences*—that is, they are willing to concur in cases even if they would reach a different result if they were in the majority. A simple way to demonstrate ideological dampening is to compare the voting patterns of Republican appointees on Republican-Democratic-Democratic (RDD) panels with those of Democratic appointees on Democratic-Republican-Republican (DRR) panels. In many areas of the law, those patterns are essentially identical.[19] Even when there is a significant overall difference between Republican and Democratic appointees, that difference is in that sense essentially wiped out because of panel effects.

For example, Democratic appointees vote for sex discrimination plaintiffs 42% of the time on RRD panels, while Republican appointees vote for such plaintiffs 44% of the time on RDD panels.[20] Note that even on such panels, Democratic appointees show more liberal voting rates than do Republican appointees. On RRD panels, for example, Republican appointees vote for sex discrimination plaintiffs 37% of the time, well below the 42% rate for Democratic appointees on such panels.[21] But ideological dampening is nonetheless significant, in the sense that the ideological tendencies of both sets of appointees are muted.

The third phenomenon is *ideological amplification*. When sitting on panels consisting solely of appointees from the same political party (DDD or RRR panels), federal judges show significantly more ideological voting patterns than when sitting on mixed pan-

---

[17] Landes and Posner, *Rational Judicial Behavior* (cited in note 14).

[18] Sunstein et al, *Are Judges Political?* at 26–27 (cited in note 14).

[19] Id.

[20] Id at 26.

[21] Id.

els.[22] A simple way to show this difference is to compare the overall difference between Republican and Democratic appointees with the difference on unified panels, with the latter counting as the "polarized difference."[23] The polarized difference is often double or even triple the overall difference. For example, Republican appointees show a liberal voting rate of 37% in sex discrimination cases, well below the Democratic rate, which is 52%.[24] But on RRR panels, Republican appointees show a liberal voting rate of 30%, and on DDD panels, Democratic appointees show a liberal voting rate of 60%. The polarized difference of 30% is of course double the overall difference of 15%. Differences of this magnitude are typical; they are the rule, not the exception.[25]

In numerous areas of federal law, ideological voting, ideological dampening, and ideological amplification are the basic findings.[26] It follows that the political affiliation of the appointing president is a relatively good predictor of judicial voting in ideologically contested cases—but that the political affiliation of the president who appointed the other two judges on the panel is at least as good a predictor of judicial voting in such cases! These findings suggest that the standard figure, for judicial voting behavior, looks roughly like the graph presented in figure 1.

In a few areas, however, these patterns are not observed. First, ideological voting cannot be found in certain domains in which it might be expected; for example, there is no significant difference between Democratic and Republican appointees in criminal appeals and in cases involving the Takings Clause, congressional power under the Commerce Clause, punitive damages, and standing to sue.[27] It is possible that existing doctrine imposes significant discipline on judges in such cases, in such a way as to ensure that ideological predispositions do not matter to judicial votes. It is also possible that federal judges do not much disagree, across party lines, in such cases, and hence ideological voting is not observed.

Second, panel effects cannot be found in cases involving abor-

---

[22] Id.

[23] Id at 20–21.

[24] Id at 20.

[25] Id at 26–27.

[26] See id.

[27] Id at 49.

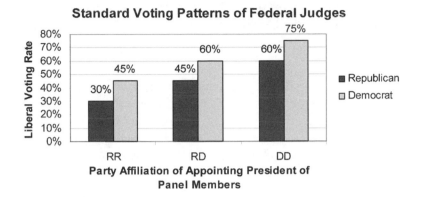

FIG. 1.—Standard voting patterns of federal judges

tion and capital punishment.[28] In those domains, ideological voting is unmistakable, in the sense that the disparity between Democratic and Republican appointees is substantial. But the votes of federal judges are unaffected by panel composition. Apparently judicial convictions are especially strong in this context, and hence neither ideological dampening nor ideological amplification is observed. How can the absence of those standard findings be explained? I shall turn to that question in Part II.

Interestingly, and contrary to a reasonable prediction, the extent of the overall difference between Republican and Democratic appointees does not predict the existence of panel effects. In abortion cases, the overall difference in liberal voting is 16%. In capital punishment cases, it is 24%. The difference in liberal voting rates is even higher in the domain of affirmative action (28%) than in either of these areas, and it is also high in cases involving the National Environmental Policy Act (24%), abrogation of state immunity under the Eleventh Amendment (21%), sex discrimination (17%), and disability discrimination (16%).[29] But in those four areas, panel effects are substantial, as both ideological dampening and amplification are found.[30] What matters, then, is not the extent of the difference between the two sets of appointees, but the tenacity with which they maintain their convictions, and

---

[28] Id.

[29] Id at 20–21.

[30] Id at 26–27.

the former does not predict the latter. With this background, let us turn to the national security cases.

B. METHOD

The data set consists of 111 courts of appeals decisions handed down between September 11, 2001 and September 10, 2008. The data set was generated by searching databases for a series of national security–related keywords[31] and then manually eliminating cases that turned out to be irrelevant. Cases were excluded if they did not seriously engage national security issues, if they involved review of immigration or asylum decisions, or if the federal government was not a party. Because a central goal of the project is to analyze panel effects, en banc decisions were also excluded. Not surprisingly, the cases that make up the data set involve highly disparate subjects; common themes included challenges to detention, to surveillance, or to government efforts to conceal information.

Judicial votes were categorized in terms of whether they favored the government. In the overwhelming majority of cases, this measure was simple to apply, but in some cases the categorization was not straightforward because several issues were involved, and the government won on some of them but lost on others. In such cases, the government was said to have "won" if the government received most of what it wanted and lost on a minor or peripheral issue. In these few cases, a discretionary judgment had to be made on that question. In *United States v Moussaoui*,[32] for example, the coding decision was not straightforward. The court of appeals ruled that it could order the government to produce enemy combatant witnesses for depositions, that a particular witness would be material to the Moussaoui defense, and that the particular deposition substitute proposed by the government was inadequate. But the court nevertheless affirmed the government's central pro-

---

[31] The initial search string in Westlaw's "cta" database was: (FISA "EXTRAORDINARY RENDITION" ATLEAST3(TORTURE) GUANTANAMO "PATRIOT ACT" SY,DI("SEPTEMBER 11" "9/11" "NATIONAL SECURITY" TERRORISM TERRORIST TORTURE "WAR ON TERROR") ((("NATIONAL SECURITY" & TERROR!) ATLEAST3(TERROR!) ATLEAST3("NATIONAL SECURITY")) & (FOIA WIRETAP DETAIN! DETENTION SURVEILLANCE "9/11" "SEPTEMBER 11")) & da(aft 9/11/2001) & da(bef 9/14/2008) % ("IMMIGRATION JUDGE" "BOARD OF IMMIGRATION APPEALS")).

[32] 365 F2d 292 (4th Cir 2004).

posal, which was to offer a written substitute instead of producing the witness. This result was counted as a victory for the government. Discretionary judgments of this kind were necessary only in a very small subset of the cases.

By our count, the panel majority found in favor of the government in a total of 94 cases out of a total of 111. As is standard, judges were classified as Democratic or Republican appointees based on the party affiliation of the president who nominated them.[33]

C. RESULTS

The basic results are shown in figure 2. In terms of raw outcomes, measured by panel composition, consider the data provided in table 1. The most noteworthy findings are simple to describe.

1. The overall invalidation rate is low—about 15%. In terms of expected outcomes, very few areas of the law have been found to be so lopsided. For example, criminals win their appeals about one-third of the time,[34] punitive damage awards are invalidated over one-fifth of the time,[35] property owners win takings claims about 20% of the time,[36] and disability plaintiffs win discrimination suits about one-third of the time.[37] Of areas that have been studied, the only one with a more lopsided rate involves challenges to congressional power under the Commerce Clause, in which the invalidation rate is about 5%.[38]

2. It might well be expected that the difference between Republican and Democratic appointees would be compressed in this domain. The area of national security might eliminate party differences; no judge would lightly rule that the government lacks authority to do what it deems necessary to protect the country. Surprisingly, however, there is no discernible compression. In a large data set, involving many domains, the average difference between the two sets of appointees was 12%; in ideologically con-

---

[33] One judge had been nominated to a district court position by a Democrat and to his circuit court position by a Republican. Because the judge is himself a registered Democrat, he was assigned that affiliation for purposes of the analysis.

[34] Sunstein et al, *Are Judges Political?* at 49 (cited in note 14).

[35] Id.

[36] Id.

[37] Id at 26.

[38] Id at 39.

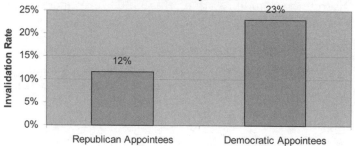

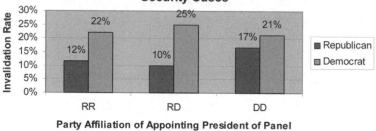

FIG. 2.—Voting patterns of federal judges in national security cases

tested cases as a whole, it was 15%.[39] The difference here is 11%, which is statistically significant and very much in line with the overall findings.[40] It is comparable to the differences in cases involving campaign finance regulation (14%), obscenity (9%), racial discrimination under Title VII (9%), and desegregation (9%).[41] It should also be emphasized that while the 11% difference is comparable in magnitude to those just described, the ratio of the rates is nearly 2 to 1, which is higher than that in *any* of these other

---

[39] See id at 21.

[40] Two-sided *p*-value from *t*-test = 0.0071. Two-sided *p*-value from exact (permutation) test = 0.0081. Note that for this and subsequent calculations, the validity of the independence assumptions behind the significant tests is in some ways debatable. However, the patterns in the data are not ambiguous, and the *p*-values presented here reflect those patterns.

[41] Sunstein et al, *Are Judges Political?* at 20–21 (cited in note 14).

TABLE 1
Invalidation Rates by Panel Composition

	Validate	Invalidate	Invalidation Rate (%)
DDD	24	9	27
DDR	69	21	23
RRD	135	15	9
RRR	54	6	10

areas. In that sense, the difference is especially stark.

To be sure, the 11% difference is lower, in absolute terms, than what is observed at the highest end of the range of domains studied to date; in cases decided under the National Environmental Policy Act, there is a 24% difference, and in affirmative action cases, the difference is 24%.[42] But the ratio remains unusually high in national security cases. In all events, it cannot be said that Democratic and Republican appointees behave essentially the same in such cases. Nor can it be said that the level of difference, in this domain, is significantly lower than what it is in most domains in which ideological voting is observed.

Note in addition that the difference in judicial voting rates at the individual level actually masks a somewhat larger difference at the level of panels. As table 1 reflects, majority Republican panels vote to invalidate government action only 9% of the time, whereas majority Democratic panels vote to invalidate government action 24% of the time. The difference between 9% and 24% is, in terms of ratios, especially noteworthy—the 267% relative difference is larger than what can be found in any other area of federal law that has been studied to date.

3. It might also be expected that national security cases would follow the standard pattern shown in figure 1, with rising liberal voting rates as the number of Democratic appointees increases, reflective of ideological dampening and ideological amplification. Because the sample size is relatively small, any conclusions on this point must remain somewhat tentative; but no such pattern is observed. The voting patterns of Democratic appointees cannot be shown to be associated with panel composition.[43] Such appointees vote to invalidate government action about one-fifth of

[42] Id at 20.
[43] ANOVA p-value = 0.8968, pair-wise two-sided p-values from exact (permutation) tests all greater than 0.70.

the time regardless of whether they are sitting with zero, one, or two Democratic appointees. In a striking contrast to other areas of the law, Republican appointees show the same voting patterns on RRD and RRR panels.[44] To be sure, such appointees seem to show a modest shift in the liberal direction on RDD panels, but the difference is not statistically significant.[45] The more general point is that none of the panel effects even approaches statistical significance.

4. We might anticipate that in the immediate aftermath of the 9/11 attacks, say between 2002 and 2004, judges would show a high rate of deference to the executive branch, and that validation rates would decrease from 2006 to 2008. In the aftermath of the attacks, the threat would be immediate, and courts might well be reluctant to invalidate government action that was initiated in order to reduce the relevant risks. As the immediacy of the attacks receded, perhaps judges would come to think that the danger had been overstated; perhaps they could be more willing to invalidate government action.

No such pattern is observed. The rate of validation is essentially constant over the two time periods.[46] The three plots in figure 3 show the trend in invalidation rates; for clarity of exposition, they divide the relevant time period in different ways. The first plot divides the cases into three periods and calculates the rates within each period; the second gives annual invalidation rates; the third divides the cases into eleven time periods and calculates the rate within each period.

Not surprisingly, the shorter time intervals show more variable invalidation rates, but this is due to the small number of cases. The general point is that there is no measurable increase in invalidation rates over the time period studied; if anything, the invalidation rate actually decreases, but the trend is not statistically significant.

---

[44] Two-sided p-value from t-test = 0.747; two-sided p-value from exact (permutation) test = 0.0764.

[45] Two-sided p-value from t-test = 0.416; two-sided p-value from exact (permutation) test = 0.330.

[46] Invalidation rate for cases 2001–2004 = 17.0%. Invalidation rate for cases 2005–2008 = 14.1%. Two-sided p-value from t-test is 0.676.

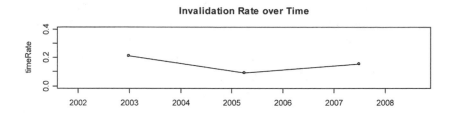

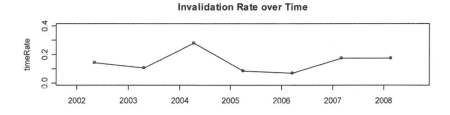

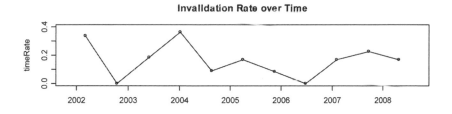

FIG. 3.—Invalidation rate over time

II. Explanations and Observations

What lessons can be drawn from these findings? How do they compare with other domains of the law? What might be said about the approach of federal courts of appeals, after 9/11, to actions of government that are challenged in court?

A. INVALIDATION RATES

1. *Two conclusions.* The invalidation rate seems to suggest two conclusions. First, federal judges have been showing a high rate

of deference to the executive branch.[47] Second, the rate of deference is not nearly as high as it might be expected to be. Judges
have not adopted anything like an irrebuttable presumption in
government's favor. In other words, the existing voting patterns
seem to suggest that federal courts have repudiated both of the
polar positions in the academic debate.

2. *Selection effects*. These conclusions are reasonable and probably
even correct, but we need to be careful with specific inferences.
To evaluate the findings, it is necessary to ask two questions. What
exactly is government doing in the relevant cases? And when are
litigants willing to challenge government action? Without answers
to these questions, any evaluations must be tentative.

We could easily imagine a world in which total invalidation rates
were significantly higher—say, 25%. But perhaps the higher invalidation rates, in that world, would be a product not of a more
aggressive judiciary, but of greater litigant selectivity in deciding
when to challenge government action. Such selectivity might stem
from multiple sources. Perhaps social pressures are leading people
to challenge government action, in this domain, only when it is
clearly unlawful; or perhaps litigants are highly risk-averse, fearing
that adverse rulings could entrench bad law. In short, a relatively
high invalidation rate might reflect the selection of cases for litigation, and might not tell us that federal courts are not being
deferential.

Alternatively, we could imagine a world in which total invalidation rates were significantly lower than they are now—say, 5%.
But perhaps the lower rates, in such a world, would be a product
of greater litigant willingness to challenge government action—
and also of greater caution, on the part of government, about
testing the legal frontiers. Perhaps ideological litigants, in such a
world, would challenge government action not only when they
had a significant chance of success, but also for political or expressive reasons; perhaps they would not greatly fear validation.
Perhaps government, in such a world, would stay well within the
legal boundaries, fearing the consequences of invalidation in terms
of frustration of its objectives, adverse public reactions, or both.

---

[47] For an interesting hypothesis about high deference rates from the lower courts, compared to the Supreme Court, see Adrian Vermeule, *Our Schmittian Administrative Law*,
122 Harv L Rev (forthcoming Feb 2009).

If so, a low invalidation rate would not suggest a high level of judicial deference.

Which world is closer to ours? Without knowing, we cannot draw clear inferences about judicial aggressiveness. There is another possibility. Perhaps the government is especially troubled by the prospect of judicial invalidation in national security cases, and perhaps it has taken strong steps to avoid losses in court. If so, it will sometimes take relatively moderate positions and work hard to ensure that it does not lose in the courts of appeals. Of course the Bush administration is generally thought to have taken aggressive positions, not moderate ones, so this explanation probably does not work in this context. What is clear is that the 15% invalidation rate suggests both that courts are not adopting a broad rule of deference and that they are usually giving the government the benefit of the doubt.

3. *No changes over time.* As I have suggested, it might be expected that invalidation rates would increase over time. In the period immediately following the 9/11 attacks, we might expect courts to adopt a general rule of deference, perhaps on the theory that any "balancing" should be tipped in the government's favor. The salience of the attacks would seem likely to produce such deference. But as the attacks receded in time, and as no fresh attack occurred, a somewhat more aggressive posture might be expected. Alongside the passage of time, signals from the Supreme Court seemed inconsistent with complete deference.[48] For this reason as well, a higher rate of invalidation should be expected in the more recent period.

The absence of any discernible change over time is a genuine puzzle. We can imagine five explanations. First, the hypothesis about salience effects might be wrong. It might simply be the case that the judicial posture in 2002 was not different from the judicial posture in 2007. Second, selection effects might be responsible for the absence of changes over time. In the immediate aftermath of the attacks, litigants might have been reluctant to challenge government action unless it was clearly unlawful; more recently, they might be bringing closer cases. Third, the government might be sensitive to changes in public opinion and in anticipated judicial attitudes. Perhaps the government was willing to be quite ag-

---

[48] The most prominent of these is *Hamdi v Rumsfeld*, 542 US 407 (2004).

gressive in 2003, but less so in 2007, and the constant judicial voting patterns therefore reflect decreased government aggressiveness in light of greater judicial scrutiny.

Fourth, the invalidation rates might mask important qualitative differences. Perhaps judges have indeed been taking a more aggressive approach, but perhaps their aggressiveness manifests itself, not in a higher invalidation rate, but in a willingness to strike down a few especially important programs, which they might have validated a few years before. Fifth, the absence of a discernible change might reflect the growing number of Republican (Bush) appointees to the federal courts, which might produce a shift in favor of the government in national security cases. Because the composition of the courts is not constant over time, a general decrease in salience effects, and hence greater judicial willingness to scrutinize government action, might be counteracted by new appointments to the federal bench.

The data do not permit us to choose finally among these five accounts. But the latter hypothesis, an apparently promising one, is not supported by the evidence. In fact, the proportion of Republican-appointed judges voting in the cases in the data set does not increase over time; if anything, it slightly decreases. Moreover, there does not appear to be a change in invalidation rates over time for either Democrat- or Republican-appointed judges. Finally, a close reading of the cases does suggest that there are not fundamental differences in the posture of courts across the various periods; any such differences, if they even exist, are far more subtle than might be anticipated.

4. *A future inquiry (about the past).* The study here is limited to national security cases after 9/11. It would be most valuable to ask the following question: What is the invalidation rate, in such cases, *before* 9/11? Suppose that in the relevant period, the invalidation rate is 40%. If so, we might be confident that there has been a "9/11 effect," in the sense that courts are now far more deferential than they were.

A study of this sort would be quite valuable, and it would cast some light on the findings here. But it would raise its own puzzles. First, the number of national security cases, in the decades before 9/11, is relatively small; it would not be simple to obtain a sufficiently large sample to produce helpful comparisons. Second, the national security cases before 9/11 are hardly the same as the national security cases after 9/11. To put the point provocatively, a comparison between the two might be a bit like comparing punitive damages cases with national security cases. The reason is that the issues in the pre-9/11 era were so fundamentally different from those in the post-9/11 era that to treat them all as part of a unitary category called "national security cases" is probably unhelpful. Third, selection effects would confound comparisons. Litigants may well have different inclinations after 9/11, and hence it would not be easy to offer confident comparisons of invalidation rates in the different periods.

B. IDEOLOGICAL VOTING

1. *No compression.* A reasonable prediction would be that in the aftermath of the attacks of 9/11, Democratic and Republican appointees would not be fundamentally different from one another. The hypothesis would be that the tragic consequences of the attacks, especially in the first decade after they occurred, would greatly compress ideological differences. There are at least crude analogies in the past. The Court's decision in *Brown v Board of Education*, for example, led to an apparent consensus between Republican and Democratic appointees, for a long period, in segregation cases; between 1945 and 1965, the two sets of appointees agreed with one another.[49]

Notably, no such compression is observed. Strikingly, the different inclinations of the two sets of appointees are strong enough to break out even in the aftermath of a national catastrophe. As we have seen, the 11% difference is not massive in absolute terms, but it is very large in relative terms. In absolute terms, it is within the general range of differences observed in other areas of the law; in relative terms, it is impressively and unusually large.

2. *A future inquiry (about the future)—a party effect?* In all of the relevant cases, federal judges confronted a Republican administration. Is this relevant? Would different judicial voting patterns be found if the pertinent measures had been undertaken by a Democratic administration? A plausible hypothesis would be that judges display an independent *party effect*—in the sense that Republican appointees are more skeptical of Democratic adminis-

---

[49] See Sunstein et al, *Are Judges Political?* at 41 (cited in note 14).

TABLE 2
VALIDATION RATES OF COURT OF APPEALS JUDGES BY PARTY OF APPOINTING AND CURRENT
PRESIDENT IN CHEVRON CASES

Party of Appointing President	Total (1)	Party of Current President		
		Democratic (2)	Republican (3)	Difference of (2) − (3)
(A) Democrat	.640	.698	.605	**.093***
	(.027)	(.043)	(.035)	**(.056)**
	[311]	[116]	[195]	
(B) Republican	.637	.592	.675	**−.083***
	(.025)	(.038)	(.033)	**(.050)**
	[369]	[169]	[200]	
Difference of (A) − (B)	**.003**	**.107***	**−.070**	. . .
	(.037)	**(.058)**	**(.048)**	

NOTE.—Means, standard errors in parentheses, and number of observations in brackets. Differences may not match exactly due to rounding.
* Denotes difference significant at 10% level.

trations than of Republican administrations, while Democratic appointees show the opposite pattern.

In important domains of administrative law, a party effect is indeed demonstrated. In reviewing interpretations of law by the Environmental Protection Agency and the National Labor Relations Board, federal judges are especially willing to uphold decisions headed by a president of the same political party as the president who appointed them.[50] Consider table 2.[51] It would not be surprising if a similar effect were observed in the domain of national security. Perhaps Republican appointees would be less deferential to government intrusions on the domain of liberty if those intrusions were undertaken by a Democratic administration. Perhaps Democratic appointees would be more deferential to government if a Democratic president headed the executive branch. It would be most valuable to see whether ideological compression would be observed under those circumstances;[52] some kind of answer will emerge in the next years.

---

[50] See Thomas J. Miles and Cass R. Sunstein, *Do Federal Judges Makes Regulatory Policy? An Empirical Analysis of Chevron*, 73 U Chi L Rev 823, 850 (2006).

[51] Id.

[52] For striking evidence of a significant party effect among citizens, see Geoffrey Cohen, *Party Over Policy: The Dominating Impact of Group Influence on Political Beliefs*, 85 J Personality and Social Psych 808 (2003).

C. PANEL EFFECTS

To understand the absence of discernible panel effects, we need to know something about ideological dampening and ideological amplification.

1. *Dampening*. What causes ideological dampening? There are several answers. In some cases, the isolated judge is undoubtedly convinced by his colleagues notwithstanding a possible disposition to rule the other way. Sitting with two Republican appointees in an affirmative action case, the Democratic appointee might be persuaded that under existing law, the program is indefensible. In other cases, ideological dampening is likely a product of internal dynamics in which the isolated judge accepts the result in return for some concessions in the analysis. Sitting with two Democratic appointees in a campaign finance case, the Republican appointee might vote to uphold the program so long as the opinion is narrow and does not venture far beyond the particular facts. To this extent, ideological dampening, measured only in terms of votes, probably understates the role of the isolated judge. Even if Rs look like Ds when they sit on majority D panels, and even if Ds look like Rs when they sit on majority R panels, they might have succeeded in moving the opinion in their preferred directions.

In still other cases, the isolated judge may privately disagree with the result, but may conclude that it is not worthwhile to dissent. By hypothesis, a dissenting opinion will not change the outcome, and its production will take some work and may ruffle some feathers. It is true that on some occasions, a dissenting opinion might increase the likelihood of en banc or Supreme Court review, but both of these are relatively rare. For this reason, a judge might conclude that it is better to join the majority, on the ground that something is gained and nothing is lost. A form of internal cost-benefit balancing may argue in favor of the collegial concurrence even if the judge does not, in fact, agree with the majority's conclusion.

Finally, many judges appear to follow an informal rule of reciprocity, in accordance with which they will not always or even ordinarily dissent from opinions with which they do not agree, in the understanding that other judges will follow the same rule. The basic norm might well be to accept the majority's conclusion, at least if the stakes are not terribly high, with the understanding that this norm is generally held. A rule of reciprocity would seem to fit well with the internal calculation in the usual run of cases: A dissenting opinion imposes burdens and by hypothesis is likely to produce no change, and hence it may make sense for judges not to dissent despite their private disagreements.

We might see ideological dampening as a reflection of the more general power of conformity pressures.[53] When people find themselves isolated with a different view from that of unanimous others, they often tend to yield.[54] They do so either because those views carry information about what is true, or because they do not want to appear wrong or confused to others.[55] The dynamic among federal judges is not at all the same, but it is overlapping. The evidence suggests that judges are apparently influenced by the views of their colleagues and they might well be attempting to avoid the disapproval, and occasional unpleasantness, that can be produced by a dissenting opinion. Note in this regard that ideological dampening can be found on every federal court of appeals— with the single exception of the United States Court of Appeals for the Sixth Circuit.[56] According to informal lore, Republican and Democratic appointees do not get along well on that circuit,[57] and the absence of a norm of reciprocity may be partly cause and partly effect of that fact.

2. *Amplification.* At first glance, ideological amplification seems more mysterious. Two Democratic appointees, on a three-judge panel with one Republican appointee, should be able to obtain the result they prefer. Why do they show significantly more moderate patterns on mixed panels than on unified ones?

One explanation points to group polarization. It is well known that like-minded people typically end up in a more extreme position in line with their predeliberation tendencies.[58] Perhaps RRR and DDD panels participate in a process of group polarization, in which judges move one another to more extreme voting patterns. The standard explanation of group polarization supports

---

[53] See Solomon Asch, *Opinions and Social Pressure*, in *Readings About the Social Animal* 13 (1995).

[54] Id.

[55] Id.

[56] Sunstein et al, *Are Judges Political?* at 113 (cited in note 14).

[57] See, e.g., the remarks of Judge Gilbert Merritt in http://www.enquirer.com/editions/2003/09/03/loc_ohcourtplayers03.html.

[58] See Roger Brown, *Social Psychology: The Second Edition* (1985); Cass R. Sunstein, *Going to Extremes* (forthcoming 2009).

this account. On that account, such polarization is produced by the exchange of information within the relevant group.[59] If, for example, a group of people is discussing climate change, and is antecedently inclined to believe that it poses serious risks, the pool of arguments favors that antecedent belief. As those arguments are revealed, people tend to shift. It is easy to imagine a similar process within a judicial panel, as different arguments, in (say) a case involving disability discrimination, move people toward more extreme points on unified panels.

An alternative explanation points not toward the relatively extreme behavior of judges on unified panels, but to the more moderate behavior of judges who constitute a majority on mixed panels. On this view, that more moderate behavior is what must be explained. The simplest account would stress a *whistleblower effect*.[60] The presence of a Republican appointee imposes a discipline on two Democratic appointees, just as the presence of a Democratic appointee imposes a discipline on two Republican appointees. Perhaps legally doubtful results are more possible on unified panels than on mixed ones, because of the absence of a whistleblower on the former. If this is so, that absence helps to explain the relatively extreme behavior of like-minded judges on unified panels. A softened version of the whistleblower argument would point not to results that are legally doubtful in any strong sense, but to the fact that the presence of a minority member may raise arguments and impose discipline on the majority, producing more moderate voting patterns.

Note that whatever the explanation for ideological amplification, its actual effects are likely to be larger than what can be picked up by a quantitative examination of judicial voting patterns. Opinions matter, not merely votes, and if amplification is occurring, DDD and RRR panels are likely to show relatively extreme opinions. The empirical finding of ideological dampening is probably overstated in an important respect, because it does not speak to opinions, on which the isolated judge likely has an effect. By contrast, the empirical finding of amplification is probably understated, because there is every reason to think that opinions are unusually extreme on unified panels.

---

[59] See Brown, *Social Psychology* (cited in note 58).

[60] See Frank Cross and Emerson Tiller, *Judicial Partisanship and Obedience to Legal Doctrine: Whistleblowing on the Federal Courts of Appeals*, 107 Yale L J 2155 (1998).

3. *No dampening, no amplification.* How, then, can the apparent absence of panel effects be explained in national security cases post-9/11? The best answer is that judicial judgments are firm— so much so that the views of panel members do not matter. In the domain of national security, differences between Republican and Democratic appointees appear to be so strongly held that the views of panel members simply do not matter.

Ideological dampening does not occur for that reason. Compare the only other domains, to date, in which dampening has been found not to occur: capital punishment and abortion.[61] In those domains, the absence of dampening is not entirely surprising. If antecedent convictions are deeply held, none of the mechanisms that account for dampening will be strong enough to move judicial votes. In such areas, judges will not be convinced by their colleagues. They will be willing to do the work that is necessary to produce a dissent, perhaps in the hope of attracting Supreme Court attention or influencing future courts. They will be willing to create the kinds of disruption that might attend dissenting opinions. Where the stakes are high, the informal norm of reciprocity, reducing dissenting opinions, is qualified or breaks down. A key finding here is that the area of national security falls in the same category as abortion and capital punishment.

I have suggested that amplification occurs either because of group polarization or because of an absence of a whistleblower effect. But if judges already have quite strong convictions, then they are not likely to be polarized by internal discussions. And if judges do not trust those who purport to be whistleblowers, then they are not likely to be moved by them. These points help to explain why amplification is not observed here.

CONCLUSION

Some people believe that when national security is threatened, federal judges should adopt a strong presumption in favor of government action. Other people believe that when national security is threatened, federal judges need to maintain a strong hand in order to prevent official overreaching. The evidence sug-

---

[61] Sunstein et al, *Are Judges Political?* at 55 (cited in note 14). Panel effects cannot be demonstrated in the area of gay and lesbian rights, but because the sample size is so small, the lack of a demonstrated effect is not worth much. The shape of the figure suggests that both dampening and polarization might be occurring. See id.

gests that in the aftermath of the attacks of 9/11, the courts of appeals have rejected both of these polar positions. They show unusually high deference rates without providing anything like a blank check to the executive. Notably and somewhat surprisingly, the rate of invalidation has not increased over time, as vivid memories of the attacks recede, and the changing composition of the judiciary does not seem to account for this unanticipated finding.

At the same time, the significant split between Republican and Democratic appointees demonstrates that ideological differences are playing a large role in this domain. Indeed, the magnitude of the difference between the two sets of appointees is similar to that in numerous other areas of law. Contrary to a plausible hypothesis, ideological compression is not observed.

Perhaps the most striking finding involves the absence of panel effects. While the sample size is relatively small, the evidence suggests that judicial views are firmly entrenched, and hence judicial votes appear unaffected by the views of judicial colleagues. This is an unusual and noteworthy pattern. Ideological dampening and ideological amplification are pervasive on the federal courts of appeals, but they cannot be found in national security cases post-9/11.

KEITH WERHAN

THE CLASSICAL ATHENIAN ANCESTRY
OF AMERICAN FREEDOM OF SPEECH

I. Introduction

This article explores how the fundamentally different understandings of self-government in the classical Athenian democracy and under the American Constitution shaped the role and limits
of freedom of speech in the two political communities. The Athenians invented democracy (*dēmokratia*), a revolutionary system in
which the people of a community (the *dēmos*) held a monopoly on
political power (*kratos*), governing themselves and their community
as they thought best. The practice of *dēmokratia* frames the classical
era of ancient Greece, which began after the reforms of the Athenian
constitution initiated by Cleisthenes in 508/507 BCE, and concluded
with the fall of Athens as a self-governing community after the
death of Alexander the Great in 323/322 BCE.[1] Over two thousand

Keith Werhan is Ashton Phelps Chair in Constitutional Law, Tulane Law School.

AUTHOR'S NOTE: A revised version of this article will appear in my forthcoming book,
tentatively titled *The Classical Athenian Democracy and the American Constitution*, to be
published by Oxford University Press. I would like to thank participants in DePaul Law
School's workshop series and in Northwestern University's political theory colloquium
for their many helpful comments during my presentation of an early draft of this article.
I also would like to thank Adeno Addis, Daniel Farber, Stephen Griffin, Sara Monoson,
and James Sullivan for reviewing an earlier draft of this article, with special thanks to
Pamela Metzger and Geoffrey Stone for helping me to reconceive this project. Finally,
and by no means least, I would like to thank Marcy Hupp, Tulane law class of 2010, and
Scott Puckett, PhD candidate, Tulane Department of Classics, for their valuable research
assistance.

[1] Thomas R. Martin, *Ancient Greece: From Prehistoric to Hellenistic Times* 94 (Yale, 1996).

years after the demise of the classical Athenian democracy, the American *dēmos* reinvented the idea of democracy. In light of the vast differences in time and circumstance, it should not be surprising that the American idea of democracy differs substantially from the Athenian original.

The principal division separating Athenian and American democracy is the difference in participation by ordinary citizens in their government. In short, Athens adopted a direct democracy in which ordinary citizens, assembled in large groups, made all governance decisions.[2] Athens had no government in the modern meaning of the term. The Athenian *dēmos* had "a plenary competence," and it was they who governed.[3] According to the central Athenian democratic principle of *isonomia*,[4] each full citizen (i.e., adult males duly registered as Athenian citizens), regardless of economic status or social station, had an equal opportunity to participate in the political decisions that guided the city (*polis*).[5] The principal governing institutions of classical Athens—the Assembly (*ekklēsia*), the Council of 500 (*boulē*), the lawmaking boards (*nomothetai*), and the jury courts (*dikastēria*)—essentially were large assemblies of citizen volunteers (the smallest usually had 500 members, the largest probably around 6,000) who listened to debate and then voted their

---

[2] Ellen Meiksins Wood, *Demos versus "We, the People": Freedom and Democracy Ancient and Modern*, in Josiah Ober and Charles Hedrick, eds, *Demokratia: A Conversation on Democracies, Ancient and Modern* 121, 122 (Princeton, 1996).

[3] Athanassios Vamvoukos, *Fundamental Freedoms in Athens of the Fifth Century*, 26 Revue Internationale des Droits de l'Antiquité, 3d ser, 89, 95 (1979).

[4] *Isonomia*, which Herodotus praised as "the most beautiful of words," Vamvoukos, id at 97, quoting Herodotus, *The Histories* 3.80, had a rich and varied meaning for classical Athenians. The principal meaning of *isonomia* was "'equality through the law." M. I. Finley, *The Freedom of the Citizen in the Greek World*, in *Economy and Society in Ancient Greece* 77, 84 (Chatto and Windus, 1981). (The prefix *iso-* conveyed "equal," and *nomos* referred to fundamental "law" or "custom.") For classical Athenians, "equality through the law" primarily meant political equality or, more precisely, the equal opportunity of all citizens, protected by and promoted through law, to exercise their political rights. See Mogens Herman Hansen, *The Athenian Democracy in the Age of Demosthenes* 81 (Blackwell, 1991) (J. A. Crook, trans); R. K. Sinclair, *Democracy and Participation in Athens* 16 (Cambridge, 1988).

[5] Kurt A. Raaflaub, *The Discovery of Freedom in Ancient Greece* 230 (Chicago, 2004); Martin Ostwald, *Shares and Rights: "Citizenship" Greek Style and American Style*, in Ober and Hedrick, eds, *Demokratia* 49, 54–56 (cited in note 2). Thucydides had Pericles boast in his *Funeral Oration* that the law of Athens permitted each citizen "to serve the state," regardless of "the obscurity of his condition." Thucydides, *The Landmark Thucydides: A Comprehensive Guide to the Peloponnesian War* 2.37.1 at 112 (Free Press, 1996) (Richard Crawley, trans, Robert B. Strassler, ed).

conscience. These mass meetings provided the final word on law and policy in Athens.[6]

In pointed contrast to Athens, America constituted a representative democracy that, in the language of James Madison, "delegate[ed] . . . the government . . . to a small number of citizens elected by the rest."[7] "The true distinction" between classical Athenian democracy and American representative democracy, Madison wrote, "lies in the total exclusion of the people, in their collective capacity, from any share in the [American government]."[8] In American democracy, ordinary citizens themselves do not make the law or set government policy.[9] The *dēmos* instead select representatives, who in turn govern the community.[10] American citizens participate in the political life of the nation primarily by voting for their representatives in the federal government.[11] Ordinary citizens do not have a vote in the governing institutions of the United States—Congress, the institutions comprising the executive branch, and the courts—but those who govern in these institutions are ultimately accountable (to a widely varying degree) to the American *dēmos* for the choices they make.[12]

Despite the profound differences between the highly participatory direct democracy of classical Athens and the relatively restrained representative democracy of the United States, Athens and America share a basic kinship. Each is a democratic experiment

---

[6] Josiah Ober, *Mass and Elite in Democratic Athens: Rhetoric, Ideology, and the Power of the People* 7–8 (Princeton, 1989).

[7] Federalist 10 (Madison) in *The Federalist* 59 (Modern Library, 1941).

[8] Federalist 63 (Madison) in *The Federalist* at 413 (emphasis deleted) (cited in note 7).

[9] See Gordon S. Wood, *The Creation of the American Republic, 1776–1787* 595 (Norton, 1972) (originally published by North Carolina, 1969). Some American states provide a lawmaking role for their citizens through an initiative process. For a leading examination of citizen initiatives, see John G. Matsusaka, *For the Many or the Few: The Initiative, Public Policy, and American Democracy* (Chicago, 2004).

[10] Wood, *Demos versus "We, the People"* at 123–24 (cited in note 2). See also Vamvoukos, 26 Revue Internationale des Droits de l'Antiquité at 91 (cited in note 3) (today's representative democracy is "not participatory; it is a government at a distance, not in the community."); Sheldon S. Wolin, *Transgression, Equality, and Voice*, in Ober and Hedrick, eds, *Demokratia* 63, 87 (cited in note 2) (America's representative democracy "is a democracy without the demos as actor").

[11] See James Madison, *Report on the Virginia Resolutions*, in 4 *The Debates in the Several State Conventions on the Adoption of the Federal Constitution* 546, 575 (Lippincott, 2d ed 1836) (Jonathan Elliot, ed) ("the right of electing the members of the government constitutes . . . the essence of a free and responsible government").

[12] Federalist 63 (Madison) in *The Federalist* at 409–10 (cited in note 7); Federalist 71 (Hamilton) in *The Federalist* at 464 (cited in note 7).

reflecting the aspirations of a free people to seek good government through self-government, although "self-government" carried very different meanings for Athenian democrats and the American founders. And because Athens and America are democracies, freedom of speech has been a fundamental element of both political communities.

In this article, I claim that the kinship between Athens and America as democracies—different though they may be—has created a sufficiently close connection between the basic principles of freedom of speech as practiced in Athens and as protected in America that it fairly may be said that American free-speech jurisprudence is a descendant of the classical Athenian democracy. And yet, because the Athenians and the Americans tailored free-speech principles to fit their distinct democratic practices, the differences in the Athenian and American understandings of freedom of speech—which at times are fundamental—reflect, as they reveal, the different constitutional commitments of the two societies.

II. Freedom of Speech, Ancient and Modern

Classical Athenians and contemporary Americans have regarded freedom of speech as indispensable to their democracies. Justice Benjamin Cardozo described the freedom of speech protected by the First Amendment as "the matrix, the indispensable condition, of nearly every other form of freedom."[13] The American legal system has acknowledged this primacy of place for freedom of speech by enforcing stronger protections for speakers than typically are found in other contemporary democracies.[14]

Freedom of speech was among the "most treasured" of individual freedoms in classical Athens as well.[15] Indeed, the Athenians regarded freedom of speech as "a cornerstone of [their] democracy."[16] The strength of the Athenian commitment to free speech was as

---

[13] *Palko v Connecticut*, 302 US 319, 327 (1937).

[14] See Ronald J. Krotoszynski, Jr., *The First Amendment in Cross-Cultural Perspective: A Comparative Legal Analysis of the Freedom of Speech* 214 (NYU, 2006); Aviam Soifer, *Freedom of the Press in the United States*, in Pnina Lahav, ed, *Press Law in Modern Democracies: A Comparative Study* 79, 79, 117 (Longman, 1985).

[15] Hansen, *Athenian Democracy* at 77 (cited in note 4).

[16] Raaflaub, *Discovery of Freedom in Ancient Greece* at 276 (cited in note 5). In the *Republic*, Plato described a democratic city as being "full of . . . freedom of speech." Plato, *Republic*, in *Plato: Complete Works* 971, 557b, 1168 (Hackett, 1997) (G. M. A. Grube, trans, rev C. D. C. Reeve, John M. Cooper, ed).

unique in ancient Greece as is America's today.[17] Plato, for example, wrote that there was "more freedom of speech [in Athens] than anywhere else in Greece. . . ."[18] Athenian democrats took great pride in their distinctive embrace of free expression.[19] The poet Euripides spoke for many Athenians in *Hippolytus* (428 BCE) when he had Phaedra express a deep desire that her children "live in glorious Athens, as free men, free of speech [*parrhēsia*] and flourishing . . . ."[20]

Yet the differences between direct Athenian democracy and American representative democracy contributed to different conceptions of freedom in the two polities, which in turn led to differing orientations toward freedom of speech in Athens and in America. The American orientation is negative.[21] The First Amendment prohibits the government from "abridging the freedom of speech . . . ."[22] This language negates considerable governmental authority to interfere with an individual's freedom of speech, but it imposes few positive obligations on the government to facilitate free speech. The central meaning of freedom of speech as protected by the First Amendment, the Supreme Court has established, is that the American "people are guaranteed the right to express any thought, free from government censorship." According to the Justices, the anticensorship rule means, at least as a default, "that government has no power to restrict expression because of its message, its ideas, its subject matter, or its content."[23]

---

[17] Max Radin, *Freedom of Speech in Ancient Athens*, 48 Am J Philology 215, 215 (1927). See Robert W. Wallace, *The Athenian Laws Against Slander*, in Gerhard Thür, ed, *Symposium 1993* 109, 110 (Böhlau Verlag, 1993) ("In the ancient world, free speech was uniquely democratic, and even uniquely Athenian.").

[18] Plato, *Gorgias*, in *Plato: Complete Works* 791, 461e, at 806 (cited in note 16) (Donald J. Zehl, trans, John M. Cooper, ed).

[19] See Stephen Halliwell, *Comic Satire and Freedom of Speech in Classical Athens*, 111 J Hellenic Studies 48, 48 (1991); Wallace, *Athenian Laws Against Slander* at 110 (cited in note 17). For an argument that the classical Athenian attitude toward free speech was more ambivalent than most classical scholars have found, see D. M. Carter, *Citizen Attribute, Negative Right: A Conceptual Difference Between Ancient and Modern Ideas of Freedom of Speech*, in Ineke Sluiter and Ralph M. Rosen, eds, *Free Speech in Classical Antiquity* 197 (Brill, 2004).

[20] Euripides, *Hippolytus* 423, in *Euripides II* 125, 165 (Loeb, 1995) (David Kovacs, trans).

[21] Carter, *Citizen Attribute, Negative Right* at 198 (cited in note 19). I adopt here Isaiah Berlin's definition of negative political liberty as "the area within which a [person] can act unobstructed by others." Isaiah Berlin, *Two Concepts of Liberty*, in *Four Essays on Liberty* 119, 122 (Oxford, 1969).

[22] US Const, Amend I.

[23] *Police Department of Chicago v Mosley*, 408 US 92, 95 (1972).

In Athens, freedom of speech had a more positive orientation.[24] It meant, in essence, that each full citizen was equally entitled to address the political institutions of the *polis* and to say everything he wanted to say when making such an address.[25] Thus conceived, freedom of speech was an attribute of citizenship, not a natural right.[26]

In the classical Athenian conception, freedom of speech not only facilitated democracy. It was "virtually equivalent to democracy itself."[27] Demosthenes, the leading Athenian orator of the fourth century BCE, once characterized the Athenian political system as being based on speech (*politeia en logois*).[28] Speech was the principal means of communication in Athenian political institutions.[29] Each of these institutions reached public decisions similarly: Citizen volunteers (*hoi boulomenoi*, "whoever wishes to do so") addressed a large group of ordinary citizens who decided on a course of action for the *polis* after deliberating on the relative merits of the speeches (and speakers) they had heard. In such a system, full citizen participation demanded that every citizen be afforded an equal opportunity to persuade the *dēmos* to his point of view. In classical Athens, "speech was power."[30]

In the United States, by contrast, the original focus was on written rather than oral expression, and thus there was a tendency in early America to privilege freedom of the press over freedom of speech by the general citizenry. For example, the Virginia Bill of Rights, which was the first bill of rights adopted in the emerging United States, provided, "the freedom of the press is one of the great bulwarks of liberty, and can never be restrained but by despotick

---

[24] Carter, *Citizen Attribute, Negative Right* at 217 (cited in note 19).

[25] Kurt A. Raaflaub, *Aristocracy and Freedom of Speech in the Greco-Roman World*, in Sluiter and Rosen, eds, *Free Speech in Classical Antiquity* 41, 58 (cited in note 19); Robert W. Wallace, *The Power to Speak—and Not to Listen—in Ancient Athens*, in Sluiter and Rosen, eds, *Free Speech in Classical Antiquity* 221, 225 (cited in note 19).

[26] Carter, *Citizen Attribute, Negative Right* at 198 (cited in note 19).

[27] Raaflaub, *Aristocracy and Freedom of Speech* at 58 (cited in note 25).

[28] Emily Greenwood, *Making Words Count: Freedom of Speech and Narrative in Thucydides*, in Sluiter and Rosen, eds, *Free Speech in Classical Antiquity* 175, 176 (cited in note 19), quoting Demosthenes 19.184.

[29] Joseph Roisman, *Speaker-Audience Interactions in Athens: A Power Struggle*, in Sluiter and Rosen, eds, *Free Speech in Classical Antiquity* 261, 261 (cited in note 19). See also Mark Munn, *The School of History: Athens in the Age of Socrates* 293 (California, 2000) ("All significant enactments of law, politics, philosophy, and poetry relied on living speech before their respective audiences.").

[30] Roisman, *Speaker-Audience Interactions in Athens* at 261 (cited in note 29).

governments."[31] The document did not mention freedom of speech. Virginia's focus on securing a free press rather than freedom of speech followed the English common law example set by Blackstone,[32] and it created a model that would be followed in most of the original state bills of rights.[33] Similarly, in the final days of the United States Constitutional Convention of 1787, two delegates moved to include protection of a free press (but not free speech), albeit unsuccessfully, in the federal Constitution.[34]

The failure of the state and federal constitutions to address freedom of speech did not mean that Americans of the founding generation believed that they lacked the freedom "to speak their minds."[35] Early American constitution makers focused on securing a free press because they believed that the press had a special role to play in the representative democracy they were constructing.[36] A free press was necessary to expose, and thereby to check, the feared tendency of government officials to abuse the powers that the people had entrusted to them in the new constitutions.[37] The central mission of the press, in this view, was to publish information and opinion that informed the people about the conduct of gov-

---

[31] *The Virginia Bill of Rights*, June 12, 1776, § 12, in Henry Steele Commager, ed, *Documents of American History* 103, 104 (Crofts, 1935).

[32] See William Blackstone, 4 *Blackstone's Commentaries on the Laws of England* *152, at 120 (Cavendish, 2001) (Wayne Morrison, ed) ("Every freeman has an undoubted right to lay what sentiments he pleases before the public: to forbid this, is to destroy the freedom of the press.").

[33] See Leonard W. Levy, *Emergence of a Free Press* 183–90 (Oxford, 1985).

[34] See Max Farrand, ed, 2 *The Records of the Federal Convention of 1787* 617–18 (Yale, 1966) (originally published, 1911). The recorded debate on the motion consists only of a statement by Roger Sherman, who opposed including a free-press guarantee, arguing that it was "unnecessary" because the enumerated powers of Congress in Article I "[did] not extend to the Press." Id at 618. The Anti-Federalists who opposed ratification of the Constitution especially criticized the absence of explicit protection for the "grand palladium of freedom, the liberty of the press." See, for example, Centinel, No 2, Oct 24, 1787, in Neil H. Cogan, ed, *The Complete Bill of Rights: The Drafts, Debates, Sources, & Origins* 103 (Oxford, 1997).

[35] Levy, *Emergence of a Free Press* at 188 (cited in note 33). Professor Levy explains, "On the contrary, . . . [people] were as outspoken in their criticisms of public measures and public officials as if they had had an iron-clad guarantee of the freedom to speak. . . . The presence or absence of constitutional guarantees did not alter a citizen's propensity to say what he thought." Id.

[36] Lucas A. Powe, Jr., *The Fourth Estate and the Constitution: Freedom of the Press in America* 50 (California, 1991); David A. Anderson, *The Origins of the Press Clause*, 30 UCLA L Rev 455, 486–94 (1983).

[37] Vincent Blasi, *The Checking Value in First Amendment Theory*, 1977 Am Bar Found Res J 521, 527–28, 529–44; Anderson, 30 UCLA L Rev at 491, 493, 534 (cited in note 36).

ernment officials so that voters could hold them accountable when they stood for reelection.[38] For Americans, the first priority in free expression was to protect the press because it informed the people about the actions of their government. For classical Athenians, the priority was to protect the freedom of speech of all citizens because it permitted them to participate actively and fully in their government.

The classical Athenians adopted two free-speech concepts that were central to their democracy.[39] The first was *isēgoria*, which described the equal opportunity of all Athenian citizens to speak in the principal political institution of the democracy, the Assembly.[40] The second was *parrhēsia*, which described the practice of Athenians to speak openly and frankly once they had the floor.[41] Although the Athenians carefully tailored *isēgoria* and *parrhēsia* to fit their democratic practices, I shall show that these classical Athenian principles resonate powerfully in contemporary American free-speech jurisprudence.

A. ATHENIAN ISĒGORIA

As practiced in the classical Athenian democracy, the principle of *isēgoria* offered every full citizen in good standing an equal opportunity to make proposals and to speak before the Assembly (*ekklēsia*).[42] The *ekklēsia* was the centerpiece of the classical Athenian democracy.[43] It settled the most fundamental policy issues facing the *polis*, along with a great many minor matters, across the

---

[38] See Madison, *Report on the Virginia Resolutions* at 571–75 (cited in note 11). Madison wrote, "[I]nformation and communication among the people . . . is indispensable to the just exercise of their electoral rights." Id at 574.

[39] See Wallace, *Power to Speak* at 221 (cited in note 25).

[40] See text at notes 42–71.

[41] See text at notes 135–72.

[42] G. T. Griffith, *Isēgoria in the Assembly at Athens*, in *Ancient Society and Institutions* 115, 115 (Blackwell, 1966); J. D. Lewis, *Isegoria at Athens: When Did It Begin?* 20 Historia 129, 129 (1971). For an argument that the Council of 500 also must have observed the practice of *isēgoria*, see A. G. Woodhead, *Isēgoria and the Council of 500*, 16 Historia 129, 134 (1967).

[43] Claude Mossé, *Inventing Politics*, in Jacques Brunschwig and Geoffrey E. R. Lloyd, eds, *Greek Thought: A Guide to Classical Knowledge* 147, 154 (Belknap, 2000) (Elizabeth Rawlings and Jeannine Pucci, trans); Ober, *Mass and Elite in Democratic Athens* at 134 (cited in note 6). The leading work on the Athenian Assembly is Mogens Herman Hansen, *The Athenian Assembly in the Age of Demosthenes* (Blackwell, 1987). For good, brief discussions, see Hansen, *Athenian Democracy* at 125–60 (cited in note 4); Ober, *Mass and Elite in Democratic Athens* at 132–38 (cited in note 6).

entire range of public concern.[44] During Athens's mature democracy, the *ekklēsia* met at a rate of once every nine or ten days (not counting possible special sessions).[45] Some leading classical scholars believe that the typical Assembly session drew around 6,000 attendees (*ekklēsiastai*), which was the approximate seating capacity of the natural amphitheater in the heart of Athens where the sessions were held.[46] Every full citizen of Athens had the right to attend Assembly sessions and to vote on every item presented to the *ekklēsia*.[47] The procedural rules of the *ekklēsia* did not limit the number of speakers or restrict the length of speeches.[48] As a matter of principle, the Athenians regarded the Assembly's actions as decisions of the full citizen body, pure and simple.[49]

The opportunity that *isēgoria* afforded Athenian citizens to speak on matters of public concern was a defining practice of the classical democracy.[50] Herodotus used *isēgoria* synonymously with democ-

---

[44] See Sinclair, *Democracy and Participation in Athens* at 19, 67–68, 75 (cited in note 4).

[45] The Assembly had forty regular sessions a year (Athens observed a lunar year of 354 days). See Hansen, *Athenian Democracy* at 128–29, 133–36 (cited in note 4); A. H. M. Jones, *Athenian Democracy* 3 (Johns Hopkins, 1986) (originally published in 1957).

[46] See Hansen, *Athenian Assembly* at 125 (cited in note 43) (estimate of about 6,000); Jones, *Athenian Democracy* at 109 (cited in note 45) (estimate of "well over 5,000"). But see Sinclair, *Democracy and Participation in Athens* at 119 (cited in note 4) (arguing that the evidence is insufficient to support calculations of the level of attendance in the Assembly). If the 6,000 attendance figure is accurate, it would constitute about 15 percent of the highest estimates of the number of full citizens in Athens before the Peloponnesian War, around 40,000. For other proportional estimates of Assembly attendance, see Ober, *Mass and Elite in Democratic Athens* at 132 (cited in note 6) (between one- and two-fifths of the eligible citizenry); David Stockton, *The Classical Athenian Democracy* 84 (Oxford, 1990) ("at most somewhere between one-seventh and one-fifth of the total number eligible to attend"). The Athenian Assembly met on the Pnyx, a low hill near the Acropolis and the *agora*, the public square and marketplace of Athens. Hansen, *Athenian Assembly* at 12–14 (cited in note 43).

[47] Hansen, *Athenian Assembly* at 12–14 (cited in note 43); Sinclair, *Democracy and Participation in Athens* at 19, 67 (cited in note 4). There was no fixed membership of the Assembly: It consisted of the full citizens who arrived for the session. M. I. Finley, *Democracy Ancient and Modern* 52 (Rutgers, 1985) (rev ed) (originally published 1973). Athenian law provided for the disenfranchisement (*atimia*) of citizens who committed certain offenses. These *atimoi* lost the right to attend and to vote in the *ekklēsia*. Hansen, *Athenian Assembly* at 7 (cited in note 43); S. C. Todd, *The Shape of Athenian Law* 142–43 (Clarendon, 1993).

[48] Hansen, *Athenian Assembly* at 91 (cited in note 43); Wallace, *Power to Speak* at 225 (cited in note 25).

[49] Hansen, *Athenian Democracy* at 130 (cited in note 4). The Athenians often used the term *ekklēsia* synonymously with *dēmos*. Id at 125; Sinclair, *Democracy and Participation in Athens* at 15 (cited in note 4). Assembly speakers addressed the *ekklēsiastai* as *ho dēmos*, "the people." Ober, *Mass and Elite in Democratic Athens* at 134 (cited in note 6).

[50] Jeffrey Henderson, *Attic Old Comedy, Frank Speech, and Democracy*, in Deborah Boedeker and Kurt A. Raaflaub, eds, *Democracy, Empire, and the Arts in Fifth-Century Athens*

racy,[51] and Demosthenes spoke eloquently of democratic citizens as having "chosen a life of *isēgoria*."[52] Aeschines, an orator of fourth-century Athens, invoked *isēgoria* more pointedly to distinguish between democracy and oligarchy in ancient Greece. In an oligarchy, Aeschines explained, only "a man in authority . . . addresses the people," whereas in a democracy, any citizen may do so "whenever it seems right to him."[53] By empowering common citizens to address the Assembly, *isēgoria* helped to ensure that the *polis* served "the many instead of the few," Pericles' definition of *dēmokratia*.[54] *Isēgoria* made popular sovereignty a reality in classical Athens by enabling the *dēmos* to rule.

The herald (*ho keryx*) of the Assembly invoked *isēgoria* by commencing every debate with the simple question, "Who wishes to speak?"[55] Euripides described the herald's invitation to open public debate as "the call of freedom."[56] *Isēgoria* was a positive political

---

255, 256 (Harvard, 1998); Ober, *Mass and Elite in Democratic Athens* at 72–73 (cited in note 6). See also Jeremy McInerney, *Nereids, Colonies and the Origins of Isēgoria* , in Sluiter and Rosen, eds, *Free Speech in Classical Antiquity* 21, 21 (cited in note 19) ("The capacity of a free man to address the People was fundamental to the democracy, and to prevent a man from speaking was an assault not only on the 'rights' of the individual, but on the democracy itself."). Athens was unusual in this respect. Many Greek *poleis* never extended to their citizens a general right to speak in political meetings. Arnaldo Momigliano, *Freedom of Speech in Antiquity*, in Phillip Weiner, ed, 2 *Dictionary of the History of Ideas* 252, 257 (Scribner's, 1973); Wallace, *Athenian Laws Against Slander* at 110 (cited in note 17).

[51] See Herodotus, *The History* 5.78 at 389 (Chicago, 1987) (David Grene, trans) ("It is not only in respect of one thing but of everything that equality and free speech are clearly good . . . .). G. T. Griffith has speculated that Herodotus may have used *isēgoria* in place of the more inclusive *dēmokratia* to describe the Athenian political regime because *isēgoria* as practiced in Athens was "an unusual freedom not shared as yet by the generality of Greek democracies." Griffith, *Isēgoria in the Assembly* at 131 (cited in note 42). For a relatively recent investigation of the meaning of *isēgoria* in Herodotus' *Histories*, citing the considerable scholarship on this question, see Yoshio Nakategawa, *Isēgoria in Herodotus*, 37 Historia 257 (1988).

[52] Demosthenes 15.18, in *Demosthenes I* 423 (Harvard, 1935) (J. H. Vance, trans).

[53] Raaflaub, *Aristocracy and Freedom of Speech* at 53 (cited in note 25), quoting Aeschines, 3.220.

[54] Thucydides, *Landmark Thucydides* 2.37.1 at 112 (cited in note 5). See also [Pseudo] Xenophon, *The Constitution of the Athenians* 6–9, in *Aristotle and Xenophon on Democracy and Oligarchy* 37, 38–39 (California, 1975) (J. M. Moore, trans) (the Athenians practiced *isēgoria* because the *dēmos* wished "to be free and to rule the city").

[55] Hansen, *Athenian Democracy* at 142 (cited in note 4). See also Ryan K. Balot, *Free Speech, Courage, and Democratic Deliberation*, in Sluiter and Rosen, eds, *Free Speech in Classical Antiquity* 233, 233 (cited in note 19) (describing the herald's call as a "well-known symbol" of free speech); Carter, *Citizen Attribute, Negative Right* at 199–200 (cited in note 19) (describing the herald's call as "[t]he most obvious expression of Athenian equality of speech . . . .").

[56] Euripides, *The Suppliant Women*, 437, in Euripides IV, 57, 74 (Chicago, 1958) (Frank Jones, trans, David Grene and Richard Lattimore, eds).

freedom which ensured that common citizens attending the Assembly could speak as well as listen, and thus become full partners in the formation of public policy.[57] *Isēgoria* also enforced the Athenian commitment to equal citizenship that formed the core of the Athenian democratic constitution.[58] For Demosthenes, *isēgoria*'s combination of civic freedom and political equality made it the preeminent civil liberty in classical Athens.[59]

In the classical Athenian imagination, the ideal Assembly speaker (*rhētōr*) enabled by *isēgoria* was an "honest, ordinary citizen" who spoke simply and truthfully when he occasionally ascended the *bēma* (speaker's platform) to address his fellow citizens.[60] Isocrates expressed this ideal when he remarked, "[S]ometimes the wisest speakers miss the point and one of the ordinary citizens, 'deemed of little account and generally ignored,' comes up with a good idea and is judged to speak the best."[61] It is unclear how frequently debate in the Assembly realized the Athenian ideal, however. Demosthenes, for example, once observed that "the majority of [*ekklēsiastai*] do not avail [them]selves of . . . [their] right to speak."[62] The surviving evidence on speaker participation in the Assembly pulls in different directions. On one hand, there is evidence that common Athenians regularly participated in Assembly debate, and that at least on some occasions, many Athenians spoke.[63] One classicist has estimated that there were between 200 and 300 speakers (*rhētōres*) at any given session of the Assembly.[64] On the other hand, it also is attested that only a small, relatively select group of *rhētōres*, or "orators," regularly participated in, and typically dominated, Assembly debate.[65]

---

[57] Henderson, *Attic Old Comedy* at 256 (cited in note 50); Woodhead, 16 Historia at 131 (cited in note 42).

[58] Griffith, *Isēgoria in the Assembly* at 115 (cited in note 42); Raaflaub, *Discovery of Freedom in Ancient Greece* at 95 (cited in note 5).

[59] See Demosthenes 21.123–24, in *Demosthenes I* 89 (cited in note 52).

[60] Hansen, *Athenian Assembly* at 58, 61–62 (cited in note 43).

[61] Wallace, *Athenian Laws Against Slander* at 109 (cited in note 17), quoting Isocrates 12.24.

[62] Demosthenes 22.30, in *Demosthenes III* 177 (Harvard, 1935) (J. H. Vance, trans).

[63] Wallace, *Power to Speak* at 221 (cited in note 25); Woodhead, 16 Historia at 129 (cited in note 42).

[64] Sinclair, *Democracy and Participation in Athens* at 140–41 (cited in note 4).

[65] See Hansen, *Athenian Democracy* at 142–46 (cited in note 4); Ober, *Mass and Elite in Democratic Athens* at 112–18 (cited in note 6). R. K. Sinclair has estimated that at any one time there were between twenty and thirty *rhētōres* who regularly participated in Assembly debate. Sinclair, *Democracy and Participation in Athens* at 140 (cited in note 4).

The Athenians' use of the word *rhētōr* reflects this tension between ordinary and elite Assembly speakers. Under Athenian law,
the meaning of *rhētōr* was fully inclusive: Anyone who addressed
the Assembly, or any of the institutions of *polis* government, was
a *rhētōr*.[66] In common usage, however, *rhētōr* meant "orator," one
of the few political leaders who regularly spoke in the Assembly
and who typically dominated debate.[67] These leaders were not
ordinary citizens. They were members of the wealth elite who
possessed the skill and courage that debate in the Athenian Assembly demanded.[68] Unlike modern democratic leaders, *rhētōres*
were unelected, and they possessed no decision-making authority.[69] *Rhētōres* were volunteers who offered themselves as "coun-
selors" or "advisors" of the *dēmos*.[70] Their only power was the
power of persuasion, and their status as *rhētōr* was "only as secure
as [their] latest speech."[71]

B. AMERICAN ISĒGORIA

Athenian *isēgoria* was both narrower and more powerful than
the freedom of speech protected by the First Amendment. *Isēgoria*
was narrower than American freedom of speech because it was
purely political, and thus was restricted to full citizens in good

---

[66] Hansen, *Athenian Assembly* at 50–51 (cited in note 43); Sinclair, *Democracy and Participation in Athens* at 136 (cited in note 4). The word *rhētōr* is derived from the verb *eipein*,
which means "to speak." Hansen, *Athenian Assembly* at 55 (cited in note 43).

[67] Finley, *Democracy Ancient and Modern* at 56–62 (cited in note 47); Hansen, *Athenian
Democracy* at 142–46 (cited in note 4).

[68] Griffith, *Isēgoria in the Assembly* at 124 (cited in note 42); Hansen, *Athenian Assembly*
at 58 (cited in note 43). Assembly orations have been described as a form of "performance-
art," Stephen Halliwell, *Aischrology, Shame, and Comedy*, in Sluiter and Rosen, eds, *Free
Speech in Classical Antiquity* 115, 126 (cited in note 19), and thus Thucydides had the fifth-
century politician-*rhētōr* Cleon accuse the *ekklēsiastai* of "go[ing] to see an oration as you
would to see a sight," Thucydides, *Landmark Thucydides* 3.38.4 at 427 (cited in note 5).
See also S. Sara Monoson, *Plato's Democratic Entanglements: Athenian Politics and the Practice
of Philosophy* 59 (Princeton, 2000) ("the Athenians delighted in excellent oratory, for the
most part taking enormous pleasure in hearing competing views argued intensely and
beautifully . . . .").

[69] Hansen, *Athenian Assembly* at 49–50 (cited in note 43). The status of *rhētōr* was not
a public office. Balot, *Free Speech, Courage, and Democratic Deliberation* at 243 (cited in
note 55).

[70] See, for example, Demosthenes 15.1, in *Demosthenes I* at 413 (cited in note 52); Thucydides, *Landmark Thucydides* 3.43 at 180 (cited in note 5).

[71] Balot, *Free Speech, Courage, and Democratic Deliberation* at 243 (cited in note 55).

legal standing.[72] The First Amendment, and indeed the entire Bill
of Rights, is not so limited.[73] Yet (and I believe, relatedly) Athenian
isēgoria was more powerful than American freedom of speech because *isēgoria* was a positive freedom of political participation,
while the First Amendment largely recognizes a negative right
against government censorship.[74] *Isēgoria* entitled citizens to make
proposals and to speak in the political institutions of Athens that
made public policy. In the political sphere, the First Amendment
simply frees individuals to speak to or about public officials and
their policies. These differences are fundamental. They demonstrate how Athens and America tailored the concept of freedom
of speech to fit the form of democracy that each polity practiced—
a highly participatory direct democracy in Athens, and a far more
restrained representative democracy in the United States.

Yet there are important—and revealing—similarities, in theory
as well as in doctrine, that link the ancient and modern understandings of freedom of speech. While the differences between
Athenian *isēgoria* and American freedom of speech followed from
the different forms of democracy embraced in the ancient and
modern systems, the kinship between the free-speech principles
of Athens and America is the product of the democratic commitments they share in common: the commitments to popular sovereignty and to self-government (albeit differently understood).
Indeed, the commonalities between Athenian *isēgoria* and American freedom of speech are so suggestive that we might identify
a concept of American *isēgoria* residing within the core of First
Amendment jurisprudence.

1. *Theory: Free speech and democracy*. The classical Athenians appreciated *isēgoria* as an essential element of their democracy,[75] and
the argument from democracy has long been widely accepted as
providing a strong, albeit partial, justification for the special pro-

---

[72] Raaflaub, *Discovery of Freedom in Ancient Greece* at 96 (cited in note 5); Josiah Ober,
The Polis as a Society: Aristotle, John Rawls, and the Athenian Social Contract, in *The Athenian
Revolution: Essays on Ancient Greek Democracy and Political Theory* 161, 181 (Princeton, 1996).

[73] See *Bridges v Wixon*, 326 US 135, 148 (1945) ("Freedom of speech and of press is
accorded aliens residing in this country."). See also *Landon v Plasencia*, 459 US 21, 82
(1982) ("once an alien gains admission to our country and begins to develop the ties that
go with permanent residence his constitutional status changes accordingly").

[74] See text at notes 21–23.

[75] See text at notes 50–54.

tection that the First Amendment affords freedom of speech.[76]
The earliest American justification for free-speech protection held
that in a democracy premised on the concept of popular sovereignty, the people, by definition, must remain free to speak out
on the performance of government officials, as well as on other
matters of public concern.[77] The Supreme Court has long recognized that a central purpose of the First Amendment's protection of freedom of speech is to facilitate self-government.[78] For
that reason, the Justices have placed political speech at the core
of First Amendment protection, reviewing with the highest skepticism government efforts to control the content of such speech.[79]

Intriguingly, the most influential arguments for a democratic
understanding of American freedom of speech were advanced by
two individuals who shared a deep affinity for classical Athenian
democracy and who drew on their understanding of Athenian political theory and practice in making their case. Justice Louis D.
Brandeis breathed life into free-speech jurisprudence early in the
twentieth century by offering, in the words of his biographer, a

---

[76] The leading scholarly treatment advocating a democratic justification for strongly
protecting freedom of speech is Alexander Meiklejohn, *Free Speech and Its Relation to Self-
Government*, in *Political Freedom: The Constitutional Powers of the People* 3 (Harper, 1960)
(originally published 1948). See also Alexander Meiklejohn, *The First Amendment Is an
Absolute*, 1961 Supreme Court Review 245 (elaborating his theory and responding to
critics). For influential critiques of Meiklejohn's theory, see Zechariah Chafee, *Book Review*,
62 Harv L Rev 891 (1948); Robert Post, *Meiklejohn's Mistake: Individual Autonomy and the
Reform of Public Discourse*, 64 U Colo L Rev 1109 (1993). Free-speech scholars from widely
different jurisprudential perspectives have followed Meiklejohn in emphasizing a demo-
cratic understanding of freedom of speech. See, for example, Lilian BeVier, *The First
Amendment and Political Speech: An Inquiry into the Substance and Limits of Principle*, 30 Stan
L Rev 299 (1978); Robert H. Bork, *Neutral Principles and Some First Amendment Problems*,
47 Ind L J 1 (1971); Owen M. Fiss, *The Irony of Free Speech* (Harvard, 1996); Burt Neuborne,
Toward a Democracy-Centered Reading of the First Amendment, 93 Nw U L Rev 1055 (1999);
Robert Post, *Constitutional Domains: Democracy, Community, Management* (Harvard, 1995);
Cass R. Sunstein, *Democracy and the Problem of Free Speech* (Free Press, 1993). For excellent
critiques of the democratic justification of free speech, see Lee Bollinger, *The Tolerant
Society: Freedom of Speech and Extremist Speech* 46–53 (Oxford, 1986); Frederick Schauer,
Free Speech: A Philosophical Enquiry 35–46 (Cambridge, 1982).

[77] See Levy, *Emergence of a Free Press* at 309–49 (cited in note 33); Keith Werhan, *Freedom
of Speech* 11–14 (Praeger, 2004).

[78] See, for example, *Mills v Alabama*, 384 US 214, 218 (1966) ("Whatever differences
may exist about interpretations of the First Amendment, there is practically universal
agreement that a major purpose of that Amendment was to protect the free discussion of
governmental affairs."). See also *Brown v Hartlage*, 456 US 45, 60 (1982) (describing the
First Amendment's protection of free speech as "the guardian of our democracy"); *Roth
v United States*, 354 US 476, 484 (1957) (the First Amendment's protection of free speech
"was fashioned to assure unfettered interchange of ideas for the bringing about of political
and social changes desired by the people").

[79] *Buckley v Valeo*, 424 US 1, 48–49 (1976).

"soaring . . . explication of the democratic value of free speech
. . . ."[80] Then, at mid-century, Alexander Meiklejohn helped to
revitalize free-speech jurisprudence after it had fallen into des-
uetude during the anticommunist furor following the Second
World War. Brandeis's and Meiklejohn's democratic rethinking of
American freedom of speech introduced *isēgoria* into First Amendment jurisprudence.

Justice Louis D. Brandeis. Justice Brandeis laid the democratic
foundation for American free-speech jurisprudence primarily in
his influential concurring opinion in *Whitney v California*,[81] which
First Amendment scholars widely have recognized as among the
most important judicial opinions ever written on American freedom of speech.[82] In his *Whitney* concurrence, Justice Brandeis
endeavored to make the (for many, counterintuitive) case that democratic states like the United States generally lack "the power to
prohibit dissemination of social, economic and political doctrine
which a vast majority of its citizens believes to be false and fraught
with evil consequences."[83]

In making this case, Brandeis drew on his understanding of

---

[80] Philippa Strum, *Louis D. Brandeis: Justice for the People* 335 (Harvard, 1984) (referring
to Brandeis's *Whitney* opinion). See also G. Edward White, *The First Amendment Comes
of Age: The Emergence of Free Speech in Twentieth-Century America*, 95 Mich L Rev 299,
325 (1996) (describing Brandeis's *Whitney* opinion as "marking the first impressive appearance of the self-governance rationale in First Amendment theory").

[81] 274 US 357, 372 (1927) (Brandeis concurring). In *Whitney*, the Supreme Court upheld
the conviction of Charlotte Anita Whitney (who, incidentally, was a niece of Supreme
Court Justice Stephen J. Field) for her role in helping to organize the Communist Labor
Party of California, a radical offshoot of the Socialist Party, and for her support of the
Industrial Workers of the World (IWW, or, more popularly, the "Wobblies"). See Ashutosh
A. Bhagwat, *The Story of Whitney v. California: The Power of Ideas*, in Michael C. Dorf, ed,
Constitutional Law Stories 407, 408–14 (Foundation, 2004). Although Justice Brandeis in
his concurring opinion advocated a far more speech-protective doctrine than the majority
of Justices in *Whitney* would accept, he nevertheless voted to affirm the conviction of
Whitney on his own terms. See *Whitney*, 274 US at 379–80 (Brandeis concurring). The
governor of California pardoned Whitney shortly after the Supreme Court affirmed her
conviction. Bhagwat, *Story of Whitney* at 421–22 (cited earlier in this note).

[82] See, for example, Vincent Blasi, *The First Amendment and the Ideal of Civic Courage:
The Brandeis Opinion in Whitney v. California*, 29 Wm & Mary L Rev 653, 660 (1988)
(describing Brandeis's *Whitney* concurrence as "what may be the most important judicial
opinion ever written on the subject of freedom of speech"); Bradley C. Bobertz, *The
Brandeis Gambit: The Making of America's "First Freedom," 1909–1931*, 40 Wm & Mary L
Rev 557, 645 (1999) (describing Brandeis's *Whitney* concurrence as providing "the dom-
inant theoretical underpinnings of the [Supreme] Court's free speech jurisprudence");
David M. Rabban, *Free Speech in Its Forgotten Years* 369 (Cambridge, 1997) (describing
Brandeis's *Whitney* opinion as "probably the most effective judicial interpretation of the
First Amendment ever written").

[83] *Whitney*, 274 US at 374 (Brandeis concurring).

classical Athenian political thought,[84] essentially smuggling *isēgoria* into free-speech theory through the American founding.[85] The most striking feature of Brandeis's *Whitney* opinion was its description of the democratic function of American freedom of speech, which was written as if the United States was a highly participatory direct democracy resembling Athens, rather than the considerably more restrained representative democracy that the American founders had constituted.[86] In an earlier free-speech opinion, Justice Brandeis had written of the "right of a citizen of the United States to take part . . . in the making of federal laws and in the conduct of the government,"[87] an apt description of the citizens of classical Athens, but a direct refutation of Madison's account of the indirect role that American citizens play in their governance.[88] Brandeis carried his preference for the Athenian conception of democratic citizenship over the more limited Madisonian understanding into his *Whitney* concurrence.

Brandeis's theory of free speech, like *isēgoria*, was grounded on the democratic premise of popular sovereignty.[89] For Brandeis, as for Athenian democrats, freedom of speech was a form of political participation in which every citizen was equally entitled to share. Brandeis found a kind of American *isēgoria* to be embedded in that broad participatory freedom. He argued that each American citizen possessed the right "to endeavor to make his own opinion

---

[84] Pnina Lahav, *Holmes and Brandeis: Libertarian and Republican Justifications for Free Speech*, 4 J L & Pol 451, 458–66 (1988). See also Strum, *Louis D. Brandeis* at 237–38 (cited in note 80) ("Brandeis held the Greeks of fifth century Athens" in "high esteem . . . . [T]o discover how the model political human being would function in the model political society, Brandeis turned to the Athenians."); Philippa Strum, *Introduction*, in Philippa Strum, ed, *Brandeis on Democracy* 1, 14 (Kansas, 1995) (Brandeis considered "Periclean Athens . . . to be the acme of democratic civilization").

[85] See *Whitney*, 274 US at 375 (Brandeis concurring) (referring to "[t]hose who won our independence"). See also Bobertz, 40 Wm & Mary L Rev at 646 (cited in note 82) (describing Brandeis's attribution of his understanding of free speech to the American founders as "a brilliant rhetorical maneuver," but "bad history").

[86] See Robert M. Cover, *The Left, the Right and the First Amendment, 1918–1928*, 40 Md L Rev 349, 385 (1981) ("The most striking new element in Brandeis' thought that is revealed by the *Whitney* concurrence is the shift from a focus upon legislative process to a more inclusive public politics."). See also Bork, 47 Ind L J at 24, 32 (cited in note 76) (criticizing Brandeis's *Whitney* concurrence for suggesting a theory of free speech that intrudes on the prerogatives of elected representatives); Lahav, 4 J L & Pol at 465 (cited in note 84) (characterizing Brandeis's *Whitney* concurrence as presenting an "almost utopian vision" of free speech).

[87] *Gilbert v Minnesota*, 254 US 325, 337 (1920) (Brandeis dissenting).

[88] See text at notes 7–12.

[89] Bhagwat, *Story of Whitney v. California* at 427 (cited in note 81).

concerning laws existing or contemplated prevail . . . ."[90] Brandeis also followed Athenian democrats in conceiving of freedom of speech not only as a privilege of citizenship, but also as an obligation of citizens with something to say for the benefit of the community.[91]

The ultimate purpose of freedom of speech in Brandeis's democracy, as in the classical Athenian democracy, was to benefit the community by enhancing the collective decision making of free citizens.[92] "[W]ithout free speech," Brandeis wrote, "assembly discussion would be futile."[93] Brandeis's reference to "assembly discussion" not only invoked *isēgoria*, it also opened a window on Brandeis's vison of freedom of speech in a democracy. In his portrayal, the purpose of the "public discussion" fostered by the First Amendment was not what Madison had described as appropriate for a representative democracy, that is, to inform the people about governmental officials and their policies,[94] or even to inform the government of popular will. Rather, it was to enable the citizen body, as the sovereign "ruling class,"[95] to deliberate toward the "political truth" that would define themselves as a people and would chart their collective course as a community.[96]

Although Brandeis attributed his democratic theory of freedom of speech to America's founding generation, his primary inspiration seems to have been Pericles' *Funeral Oration.*[97] Pericles and Brandeis expressed similar visions of Athens and America, respectively, as highly participatory democracies in which the people govern themselves. Thus, while Pericles had said that the Athenians regarded "the citizen who takes no part in . . . [public]

---

[90] *Gilbert*, 254 US at 337–38 (Brandeis dissenting).

[91] *Whitney*, 274 US at 375 (Brandeis concurring) ("public discussion is a political duty").

[92] Id at 375 (describing freedom of speech as facilitating "the discovery and spread of political truth").

[93] Id.

[94] See text at note 38.

[95] See Louis D. Brandeis, *Address to the Civic Federation of New England* (1906), excerpted in Vincent Blasi, *Ideas of the First Amendment* 669, 669 (Thomson West, 2006) ("every man is of the ruling class"). Compare Euripides, *Suppliant Women* 351–52, at 71 (cited in note 56) (describing the Athenian *dēmos* as the "[s]ole rulers" of Athens).

[96] *Whitney*, 274 US at 375 (Brandeis concurring).

[97] Paul A. Freund, *Mr. Justice Brandeis: A Centennial Memoir*, 70 Harv L Rev 769, 789 (1957); Strum, *Louis D. Brandeis* at 237 (cited in note 80). See Lahav, 4 J L & Pol at 462–64 (cited in note 84) (comparing Brandeis's *Whitney* concurrence with Pericles' *Funeral Oration*).

duties [*apragmon*] . . . as useless [*achreios*],"[98] Brandeis echoed that "the greatest menace to freedom is an inert people."[99] Brandeis's understanding of the democratic function of freedom of speech was Periclean to the core. Pericles had said, "[I]nstead of looking on discussion as a stumbling-block in the way of action, we think it an indispensable preliminary to any wise action at all."[100] Brandeis wrote similarly that "public discussion" unleashed "the power of reason," which in turn enabled "the deliberative forces" of society to "prevail over the arbitrary."[101] Finally, and perhaps most strikingly, both Pericles and Brandeis emphasized the interrelation between freedom and courage. Pericles said, "[H]appiness . . . [is] the fruit of freedom and freedom of valor . . . ."[102] While for Brandies, "liberty . . . [is] the secret of happiness and courage is the secret of liberty."[103] As Pnina Lahav observed, Brandeis's *Whitney* concurrence "transplanted Pericles' speech to American soil."[104]

Alexander Meiklejohn. Alexander Meiklejohn, like Justice Brandeis, viewed American freedom of speech through a classical Athenian lens,[105] reimagining America's representative democracy as an assembly democracy dependent upon direct citizen participation in the formation of law and policy. Meiklejohn built on Brandeis's *Whitney* concurrence in his influential *Free Speech and*

---

[98] Thucydides, *Landmark Thucydides* 2.40.2 at 113 (cited in note 5).

[99] *Whitney*, 274 US at 375 (Brandeis concurring).

[100] Thucydides, *Landmark Thucydides* 2.40.2 at 113 (cited in note 5). See also Isocrates 1.34, in *Isocrates I* 25 (Loeb, 1928) (George Norlin, trans) ("Be slow in deliberation, but be prompt to carry out your resolves.").

[101] *Whitney*, 274 US at 375 (Brandeis concurring).

[102] Thucydides, *Landmark Thucydides* 2.43.4 at 115 (cited in note 5). For a discussion of the Athenian understanding of the relationship between freedom of speech and courage, see text at notes 165–72.

[103] *Whitney*, 274 US at 375 (Brandeis concurring). Vincent Blasi has written evocatively on Brandeis's claim that freedom of speech cultivates within citizens the individual character that is required for effective self-government. See Vincent Blasi, *Free Speech and Good Character: From Milton to Brandeis to the Present*, in Lee C. Bollinger and Geoffrey R. Stone, eds, *Eternally Vigilant: Free Speech in the Modern Era* 61 (Chicago, 2002); Vincent Blasi, *Free Speech and Good Character*, 46 UCLA L Rev 1567 (1999); Blasi, 29 Wm & Mary L Rev at 676–97 (cited in note 82).

[104] Lahav, 4 J L & Pol at 464 (cited in note 84).

[105] See Arlene W. Saxonhouse, *Free Speech and Democracy in Ancient Athens* 25 (Cambridge, 2006) (Meiklejohn was "deeply devoted to the study of the classics," and for him, "[t]he health of modern democracy derived . . . from the understanding of Athenian democracy.").

Its Relation to Self-Government (1948),[106] where he argued, as would any classical Athenian democrat, that "[t]he principle of the freedom of speech springs from the necessities of the program of self-government."[107]

Meiklejohn modeled his theory of free speech on "the traditional American town hall meeting,"[108] the American political institution that is most evocative of the classical Athenian Assembly. The particulars of Meiklejohn's account of a town hall meeting described the workings of the *ekklēsia*, making clear his translation of American self-government into classical Athenian terms. Meiklejohn wrote, "In the town meeting the people of a community assemble to discuss and act upon matters of public interest. . . . Every man is free to come. They meet as political equals. Each has a right and a duty to think his own thoughts, to express them, and to listen to the arguments of others. The basic principle is that the freedom of speech shall be unabridged."[109] For Meiklejohn, as for Brandeis, this "basic principle" of free speech existed in the United States for the very reason that the Athenians practiced *isēgoria*: It was a necessary means toward the end of effective self-government.[110] "The final aim of the meeting," Meiklejohn wrote, "is the voting of wise decisions."[111]

Meiklejohn's focus on the relationship between freedom of speech and democracy, together with his understanding of free speech as a means of enhancing public decision making rather than of self-expression, connects him with the classical Athenian concept of *isēgoria*. In line with classical Athenian thought (and in opposition to the thinking of the American founding generation[112]) Meiklejohn dismissed any claim that freedom of speech was "a

---

[106] Cited in note 76.

[107] Meiklejohn, *Free Speech and Its Relation to Self-Government* at 27 (cited in note 76). For Meiklejohn, as for Athenian democrats, the "wisdom" required for sound public decision making resided "only in the minds of . . . individual citizens," and not in some elite ruling group. Id at 26.

[108] Id at 24. It was in the town meeting that Meiklejohn discovered "self-government in its simplest, most obvious form." Id at 24. See id at 24–28.

[109] Id at 24. For a brief description of the Athenian Assembly that perfectly parallels Meiklejohn's town meeting, see text at notes 42–49.

[110] Meiklejohn, *Free Speech and Its Relation to Self-Government* at 24–25 (cited in note 76.

[111] Id at 26.

[112] See text at notes 282–92.

Law of Nature or of Reason . . . ."[113] If the goal of democratic freedom of speech is to inform citizens adequately for public decision making, Meiklejohn reasoned, it was not "essential . . . that everyone shall speak, but that everything worth saying shall be said."[114] This, of course, was a central function of *isēgoria*.

2. *Doctrine: Free speech and equality.* The Brandeis-Meiklejohn account of free speech resonated with Athenian *isēgoria* not only at the level of theory, justifying American freedom of speech as if it served a highly participatory assembly democracy as had existed in classical Athens, but also at the doctrinal level, stressing that free speech in America, like *isēgoria* in Athens, embodied a strong equality principle. For contemporary Americans, the freedom of speech protected by the First Amendment, in large part, means what *isēgoria* meant in classical Athens, an equal opportunity of individuals to speak out on matters of public concern.

For Justice Brandeis, protecting an individual's "freedom to think as you will and to speak as you think"[115] required that the government remain neutral, at least formally, in public discussion. In Brandeis's democracy, members of the government, including, of course, the people's representatives, participated in public debate, but they could not enlist the coercive power of government to silence speakers or speech that they regarded as dangerous or wrongheaded. According to Brandeis, "silence coerced by law" not only stifled "the discovery and spread of political truth,"[116] it also was fundamentally inconsistent with the principle of popular sovereignty on which democracy and freedom of speech (American as well as Athenian) rested.

Meiklejohn elaborated the principle of government neutrality toward speech that Justice Brandeis had sketched in his *Whitney* concurrence. Meiklejohn, like the classical Athenians, entwined the right to speak in the citizen assembly (*isēgoria*) with the political equality (*isonomia*) of the members of a self-governing community.[117] The citizens attending Meiklejohn's town meeting, like the

---

[113] Meiklejohn, *Free Speech and Its Relation to Self-Government* at 27 (cited in note 76).

[114] Id at 26.

[115] *Whitney*, 274 US at 375 (Brandeis concurring).

[116] Id at 375–76.

[117] See Griffith, *Isēgoria in the Assembly* at 115 (cited in note 42) (*isēgoria* "must be presumed to be a part [of *isonomia*]"); Nakategawa, 37 Historia at 270 (cited in note 51) (*isēgoria* conveys "a sense that the citizens possess their *polis* in equal shares, and share equal responsibility for its flourishing").

classical Athenian *ekklēsiastai*, "meet as political equals. Each has a right and a duty to think his own thoughts, to express them, and to listen to the arguments of others."[118] In this "method of political self-government" grounded on the political equality of each citizen, Meiklejohn argued, "the vital point" is that the government may not deny a hearing to any "suggestion of policy . . . because it is on one side of the issue rather than another."[119] For Meiklejohn, "this equality of status in the field of ideas lies deep in the very foundations of the self-governing process."[120] He explained,

> When men govern themselves, it is they—and no one else— who must pass judgment upon unwisdom and unfairness and danger. . . . Just so far as, at any point, the citizens who are to decide an issue are denied acquaintance with information or opinion or doubt or disbelief or criticism which is relevant to that issue, just so far the result must be ill-considered, ill-balanced planning for the general good. It is that mutilation of the thinking process of the community against which the First Amendment to the Constitution is directed.[121]

Meiklejohn underscored his "vital" rule against viewpoint discrimination with an evocation of Demosthenes. Just as Demosthenes had celebrated the Athenians for permitting their fellow citizens to praise the Spartan constitution over the Athenian constitution,[122] Meiklejohn, near the dawn of the Cold War, argued that the United States must allow its communists to criticize the fundamentals of American constitutionalism.[123] Meiklejohn also drew upon the classical Athenian theme of civic courage that Pericles and Brandeis had identified as the secret of a free and democratic people. "When a question of policy is 'before the house,'" Meiklejohn concluded, "free men choose to meet it not with their

---

[118] Meiklejohn, *Free Speech and Its Relation to Self-Government* at 24 (cited in note 76).

[119] Id at 26–27. For Meiklejohn, this rule against viewpoint discrimination "means that though citizens may, on other grounds, be barred from speaking, they may not be barred because their views are thought to be false or dangerous. . . . No speaker may be declared 'out of order' because we disagree with what he intends to say." Id at 27.

[120] Id at 27.

[121] Id (emphasis deleted).

[122] Demosthenes 20.106, in *Demosthenes I* at 563 (cited in note 52).

[123] Meiklejohn, *Free Speech and Its Relation to Self-Government* at 27 (cited in note 76).

eyes shut, but with their eyes open. To be afraid of ideas, any idea, is to be unfit for self-government."[124]

The Supreme Court has given doctrinal primacy to Brandeis's principle of government neutrality and Meiklejohn's principle of ideological equality by making the so-called "content distinction" a dominant feature of contemporary free-speech methodology. The content distinction obligates courts to review carefully and skeptically government restrictions imposed on speakers or speech because officials disapprove, or fear the consequences of, the content of the restricted speech.[125] "[A]bove all else," the Court declared in *Police Department of City of Chicago v Mosley*, "the First Amendment means that government has no power to restrict expression because of its message, its ideas, its subject matter, or its content."[126] As a general rule, such a "content-based" restriction presumptively violates the First Amendment.[127]

The Justices in *Mosley* made clear their reliance on Meiklejohn by explicitly adopting his principle of the "equality of status in the field of ideas."[128] The Court's importation of that equality principle into First Amendment jurisprudence led the Justices to Meiklejohn's conclusion: "[G]overnment must afford all points of view an equal opportunity to be heard."[129] Thus, just as Meiklejohn had argued for an absolute rule against viewpoint discrimination by the government (i.e., "deny[ing] a hearing" to a policy suggestion "because it is on one side of the issue rather than an-

---

[124] Id at 28.

[125] I have described the content distinction and its place in First Amendment jurisprudence in Werhan, *Freedom of Speech* at 72–79 (cited in note 77). A small sampling of leading commentary on the content distinction includes John Hart Ely, *Flag Desecration: A Case Study in the Roles of Categorization and Balancing in First Amendment Analysis*, 88 Harv L Rev 1482 (1975); Elena Kagan, *Private Speech, Public Purpose: The Role of Government Motive in First Amendment Doctrine*, 63 U Chi L Rev 413 (1996); Kenneth L. Karst, *Equality as a Central Principle in the First Amendment*, 43 U Chi L Rev 20 (1975); Geoffrey R. Stone, *Content Regulation and the First Amendment*, 25 Wm & Mary L Rev 189 (1983). Important criticisms of the content distinction are to be found in Morton J. Horowitz, *Foreword: The Constitution of Change: Legal Fundamentality Without Fundamentalism*, 107 Harv L Rev 30 (1993); Martin H. Redish, *The Content Distinction in First Amendment Analysis*, 34 Stan L Rev 113 (1981).

[126] 408 US 92, 95 (1972).

[127] *City of Renton v Playtime Theatres, Inc.*, 475 US 41, 46–47 (1986).

[128] *Mosley*, 408 US at 96 & n 4, quoting Meiklejohn, *Free Speech and Its Relation to Self-Government* at 27 (cited in note 76).

[129] *Mosley*, 408 US at 96.

other"),[130] contemporary free-speech jurisprudence has made it virtually impossible to justify any speech or speaker restriction that is based on government disapproval of the viewpoint expressed.[131] And, by the same token, the courts lower their guard against content-neutral speech restrictions, that is, restrictions that do not discriminate between speakers because of the content of their expression,[132] as well as against content-based restrictions that pose only an attenuated risk of government censorship.[133] The dominance of the content distinction in free-speech jurisprudence has made equality a "central principle" of the First Amendment,[134] just as it was in Athenian *isēgoria*.

The incorporation of Athenian *isēgoria* into the heart of First Amendment theory and doctrine emphasizes what Athens and America share in common—their commitment to self-government premised on popular sovereignty. This common commitment draws the Athenian and American understandings of free speech closer than one might have suspected, in light of the fundamental differences between Athenian and American democracy. Brandeis and Meiklejohn, two pioneers of American free-speech theory, explicitly bridged the gap between Athens and America when they reimagined the United States as a pure assembly democracy for the purposes of laying the foundation of modern First Amendment theory and doctrine. Even when one returns to the reality of the United States as a representative democracy, where citizens vote for their representatives in government rather than for law and policy, the idea of popular sovereignty nevertheless implies principles of equality among citizens and of citizen control over the government that have led Americans to adapt the essence of Athenian *isēgoria*—the equal right to speak on matters of public concern—to their political environment.

C. ATHENIAN PARRHĒSIA

The second classical Athenian term for freedom of speech was

---

[130] Meiklejohn, *Free Speech and Its Relation to Self-Government* at 26–28 (cited in note 76).

[131] Kathleen M. Sullivan and Gerald Gunther, *First Amendment Law* 212 (Foundation, 3rd ed 2007). For an analysis of the Court's handling of viewpoint-discrimination cases, see Marjorie Heins, *Viewpoint Discrimination*, 24 Hastings Const L Q 99 (1996).

[132] See *Renton*, 475 US at 47.

[133] *Davenport v Washington Education Assoc.*, 127 S Ct 2372, 2381 (2007).

[134] Karst, 43 U Chi L Rev at 20 (cited in note 125).

parrhēsia, but as was with *isēgoria*, the language "freedom of speech" is far too bland to capture the rich and nuanced meaning of Athenian *parrhēsia*. *Parrhēsia* ("the ability to say everything") described the freedom to speak one's mind frankly and with complete openness, to say the whole truth as one understands the truth.[135] The truth-telling prescribed by *parrhēsia* typically had a confrontative, critical bite.[136] *Parrhēsia* connoted strong admonishment or well-intentioned advice, stemming from a sincere concern to correct the listener's conduct.[137] In the political context, my focus here, *parrhēsia*, at least in principle, freed ordinary Athenians to challenge the policy preferences of *polis* leaders, as well as the ideas and beliefs of their fellow citizens.[138]

For some classical Athenians, especially aristocrats who were critical of democracy, *parrhēsia* had a decidedly negative connotation. It implied crude, profane, or offensive language that threatened to coarsen public discourse, and thereby to undermine traditional Greek notions of public decorum.[139] For these critics, the

---

[135] Monoson, *Plato's Democratic Entanglements* at 52–53 (cited in note 68); Raaflaub, *Discovery of Freedom in Ancient Greece* at 223 (cited in note 5). The orator Isocrates used *parrhēsia* in this most basic sense when telling his listeners, "I am going to speak to you absolutely without reserve. . . . Be assured, therefore, you shall hear from me the whole truth . . . ." Isocrates 15.43–44, in *Isocrates II* 211 (Loeb, 1929) (G. P. Gould, trans.).

[136] See Michel Foucault, *Fearless Speech* 17 (Semiotext(e), 2001); Monoson, *Plato's Democratic Entanglements* at 53 (cited in note 68).

[137] Henderson, *Attic Old Comedy* at 256 (cited in note 50); Roisman, *Speaker-Audience Interactions in Athens* at 268–75 (cited in note 29). Demosthenes described the parrhesiast as speaking "the truth . . . with all freedom, simply in goodwill and for the best . . . ." Demosthenes 10.76, in *Demosthenes I* at 313 (cited in note 52).

[138] Roisman, *Speaker-Audience Interactions in Athens* at 268 (cited in note 29). The exercise of *parrhēsia*, unlike *isēgoria*, was not limited to full citizens participating in the political institutions of Athens. It was a personal as well as a political freedom, Robert W. Wallace, *Private Lives and Public Enemies: Freedom of Thought in Classical Athens*, in Alan L. Boegehold and Adele C. Scafuro, eds, *Athenian Identity and Civic ideology* 127, 127 (Johns Hopkins, 1994), and thus the Athenians practiced *parrhēsia* in their daily lives, Henderson, *Attic Old Comedy* at 257 (cited in note 50); Raaflaub, *Aristocracy and Freedom of Speech* at 43 (cited in note 25). And *parrhēsia*, again unlike *isēgoria*, was not limited to citizens: Everyone living in Athens enjoyed considerable freedom to speak his or her mind. Carter, *Citizen Attribute, Negative Right* at 215 (cited in note 19); Wallace, *Athenian Laws Against Slander* at 109 (cited in note 17). Indeed, Demosthenes remarked that the metics (resident aliens) and slaves of Athens practiced greater *parrhēsia* than the full citizens of many other *poleis*. Demosthenes 9.3, in *Demosthenes I* at 227 (cited in note 52). See also Isocrates 5.97, in *Isocrates I* at 405 (cited in note 100) ("[I]t is disgraceful that we, who in former times would not allow even free men the right of equal speech [*isēgoria*], are now openly tolerating license of speech [*parrhēsia*] on the part of slaves."); [Pseudo] Xenophon, *Constitution of the Athenians* 1.12 at 39 (cited in note 54) ("in the matter of free speech we have put slaves and free men on equal terms; we have also done the same for metics and citizens . . .").

[139] Carter, *Citizen Attribute, Negative Right* at 201 (cited in note 19); Halliwell, *Aischrology, Shame, and Comedy* at 127–30 (cited in note 68).

license afforded by *parrhēsia* to "say everything" freed Athenians
to say too much, to say things that traditional norms of respect
and shamefulness (*aidōs*) decreed should be left unsaid.[140] In the
Areopagiticus, for example, Isocrates charged that classical Athenian
democracy "trained the citizens in such fashion that they looked
upon insolence as democracy . . . [and] impudence of speech [*parrhēsia*] as equality . . . ."[141] In this vein, some ancient sources
likened *parrhēsia* to the kind of frank speech that is unleashed
when one becomes intoxicated.[142]

As with *isēgoria*, the classical Athenians closely associated *parrhēsia* with democracy,[143] so much so that they named a trireme
(warship) *Parrhēsia*.[144] In the *Republic*, for example, Plato's Socrates
described democracy as "a city full of freedom [*eleutheria*] and
freedom of speech [*parrhēsia*]."[145] The Athenians regarded *parrhēsia* as essential to their democracy because their primary political practice of group decision making, following a series of
speeches, depended on authentic public debate among citizens
who honestly and forthrightly spoke their minds.[146] The Athenians

---

[140] Carter, *Citizen Attribute, Negative Right* at 201 (cited in note 19); Halliwell, *Aischrology,
Shame, and Comedy* at 127–30 (cited in note 68). Isocrates, for example, once complained,
"[M]y father's private life they revile with excessive indecency and audacity, and they are
not ashamed, now that he is dead, to use a license of speech [*parrhēsia*] concerning him
which they would have feared to employ while he lived."). Isocrates 16.22, in *Isocrates III*
189 (Loeb, 1945) (La Rue Van Hook, trans).

[141] Isocrates 7.20, in *Isocrates II* at 115–17 (cited in note 135). See also Raaflaub, *Aristocracy
and Freedom of Speech* at 50 (cited in note 25) (to Athenian aristocrats, *parrhēsia* "symbolized
the lack of discipline and order that was typical of democracy").

[142] See Plato, *Laws* 649b, in *Plato: Complete Works* 1318, 1342–43 (cited in note 16)
(Trevor J. Saunders, trans) (becoming intoxicated, "the fellow loses all his inhibitions and
becomes completely fearless: he'll say and do anything, without a qualm"); Xenophon,
Symposium 8.24–25, in *Xenophon IV* 534, 623 (Loeb, 1923) (E. C. Marchant and O. J.
Todd, trans) ("Do not be surprised at my plain speaking; the wine helps to incite me, and
the kind of love that ever dwells with me spurs me on to say what I think [*parrhēsiazesthai*]
about its opposite.").

[143] Monoson, *Plato's Democratic Entanglements* at 51, 54 (cited in note 68); Saxonhouse,
Free Speech and Democracy in Ancient Athens at 8 (cited in note 105).

[144] Mogens Herman Hansen, *The Ancient Athenian and the Modern Liberal View of Liberty
as a Democratic Ideal*, in Ober and Hedrick, eds, *Demokratia* at 91, 92 (cited in note 2).
The Athenians named several other triremes *Eleutheria* ("freedom"). Barry S. Strauss, *The
Athenian Trireme, School of Democracy*, in Ober and Hedrick, eds, *Demokratia* at 313, 318
(cited in note 2).

[145] Plato, *Republic* 557b, at 1168 (cited in note 16). Demosthenes went further, declaring
in his *Funeral Oration* that one of the "just and noble features" of democracy was the
impossibility of stifling *parrhēsia*. Demosthenes 60.26, in *Demosthenes VII* 25–27 (Loeb,
1940) (N. W. and N. J. Dewitt, trans).

[146] Monoson, *Plato's Democratic Entanglements* at 52 (cited in note 68); Saxonhouse, *Free
Speech and Democracy in Ancient Athens* at 87–88 (cited in note 105).

appreciated *parrhēsia* more generally for contributing to the atmosphere of individual freedom that democracy required in order to flourish.[147] For example, Demades, a fourth-century orator (and demagogue), described *parrhēsia* as "the sound of freedom."[148]

Classical Athenians also understood that *parrhēsia* supported democracy by serving the kind of checking function that the American Founders had ascribed to a free press.[149] Demosthenes explained that "of all states," democracies were "the most antagonistic" to political leaders "of infamous habits" because "every man is at liberty to publish their shame."[150] This description of *parrhēsia* in classical Athens foreshadowed the function of American freedom of the press in the Internet age. And when Demosthenes said that in a democracy committed to freedom of expression, "even the lone individual, uttering the deserved reproach, makes the guilty wince,"[151] he anticipated the First Amendment principle that "liberty of the press is the right of the lonely pamphleteer . . . just as much as of the large metropolitan publisher . . . ."[152] Demosthenes stated an American as well as an Athenian ideal when he observed that democracies could not "deter freedom of speech, which depends upon speaking the truth, from exposing the truth."[153]

The classical Athenians thus nurtured a political culture that not only invited all citizens to address political institutions (*isēgoria*),

---

[147] Jeff Miller, *Democratic Characterizations of Democracy: Liberty's Relationship to Equality and Speech in Ancient Athens*, 22 Hist Pol Thought 400, 415–16 (2001). See also Raaflaub, *Discovery of Freedom in Ancient Greece* at 276 (cited in note 5) ("The coining of *parrhēsia* . . . confirms . . . the deep connection between the democratic concept of freedom and the values and characteristics essential for the freeman's liberty."). Euripides wrote that *parrhēsia* was part of the "rich and glorious life in Athens" that made the *polis* "famous." Euripides, *Hippolytus* 420–22, at 181 (cited in note 20).

[148] Demades, *Fragment* 125.3 (translated by Scott Puckett).

[149] See Monoson, *Plato's Democratic Entanglements* at 55 (cited in note 68); Wallace, *Athenian Laws Against Slander* at 123 (cited in note 17). See text at notes 36–38.

[150] Demosthenes 22.31, in *Demosthenes III* at 177 (cited in note 62). See also Henderson, *Attic Old Comedy* at 257 (cited in note 50) ("*parrhēsia* . . . allowed any member of the *demos*, [no matter how inconsequential,] publicly to expose the misbehavior, dishonesty, bad counsel, or incompetence of anyone, however powerful, who threatened the integrity or well-being of the community").

[151] Demosthenes 60.26, in *Demosthenes VII* at 25–27 (cited in note 145).

[152] *Branzburg v Hayes*, 408 US 665, 704 (1972). See also *Mills v Alabama*, 384 US 214, 219 (1966) ("[T]he press . . . includes not only newspapers, books, and magazines, but also humble leaflets and circulars . . . ."); *Lovell v City of Griffin*, 303 US 444, 452 (1938) ("The press in its historic connotation comprehends every sort of publication which affords a vehicle of information and opinion.").

[153] Demosthenes 60.25, in *Demosthenes VII* at 25 (cited in note 145).

but also to speak forthrightly when doing so (*parrhēsia*).[154] In the Athenian Assembly (*ekklēsia*) the exercise of *parrhēsia* by *rhētōres* (Assembly speakers) complemented, or, rather, completed, *isēgoria*.[155] *Isēgoria* was a positive, procedural freedom that guaranteed Athenian citizens an equal opportunity to address the *ekklēsia*. *Parrhēsia* was a positive, substantive freedom that shaped the content of each *rhētōr*'s speech. Demosthenes thus described *parrhēsia* as a "privilege" of the *bēma*, the speaker's platform in the *ekklēsia*.[156] *Parrhēsia* freed *rhētōres*—indeed, it morally obligated them—to speak their mind completely and frankly.[157] In the Athenian Assembly, *isēgoria* enabled *parrhēsia*; *parrhēsia* was the free speech enabled by *isēgoria*.[158]

The interaction of *isēgoria* and *parrhēsia* in the Athenian Assembly represented an ideal of classical democratic deliberation that the Athenians regarded as essential for wise and legitimate public decision making.[159] In this idealized Assembly debate, ordinary citizens took their turn and spoke their mind, fully and frankly, before the *dēmos* decided the issues of the day.[160] The Athenians expected this highly participatory public debate to educate the *dēmos* fully about the implications of their policy options, and thereby enable the *ekklēsia* to settle on the proper decision.[161] As Thucydides had Pericles say in his *Funeral Oration*, "[I]nstead of looking on discussion as a stumbling-block in the way of action, we think it an indispensable preliminary to any wise action at all."[162] Debate structured

---

[154] Monoson, *Plato's Democratic Entanglements* at 51–52 (cited in note 68).

[155] See Halliwell, *Aischrology, Shame, and Comedy* at 129–30 (cited in note 68); Henderson, *Attic Old Comedy* at 256 (cited in note 50).

[156] Demosthenes 7.1, in *Demosthenes I* at 151 (cited in note 52).

[157] Miller, 22 Hist Pol Thought at 414–16 (cited in note 147). Michel Foucault described *parrhēsia* not only as "a guideline for democracy," but also as "an ethical and personal attitude characteristic of the good citizen." Foucault, *Fearless Speech* at 22 (cited in note 136).

[158] See Nakategawa, 37 Historia at 262 (cited in note 51) (*isēgoria* made "free speech in the assembly possible"); Saxonhouse, *Free Speech and Democracy in Ancient Athens* at 94 (cited in note 105) ("*isēgoria* captures the equality of opportunity to practice *parrhēsia*").

[159] See Monoson, *Plato's Democratic Entanglements* at 54, 56–63 (cited in note 68).

[160] Balot, *Free Speech, Courage, and Democratic Deliberation* at 233 (cited in note 55); Hansen, *Athenian Assembly* at 58, 61–62 (cited in note 43).

[161] Monoson, *Plato's Democratic Entanglements* at 56, 58, 61–62 (cited in note 68); Roisman, *Speaker-Audience Interactions in Athens* at 268 (cited in note 29).

[162] Thucydides, *Landmark Thucydides* 2.40.2 at 113 (cited in note 5). Thucydides had Diodotus emphasize the same point in the Mytilenian Debate. Diodotus said, "As for the argument that speech ought not to be the exponent of action, the man who uses it must

by the interplay of *isēgoria* and *parrhēsia* also legitimated Assembly decrees because these free-speech principles had offered every citizen an equal opportunity to speak his mind, which in turn enabled the *ekklēsia* to "speak" as the legitimate voice of the *dēmos*.[163] If everyone (*isēgoria*) had said all (*parrhēsia*), the *dēmos* had heard everything it needed to know before deciding on a course of action for the *polis*.

Political *parrhēsia*—the freedom to speak openly, fully, and forthrightly in the Assembly—gave *rhētōres* wide-ranging freedom to criticize opposing viewpoints, to attack and to demean their political competitors, and to challenge, even chastise, the assembled *dēmos*.[164] At the same time, the classical Athenian ideal of political *parrhēsia* implied a set of norms that the *dēmos* used to evaluate the democratic integrity of *rhētōres* who advised them in Assembly debate. First and foremost, the political parrhesiastic ideal implied a virtuous speaker, the "parrhesiast" (*parrhēsiastes*), an individual with the courage and the character to speak the truth, regardless of personal risk, for the public good rather than for self-serving motives.[165] Demosthenes spoke to this speech norm when he described the "truly brave" and "useful citizen" as one who "often opposes [the] wishes [of the *dēmos*] for the sake of what is best, and never speaks to win favor, but to promote [the] best interests" of the *polis*.[166]

The brave and honest parrhesiast, devoted to enhancing the welfare of the *polis* rather than his own power and prestige, would never stoop to ingratiating himself with his audience. He would neither

---

be either senseless or personally interested: senseless if he believes it possible to deal with the uncertain future through any other medium; interested if wishing to carry a disgraceful measure and doubting his ability to speak well in a bad cause . . . ." Id 3.42.2 at 179.

[163] Monoson, *Plato's Democratic Entanglements* at 57 (cited in note 68).

[164] Henderson, *Attic Old Comedy* at 256 (cited in note 50); Roisman, *Speaker-Audience Interactions in Athens* at 272 (cited in note 29). See also Wallace, *Power to Speak* at 222 (cited in note 25) ("Athenians were free to say almost anything, including blatant vituperation[,]" in the Assembly as well as in the courts).

[165] See Balot, *Free Speech, Courage, and Democratic Deliberation* at 234, 246–53 (cited in note 55); Monoson, *Plato's Democratic Entanglements* at 60–61 (cited in note 68). Sara Monoson has described the "climate of personal risk" in which the Assembly conducted debate. In her description, *rhētōres* "risked being disliked, shouted down, humiliated, fined, or brought up on any one of a variety of charges, some of which could carry stiff penalties." Monoson, *Plato's Democratic Entanglements* at 60 (cited in note 68). For an evaluation of how these risks limited freedom of speech in the Assembly, see text at notes 249–66, 293–315.

[166] Demosthenes 8.68–70, in *Demosthenes I* 213 (cited in note 52).

flatter his listeners nor appeal to their prejudices.[167] To do so would constitute an abuse rather than an exercise of *parrhēsia*, because such a speaker would have focused on pleasing his audience rather than on confronting it with the truth.[168] The ideal parrhesiast would not hold back truths that might offend. He endeavored to persuade the *dēmos* by honest and forthright argument, and not by deceptive rhetorical tricks.[169] Nor would he express views that he did not hold.[170] Deinarchos, for example, said that *rhētōres* who took bribes had "sold . . . [their] *parrhēsia*."[171]

The political parrhesiastic ideal required courage and character not only of Assembly speakers, but also, and just as importantly, of Assembly audiences, the *ekklēsiastai*. Just as *parrhēsia* demanded that *rhētōres* speak in service of the public good rather than their individual interests, it required that the *ekklēsiastai* open themselves to critical oratory for the good of the community, overcoming their personal displeasure at being chastised or at listening to what they did not wish to hear.[172]

D. AMERICAN PARRHĒSIA

Athenian *parrhēsia*, like Athenian *isēgoria*, has been woven into the theory and doctrine of American freedom of speech. The classical Athenian principle that licensed—and obligated—the parrhesiast to speak the truth as he saw it has informed the theoretical claim that justifies strong First Amendment protection on the

---

[167] See, for example, Demosthenes 10.76, in *Demosthenes I* 313 (cited in note 52) (describing his speech as having spoken the truth "with all freedom" and as not having been "packed by flattery").

[168] See Greenwood, *Making Words Count* at 183 (cited in note 28). It was a common feature of Assembly oratory for the speaker to credit himself for summoning the courage to speak frankly for the good of the community, rather than to pander to the *dēmos* in order to enhance his own political standing. Balot, *Free Speech, Courage, and Democratic Deliberation* at 243–44 (cited in note 55). Isocrates, for example, wrapped himself in the mantle of the ideal parrhesiast when he wrote, "I am accustomed always to speak with the utmost frankness [*meta parrhēsias*] and I should prefer to be disliked for having justly censured than to win favor through having given unmerited praise." Isocrates 9.12, in *Isocrates III* 479 (cited in note 140).

[169] Foucault, *Fearless Speech* at 12 (cited in note 136); Saxonhouse, *Free Speech and Democracy in Ancient Athens* at 92 (cited in note 105). See, for example, Demosthenes 10.76, in *Demosthenes I* at 313 (cited in note 52) (describing his speech as having spoken the truth "with all freedom" and as not having been "packed . . . with mischief and deceit").

[170] Foucault, *Fearless Speech* at 12–13 (cited in note 136); Saxonhouse, *Free Speech and Democracy in Ancient Athens* at 87–88 (cited in note 105).

[171] Dinarchos 2.1, in *Minor Attic Orators II* 265 (Loeb, 1954) (J. O. Burtt, trans.).

[172] Monoson, *Plato's Democratic Entanglements* at 61–62, 102 (cited in note 68).

ground that freedom of speech is a necessary condition for a society's collective search for truth. American courts similarly have incorporated into free-speech doctrine the associated classical Athenian principle that the parrhesiast at times must frankly confront or offend an audience, and that the audience, in the exercise of democratic citizenship, cannot have the parrhesiast punished for having had his say.

1. *Theory: Free speech and the search for truth.* It long has been claimed that a central function of the First Amendment is to create a hospitable environment for open inquiry, rigorous critique, and the free exchange of ideas—in other words, to grant a constitutional right of *parrhēsia*—in order for the society to progress in a never-ending quest for truth. On this view, the First Amendment signifies what Michel Foucault has called a "parrhesiastic contract," through which the sovereign people acquire the truth they need for self-government, in exchange for a promise not to punish speakers who speak the truth, "no matter what this truth turns out to be. . . ."[173]

Early versions of the search-for-truth justification of freedom of speech were grounded on the highly dubious conceit that truth invariably would triumph over falsity in unfettered debate. In *Areopagitica* (1644), the earliest Anglo-American exposition of the search-for-truth rationale, John Milton wrote, "let [Truth] and Falsehood grapple; who ever knew Truth put to the worse, in a free and open encounter?"[174] And Virginia's *Act for Establishing Religious Freedom* (1786), written by Thomas Jefferson, similarly promised that "truth is great and will prevail if left to herself."[175] But John Stuart Mill, who in his essay *On Liberty* (1859) wrote the classic nonjudicial statement of the search-for-truth rationale, regarded the easy assumption that truth would trump falsehood in a free society as nothing more than "a piece of idle sentimentality."[176] Nor did Mill argue, as Milton and Jefferson at least had

---

[173] Foucault, *Fearless Speech* at 32–33 (cited in note 136).

[174] John Milton, *Areopagitica* 51–52 (Clarendon, 1904) (John W. Hales, ed). Milton borrowed the title of his pamphlet from Isocrates' *Areopagiticus*. John W. Hales, *Introduction*, in John Milton, *Areopagitica* xxix (cited earlier in this note).

[175] *Virginia Statute of Religious Liberty*, Jan 16, 1786, § I, in Commager, ed, *Documents of American History* 125, 126 (cited in note 31).

[176] John Stuart Mill, *On Liberty* (1859), in *On Liberty and Other Writings* 5, 31 (Cambridge, 1989) (Stefan Collini, ed).

implied, that freedom of speech would lead to the discovery of truth in any absolute or objective sense.

Mill's claim was more subtle, and more in line with Athenian *parrhēsia*, which did not necessarily suggest that speaking the truth as one sees it expressed truth in any absolute sense.[177] Mill's aspiration was not that societies attain objective truth, but rather "truth for purposes of action," that is, that societies acquire sufficient confidence in their opinions to legitimate their actions as rational decisions rather than arbitrary assertions of power.[178] According to Mill, societies reached that level of confidence only by permitting "[c]omplete liberty of contradicting and disproving . . . [any] opinion" that was the predicate to collective action.[179] This was the purpose of Assembly debate that Pericles highlighted in his *Funeral Oration*—to criticize proposals and to air fully all points of view before settling on a course of action.[180] Free, frank, and open debate did not guarantee a correct decision. It simply was the best that any society could do.[181]

It was no accident that Mill's theory of free speech coincided so closely with the classical Athenian principle of political *parrhēsia*. Like Brandeis and Meiklejohn, Mill was deeply influenced by his understanding of the democratic thought and practice of classical Athens, so much so that Mill's first biographer, Alexander Bain, wrote of his "Greek intoxication."[182] Mill's study of Athens was purposeful. He was a participant in the intellectual debate of the early nineteenth century over whether Sparta and Rome, on one hand, or Athens, on the other, provided the better classical model for the development of representative governments in Europe in the wake of the American and French revolutions.[183] Mill drew on Athens to push European governments in a more democratic direction.[184] In so doing, political theorist Nadia Urbinati

---

[177] Monoson, *Plato's Democratic Entanglements* at 53 (cited in note 68).

[178] Mill, *On Liberty* at 23 (cited in note 176).

[179] Id at 23–24.

[180] See text at note 100.

[181] Mill, *On Liberty* at 24, 31 (cited in note 176).

[182] Nadia Urbinati, *Mill on Democracy: From the Athenian Polis to Representative Government* 3 (Chicago, 2002), quoting Alexander Bain, *John Stuart Mill: A Criticism; with Personal Recollections* (Longmans Green, 1882).

[183] Urbinati, *Mill on Democracy* at 14–41 (cited in note 182).

[184] Id at 4–5 (Mill "sought a democratic model of inspiration, which he found precisely in [Athens]"). Professor Urbinati wrote, "Mill . . . belonged to an age in which the ancients

has argued, Mill introduced classical Athenian democracy to "modernity."[185]

Justice Oliver Wendell Holmes, Jr., in his dissenting opinion in *Abrams v United States*,[186] built on Mill's search-for-truth justification of free speech and thereby introduced Athenian *parrhēsia* into First Amendment theory.[187] Justice Holmes, in the first, and perhaps the most eloquent, judicial defense of strong First Amendment protection of freedom of speech, wrote, "[W]hen men have realized that time has upset many fighting faiths, they may come to believe even more than they believe the very foundations of their own conduct that the ultimate good desired is better reached by free trade in ideas—that the best test of truth is the power of the thought to get itself accepted in the competition of the market, and that truth is the only ground upon which their wishes safely may be carried out."[188] Holmes, following Mill, believed that truth was "the only ground" for legitimate societal action. But also like Mill, he did not claim that "free trade in ideas" inexorably led a society to truth in any objective sense. Indeed, Holmes was a confirmed skeptic of such claims.[189] Holmes simply argued, as had Mill and Pericles, that collective acceptance or rejection of any idea after free debate was the best that any society could do in approximating truth.

The Mill/Holmes search-for-truth justification evoked not only the classical Athenian democratic principle of political *parrhēsia*, but also the practice of philosophical *parrhēsia* by perhaps the most famous critic of the ancient democracy, Socrates.[190] The Socrates

conveyed a strong ideological meaning. In reasserting the superiority of Athens, they *discovered* Athens and contributed to the renaissance of democracy both as a historical event and a political project," id at 18.

[185] Id at 5. Urbinati characterized Mill's *On Liberty*, which has had a profound effect on the development of American free-speech jurisprudence, "as an attempt to articulate in modern terms the ancient notion of democratic *eleutheria* [freedom] . . . ." Id at 28.

[186] 250 US 616, 624 (1919).

[187] See Lahav, 4 J L & Pol at 455 (cited in note 84) (Holmes's defense of freedom of speech "relied upon," but did "not merely echo[] Mill").

[188] *Abrams*, 250 US at 630 (Holmes dissenting).

[189] Lahav, 4 J L & Pol at 456–57 (cited in note 84).

[190] See, for example, Plato, *Protagoras* 319b, in *Plato: Complete Works* 746, 755 (cited in note 16) (Stanley Lombardo and Karen Bell, trans) (where Socrates told one of his interlocutors, "There is no point in my saying to you anything other than exactly what I think"). Plato described the practice of philosophy as a type of *parrhēsia* in several dialogues. Monoson, *Plato's Democratic Entanglements* at 17 (cited in note 68); Marlein van Raalte, *Socratic Parrhesia and Its Afterlife in Plato's Laws*, in Sluiter and Rosen, eds, *Free Speech in*

we know is based primarily on Plato's portrait of him as "the ideal philosopher."[191] Plato's Socrates was a "lover of inquiry,"[192] a seeker of truth[193] who questioned the orthodoxies of his time by engaging the reputed wise men of Athens in public, adversarial dialogue.[194] Socrates' aim was devastatingly simple: to prove to his interlocutor of the moment, as well as to spectators, that the interlocutor did not know what he claimed to know.[195] By the end of the dialogue, Socrates typically had exposed the pretensions of those who had clung dogmatically to conventional wisdom.[196] He also had contributed some measure of wisdom by exposing the errors and contradictions of the ideas and beliefs his interlocutors had defended.[197] Yet Plato's Socratic dialogues often end inconclusively, with Socrates' dialogue partner utterly confused (*aporia*),

---

Classical Antiquity 282–86 (cited in note 19). See also Foucault, *Fearless Speech* at 20 (cited in note 136) (Plato's Socratic dialogues enact "a major technique" of practicing *parrhēsia*).

[191] C. C. W. Taylor, *Socrates* 1 (Oxford, 1998). See Munn, *School of History* at 293 (cited in note 29) ("Plato was the historian of Socrates."). Although the question has long been debated, it likely never will be known whether and to what degree Plato's Socrates resembled the historical Socrates. Christopher Rowe, *Democracy and Sokratic-Platonic Philosophy*, in Boedeker and Raaflaub, eds, *Democracy, Empire, and the Arts in Fifth-Century Athens*, 241, 245 (cited in note 50).

[192] Plato, *Euthyphro* 14c, in *Plato: Complete Works* 1, 14 (cited in note 16) (G. M. A. Grube, trans).

[193] See, for example, Plato, *Euthyphro* 14e, at 14 (cited in note 192) (where Socrates said, "I prefer nothing, unless it is true"). Robert Wallace has defined the Platonic conception of a philosopher as one who "investigated metaphysical, political, and ethical questions in search of the truth." Robert W. Wallace, *Plato's Sophists, Intellectual History after 450, and Sokrates*, in Loren J. Samons II, ed, *The Cambridge Companion to the Age of Pericles* 215, 215 (Cambridge, 2007). See also Rowe, *Democracy and Sokratic-Platonic Philosophy* at 241–53 (cited in note 191) (describing "the figure of the philosopher as (Sokratic) *searcher* for knowledge . . . [as] the key element in the argument of Plato's political dialogues as a whole").

[194] Thomas C. Brickhouse and Nicholas D. Smith, *Plato's Socrates* 3–4 (Oxford, 1994); Saxonhouse, *Free Speech and Democracy in Ancient Athens* at 14 (cited in note 105). See Plato, *Crito* 50c, in *Plato: Complete Works* 37, 44 (cited in note 16) (G. M. A. Grube, trans) (Socrates is "accustomed to proceed by question and answer"). Socrates' dialogues often took place in the Athenian *agora*, making the Athenian marketplace a "literal marketplace of ideas." Saxonhouse, *Free Speech and Democracy in Ancient Athens* at 28 (cited in note 105).

[195] Foucault, *Fearless Speech* at 126–27 (cited in note 136). For Socrates, there was nothing "quite so bad for a person as having false belief about [moral truths]." Plato, *Gorgias* 458a, at 802 (cited in note 18).

[196] Brickhouse and Smith, *Plato's Socrates* at 3–4 (cited in note 194); Saxonhouse, *Free Speech and Democracy in Ancient Athens* at 37–38 (cited in note 105). See Gregory Vlastos, *Introduction: The Paradox of Socrates*, in Gregory Vlastos, ed, *The Philosophy of Socrates: A Collection of Critical Essays* 1, 7 (Notre Dame, 1971) (observing that Socrates left his dialogue partner with a "shipwrecked argument").

[197] See Brickhouse and Smith, *Plato's Socrates* at 3–4, 16–17 (cited in note 194); Saxonhouse, *Free Speech and Democracy in Ancient Athens* at 37 (cited in note 105).

and at times, deeply hurt or angry.[198] Having freed his interlocutor from the grip of orthodoxy, Socrates claimed that he did not possess the knowledge to replace it with the truth.[199]

Socrates' claimed lack of knowledge of moral truth resonates powerfully with the later positions of Mill and Holmes regarding political and societal orthodoxy.[200] For Socrates, it is the human condition never to be certain of our knowledge of moral truth, and therefore never to know whether our beliefs regarding what is true are correct.[201] Thus, just as Mill and Holmes would require that communities subject their "fighting faiths" to continual critique and revision, Socrates insisted that community leaders allow their beliefs to be tested in adversarial dialogue, and to revise their understanding of the truth if they are refuted.[202]

Socrates, as Arlene Saxonhouse has written, embodied the "practice [of] freedom of speech" envisioned by Mill and Holmes: an unflinching seeker of truth who "challenged the life of the community" so that individuals may "discover their errors and move forward toward understanding what is true."[203] Yet despite its allure, the search-for-truth rationale has been criticized for over-relying on the "process of rational thinking,"[204] and thus for pre-

---

[198] Brickhouse and Smith, *Plato's Socrates* at 3–4, 16–17 (cited in note 194); Foucault, *Fearless Speech* at 126 (cited in note 136). See, for example, Plato, *Euthyphro* 11b, at 11 (cited in note 192) (where Socrates' interlocutor said, "I have no way of telling you what I have in mind, for whatever proposition we put forward goes around and refuses to stay put where we establish it"). Gregory Vlastos, a leading Platonist, has argued that "what is ground-breakingly new" in Plato's Socratic dialogues is that the goal of the Socratic method "cannot be final." Gregory Vlastos, *Socrates, Ironist and Moral Philosopher* 4 (Cornell, 1991).

[199] Brickhouse and Smith, *Plato's Socrates* at 3–4 (cited in note 194). See also Saxonhouse, *Free Speech and Democracy in Ancient Athens* at 37 (cited in note 105) ("the eternal question in Platonic scholarship is whether Socrates or Plato ever provides an adequate replacement for past beliefs and tradition as the source of knowledge").

[200] For an exploration of a "Socratic ethos" in Mill's political thought, see Urbinati, *Mill on Democracy* at 123–54 (cited in note 182).

[201] See Plato, *Apology* 21d, in *Plato: Complete Works* 17, 21 (cited in note 16) (G. M. A. Grube, trans) (humans do not "know[] anything worthwhile"). Socrates believed that only a god could possess true wisdom. Plato, *Phaedrus* 278d, in *Plato: Complete Works* 506, 555 (cited in note 16) (Alexander Nehamas and Paul Woodruff, trans).

[202] According to Socrates, "What's true is never refuted." Plato, *Gorgias* 473b, at 817 (cited in note 18). Because we lack knowledge of the truth, Socrates believed that our beliefs of the truth "can always be sensibly re-opened." Vlastos, *Paradox of Socrates* at 10 (cited in note 196).

[203] Saxonhouse, *Free Speech and Democracy in Ancient Athens* at 28, 30 (cited in note 105). See also van Raalte, *Socratic Parrhesia* at 301 (cited in note 190) (describing "Socratic *parrhēsia*" as "freedom of speech in service of the truth and the good").

[204] Schauer, *Free Speech* at 30 (cited in note 76).

senting a false, or at least a simplistic, account of the development of public opinion in society. This is a telling criticism. Holmes's marketplace metaphor suggests that society is a collective *homo economicus*, which rationally and dispassionately selects the best idea from a full selection of alternatives based on complete and unbiased information about them. This is hardly an accurate description of how opinions become dominant in society. To compensate for this weakness in the search-for-truth justification, the Supreme Court incorporated Athenian *parrhēsia* into free-speech doctrine.

2. *Doctrine: Free speech and provocative speech.* The reality of *parrhēsia* in the Athenian Assembly was considerably less tidy than Meiklejohn's idealized town hall meeting, which posited a strong presiding officer actively enforcing strict rules of decorum. While Athenian *rhētōres* enjoyed full rein to attack their opponents as well as their opponents' ideas in debate, Meiklejohn's presiding officer would limit speakers to the relevant agenda items, ruling extraneous or abusive remarks out of order.[205] And while the *ekklēsiastai*, perhaps in violation of Athenian law, actively participated in political debate by interjecting cheers, jeers, shouts, heckling, and laughter,[206] Meiklejohn's presiding officer would permit no audience interruptions of speakers except as allowed by the rules of the meeting.[207]

Meiklejohn's tightly controlled town meeting captured the reality of free speech in the United States no better than it described political debate in the *ekklēsia*. As a consequence, when the Supreme Court began to adopt serious protections of free-speech rights under the First Amendment, the Justices rejected Meiklejohn's call for strict decorum rules controlling public discourse. Instead, the Court purposefully developed First Amendment doctrine "against the background of a profound national commitment to the principle that debate on public issues should be uninhibited, robust, and wide-open."[208] In other words, American free-speech

---

[205] Meiklejohn, *Free Speech and Its Relation to Self-Government* at 24–25 (cited in note 76).

[206] See text at notes 249–66.

[207] Meiklejohn, *Free Speech and Its Relation to Self-Government* at 24 (cited in note 76). Meiklejohn mentioned these types of restrictions on free speech in a town meeting to illustrate the types of abridgments on expression generally permitted by the First Amendment. Id at 24–25.

[208] *New York Times Co. v Sullivan*, 376 US 254, 270 (1964).

jurisprudence, like Athenian democratic practice, created a concept of *parrhēsia* to complement its incorporation of *isēgoria*, the equal freedom of individuals to speak on matters of public concern.

Justice Brandeis introduced Athenian *parrhēsia* into American free-speech jurisprudence in his *Whitney* concurrence when he wrote that the First Amendment protected "the freedom . . . to speak as you think" as essential to democracy.[209] American *parrhēsia* protects "vehement, caustic, and sometimes unpleasantly sharp attacks on government and public officials."[210] Like its Athenian ancestor, American *parrhēsia* licenses speakers to express themselves frankly, even if what they say offends, angers, or otherwise disturbs their audience.[211] "[I]t is a prized American privilege to speak one's mind," declared the Court in *Bridges v California*, "although not always with perfect good taste, on all public institutions."[212]

The Justices delineated the doctrinal rules protecting *parrhēsia* in one of the oldest lines of free-speech cases, those involving criminal prosecutions of "provocative" speakers.[213] A provocative speaker is one whose speech offends or enrages audience members to such a degree that there exists the threat of violence or disorder. The Court's provocative-speech decisions established that government officials may not punish speakers for "the peaceful expression of unpopular views."[214] Protected expression may be "provocative and challenging" because, like Socratic dialogue, it "strike[s] at prejudices and preconceptions" and thereby yields "profound unsettling effects" on listeners. Such audience effects, the Court has held, are to be nurtured, not avoided, because they

---

[209] *Whitney*, 274 US at 375 (Brandeis concurring).

[210] *New York Times*, 376 US at 270.

[211] See, for example, *Terminiello v City of Chicago*, 337 US 1, 4 (1949) ("[A] function of free speech under our system of government is to invite dispute. It may indeed best serve its high purpose when it induces a condition of unrest, creates dissatisfaction with conditions as they are, or even stirs people to anger."); *Cantwell v Connecticut*, 310 US 296, 310 (1940) ("To persuade others to his own point of view, the pleader, as we know, at times, resorts to exaggeration, to vilification of men who have been, or are, prominent in church or state, and even to false statement.").

[212] 314 US 252, 270 (1941).

[213] For a discussion of provocative-speech jurisprudence, see Werhan, *Freedom of Speech* at 82–98 (cited in note 77).

[214] See *Edwards v South Carolina*, 372 US 229, 237 (1963). See also *Cantwell*, 310 US at 308 (speakers enjoy a First Amendment "right peacefully to impart [their] views to others").

signal that speech is serving "its high purpose" under the First Amendment.[215]

Audience anger or offense at the content of a speaker's expression therefore generally is not a legitimate ground for punishment.[216] In striking down a state statute prohibiting "flag desecration," which for many Americans is the prototypical example of provocative expression, the Court declared, "If there is a bedrock principle underlying the First Amendment, it is that the government may not prohibit the expression of an idea simply because society finds the idea itself offensive or disagreeable."[217] Nor does a speaker's disregard of community norms governing proper public discourse, by itself, provide sufficient ground for criminal prosecution.[218] The First Amendment by and large empowers speakers to decide for themselves what to say and how to say it.[219] It is only when a provocative speaker directs his provocation to inciting disorder or a violent audience reaction, and is at least on the threshold of producing such a reaction, that a speaker can be held criminally responsible for the violence or disorder caused or threatened by his speech.[220]

The Supreme Court developed strong First Amendment protections of provocative speakers so that legislators and government officials could not register their fear of civil unrest (what the ancient Greeks called *stasis*) reflexively by stifling unsettling expression.[221] In this sense, the provocative-speech jurisprudence is an outgrowth of Justice Brandeis's concurring opinion in *Whitney*, where he, drawing on Pericles' *Funeral Oration*, emphasized that "courage" is "the secret of liberty."[222] The provocative-speech de-

---

[215] *Terminiello*, 337 US at 4.

[216] See, for example, *Texas v Johnson*, 491 US 397, 410 (1989); *Cohen v California*, 403 US 15, 18 (1971); *Cantwell*, 310 US at 308.

[217] *Johnson*, 491 US at 414.

[218] *Cohen*, 403 US at 21.

[219] Id at 24.

[220] See, for example, *Johnson*, 491 US at 410; *Cohen*, 403 US at 18, 22; *Edwards*, 372 US at 236; *Feiner v New York*, 340 US 315, 321 (1951); *Cantwell*, 310 US at 308.

[221] See, for example, *Johnson*, 491 US at 409 ("We have not permitted the government to assume that every expression of a provocative idea will incite a riot, but have instead required careful consideration of the actual circumstances surrounding such expression."); *Tinker v Des Moines Independent Community School District*, 393 US 503, 508 (1969) ("undifferentiated fear or apprehension of disturbance is not enough to overcome the right of free expression"); *Whitney*, 274 US at 376 (Brandeis concurring) ("Fear of serious injury cannot alone justify suppression of free speech and assembly.").

[222] *Whitney*, 274 US at 375 (Brandeis concurring); see text at notes 102–03.

cisions also reflect the Justices' internalization of the classical Athenian parrhesiastic ideal, which not only honored speakers with the courage to confront their audiences with the truth as they saw it, but also demanded of audiences the courage to remain open to the most unsettling discourse. Indeed, in this important sense, American *parrhēsia* is stronger than the Athenian original, for Athens had no law like the First Amendment that generally protected speakers from being held criminally responsible for the violent reactions of their audience.[223] In Athens, unlike in America, the assessment of responsibility in such circumstances was largely entrusted to juries.

Just as the principles of *isēgoria* and *parrhēsia* interacted in the classical Athenian democracy to generate a powerful free-speech practice inviting every full citizen to speak his mind in public debate, the American variations of *isēgoria* and *parrhēsia* combine to create what is perhaps the guiding principle of American free-speech jurisprudence: the equal right of all individuals to speak out fully and frankly on matters of public concern.

III. Limits on Freedom of Speech, Ancient and Modern

Freedom of speech was never absolute in classical Athens.[224] Nor has the First Amendment's protection of free speech in America ever been absolute.[225] As with the ancient and modern understandings of freedom of speech, there are fundamental similarities and differences between the Athenian and the American approaches to limiting free speech. The essential similarity is that

---

[223] See Carter, *Citizen Attribute, Negative Right* at 206 (cited in note 19) (stating that there is no evidence in the surviving record of any Athenian law protecting freedom of speech); Foucault, *Fearless Speech* at 72 (cited in note 136) ("[T]here was no law . . . protecting the [parrhesiast] from potential retaliation or punishment for what he said.").

[224] Henderson, *Attic Old Comedy* at 257–60 (cited in note 50); Wallace, *Athenian Laws Against Slander* at 110 (cited in note 17).

[225] See, example, *Chaplinsky v New Hampshire*, 315 US 568, 571 (1942) ("the right of free speech is not absolute at all times and under all circumstances"). Justice Hugo L. Black was the notable contrarian on this point. He read the First Amendment as having established an "unequivocal command" that absolutely prevented the government from restricting the right of free speech in favor of competing societal interests. *Konigsberg v State Bar of California*, 366 US 36, 61 (1961) (Black dissenting). For Justice Black, the purpose of the First Amendment, and, indeed, of the entire Bill of Rights, was "to put the freedoms protected there completely out of the area of any congressional control." Id. But Black's emphasis on the clarity of part of the First Amendment text ("no law") ignored the ambiguity of other language, however, such as "abridging" and "freedom of speech." Justice Black's absolutist interpretation of the First Amendment's protection of free speech has never come close to swaying a majority of the Justices.

both Athens and America observed a strong default rule favoring freedom of speech. The basic difference lies in the means by which the two polities observed this default rule. In America, of course, the First Amendment provides explicit, and powerful, constitutional protection of free speech, subject to exceptions that the courts have carved out over the years.[226]

The legal status of the two free-speech principles in Athens—*isēgoria* and *parrhēsia*—is less clear. Classical scholars do not know whether the Athenians adopted a law protecting *isēgoria*—the equal opportunity of citizens to speak in the Assembly—or whether *isēgoria* was a practice that became recognized over time as an inviolable principle of the classical democracy.[227] By contrast, it seems clear that Athenian *parrhēsia*—the freedom of Athenians to speak openly and frankly—was not a legal right.[228] *Parrhēsia* existed at the sufferance of the Athenian *dēmos*, who could withdraw it at any time. The classical Athenians proved their commitment to free speech by their remarkable forbearance. Although the *polis* possessed the constitutional power to punish any individual for anything he might say, it seldom chose to do so.[229] And yet, it hardly can be doubted that the lack of legal protection for Athenian *parrhēsia* created what American free-speech jurisprudence describes as a "chilling effect" on speakers. Athenian speakers knew that they spoke freely at their own risk.[230]

In the political realm, Athens and America followed the same

---

[226] See *Chaplinsky*, 315 US at 571–72. For a discussion, see Werhan, *Freedom of Speech* at 70–72 (cited in note 77).

[227] Griffith, *Isēgoria in the Assembly* at 126–27, 131 (cited in note 42); Vamvoukos, 26 Revue Internationale des Droits de l'Antiquité, 3d ser, at 100–01 (cited in note 3).

[228] See Wallace, *Athenian Laws Against Slander* at 124 (cited in note 17) ("*parrhēsia* at Athens did not mean protected speech"); note 223.

[229] See Raaflaub, *Aristocracy and Freedom of Speech* at 49 (cited in note 25) (Athenian law made speech actionable only "on rare occasions"). The best known prosecution of an Athenian whom the *dēmos* regarded as subversive of their democracy occurred in 399 BCE, when Socrates was convicted and executed for the crime of impiety (*asebeia*). But the conviction and execution of Socrates for *asebeia* was aberrational, the product of a perfect storm that made Socrates' distinctive practice of philosophical *parrhēsia*, which the Athenians had tolerated for his entire adult life, suddenly intolerable. For discussion of the trial of Socrates in historical context, see Mogens Herman Hansen, *The Trial of Sokrates—from the Athenian Point of View* (Royal Danish Academy of Sciences and Letters, 1995); Thomas C. Brickhouse and Nicholas D. Smith, *Socrates on Trial* (Princeton, 1989). Indeed, the trial of Socrates stands as the only attested instance of the Athenians convicting an individual because of the beliefs he had expressed. Hansen, *Trial of Sokrates* at 20–21 (cited above).

[230] See Monoson, *Plato's Democratic Entanglements* at 55 (cited in note 68) ("Speaking with parrhesia in the democratic political context retained a strong association with risk.").

guiding principle when drawing the boundaries of free expression: Individuals were free to speak their minds on matters of public concern unless the speech unduly threatened harm to the community. In the direct democracy of classical Athens, the crucial political speech came from *rhētōres* in Assembly debate, and therefore the Athenians focused their relatively few restrictions on political speech on *rhētōres*. By contrast, in America's representative democracy, members of Congress possess constitutional immunity for what they say in legislative debate.[231] The relatively few restrictions on political speech in America by and large fall on ordinary citizens outside the corridors of government. In the remainder of this article, I briefly examine the similarities and differences between the classical Athenian and modern American limits on political speech.

A. SILENCING SPEAKERS

The Athenian *dēmos* were deeply ambivalent toward *rhētōres*.[232] On one hand, they looked to *rhētōres* for guidance and regularly honored those who had led the Assembly to take actions that had benefited the *polis*.[233] On the other hand, the Athenians constantly worried over the possibility that *rhētōres* might misuse their oratorical skills to fool the *dēmos* into furthering the personal interests of the *rhētōres* rather than the public interest.[234] Demosthenes explained the Athenian concern: "[I]t would be dangerous if there ever happened to coexist a considerable number of men who were bold and clever speakers, but full of . . . disgraceful wickedness. For the people would be led astray by them to make many mistakes."[235]

The American representative democracy addresses Demosthenes' concern by limiting the power to speak in Congress, the federal legislative assembly, to members of Congress. While any

---

[231] See note 316.

[232] Hansen, *Athenian Assembly* at 62 (cited in note 43); Roisman, *Speaker-Audience Interactions in Athens* at 268 (cited in note 29).

[233] Hansen, *Athenian Assembly* at 63 (cited in note 43). Every year, the *dēmos* in the Assembly passed decrees recognizing, and presented golden crowns to, *rhētōres* who "'continually move proposals and do what is best for the people.'" Id.

[234] Id at 62–63; Roisman, *Speaker-Audience Interactions in Athens* at 261–62, 268 (cited in note 29). See text at notes 164–71.

[235] Demosthenes 22.30–32, in *Demosthenes III* at 175–77 (cited in note 62).

citizen volunteer could speak in the *ekklēsia*, the American *dēmos* pre-clear Assembly speakers by electing them as representatives to speak on behalf of the people at the decisive moment when law and policy are made. Because *rhētōres* were unelected, the Athenian *dēmos* were required to develop other means of controlling Assembly debate.

1. *Prior restraints, Athenian style.* The Athenians expressed their wariness of *rhētōres* at the beginning of every session of the Assembly when the very herald who invited all Athenians to speak also pronounced a curse (*ara*) on *rhētōres* who would deceive the *ekklēsiastai.*[236] The Athenians more tangibly addressed their concern over the threat of corrupt *rhētōres* misleading the *dēmos* into harmful action by denying *isēgoria* to citizens who had engaged in certain types of misconduct.[237] Some citizens lost their entitlement to address the Assembly as punishment for having committed certain specified crimes.[238] For example, a citizen found guilty of having addressed the Assembly in return for a bribe might lose his freedom to participate in future Assembly debates.[239] And *isēgoria* might be withdrawn from a citizen found guilty for the third time of having proposed illegal (*paranomōn*) decrees to the Assembly.[240]

Athenian law also provided for the denial of *isēgoria* to a citizen who had engaged in certain dishonorable noncriminal conduct, such as owing money to the state, abusing or failing to support one's parents, evading military service or showing cowardice during battle, squandering one's inheritance, or being a prostitute.[241]

---

[236] Hansen, *Athenian Assembly* at 90 (cited in note 43); Monoson, *Plato's Democratic Entanglements* at 59 (cited in note 68). The same curse opened sessions of the Council of 500 and the jury courts. Robert J. Bonner, *Aspects of Athenian Democracy* 76 (California, 1933); Vamvoukos, 26 Revue Internationale des Droits de l'Antiquité, 3d ser, at 101 (cited in note 3).

[237] In addition to these ex ante controls, Athenian law provided for stiff penalties, including death, for a *rhētōr* whom they found to have misled the *dēmos* into action harmful to the *polis*. See text at notes 294–315.

[238] Momigliano, *Freedom of Speech in Antiquity* at 252 (cited in note 50); Vamvoukos, 26 Revue Internationale des Droits de l'Antiquité, 3d ser, at 102 (cited in note 3). See also Henderson, *Attic Old Comedy* at 257–58 (cited in note 50) (also mentioning a catchall consideration, "posing any comparable threat to the integrity of the democratic process").

[239] Bonner, *Aspects of Athenian Democracy* at 80 (cited in note 236); Vamvoukos, 26 Revue Internationale des Droits de l'Antiquité, 3d ser, at 117–19 (cited in note 3).

[240] Momigliano, *Freedom of Speech in Antiquity* at 252 (cited in note 50); Wallace, *Athenian Laws Against Slander* at 115 (cited in note 17).

[241] Momigliano, *Freedom of Speech in Antiquity* at 252 (cited in note 50); Wallace, *Athenian*

In Athenian culture, the character of any citizen engaging in the types of conduct described by the disqualifying offenses would have been severely compromised.[242] Denying *isēgoria* to citizens who had engaged in such conduct therefore served the screening function of congressional elections: It protected the *polis* by silencing would-be Assembly speakers whose conduct had proven them unfit to lead.[243]

American courts would regard the silencing of speakers because of poor character or past misconduct as impermissible "prior restraints upon the right to speak."[244] Anglo-American history has taught that prior-restraint systems operate as an "apparatus of censorship,"[245] the central evil against which the First Amendment is directed. American free-speech jurisprudence thus permits potentially threatening expression to go forward except under narrow and extraordinary circumstances.[246]

Yet the Athenian and American approaches to silencing *rhētōres* whose character had been severely compromised are not as distant as they may seem. Athenian "prior restraints" only silenced speech in the Assembly. Citizens who had been stripped of *isēgoria* remained as free as any other Athenian to speak their minds in the *agora*, the public square and central marketplace of Athens. And for its part, the American Constitution provides auxiliary protec-

---

Laws Against Slander at 114, 119 (cited in note 17). Any citizen could challenge the qualifications of a *rhētōr* by initiating a judicial proceeding called *dokimasia rhētoron* ("scrutiny of a speaker"). See S. C. Todd, *Lysias* 104 n 2 (Texas, 2000); Wallace, *Athenian Laws Against Slander* at 120 (cited in note 17). If a jury found the *rhētōr* guilty of having committed disqualifying conduct, he was permanently barred from practicing *isēgoria*. Bonner, *Aspects of Athenian Democracy* at 81 (cited in note 236). It does not appear that the *dokimasia rhētoron* often was used to disqualify *rhētōres*, however, id at 82, which is as it should be in a full, direct democracy such as existed in Athens, which observed a strong default rule opening opportunities of public participation to every citizen, subject to override only in extraordinary circumstances.

[242] See Aeschines 1.31, in *The Speeches of Aeschines* 30 (Loeb, 1919) (C. D. Adams, trans). See also Saxonhouse, *Free Speech and Democracy in Ancient Athens* at 95 (cited in note 105) ("These . . . limitations . . . were supposed to focus on the moral character of the citizen."); Wallace, *Athenian Laws Against Slander* at 119, 122 (cited in note 17) (describing the disqualifying offenses as "especially reprehensible" to Athenians).

[243] Monoson, *Plato's Democratic Entanglements* at 59 (cited in note 68); Wallace, *Athenian Laws Against Slander* at 113 (cited in note 17).

[244] *Kunz v New York*, 340 US 290, 294 (1951) (invalidating a city's denial of an application for a meeting permit where the denial was based on the city's good-cause revocation of a prior permit to the applicant). See also *Near v Minnesota*, 283 US 697 (1931) (invalidating an injunction against defamatory speech by a newspaper that had made prior defamatory statements).

[245] *Freedman v Maryland*, 380 US 51, 57 (1965).

[246] See *New York Times Co. v United States*, 403 US 713 (1971).

tions against bad actors in the halls of Congress by authorizing each House of Congress to punish and even to expel its members for misconduct while in office.[247] The Constitution also permits the states to strip convicted felons permanently of the principal participatory right of American citizens, the right to vote.[248]

2. *Audience thorubos and the heckler's veto.* Notwithstanding the classical Athenian parrhesiastic ideal that Assembly audiences open themselves to oratory with which they strongly disagreed,[249] the *ekklēsiastai*, by all accounts, did not listen silently during Assembly debate.[250] They felt free to interject themselves into the debate at any time, noisily demonstrating their approval or disapproval of the *rhētōres* who stood to counsel them.[251] The Athenians referred to these audience interruptions as *thorubos* ("clamor," "tumult," "hubbub"),[252] the same word they used to describe the shouts and screams that soldiers used to intimidate their enemies on the battlefield.[253] According to Demosthenes, *thorubos* during Assembly debate was only to be expected.[254] Every *rhētōr* assumed the risk of angering or otherwise disappointing the *ekklēsiastai*, thereby opening himself to being shouted down or even being pulled off

---

[247] See US Const, Art I, § 5, cl 2 ("Each House may . . . punish its Members for disorderly Behavior, and, with the Concurrence of two-thirds, expel a Member.").

[248] See *Richardson v Ramirez*, 418 US 24, 41–56 (1974).

[249] See text at note 172.

[250] Roisman, *Speaker-Audience Interactions in Athens* at 264 (cited in note 29); Wallace, *Power to Speak* at 223 (cited in note 25). Audience interruptions of *rhētōres* were forbidden by law, but the law was neither observed nor enforced. Hansen, *Athenian Assembly* at 71 (cited in note 43); Judith Tacon, *Ecclesiastic Thorubos: Interventions, Interruptions, and Popular Involvement in the Athenian Assembly*, 48 Greece & Rome 173, 173–74 (2001). See Aeschines 1.35, in *Speeches of Aeschines* 33 (cited in note 242) (reporting that interruptions of, or speaking out of order in, Assembly proceedings were punishable by fine); Aeschines 3.2, in *Speeches of Aeschines* 309 (cited in note 242) (expressing the wish that "the assemblies of the people were properly conducted . . . , and the laws enforced" so that *rhētōres* could speak "uninterrupted by shouting and tumult [*thorubos*] . . . ."). But see Roisman, *Speaker-Audience Interactions in Athens* at 267–68 (cited in note 29) (noting evidence that the Assembly in 346–45 may have adopted a decree to limit heckling, but stating that any such decree was directed against other orators, and not at the audience).

[251] Hansen, *Athenian Assembly* at 70 (cited in note 43); Roisman, *Speaker-Audience Interactions in Athens* at 264–65 (cited in note 29).

[252] Roisman, *Speaker-Audience Interactions in Athens* at 264–65 (cited in note 29); Tacon, 48 Greece & Rome at 173 (cited in note 250). For a discussion of the different forms of *thorubos* in the Assembly, see Tacon, 48 Greece & Rome at 181–86 (cited in note 250).

[253] Foucault, *Fearless Speech* at 65–66 (cited in note 136).

[254] Wallace, *Power to Speak* at 223 (cited in note 25), quoting Demosthenes 24.151. Mogens Hansen has written that *thorubos* in one form or another may have erupted in every Assembly session. Hansen, *Athenian Assembly* at 70 (cited in note 43).

the *bēma*.[255] Xenophon, for example, described how Plato's brother Glaucon, when he was not yet twenty years old, insisted on addressing the Assembly, only to be "dragged from the platform" and made "a laughing stock."[256]

The interaction of audience *thorubos* with *isēgoria* and *parrhēsia* reveals a richer, more nuanced understanding of freedom of speech in the Athenian Assembly. *Thorubos* tempered *isēgoria*, which in principle gave each full citizen the right to address the *ekklēsia* for as long as he wished,[257] by handing the *ekklēsiastai* an informal (yet highly effective) veto over what they would hear.[258] *Thorubos* also supplemented *isēgoria* by providing ordinary citizens a means of participating in debate without assuming the risks of ascending the *bēma*.[259] Perhaps most fundamentally, *thorubos* itself constituted a form of audience *parrhēsia*, enabling members of the *dēmos* to "talk back" to *rhētōres* freely, openly, and with brutal honesty.[260] *Thorubos* enabled ordinary citizens to rebut or to reshape the messages communicated in orations without risking head-to-head competition with skilled *rhētōres*.

And yet, it must be said, *thorubos* discouraged the frank speech from *rhētōres* that political *parrhēsia* demanded.[261] By effectively silencing speakers who displeased the *dēmos*, *thorubos*, in Michel Foucault's language, "'protected' [the Assembly] against the truth."[262] Isocrates, for example, admonished the *ekklēsiastai* for "hav[ing] formed the habit of driving all orators from the platform

---

[255] Bonner, *Aspects of Athenian Democracy* at 74–75 (cited in note 236); Hansen, *Athenian Assembly* at 70 (cited in note 43). See also Plato, *Protagoras* 319c at 755 (cited in note 190) (if a *rhētōr* attempts to speak on a technical matter on which he lacks expertise, the Athenians "laugh at him and shout him down . . . .").

[256] Xenophon, *Memorabilia* III 6.1, in *Xenophon IV* at 203 (cited in note 142).

[257] See text at note 48.

[258] Wallace, *Power to Speak* at 225 (cited in note 25). See also Monoson, *Plato's Democratic Entanglements* at 58 (cited in note 68) ("The right to speak did not guarantee one a hearing."). According to classical scholar Robert Wallace, the surviving record suggests that the *ekklēsiastai* handled this veto power responsibly. Wallace, *Power to Speak* at 227 (cited in note 25).

[259] See Tacon, 48 Greece & Rome at 180 (cited in note 250) (*thorubos* "may be regarded as the vital way, aside of course from the voting process itself, in which ordinary people could make their thoughts known").

[260] See Halliwell, *Aischrology, Shame, and Comedy* at 130 (cited in note 68); Roisman, *Speaker-Audience Interactions in Athens* at 266 (cited in note 29).

[261] Balot, *Free Speech, Courage, and Democratic Deliberation* at 244–45 (cited in note 55).

[262] Foucault, *Fearless Speech* at 18–19 (cited in note 136).

except those who support your desires."[263] The surviving oratory
is crowded with pleas by *rhētōres* that the *ekklēsiastai* become quiet
and permit them a fair hearing.[264] The mere prospect of *thorubos*
must have discouraged many Athenians from participating in Assembly debate, and it certainly encouraged those citizens who
spoke to violate the norms of the political parrhesiastic ideal by
pandering to the *ekklēsiastai* instead of confronting them with the
truth.[265] In the Mytilenian Debate, Thucydides had Diodotus say
that even the best speakers must "lie in order to be believed."[266]

Thorubos constituted what American free-speech jurisprudence
has labeled a "heckler's veto," that is, a hostile audience reaction
that effectively silences a speaker.[267] As a formal matter, of course,
such an audience reaction, by itself, does not violate the First
Amendment because it is private rather than state action.[268] A more
difficult question is whether the First Amendment should protect
audience *thorubos*. Although the U.S. Supreme Court has never
ruled on the issue, some American courts have recognized a limited

---

[263] Wallace, *Power to Speak* at 224 (cited in note 25), quoting Isocrates 8.3. See also
Demosthenes 3.32, in *Demosthenes I* at 61 (cited in note 52) (the *ekklēsiastai* do "not allow
liberty of speech [*parrhēsia*] on every subject . . . ."); Demosthenes 10.54, in *Demosthenes
I* at 301 (cited in note 52) (an error of the Athenians, which has led to other errors, was
their being "offended" if a speaker "speak[s] the truth boldly"); Isocrates 8.14, in *Isocrates
II* at 15 (cited in note 135) ("[I]t is hazardous to oppose your views . . . . [Y]ou are ill-
disposed to those who rebuke and admonish you as you are to men who work injury to
the state.").

[264] Balot, *Free Speech, Courage, and Democratic Deliberation* at 244–45 (cited in note 55);
Tacon, 48 Greece & Rome at 179–80 (cited in note 250). See, for example, Demosthenes
8.32, in *Demosthenes I* at 193 (cited in note 52) ("[I]n Heaven's name, when I am pleading
for your best interests, allow me to speak freely"); Demosthenes 13.3, in *Demosthenes I* at
357 (cited in note 52) ("do not shout me down, but hear me before you judge").

[265] Balot, *Free Speech, Courage, and Democratic Deliberation* at 244 (cited in note 55)
("speakers were strongly discouraged from making bold and independent resolutions that
challenged the assumptions and preconceptions of their audiences—that is, from doing
their part in the ideal workings of the democratic Assembly"); Roisman, *Speaker-Audience
Interactions in Athens* at 265 (cited in note 29) (classical Athenians acknowledged "the
power of the crowd to intimidate a speaker or to move him to seek popular approval at
the expense of advocating sound, but unpopular policy").

[266] Thucydides, *Landmark Thucydides* 3.43.2 at 180 (cited in note 5). See also Henderson,
Attic Old Comedy at 260 (cited in note 50) ("under the conditions of democratic competition,
politicians could often get farther by flattering the demos, by catering to its whims and
prejudices, than by telling it the truth.").

[267] For a discussion of the hostile-audiences problem in American free-speech jurisprudence, see Weihan, *Freedom of Speech* 83–88 (cited in note 77).

[268] See *Lloyd Corp. v Tanner*, 407 US 551 (1972) (the First Amendment does not obligate
a privately owned shopping center to permit leafleting). A serious First Amendment issue
is raised, however, when government officials silence a speaker because of a hostile audience
reaction. See text at notes 205–23.

First Amendment right of audience *thorubos*. The leading decision is *In re Kay*,[269] where the Supreme Court of California overturned a conviction, and a four-month prison sentence, of several hecklers who had engaged in shouting and rhythmic clapping for about five to ten minutes of a Fourth of July speech by a member of Congress.[270]

The court in *Kay* accepted audience *thorubos* as an element of the "happy cacophony of democracy," and thus worthy of First Amendment protection.[271] The California High Court, like the classical Athenians, understood that *thorubos* provided some audience members their only practical means of participating in public debate.[272] The court therefore held that "[a]udience activities, such as heckling, interrupting, harsh questioning, and booing, even though they may be impolite and discourteous, can nonetheless advance the goals of the First Amendment."[273]

But the court in *Kay* stopped short of the Athenians' complete embrace of audience *thorubos*. The court permitted the state to punish hecklers when their *thorubos* "substantially impairs the effective conduct of a meeting."[274] This limitation reflected the court's balancing of the expressive interests of hecklers against the First Amendment right of speakers to have their say and the interest of other audience members to hear them.[275] Notwithstanding the *Kay* court's protection of audience *thorubos* on the facts of that case,[276] lower courts have invoked *Kay* to uphold the conviction of audience hecklers for *thorubos* that both violated the customs and usages of a particular speech environment and substan-

---

[269] 464 P2d 142 (Cal 1970).

[270] The hecklers' demonstration was a spontaneous protest against the congressman's failure to support a consumer boycott of nonunion table grapes. Id at 145–46.

[271] Id at 146–48.

[272] Id at 147.

[273] Id.

[274] Id at 150.

[275] Id at 149–50. The court explained, "Freedom of everyone to talk at once can destroy the right of anyone effectively to talk at all. Free expression can expire as tragically in the tumult of license as in the silence of censorship." Id at 149.

[276] In *Kay*, the court protected the audience hecklers in large part because the *thorubos* they created was consistent with the "customs and usages" of a city-sponsored speech in a public park, and did not actually interfere with the conduct of the city's Fourth of July program. The *thorubos* lasted but a few minutes, and the speaker completed his speech, which the audience largely was able to hear. In the end, the court in *Kay* concluded that the audience *thorubos* there at issue was "a legitimate element" of the congressman's speech. Id at 150–52.

tially impaired a speaker's communication with an audience.[277]

The *Kay* court's refusal to protect *thorubos* that substantially impairs a speaker's ability to communicate with an audience highlights a fundamental distinction between the American and Athenian understandings of freedom of speech. The First Amendment protects a speaker's interest in expressing a point of view to an audience as a fundamental right, and audience *thorubos* that unduly silences a speaker eviscerates that right.[278] The Athenians, by contrast, did not understand the silencing of a speaker through audience *thorubos* as having violated the speaker's freedom of speech. To them, *thorubos* was a means of holding speakers accountable to the *dēmos*.[279] Indeed, the Athenians regarded a speaker's refusal to stand down in the face of overwhelming *thorubos* to be an abuse of *parrhēsia*,[280] because any such refusal elevated an individual's desire to speak over the spoken will of the *dēmos* not to hear him, a form of hubris that breached a clear boundary of the classical Athenian conception of individual freedom.[281]

B. PUNISHING SUBVERSIVE SPEECH

Athens punished, often harshly, speakers whose speech caused, or threatened to cause, serious harm to the community.[282] This ancient limitation on freedom of speech was fundamental, inhering in the classical Athenian understanding of the relationship between the individual and the state. The Athenians, together with the ancient Greeks generally, believed in the essential identity of the

[277] See, for example, *State v Hardin*, 498 NW2d 677 (Iowa 1993) (upholding conviction of an audience heckler for disrupting a speech of President George H. W. Bush by chanting antiwar sentiments); *State v Morgulis*, 266 A2d 136 (NJ Super Ct App Div 1970) (upholding conviction of an audience heckler for shouting obscenities at a high school sporting event). But see *City of Spokane v McDonough*, 485 P2d 449 (Wash 1971) (overturning conviction of an audience heckler for shouting "warmonger" at a noisy, partisan rally that included a tacit invitation to the audience to demonstrate through "applause, cheers, and friendly expletives").

[278] *Whitney v California*, 274 US 357, 375 (1927) (Brandeis concurring) ("the fitting remedy for evil counsels is good ones").

[279] Roisman, *Speaker-Audience Interactions in Athens* at 261–62 (cited in note 29).

[280] Wallace, *Power to Speak* at 227 (cited in note 25), quoting Aeschines 1.34 (saying that it is "shameless[]" for a speaker not to step down when confronted with *thorubos*).

[281] Balot, *Free Speech, Courage, and Democratic Deliberation* at 245 (cited in note 55); Wallace, *Power to Speak* at 226–27 (cited in note 25).

[282] Carter, *Citizen Attribute, Negative Right* at 207 (cited in note 19); Raaflaub, *Aristocracy and Freedom of Speech* at 49 (cited in note 25).

polis and its citizens.[283] On this understanding, the individual citizen was but one part of the whole citizen body. He flourished only if his community flourished.[284] In Athens, and throughout classical Greece, the *polis* therefore took primacy over the individual.[285] Against this background understanding, it should not be surprising that the Athenians valued individual freedom (*eleutheria*), including freedom of speech, not as an aspect of individual autonomy, but because it benefited the *polis* and its democracy.[286] Because the Athenians only conceived of *isēgoria* and *parrhēsia* instrumentally, they regarded speech that undermined the collective interests of the *polis* as an abuse of these freedoms.[287]

The American understanding of individual freedom projects a mirror image of the ancient Greek relationship between the individual and the state. The social compact theory of John Locke, which greatly influenced the thinking of the American founding generation,[288] posits a strict separation between the state and its citizens.[289] According to Locke, individuals, living free and equal under the "Law of Nature," create a political community by entering into an "original Compact" (in the American understanding, a constitution), and thereby consent to the exercise of political power over them.[290] The essential purpose of this political community is to protect the rights that the individual members of the community had possessed under natural law, which, for Locke, fell under the broad categories of life, liberty, and property.[291] Read

---

[283] Philip Brook Manville, *The Origins of Citizenship in Ancient Athens* 6 (Princeton, 1990); Ostwald, *Shares and Rights* at 49, 55 (cited in note 5). In Aristotle's suggestive language, the ancient Greek *polis* was "a partnership [*koinōnia*] of citizens." Aristotle, *The Politics* 1276a40–1276b1, at 89 (Chicago, 1984) (Carnes Lord, trans).

[284] Vamvoukos, 26 Revue Internationale des Droits de l'Antiquité, 3d ser, at 96–97 (cited in note 3).

[285] Wallace, *Private Lives and Public Enemies* at 144 (cited in note 138).

[286] Henderson, *Attic Old Comedy* at 259 (cited in note 50).

[287] See Saxonhouse, *Free Speech and Democracy* at 31 (cited in note 105) ("*parrhēsia* was double edged . . . in terms of whether the community benefited or suffered from it.").

[288] See Leonard W. Levy, *Origins of the Bill of Rights* 3 (Yale, 1999); Wood, *Creation of the American Republic* at 282–91 (cited in note 9).

[289] Wood, *Creation of the American Republic* at 283 (cited in note 9).

[290] John Locke, *An Essay Concerning the True Original, Extent, and End of Civil Government (Second Treatise of Government)*, in *Two Treatises of Government* 267, II.4.1–8, II.7.12, at 269, 272, VIII.95, at 332, 350 (Cambridge, 1960) (Peter Laslett, ed) (originally published, 1690).

[291] Id IX.123, at 330–31; see Levy, *Origins of the Bill of Rights* at 3–4 (cited in note 288); Wood, *Creation of the American Republic* at 283–84 (cited in note 9).

in the light of Locke's social compact theory, the purpose of the
First Amendment was to make explicit that freedom of speech was
among the particular natural rights that the new American government was obligated to protect.[292]

1. *The Athenian law against misleading the dēmos*. Athens, like
political communities before and since, adopted laws that dealt
harshly with those who would overthrow or otherwise subvert the
democracy.[293] Perhaps the most distinctive Athenian provision
against subversion was the law, dating perhaps from the early years
of the classical democracy, that prescribed the death penalty for
Assembly speakers who misled the *dēmos*.[294] Every citizen had legal
standing to commence such a prosecution,[295] which could be
lodged against any *rhētōr* who had advocated an Assembly decision
resulting in harm to the *polis*.[296] The Athenians regarded an Assembly action gone awry as the product of the *dēmos* having been
deceived by "mischievous advice."[297] When an action turned out
badly, the speaker's deception was revealed.[298] In the Athenian
view, an Assembly speaker who misled the *dēmos* into acting to the
detriment of the *polis* engaged in misconduct tantamount to treason, on a par with those who sought to subvert the democracy or
who betrayed Athens to one of its enemies.[299]

---

[292] Levy, *Origins of the Bill of Rights* at 3–4 (cited in note 288).

[293] See Douglas M. MacDowell, *The Law in Classical Athens* 175–79 (Cornell, 1978).

[294] Demosthenes 20.100, in *Demosthenes I* 559 (cited in note 52); [Pseudo] Xenophon,
Constitution of Athenians 17 at 44 (cited in note 54); Thucydides, *Landmark Thucydides*
3.43.4 at 180 (cited in note 5). See MacDowell, *Law in Classical Athens* at 179–80 (cited
in note 293). The same crime applied to those who spoke in the Council of Five Hundred
and in the courts. Id at 179, 185.

[295] See Bonner, *Aspects of Athenian Democracy* at 79 (cited in note 236) ("In Athens the
task of prosecuting criminals was the privilege of any citizen.").

[296] Demosthenes 20.100, in *Demosthenes I* 559 (cited in note 52); [Pseudo] Xenophon,
Constitution of Athenians 17 at 44 (cited in note 54); Thucydides, *Landmark Thucydides*
3.43.4 at 180 (cited in note 5). See Bonner, *Aspects of Athenian Democracy* at 77 (cited in
note 236).

[297] Ineke Sluiter and Ralph Rosen, *General Introduction*, in Sluiter and Rosen, eds, *Free
Speech in Classical Antiquity* 1, 11 n 33 (cited in note 19), quoting Lysias 20.20. See also
Roisman, *Speaker-Audience Interactions in Athens* at 272–73 (cited in note 29) (the crime
of misleading the *dēmos* "exonerated the people from the responsibility for, and the shame
of, reaching wrong conclusions"); Claire Taylor, *Bribery in Athenian Politics Part II: Ancient
Reaction and Perceptions*, 48 Greece & Rome 154, 164 (2001) ("The *dēmos* was, by definition,
always right and if it made a bad decision the blame was laid with the proposer of a decree
. . . , who was duly charged and brought to trial.").

[298] Sluiter and Rosen, *Introduction* at 10–11 (cited in note 297).

[299] Hypereides 7–8, 29, in *Minor Attic Orators II* at 471, 485 (cited in note 171). See
MacDowell, *Law in Classical Athens* at 184 (cited in note 293). S. C. Todd has explained,

An early and classic example of the crime of misleading the *dēmos* involved Miltiades, the general (*stratēgos*) who had led the Athenian forces to victory at the battle of Marathon. In Herodotus' account, Miltiades, basking in the glow of that triumph, convinced the Assembly to raise an expeditionary force under his command, "without saying against what country . . . [it] would be used—only that . . . [the Athenians] would grow rich if they followed him."[300] According to Herodotus, Miltiades' actual motive was personal. He sought revenge against the Parians for a past wrong.[301] The Paros expedition was an embarrassing failure.[302] Miltiades returned to Athens wounded and humiliated, whereupon the Assembly tried and convicted him for having misled the *dēmos* into approving the expedition. Miltiades avoided the death penalty, but he died of his wounds before he could pay the substantial fine that the Assembly had levied upon him.[303]

Thucydides, speaking through the perhaps fictional orator Diodotus, criticized the Athenian crime of misleading the *dēmos* as unwise and unfair. "[Y]ou visit the disasters into which the whim of the moment may have led you," said Thucydides' Diodotus, "upon the single person of your advisor, not upon yourselves, his numerous companions in error." If the people who voted for an ill-advised action "suffered equally" with the speaker who had proposed the action, Diodotus continued, the Assembly "would judge more calmly" before voting.[304] But because the Assembly usually voted by a show of hands (*cheirotonia*),[305] it is not at all clear how the Athenians could have enforced such a broad-based responsibility.[306] More fundamentally, Diodotus conceded that legal liability for bad advice created a check on Assembly speakers, encouraging them to assess carefully the potential risk and reward of actions before urging

"Athenian public discourse rests on a success-oriented model of politics in which incompetence is criminal. . . . Athenians did not distinguish as we perhaps might between political error and legal offence." Todd, *Shape of Athenian Law* at 306 (cited in note 47).

[300] Herodotus, *History* 6.132 at 461–62 (cited in note 51).

[301] Id 6.133 at 462.

[302] Id 6.134 at 462.

[303] Id 6.135–136 at 462–63. Miltiades' son, Cimon, paid his father's fine and later succeeded in rehabilitating Miltiades' reputation. Michael Grant, *The Classical Greeks* 7 (Scribner's, 1989).

[304] Thucydides, *Landmark Thucydides* 3.43.5 at 180 (cited in note 5).

[305] Hansen, *Athenian Assembly* at 41–44 (cited in note 43).

[306] See Todd, *Shape of Athenian Law* at 306 (cited in note 47) ("If a democratic decision leads to disaster, the fault must lie not with the voters, because it is impossible to put them on trial for it, but with either the proposers or the executors of this policy . . . .").

them on the citizen body.[307] Placing responsibility on *rhētōres* rather than on the assembled *dēmos* also reinforced the primacy of the *polis* over the individual. An individual whose advice harmed the community must be held accountable.[308]

There are few attested cases of the Athenians applying the law against misleading the *dēmos* to *rhētōres* whose proposals led to actions that harmed the *polis*. Far more common was resort to the *graphē paranomōn*, which may be understood as a subcategory of the crime of misleading the *dēmos*.[309] The *graphē paranomōn* was a criminal proceeding that allowed for the imposition of a substantial fine on a *rhētōr* who proposed that the Assembly enact a decree that violated the higher law (*nomos*) of Athens.[310] Athens introduced the *graphē paranomōn* at least by 415 BCE,[311] and these proceedings were a common feature in the democracy of the fourth century BCE.[312]

Because conviction of the *rhētōr* invalidated the decree in question, the *graphē paranomōn* provided a process of judicial review of Assembly action.[313] But the imposition of criminal liability on the *rhētōr* marks this judicial review process as distinctively Athenian. The *graphē paranomōn*, like the more general crime of misleading the *dēmos*, checked *rhētōres* by motivating them to think carefully before proposing decrees for Assembly action.[314] And also like the crime of misleading the *dēmos*, the *graphē paranomōn* forced *rhētōres* "to accept the risks of their speech."[315]

2. *The law of subversive advocacy in the United States.* Because the Constitution immunizes the people's representatives for what they

---

[307] Thucydides, *Landmark Thucydides* 3.43.4 at 180 (cited in note 5).

[308] Wallace, *Athenian Laws Against Slander* at 124 (cited in note 17).

[309] See Bonner, *Aspects of Athenian Democracy* at 80 (cited in note 236) (the *graphē par anomōn* was "in principle a prosecution for deceiving the people").

[310] Hansen, *Athenian Democracy* at 205 (cited in note 4); Munn, *School of History*, 102 (cited in note 29). A citizen found guilty for the third time of having proposed illegal (*paranomōn*) decrees to the Assembly could lose his freedom to address the assembly or to propose any future decrees. See text at note 240. For discussions of the *graphē paranomōn*, see Hansen, *Athenian Democracy* at 205–12 (cited in note 4); Sinclair, *Democracy and Participation* at 152–56 (cited in note 4).

[311] Hansen, *Athenian Democracy* at 205 (cited in note 4); Munn, *School of History*, 102 (cited in note 29).

[312] Hansen, *Athenian Democracy* at 208–09 (cited in note 4).

[313] See id at 174; Sinclair, *Democracy and Participation* at 68, 221 (cited in note 4).

[314] Finley, *Democracy Ancient and Modern* at 113–14 (cited in note 47).

[315] Id at 114. See also Bonner, *Aspects of Athenian Democracy* at 81 (cited in note 236) ("[t]he *graphē paranomōn* was . . . a check upon the abuse of freedom of speech in the assembly").

say in the chambers of Congress,[316] the American *dēmos* lacks legal recourse against any member of Congress for misleading his or her colleagues into approving actions that harm the public good. In this respect, America's representative democracy inverts the liability rules that the Athenians developed for their direct democracy. While Athenian law imposed special restraints on the advocacy of *rhētōres* to encourage them to speak in the interest of the community rather than in furtherance of their own desires, the American Constitution provides legal immunity to congressional *rhētōres* to safeguard the "deliberative autonomy" of Congress.[317]

The best American analogy to the Athenian law making *rhētōres* criminally liable for misleading the *dēmos* into taking action that was illegal (*paranomōn*) or otherwise harmful to the *polis* is the law of subversive advocacy, that is, speech advocating violence or illegal conduct.[318] The problem of subversive advocacy, like the Athenian law against misleading the *dēmos*, raises the most fundamental of all questions arising in a political community dedicated to freedom of speech: Under what circumstances, if any, may the community restrict speech that threatens societal harm?

Justice Brandeis wrote his *Whitney* concurrence to reform free-speech jurisprudence so that it could stand as a bulwark against subversive speech prosecutions. In Brandeis's hands, the First Amendment would block government restrictions of free expression unless there was proof of an *immediate* danger of *serious* harm.[319] "*Fear* of serious injury," Brandeis wrote, "cannot alone justify suppression" of the expressive freedoms of the First Amendment.[320] Nor was the mere "advocacy of violence" actionable in Brandeis's scheme. Brandeis would limit government prosecutions of subver-

---

[316] See US Const, Art I, § 6, cl 1 ("for any Speech or Debate in either House, [the Senators and Representatives] . . . shall not be questioned in any other Place"). Modern constitutional jurisprudence immunizes members of Congress and their aides from civil and criminal liability arising from their legislative conduct. See *Gravel v United States*, 408 US 606, 815–16 (1972).

[317] Laurence H. Tribe, *American Constitutional Law* 1013 (Foundation, 3d ed 2000).

[318] See *Brandenburg v Ohio*, 395 US 444, 447 (1969) ("advocacy of the use of force or of law violation").

[319] *Whitney v California*, 274 US 357, 376 (1927) (Brandeis concurring). In an earlier dissenting opinion that Justice Brandeis had joined, Justice Holmes had emphasized the need to show immediacy, but not the requirement that the threatened harm be sufficiently serious to justify restricting the exercise of a fundamental constitutional right. See *Abrams v United States*, 250 US 616, 627–28 (1919) (Holmes dissenting).

[320] *Whitney*, 274 US at 376 (Brandeis concurring) (emphasis added). Brandeis continued, "It is the function of speech to free men from the bondage of irrational fears." Id.

sive speakers to instances of "incitement," where the record proved that a speaker's call for unlawful action "would be immediately acted on."[321] For Brandeis, "Only an emergency can justify repression."[322]

The Court did not infuse subversive speech doctrine with the spirit of Brandeis until 1969—1969! In *Brandenburg v Ohio*,[323] the Justices extended First Amendment protection to the "advocacy of the use of force or of law violation except where such advocacy [1] is directed to inciting or producing imminent lawless action and [2] is likely to incite or produce such action."[324] The *Brandenburg* test adopted the immediacy requirement that was at the heart of Brandeis's approach.[325] It more subtly revised the clear-and-present-danger test that Brandeis had championed by substituting the element of likelihood for the original danger requirement. There is an important difference in having a jury determine whether a speaker's subversive advocacy, which often is frightening in the abstract, creates a "danger" of unlawful conduct or actually makes such conduct "likely" to occur. The latter formulation requires an empirical showing of a real prospect of harmful action, and not simply fear over the possible consequences of dissident speech.[326]

The *Brandenburg* test minimizes the liability of speakers for the unlawful conduct of listeners. Brandeis had written in his *Whitney* concurrence that the ordinary remedy against unlawful conduct was to punish the actor, and not to abridge First Amendment freedoms.[327] Brandeis, and *Brandenburg*, thus flipped the classical Athenian assumption that speakers were legally responsible for advocating that the *dēmos* take ill-advised action, but that the *dēmos* were blameless for taking the action. Under *Brandenburg*, a speaker may not be punished for persuading an audience to action if listeners have had time to deliberate and to make the action their own. *Brandenburg* makes people responsible for their own decisions, and for their own actions.

---

[321] Id. For Brandeis, there was a "wide difference between advocacy and incitement." Id.

[322] Id at 377.

[323] 395 US 444 (1969).

[324] *Brandenburg v Ohio*, 395 US 444, 447 (1969).

[325] *Hess v Indiana*, 414 US 105, 108 09 (1973).

[326] See *NAACP v Claiborne Hardware Co.*, 458 US 886, 928 (1982) (the First Amendment protected a speaker who used "strong language" and "emotionally charged rhetoric" that was not "followed by acts of violence").

[327] *Whitney*, 274 US at 377–78 (Brandeis concurring).

The different allocation of legal responsibility for speech leading to action that harms the community in Athenian law and in contemporary First Amendment jurisprudence reflects the difference between the Athenian and the American understandings of the relationship between the individual and the community. Because Athenians regarded the individual citizen as a constituent part of the *polis*, he was held legally responsible for actions, including speech, that harmed the community. In American constitutional theory, the individual citizen is distinct from the state, which is bound by a social compact to safeguard the fundamental rights of its citizens, including freedom of speech. For that reason, an individual advocating action harmful to the community, without more, enjoys a legal immunity that would have been unimaginable to classical Athenians. Ironically, it was the most Athenian of American Supreme Court Justices, Justice Louis D. Brandeis, who is most responsible for this fundamental discontinuity between the protection of freedom of speech in Athens and in America.

IV. CONCLUSION

This article has shown that the roots of American freedom of speech extend to classical Athens, the fountainhead of democracy. This article also has shown that these roots are strong, notwithstanding the passage of over two thousand years and the adoption of two very different approaches to democracy in Athens and in America. Perhaps the linkage between freedom of speech and democracy made some degree of kinship between Athens and America inevitable. But I have argued that the importation of classical Athenian principles into American free-speech jurisprudence resulted not only from the logic of democracy, but also from the purposeful embrace of classical Athens as a model democracy by Justice Louis D. Brandeis, Alexander Meiklejohn, and (indirectly) John Stuart Mill, each of whom helped to shape the modern American understanding of freedom of speech. The differences between the highly participatory direct democracy of classical Athens and America's relatively restrained representative democracy have dictated fundamental differences in free-speech law and practice in the two systems, which this article has explored. But the infusion of an Athenian sensibility into American freedom of speech undeniably has made the United States more democratic, as American citizens generally have been empowered, as were Athenian citizens, not simply to vote, but to participate in politics by speaking their minds fully and freely on matters of public concern.

PAUL FINKELMAN

LINCOLN, EMANCIPATION, AND THE
LIMITS OF CONSTITUTIONAL CHANGE

The Emancipation Proclamation[1] is rarely considered as a legal document and seems disconnected from the Supreme Court. The Court, after all, has never adjudicated its meaning or interpretation. It is at best a historical artifact brought out to dress up an opinion or illustrate a point that a Justice is trying to make.[2] Whatever legal significance it might have had in 1863 was superseded by the events of the Civil War and the ratification of the Thirteenth Amendment in 1865. At the end of the war, former Confederates surely had no moral standing—and uncertain legal standing—to challenge the Emancipation Proclamation. The federal courts were in disarray, and it is hard to imagine, in mid- or late 1865, how anyone in the former Confederate states would have litigated the Emancipation

---

Paul Finkelman is President William McKinley Distinguished Professor of Law and Public Policy, Albany Law School.

[1] Proclamation No 17, 12 Stat 1268 (Jan 1, 1863).

[2] For example, in *Schneiderman v United States*, 320 US 118 (1943), Justice Murphy used the Emancipation Proclamation to demonstrate that Schneiderman's support for a radical political and economic change did not prove disloyalty to the government or the Constitution. Schneiderman, a naturalized citizen who was communist, faced denaturalization on the grounds that his party membership proved he was not "attached" to the Constitution. Murphy wrote: "And something once regarded as a species of private property was abolished without compensating the owners when the institution of slavery was forbidden. Can it be said that the author of the Emancipation Proclamation and the supporters of the Thirteenth Amendment were not attached to the Constitution? We conclude that lack of attachment to the Constitution is not shown on the basis of the changes which petitioner testified he desired in the Constitution." Id at 142. For another use of the Proclamation to illustrate jurisprudence, see Justice Brennan's dissent in *Oregon v Mitchell*, 400 US 112 at 254, 255.

Proclamation, although masters might have argued that the Proclamation violated the Takings Clause of the Fifth Amendment, had they been able to get into court.[3] However, the ratification of the Thirteenth Amendment in December 1865 mooted any such legal claims, and only left the federal courts to consider whether the Proclamation affected certain antebellum property rights.[4]

Despite the lack of litigation over its implementation, the Proclamation is best understood as a legal document, albeit one promulgated under unusual circumstances. Lincoln wrote the Emancipation Proclamation believing, or fearing, that it might be litigated or challenged in the Supreme Court. As Justice Brennan noted, "even President Lincoln doubted whether his Emancipation Proclamation would be operative when the war had ended and his special war powers had expired."[5] The uncertain legality of emancipation was complicated by the makeup of the Supreme Court, which was still led by Chief Justice Roger B. Taney, an uncompromising opponent of emancipation, black rights, and the war effort. If Taney remained on the Court when the war ended he would undoubtedly hear cases on the legitimacy of the Emancipation Proclamation.

In the end, of course, none of this happened. Chief Justice Taney died in 1864 and Lincoln nominated Salmon P. Chase, a dedicated abolitionist, to replace him. Lincoln chose Chase, at least in part, because he could be counted on to support emancipation.[6] As Lincoln told New York Congressman Augustus Frank, Chase was

---

[3] The answer to such a claim might have been that the Emancipation Proclamation was the land equivalent of *The Prize Cases*, 67 US (2 Black) 635 (1863). There Justice Grier upheld the blockade of southern ports, and the seizure of private property violating the blockade, on the ground that "As a civil war is never publicly proclaimed, *eo nomine*, against insurgents, its actual existence is a fact in our domestic history which the Court is bound to notice and to know." 67 US at 667.

[4] *Osborn v Nicholson*, 13 Wall 654 (1872); Grossmeyer's Case (*Henry Grossmeyer v United States*), 4 Ct Cl 1 (1868); Mott's Case (*Randolph Mott v United States*), 4 Ct Cl 218 (1867); *French v Tumlin*, 9 F Cas 798 (1871); *Miller v Keys*, 17 F Cas 328 (1869); *Martin v Bartow Iron Works*, 16 F Cas 888 (1867).

[5] *Oregon v Mitchell*, 400 US 112 at 254 (Brennan, J, dissenting).

[6] George S. Boutwell, 2 *Reminiscences of Sixty Years in Public Affairs* 29 (1902). "There are reasons in favor of his appointment, and one very strong reason against it. First, he occupies the largest place in the public mind in connection with the office; then we wish for a Chief Justice who will sustain what has been done in regard to emancipation and the legal tenders. We cannot ask a man what he will do, and if we should, and he should answer us, we should despise him for it. Therefore, we must take a man whose opinions are known. But there is one very strong reason against his appointment. He is a candidate for the Presidency and if he does not give up that idea, it will be very bad for him and very bad for me."

"sound" on the "general issues of the war," which included emancipation.[7] Within a year after Chase's appointment, the legality of
emancipation was settled by the ratification of the Thirteenth
Amendment in 1865. The cases that raised the legal issues surrounding emancipation did not question that slavery in fact was
over.[8] Thus, for example, in *Osborn v Nicholson* (1872),[9] the Court
upheld the contract for sale of a slave that took place in March
1861, with Justice Noah Swayne concluding: "Neither the rights
nor the interests of the colored race lately in bondage are affected
by the conclusions we have reached. The opinion decides nothing
as to the effect of President Lincoln's Emancipation Proclamation.
We have had no occasion to consider that subject."[10]

However, in 1863 Lincoln assumed that there would be a legal
challenge to the Proclamation, and he wrote it with that prospect
in mind. Thus he made it as narrowly focused and as constitutionally
solid as possible. He avoided soaring language and inspiriting rhetoric.

The awkward style and structure of the Proclamation has troubled
historians. The great historian Richard Hofstadter criticized the
Proclamation as a cynical and meaningless document with "all the
moral grandeur of a bill of lading."[11] Lincoln was one of the greatest
craftsmen of the English language in American political history. But
here, in the most important moment of his life, he resorted to the
tools of the pettifogger, drafting a turgid and almost incompre-
hensible legal document. Unlike almost every other public document Lincoln wrote, the Proclamation was without style or grace.
Even historians who admire Lincoln think it was "boring" and "pe-
destrian."[12]

---

[7] Richard Aynes, *Bradwell v. Illinois: Chief Justice Chase's Dissent and the "Sphere of Women's Work*," 59 La L Rev 521 at 532, quoting John Niven, *Salmon P. Chase* 374 (Oxford, 1995).

[8] The meaning of the Proclamation was at least partially at issue in a few postwar cases, but these cases did not involve undoing emancipation. Grossmeyer's Case (*Henry Grossmeyer v United States*), 4 Ct Cl 1 (1868); Mott's Case (*Randolph Mott v United States*), 4 Ct Cl 218 (1867); *French v Tumlin*, 9 F Cas 798 (1871); *Miller v Keys*, 17 F Cas 328 (1869); *Martin v Bartow Iron Works*, 16 F Cas 888 (1867).

[9] 80 US 654 (1872).

[10] Id at 663. Chase, who was the most dedicated abolitionist on the Court, dissented in this case, presumably because he believed no contract for the purchase of a slave should ever be recognized by American law.

[11] Richard Hofstadter, *The American Political Tradition* 110, 115, 131 (Knopf, 1948).

[12] Allen C. Guelzo, *"Sublime in Its Magnitude": The Emancipation Proclamation*, in Harold Holzer and Sara Vaughn Gabbard, eds, *Lincoln and Freedom: Slavery, Emancipation, and the Thirteenth Amendment* at 66 (Southern Illinois, 2007).

In addition to its lack of rhetorical elegance, scholars have criticized the timing of the Proclamation, arguing it illustrates that
Lincoln was not seriously committed to black freedom. It took
Lincoln more than a year to even propose emancipation, and even
then Lincoln seemed to vacillate, apparently willing to withdraw
the preliminary Proclamation if the rebellious states would return
to the Union.[13] He did not issue the final Emancipation Proclamation until nearly two years into the war. When finally issued, the
Proclamation did not free all the slaves in the United States. In
fact, it did not free any of the slaves *in* the United States, but only
freed slaves in those states that claimed to be in the Confederacy
and thus not actually under the jurisdiction of the United States.
To the untrained eye, or at least the legally unsophisticated eye, the
Emancipation Proclamation seems to be chimera. Lincoln only
freed those slaves where he had no physical power to enforce his
will—in the Confederacy—and refused to free any slaves where he
had power to implement his policies—in the United States.

A careful understanding of Lincoln's own ideology and philosophy, the constraints of the Constitution, and the nature of the
Civil War illustrates that these criticisms ultimately miss their mark.
Lincoln's emancipation strategy turns out to be subtle, constitutionally innovative, and at times brilliant. Ultimately his policy
worked, as slavery came to an end everywhere in the nation without
any constitutional challenges.

I. CONSTITUTIONAL LIMITATIONS ON EMANCIPATION

A successful lawyer and lifelong student of the U.S. Constitution, Lincoln began his presidency with a strong sense of the
limitations that the Constitution placed on any emancipation
scheme. In his first inaugural he urged the seven seceding states to
return to the Union. In making this case Lincoln argued that slavery
in the southern states was safe under the Constitution and under
his administration. He reiterated a point made during the campaign:
"I have no purpose, directly or indirectly, to interfere with the

---

[13] Proclamation No 16 (Preliminary Emancipation Proclamation), 12 Stat 1267 (Sept
22, 1862). Lincoln indicated that the Proclamation would go into effect only if the Confederate states did not return to the Union. He had no expectation that any of the Confederate states would accept this offer, so his vacillation is more apparent than real. Had
the Confederate states returned to the Union before the Proclamation went into effect,
he would have had no constitutional power to end slavery in them.

institution of slavery in the States where it exists. I believe I have no lawful right to do so, and I have no inclination to do so." He underscored this position by quoting the Republican Party platform:

> *Resolved*, That the maintenance inviolate of the rights of the States, and especially the right of each State to order and control its own domestic institutions according to its own judgment exclusively, is essential to that balance of power on which the perfection and endurance of our political fabric depend. . . .

He pledged that during his administration "all the protection which, consistently with the Constitution and the laws, can be given, will be cheerfully given to all the States when lawfully demanded, for whatever cause—as cheerfully to one section as to another."[14]

Lincoln's position reflected an orthodox and almost universally accepted interpretation of the U.S. Constitution. Since 1787 virtually all constitutional theorists had understood that national government had no power to interfere with the "domestic institutions" of the states. Thus the states, and not the national government, had sole power to regulate all laws concerning personal status, such as marriage, divorce, child custody, inheritance, voting, and freedom— whether one was a slave or a free person. After the Constitutional Convention, General Charles Cotesworth Pinckney told the South Carolina House of Representatives: "We have a security that the general government can never emancipate them, for no such authority is granted and it is admitted, on all hands, that the general government has no powers but what are expressly granted by the Constitution, and that all rights not expressed were reserved by the several states."[15]

On the eve of Lincoln's presidency virtually all constitutional theorists, lawyers, and jurists accepted Pinckney's understanding of the Constitution: that it created a government of limited powers and that any powers not explicitly given to the national government were retained by the states. Antebellum constitutional jurisprudence had strengthened this understanding and also had expanded it to actually encroach on the powers of Congress, limiting the reach of

---

[14] Abraham Lincoln, "First Inaugural Address—Final Text," in Roy P. Basler, ed, *The Collected Works of Abraham Lincoln* 4:262–63 (Rutgers, 1953) (cited below as "*CW*").

[15] Pinckney, quoted in Jonathan Elliot, *The Debates in the Several State Conventions on the Adoption of the Federal Constitution*, 5 vols, 4:286 (1888; reprint, Burt Franklin, 1987). For greater discussion of this issue at the convention see Paul Finkelman, *Slavery and the Founders: Race and Liberty in the Age of Jefferson* (M. E. Sharpe, 2d ed 2001).

Congress to regulate slavery even in areas where the Constitution appeared to allow this.[16] Except for a few constitutional outliers, such as Lysander Spooner,[17] no antebellum politicians or legal scholars believed Congress had the power to regulate slavery in the states. In 1860 a claim of federal power to end slavery in the states was simply unthinkable for someone like Lincoln, who took law and constitutionalism seriously.

In *Dred Scott v Sandford* (1857), Chief Justice Roger B. Taney had asserted that Congress could never ban slavery in the federal territories. Lincoln and most other Republicans rejected the legitimacy of that portion of the decision on the grounds that once Taney found Dred Scott had no standing to sue the case became moot and everything Taney said after that was mere dicta.[18] In addition to rejecting Taney's jurisprudence on procedural grounds, Republicans like Lincoln also rejected it on substantive grounds. They argued that Congress did indeed have the power to ban slavery from the territories. But, even if Lincoln and his fellow Republicans were correct on this issue—and Chief Justice Taney was wrong— that did not affect emancipation in the states. There was a huge difference between banning slavery in new territories and taking slave property from people in the states or even in federal jurisdictions, like Washington, D.C., where slavery was legal. Thus, the accepted view was that the national government could not end slavery in the states. The only issue in dispute was whether the Republicans were right and Congress could ban slavery in the territories and the District of Columbia, or whether Chief Justice Taney was correct and Congress could not ban slavery in any federal jurisdictions.

In addition to the constitutional limitation on federal power, emancipation at the federal level also raised significant issues surrounding property rights—what modern legal scholars call "takings." The Fifth Amendment declares that "No person . . . shall be deprived of life, liberty, or property, without due process of law; nor shall private property be taken for public use without just com-

---

[16] This was the outcome in *Dred Scott v Sandford*, 19 How (60 US) 393 (1857); see Paul Finkelman, *Was Dred Scott Correctly Decided? An "Expert Report" for the Defendant*, 12 Lewis & Clark L Rev 1219 (2008).

[17] Helen J. Knowles, *The Constitution and Slavery: A Special Relationship*, 28 Slavery and Abolition 309 (2007); Randy E. Barnett, *Was Slavery Unconstitutional Before the Thirteenth Amendment? Lysander Spooner's Theory of Interpretation*, 28 Pac L J 977 (1997).

[18] Paul Finkelman, *Dred Scott v. Sandford: A Brief History* (Bedford, 1995).

pensation." An Emancipation Proclamation might violate the due process aspects of this amendment, but even if it did not, it might violate the takings provision. Lincoln, like almost all lawyers at the time, understood that even if Congress had the power to take slaves from American citizens, it could only be done through compensation, as required by the Fifth Amendment.

As a freshman congressman Lincoln had proposed a bill to end slavery in the District of Columbia through gradual emancipation, a process that would not constitute a taking because no living slaves would be freed. Under gradual abolition schemes the children of all slave women were born free, but indentured to the owners of their mothers until they reached the age of majority. This compensated the masters for raising these free-born children of slaves while not actually taking any property from the masters. Such legislation had been used to end slavery in most of the northern states in the wake of the American Revolution.[19]

Although Lincoln's bill for gradual emancipation in Washington, D.C., never reached the floor of Congress, it illustrates Lincoln's understanding that slave property could not be taken from masters without compensation. Indeed, when Congress finally did end slavery in the District of Columbia during the war, it did so through compensation, because that was the only constitutionally permissible way of immediately taking slave property from loyal masters in the nation's capital.[20] By 1862 gradual abolition was no longer realistic. No one in the government—and certainly not the slaves in Washington, D.C.—had any patience for any emancipation that was gradual.

Thus, when Lincoln entered office he fully understood that he had "no lawful right" to "interfere with the institution of slavery in the States where it exists." Because he had no "lawful right" to free slaves in the South, he could honestly tell the seceding states "I have no inclination to do so." This statement in his Inaugural Address could be interpreted to mean that Lincoln had no personal

---

[19] For a discussion of these schemes, see Arthur Zilversmit, *The First Emancipation: The Abolition of Slavery in the North* (Chicago, 1967); Paul Finkelman, *An Imperfect Union: Slavery, Federalism, and Comity* (North Carolina, 1981); Gary B. Nash and Jean R. Soderlund, *Freedom by Degrees: Emancipation in Pennsylvania and Its Aftermath* (Oxford, 1991); Shane White, *Somewhat More Independent: The End of Slavery in New York City, 1770–1810* (Georgia, 1991); and Robert Fogel and Stanley Engerman, *Philanthropy at Bargain Prices: Notes on the Economics of Gradual Emancipation*, 3 J Legal Stud 377 (1974).

[20] An Act for the Release of Certain Persons Held to Service or Labor in the District of Columbia, 12 Stat 376 (April 16, 1862).

interest or desire in ending slavery. But Lincoln chose his words carefully. His personal views on slavery were clear: he hated slavery and had always believed that "If slavery is not wrong, nothing is wrong."[21] But his personal desires could not overcome the constitutional realities of his age. Because he had no power to touch slavery in the states he could honestly say he had no inclination to attempt to do what was constitutionally impossible. Consistent with his long-standing Whig ideology, Lincoln rejected the idea of acting outside the Constitution. Reflecting his sense of the politically possible, Lincoln willingly reassured the seceding states that he had no "inclination" to do what he could not constitutionally, legally, or politically accomplish. When circumstances changed, so would Lincoln's "inclination," but in March 1861 Lincoln had no reason to think that circumstances would change.

Lincoln's constitutional understandings in 1861 were hardly new. He had articulated them in the Illinois legislature in 1837, when he was one of six members of the state legislature who opposed a proslavery resolution which attacked abolitionists and declared that slavery was "sacred to the slaveholding States." Lincoln then framed his own resolution (supported by only one other member of the assembly), asserting that slavery was "founded on both injustice and bad policy." In this protest against the actions of a majority in the legislature, Lincoln asserted the traditional understanding that the national government had "no power, under the constitution, to interfere with the institution of slavery in the different States." However, Lincoln also asserted that Congress did have "the power under the constitution, to abolish slavery in the District of Columbia."[22] This early foray into the constitutional issues of slavery suggests that even as a young man Lincoln understood the constitutional limitations as well as the constitutional possibilities of fighting slavery.

A decade later, in his single term in Congress, Lincoln proposed a bill for the gradual abolition of slavery in the District of Columbia, noted above. His emancipation scheme would have avoided the Fifth Amendment takings problem, because gradual emancipation did not free any existing slaves, but only guaranteed that their as-yet-unborn children would be free. Lincoln read the proposed

---

[21] Lincoln to Albert G. Hodges, April 4, 1864, *CW*, 7:281.

[22] "Protest in the Illinois Legislature on Slavery," *CW*, 1:74–75.

emancipation bill on the floor of Congress, but in the end did not introduce it. A powerless freshman congressman, he explained, "I was abandoned by my former backers."[23] Nevertheless, this bill, like his state legislative resolution, underscores Lincoln's early opposition to slavery and his understanding of the constitutional limitations of federal action against slavery.

This, then, was the constitutional framework Lincoln understood as he entered the White House. He personally hated slavery—he was "naturally antislavery" and could "not remember when" he "did not so think, and feel."[24] But he understood the constitutional limitations on his actions.

Lincoln also knew, as all Americans did, that slavery was the reason for secession and the cause of the Civil War. The Confederate states made this clear when they seceded. South Carolina, for example, explained that it was leaving the Union because of the "increasing hostility on the part of the non-slaveholding States to the institution of slavery."[25] South Carolina asserted the "right of property in slaves was recognized" in the Constitution but that "these ends for which this Government was instituted have been defeated, and the Government itself has been made destructive of them by the action of the non-slaveholding States."[26] The free states had "denied the rights of property" in slaves, "denounced as sinful the institution of slavery," and had "permitted the open establishment among them of societies, whose avowed object is to disturb the peace and to eloign the property of the citizens of other States."[27] The South Carolinians also complained that the northern states had "united in the election of a man to the high office of President of the United States, whose opinions and purposes are hostile to slavery."[28] The other seceding states expressed similar views. Thus, because slavery was clearly the cause of secession and the war, it would seem that attacking slavery should have been the first goal

---

[23] Benjamin Quarles, *Lincoln and the Negro* 30 (Oxford, 1962). In fact, with the acrimonious debates over the Wilmot Proviso tearing Congress apart, a serious discussion of a bill to end slavery in the district was not even remotely plausible.

[24] Lincoln to Hodges, *CW*, 7:281.

[25] Declaration of the Immediate Causes Which Induce and Justify the Secession of South Carolina, December 24, 1860, reprinted in Kermit L. Hall, Paul Finkelman, and James W. Ely, Jr., eds, *American Legal History* 250 (Oxford, 3rd ed 2005).

[26] Id at 251.

[27] Id.

[28] Id at 252.

of the Lincoln administration. Root out the problem, destroy the institution, and the Union could be restored. However, such a simplistic response did not comport with the reality of the crisis Lincoln faced. As much as he hated slavery and would have liked to destroy it—and as much as he understood that the slaveholders of the South were the cause of the crisis—Lincoln also understood that an assault on slavery required the complete or partial fulfillment of four essential preconditions.

II. The Preconditions for Emancipation: Constitutional, Political, and Military

From the moment the war began, Lincoln faced demands for emancipation. Abolitionists and antislavery Republicans wanted Lincoln to make the conflict a war against slavery. Northern free blacks were anxious to serve in a war of liberation. From the beginning of the war slaves escaped to U.S. army lines where they assumed (usually correctly) that they would find freedom. But the seriously committed opponents of slavery in the North were relatively few in number, free blacks in most of the North were politically disfranchised, and southern slaves had no political influence, at least in the first year of the war. Most northerners wanted a quick end to the conflict and a restoration of the Union. Any attempt at emancipation would prevent a speedy restoration of the Union. Moreover, any national program for emancipation beyond the territories or the District of Columbia did not fit into any generally recognized interpretation of the Constitution.

Early attempts at emancipation—such as General John C. Frémont's precipitous and near disastrous proclamation freeing slaves in Missouri—illustrate the complexity of the issue and the delicate nature of achieving black freedom. Many abolitionists (and some modern-day critics of Lincoln) have bristled at the idea that achieving freedom could be delicate.[29] From their perspective slavery was immoral, wrong, and the cause of the war. Thus, emancipation

---

[29] For modern critical assessments of Lincoln and emancipation, in addition to Hofstader, see Lerone Bennett, Jr., *Forced into Glory: Abraham Lincoln's White Dream* (Johnson, 2000); LaWanda Cox, *Lincoln and Black Freedom*, in Gabor S. Boritt and Norman O. Forness, eds, *The Historian's Lincoln: Pseudohistory, Psychohistory, and History* (Illinois, 1988); Ira Berlin, *Who Freed the Slaves? Emancipation and Its Meaning*, in David W. Blight and Brooks D. Simpson, eds, *Union and Emancipation: Essays on Politics and Race in the Civil War Era* (Kent State, 1997); Julius Lester, *Look Out Whitey! Black Power's Gon' Get Your Mama!* (Dial, 1968); Lerone Bennett, Jr., *Was Lincoln a White Supremacist?* 23 Ebony 35 (1968).

would be a great humanitarian act which would strike at the heart of traitorous Confederates. Without any regard to constitutional-ism, the early proponents of emancipation simply argued that it was justified by secession. President Lincoln, however, could not accept such facile and simplistic arguments. For Lincoln, emanci-pation required the convergence of four preconditions involving legal and constitutional theory, popular support, and military suc-cess. Without these preconditions emancipation was both mean-ingless and impossible.

First, Lincoln needed a constitutional or legal framework for taking slaves—the private property of masters—and for freeing those slaves. Mere hostility to the United States by slave owners was not a sufficient reason for taking their property. Creating a constitutional framework for emancipation was complicated by the different statuses of the slave states. Four of the slave states—Mary-land, Delaware, Kentucky, and Missouri—had not joined the Con-federacy. Their citizens still enjoyed all of the protections of the U.S. Constitution. Since neither Congress nor the president had any power to interfere with the local institutions of the states, Lin-coln had no constitutional power to end slavery in those states. Lincoln did believe Congress could end slavery in the District of Columbia, the Indian Territory, and other federal territories, like Utah and Nebraska. However, emancipation in those places pre-sumably required compensation, since the Fifth Amendment pro-hibited the taking of private property without due process of law and just compensation. This provision of the Constitution would also hold true for ending slavery in the loyal slave states, if Lincoln somehow found a constitutionally acceptable method of ending slav-ery in these states.

The status of slaves in the putative Confederate nation was much less clear. Lincoln believed that secession was unconstitutional and that the Confederacy could not legally exist. If this were true, then presumably the citizens of the Confederacy were still protected by the Constitution. However, as combatants Confederates were surely not protected by the Constitution while making war against the United States. Confederates might be entitled to due process as civilians, but they were not protected in their capacity as enemies of the United States. Personal property used in combat—a weapon, a wagon, or a horse—could of course be confiscated on the bat-tlefield. This would be true whether the combat was with Confederate soldiers in uniform or pro-Confederate guerillas in civilian clothes. Presumably, slaves used in a combat situation—as teamsters, laborers, or even cooks in military camps—might also be seized.

Thus, at the beginning of the war there was no clear legal theory on which emancipation might proceed. Lincoln believed that the Supreme Court—still dominated by Chief Justice Taney and his proslavery allies—would doubtless overturn any emancipation scheme that was not constitutionally ironclad. At the beginning of the war every one of the six Justices on the U.S. Supreme Court was a proslavery Democrat.[30] Five of the Justices, including Chief Justice Taney, had been part of the majority in *Dred Scott* and had held that the Fifth Amendment protected slave property in the territories. The sixth, Nathan Clifford, was a classic doughface—a northern man with southern principles—who could be expected to support slavery and oppose emancipation. Taney, a "seething secessionist," in fact drafted an opinion striking down emancipation just in case he had the opportunity to use it.[31] Lincoln reasonably assumed the Court would strike down any emancipation act that was not constitutionally impregnable.

Second, even if Lincoln could develop a coherent legal and constitutional theory to justify emancipation, he still needed to have political and popular support to move against slavery. Most northerners disliked slavery, but this did not mean they were prepared for a long, bloody crusade against bondage. When the war began, even Republicans who had been battling slavery all their adult lives, like Salmon P. Chase and William H. Seward, did not think there was sufficient public support to attack slavery. Lincoln, who was already on his way to becoming a master politician, needed to create the political climate to make emancipation an acceptable wartime goal. The war began as one to save the Union, which commanded support among almost all northerners. He could not afford to jeopardize that support by moving too quickly to end slavery, even though he deeply hated slavery.

Third, Lincoln needed to secure the four loyal slave states before he could move against slavery. This required a combination of po-

---

[30] There were three vacancies on the Court when Lincoln took office, and he could not fill them right away. The seats could not be filled until Congress reconfigured the circuits for Justices.

[31] Don E. Fehrenbacher, *The Dred Scott Case: Its Significance in American Law and Politics* (Oxford, 1978).

litical and military success. The demographic and geographic issues were crucial. There were more than two and a half million whites living in these states. If Missouri and Kentucky seceded they would become the second and third largest states in the Confederacy. More importantly, in terms of the crucial white population that would provide troops for the Confederacy, they would be the largest and third largest states in the Confederacy. If the border slave states left the United States they would also provide three of the four largest cities in the Confederacy—Baltimore, St. Louis, and Louisville— dwarfing all other Confederate cities except New Orleans.[32] Strategically and geographically they were even more important. If Maryland joined the Confederacy the nation's capital would be completely surrounded by the enemy. If Missouri seceded there would be a Confederate army on the upper Mississippi poised to threaten Lincoln's home state of Illinois and able to penetrate into Iowa and Minnesota.

Kentucky was the most crucial of the states. A Confederate army on the southern bank of the Ohio River would interrupt east-west commerce and troop movements, threaten the vast agricultural heartland of Ohio, Indiana, and Illinois, and endanger key cities, including Cincinnati, Chicago, Indianapolis, and Pittsburgh. With more than 200,000 slaves in the state, Kentucky was vulnerable to Confederate entreaties. A precipitous movement toward emancipation would push the bluegrass state into the hands of the enemy, and that would probably lead to secession in Missouri as well. Early in the war a group of ministers urged Lincoln to free the slaves, because God would be on his side. He allegedly responded, "I hope to have God on my side, but I must have Kentucky."[33] Early emancipation would almost certainly have cost him that crucial state and possibly the war.

This leads to the fourth precondition for emancipation: the actual possibility of a military victory. Lincoln could only move to end slavery if he could win the war; if he attacked slavery and did not win the war, then he accomplished nothing. Lincoln's reply to a group of ministers illustrates this point. In September 1862 Lincoln

---

[32] Peggy Wagner, Gary W. Gallagher, and Paul Finkelman, *The Library of Congress Civil War Desk Reference* 70–72 (Simon and Schuster, 2002).

[33] Lowell Hayes Harrison, *Lincoln of Kentucky* 135 (Kentucky, 2000); see also David Lindsey, review of *The Civil War in Kentucky* by Lowell H. Harrison, 63 J Am Hist 136 (1976).

had already decided to move against slavery, but was waiting for the right moment—a substantial military victory. He could not tell the ministers of his plans, and instead told them that emancipation was useless without a military victory. He said an emancipation proclamation without a victory would be "like the Pope's bull against the comet"; he asked how he "could free the slaves" when he could not "enforce the Constitution in the rebel States."[34]

This analysis turns modern critiques of Lincoln on their head. Critics of Lincoln argue that he eventually moved toward emancipation for military and diplomatic reasons: because he needed black troops to repopulate his army and to prevent Britain and France from giving diplomatic recognition to the Confederacy.[35] Emancipation is explained as a desperate act to save the Union, reflecting the title of Leone Bennett's book that Lincoln was "forced into glory" by circumstances.

But the chronology of emancipation and all of Lincoln's statements leading up to emancipation do not support this analysis. Both Lincoln and Congress began to move toward emancipation only after a series of U.S. victories in early 1862. Lincoln then waited to announce emancipation until after a major victory that stopped Lee's army dead in its tracks—with huge casualties—at Antietam. Early emancipation would have probably thrown Kentucky and Missouri into the Confederacy and perhaps doomed the Union cause. While emancipation may be properly seen as one of the elements of victory, it must also be seen as an outcome of the likelihood of ultimate victory. Victory would probably have been possible without emancipation, although it might have been more difficult and perhaps taken longer.[36] Victory could also have been accomplished without black troops, although they surely made a huge difference in the last years of the war, but a general eman-

---

[34] "Reply to Emancipation Memorial Presented by Chicago Christians of All Denominations," Sept 13, 1862, *CW*, 5:419–25 (quotations on 420). According to various stories, in 1456 Pope Calixtus III issued a Papal Bull against Halley's Comet. This event was recounted in a biography of Calixtus III by Pierre-Simon Laplace published in 1475. Modern scholars believe this is not a true story, but it was believed at the time of Lincoln. For one discussion of this, see Andrew Dickson White, *A History of the Warfare of Science with Theology in Christendom* 177 (D. Appleton, 1896).

[35] For modern critical assessments of Lincoln and emancipation, in addition to Hofstader, see Bennett, *Forced into Glory*; Cox, *Lincoln and Black Freedom*; Berlin, *Who Freed the Slaves?*; Lester, *Look Out Whitey!*; and Bennett, 23 Ebony 35 (1968) (all cited in note 29).

[36] It is also possible that without the Emancipation Proclamation the Confederacy would have surrendered earlier, and that the threat of ending slavery actually prolonged the war.

cipation was not a precondition to enlisting blacks. While victory was possible without emancipation, emancipation was clearly impossible without victory. Conditions looked bright after Antietam, when the preliminary Proclamation was announced, and Lincoln assumed they would look just as bright in a hundred days, when he planned to sign the Proclamation on January 1, 1863. Thus, rather than being forced into glory when he announced the Preliminary Emancipation Proclamation, Lincoln understood that moral glory—emancipation—could only be possible through military glory.

III. Constitutional Principles and Emancipation in Time of War

In the spring of 1861 none of the four preconditions for emancipation existed. However, demands for emancipation would not wait until the circumstances allowed for it. In the first half year of the war Lincoln faced three different models for attacking slavery. Two of these models satisfied the first three preconditions: there was a legal/constitutional basis for emancipation, they would not undermine northern support for the war, and they would not chase Kentucky and Missouri out of the Union. The third one, General John C. Frémont's proclamation freeing slaves in Missouri, failed all of these tests, and Lincoln wisely overruled it.

Almost immediately after the war began slaves began to abandon their masters and flee to the safety and protection of the U.S. Army. In exercising this self-emancipation these fleeing slaves created the need for a clear government policy, well before anyone in the administration was ready to develop such a policy. This set the stage for clever lawyering that ultimately created a constitutional basis for emancipation. In his second inaugural Abraham Lincoln would assert that in 1861 "All knew" that slavery "was somehow the cause of the war." However, when the war began, the administration could not attack slavery—the cause of the war—because of the lack of preconditions necessary to attack slavery. Most importantly, Lincoln still hoped to reunite the Union without a war, and when the war came he needed to keep the loyal slave states in the Union. These priorities, as well as the absence of a constitutional theory or strong popular support, led Lincoln to defer any consideration of ending slavery.

The slaves, however, were under no such constraints. They knew, even more than their masters or the blue-clad enemies of their masters, that this war was about slavery—about them and their future. While Lincoln bided his time, waiting for the moment to strike out against slavery, hundreds and then thousands of slaves struck out for freedom on their own.

From almost the beginning of the war slaves streamed into U.S. Army camps and forts. The army was not a social welfare agency and was institutionally unprepared to feed, clothe, or house masses of propertyless refugees. Initially the army returned slaves to masters who came after them. This situation undermined the morale of U.S. troops, who fully understood that they were returning valuable property to their enemies who would use that property to make war on them. Slaves grew the food that fed the Confederate Army, raised and cared for the horses the Confederates rode into battle, and labored in the workshops and factories that produced the metals and weapons necessary to fight the war.[37] As Frederick Douglass noted, "The very stomach of this Rebellion is the negro in the form of a slave." Douglass correctly understood that if the government could "arrest that hoe in the hands of the Negro," the Lincoln administration would be able to "smite the rebellion in the very seat of its life."[38] Returning slaves to Confederate masters was hardly different than returning guns or horses to them. Initially, however, some army officers did just that.

Circumstances began to change on May 23, when three slaves owned by Confederate Colonel Charles K. Mallory escaped to Fortress Monroe, under the command of General Benjamin F. Butler. A day later Butler faced the surrealistic spectacle of Confederate Major M. B. Carey, under a flag of truce, demanding the return of the slaves under the Fugitive Slave Law. Major Carey, identifying himself as Mallory's agent, argued that Butler was obligated to return the slaves under the Fugitive Slaves Clause of the Constitution and the Fugitive Slave Law of 1850. Butler, a successful Massachusetts lawyer before the war, had devoted some thought to the issue. He told Major Carey "that the fugitive slave act did not affect a foreign country, which Virginia claimed to be and she must reckon it one of the infelicities of her position that in so far at least

---

[37] Charles Dew, *Bond of Iron: Master and Slave at Buffalo Forge*, 264–311 (W.W. Norton, 1994).

[38] Douglass, quoted in James M. McPherson, *Battle Cry of Freedom: The Civil War Era* at 354 (Oxford, 1988) (cited below as "*Battle Cry of Freedom*").

she was taken at her word." Butler then offered to return the slaves to Colonel Mallory if he would come to Fortress Monroe and "take the oath of allegiance to the Constitution of the United States."[39] But until Mallory took such an oath his slaves were contrabands of war and could not be returned.[40]

This was the end of Colonel Mallory's attempt to recover his slaves, but it was the beginning of a new policy for the United States. Butler, in need of workers, immediately employed the three fugitives, who had previously been used by Mallory to build Confederate defenses. Taking slaves away from Mallory and other Confederates served the dual purposes of depriving the enemy of labor while providing labor for the United States.

Butler's new contraband policy was not applied everywhere at once. By the middle of the summer slaves poured into U.S. forts and camps, where soldiers had conflicting orders. Some officers returned slaves to all masters; others only returned them to loyal masters in Maryland, Kentucky, and Missouri. Some offered sanctuary to all slaves who entered their lines.

Clarity of sorts came from Secretary of War Simon Cameron on August 8, when he informed Butler of the president's desire "that all existing rights in all the States be fully respected and maintained" and reminded Butler the war was "for the Union and for the preservation of all constitutional rights of States and the citizens of the States in the Union." Because of this, "no question can arise as to fugitives from service within the States and Territories in which the authority of the Union is fully acknowledged." This of course meant that military commanders could not free fugitive slaves in Missouri, Kentucky, Maryland, and Delaware. All of this was consistent with Lincoln's public position at the beginning of the war. Moreover, this position would shore up support for the Union in the loyal slave states. But Cameron added a new wrinkle, which indicated an important change in administration policy. Cameron told Butler that the president also understood that "in States wholly or partially under insurrectionary control" the laws could not be enforced, and it was "equally obvious that rights dependent on the laws of the States within which military operations are conducted must be nec-

---

[39] Maj. Gen. Benjamin F. Butler to Lt. Gen. Winfield Scott, May 24/25, 1861, in *The War of the Rebellion: The Official Records of the Union and Confederate Armies*, 127 vols, index, and atlas (GPO, 1880–1901), ser 2, vol 1:752 (cited below as "*O.R.*").

[40] Benjamin F. Butler, *Butler's Book* 256–57 (A. M. Thayer, 1892).

essarily subordinated to the military exigencies created by the insurrection if not wholly forfeited by the treasonable conduct of the parties claiming them." Most importantly, "rights to services" could "form no exception" to "this general rule."[41]

Quietly Lincoln had now changed his administration's policy toward slavery in the Confederacy. Under this policy the military would return fugitive slaves from the loyal slave states, but not in the Confederate states, where of course most of the slaves were held. The slaves of loyal masters who lived in the Confederacy presented a "more difficult question." The solution was to have the army employ the fugitives, but to keep a record of such employment, so at some point loyal masters might be compensated for the use of their slaves. Speaking for the president, Secretary of War Cameron admonished Butler not to encourage slaves to abscond nor to interfere with the "servants of peaceful citizens" even in the Confederacy, nor to interfere in the voluntary return of fugitives to their masters "except in cases where the public safety" would "seem to require" such interference.[42]

By late August Butler's contraband policy had become the norm. The U.S. Army could employ any slaves who ran to its lines, provided they came from Confederate states. This was not a general emancipation policy, and, indeed, the army was not supposed to deliberately attempt to free slaves. But the army would not return fugitive slaves to masters in the Confederate states, even if the masters claimed to be loyal to the United States. Shrewdly, the Lincoln administration had become part of the process of ending slavery while professing not to be doing so. To abolitionists the administration could point to the growing thousands of "contrabands" who were being paid a salary and often wearing the only clothing available, blue uniforms.[43] But to conservatives and loyal masters still living in the United States, his administration could still point out that it had no emancipation policy and was not interfering with slavery *in the states*, it was only taking military contraband from people who claimed to be living outside the United States and were at war with the United States.

---

[41] Simon Cameron to Maj. Gen. Benjamin F. Butler, Aug 8, 1861, *O.R.*, ser 2, vol 1: 761–62.

[42] Id.

[43] Special Orders No 72, October 14, 1861, and General Orders No 34, November 1, 1861, *O.R.*, ser 2, vol 1:774–75 (setting out pay scale for black laborers).

This emerging policy began with General Butler's response to a Confederate colonel and was soon adopted by the Department of War and the president. It was not a direct attack on slavery, and it was not an emancipation policy per se. But it did protect the freedom of thousands of slaves who were developing their own strategy of self-emancipation by running to the U.S. Army. By the time Secretary of War Cameron spelled out the policy to General Butler, Congress had endorsed it and pushed it further along with the First Confiscation Act.

The First Confiscation Act, passed on August 6, allowed for the seizure of any slaves used for military purposes by the Confederacy.[44] This was not a general emancipation act and was narrowly written to allow the seizure of slaves only in actual use by Confederate forces. The law did not jeopardize the slave property of masters in the loyal slave states, even those sympathetic to the Confederacy. Freeing slaves under the Confiscation Act might have violated the Fifth Amendment, if seen as allowing a taking of private property without due process. But the law was carefully drawn as a military measure. Surely the army could seize a weapon in the hands of a captured Confederate soldier without a due process hearing, or take a horse from a captured Confederate. Similarly, slaves working on fortifications, or being used in other military capacities, might be taken.

The First Confiscation Act was ambiguous and cumbersome and did not threaten slavery as an institution. Under the law only those slaves being used specifically for military purposes—relatively few in number—could be freed. But the law did indicate a political shift toward emancipation. It was not decisive, because the emancipatory aspects of the law were limited, but it did show that Congress was ready to support some kind of emancipation. Neither Congress nor the American people were ready to turn the military conflict into an all-out war against slavery; however, Congress—which presumably reflected the ideology of its constituents—was ready to allow the government to free some slaves in the struggle against the Confederacy.

The First Confiscation Act along with the contraband policy were major steps toward eventual public support for emancipation. In the Confiscation Act, Congress embraced the principle that the

---

[44] An Act to confiscate Property used for Insurrectionary Purposes, 12 Stat 319 (Aug 6, 1861).

national government had the power to free slaves as a military necessity. The logical extension of this posture could be the total destruction of slavery. If Congress could free some slaves through the Confiscation Act, or the executive branch could free some slaves through the contraband policy, then the two branches might be able to free all slaves if the military and social conditions warranted such a result.

Just a few weeks after Lincoln signed the Confiscation Act, Major General John C. Frémont issued a "proclamation" declaring martial law in Missouri and announced that all slaves owned by Confederate activists in that state were free.[45] This proclamation went well beyond the Confiscation Act. Lincoln immediately and unambiguously urged Frémont to withdraw his proclamation, pointing out that it undermined efforts to keep Kentucky in the Union: "I think there is great danger that the closing paragraph, in relation to the confiscation of property, and the liberating slaves of traitorous owners, will alarm our Southern Union friends, and turn them against us—perhaps ruin our rather fair prospect for Kentucky." Thus he asked the general to "modify" his proclamation "on his own motion," to conform to the Confiscation Act. Aware of the exaggerated egos of his generals, Lincoln noted, "This letter is written in a spirit of caution and not of censure."[46]

While Lincoln waited for Frémont to withdraw his proclamation, politicians, generals, and border state unionists urged the president to directly countermand Frémont's order. Lincoln agreed with a Kentucky unionist who told him, "There is not a day to lose in disavowing emancipation or Kentucky is gone over the mill dam."[47] Lincoln told Senator Orville Browning that "to lose Kentucky is nearly . . . to lose the whole game."[48] Lincoln hoped that Frémont—who had been the Republican candidate for president in 1856—would be politically savvy enough to withdraw the order.

Hoping to score points with the abolitionist wing of the Republican Party, embarrass Lincoln, and set himself up to be the Republican candidate in 1864, Frémont refused to comply with the request of his commander-in-chief. Instead of withdrawing his proc-

---

[45] J. C. Frémont, Proclamation, August 30, 1861, *O.R.*, ser 1, vol 3:466–67.

[46] Lincoln to John C. Frémont, Sept 2, 1861, *CW*, 4:506.

[47] Both quotations in William E. Gienapp, *Abraham Lincoln and Civil War America: A Biography* 89 (Oxford, 2002).

[48] Lincoln to Orville H. Browning, Sept 22, 1861, *CW*, 4:531–32.

lamation, Frémont asked Lincoln to formally countermand it. This would allow Frémont to later blame the president for undermining emancipation. Lincoln "cheerfully" did so, ordering Frémont to modify the proclamation. Still playing politics, Frémont claimed he never received the order, but only read about it in the newspapers, and even then Frémont continued to distribute his original order.[49] Frémont's stubbornness, lack of political sense, and military incompetence led to his dismissal by Lincoln on November 2, 1861.[50] He would get another command, and fail there, and by the end of the war Frémont would be marginalized and irrelevant.

Some scholars have asserted that Lincoln's response to Frémont illustrates his insensitivity to black freedom. Frémont was a national hero before the war, and by supporting his abolitionist general, critics argue that Lincoln could have turned the war into a crusade against slavery. However, unlike Frémont, Lincoln understood that an unwinnable war would not end slavery; it would only destroy the Union and permanently secure slavery in the new Confederate nation. His comments to Frémont bear out his realistic assessment that if Kentucky, and perhaps Missouri, joined the Confederacy, the war might be lost. Frémont's proclamation jeopardized Kentucky, and Lincoln correctly countermanded it. The fall of 1861 was simply not the time to attack slavery, especially in the loyal slave states.

Lincoln could have responded to Frémont with a lecture on constitutional law. Freeing slaves as contrabands of war in the Confederacy was probably constitutional. Freeing slaves *within* the United States—which included Missouri—was not constitutional unless those slaves were actually being used as part of active resistance against the government. The First Confiscation Act could have been used to free slaves being used by pro-Confederate forces in Missouri for military purposes; however, this is not what Frémont wanted to do. He wanted to take slaves from anyone who supported the Confederacy, even if those slaves were not directly being used for military purposes and were the property of people living in the United States. Because Missouri had not seceded, Confederate sympathizers who were not involved in direct combat were still protected by the Constitution. But Frémont's plan was ambiguous about their status or the status of their property. Moreover, because

---

[49] Lincoln to John C. Frémont, Sept 11, 1861, *CW*, 4:517–18.

[50] General Order No 28, Nov 2, 1861, *O.R.*, Additions and Corrections to Series 2, vol 3:558–59 (GPO, 1902).

Frémont's plan would have summarily deprived American citizens living in the United States of their property without due process, it clearly violated the Fifth Amendment.

Some Republicans were deeply troubled by Lincoln's response to Frémont. Privately Lincoln assured Senator Charles Sumner that the difference between them on emancipation was only a matter of time—a month or six weeks. Sumner accepted this statement and promised to "not say another word to you about it till the longest time you name has passed by."[51] The time would in fact be more like a year, but there is little reason to doubt that Lincoln was moving toward some sort of abolition plan.

For Lincoln there were two paramount issues to consider. The first was timing. He could only attack slavery if he could win the war; if he attacked slavery and did not win the war, then he accomplished nothing. Critics of Lincoln argue that he eventually moved toward emancipation because he needed black troops to win the war. But the alternative reading—starting with his correspondence with Frémont—is that he could only move against slavery after he had secured the border states and made certain that victory was possible. Only then could emancipation actually work. Rather than a desperate act to save the war effort, emancipation becomes the logical fruit of victory. Frémont's proclamation surely did not fit that bill; consequently, Lincoln countermanded it.

IV. Military Victory, Securing the Loyal Slave States, and Emancipation

Lincoln clearly underestimated the time needed before he could move against slavery. The preconditions he needed for emancipation did not emerge in the month or six weeks he forecast to Sumner. A call for emancipation had to be tied to securing the loyal slave states and to a realistic belief that the war could be won; there was no point in telling slaves they were free if the government could not enforce that freedom. The prospect of a military victory was not great in the fall of 1861. The embarrassing defeats at the First Battle of Bull Run and Ball's Bluff did not bode well for the future.[52]

In November 1861 the course of the war began to change, as

---

[51] Stephen Oates, *With Malice Toward None: The Life of Abraham Lincoln* 292 (Mentor, 1978).

[52] McPherson, *Battle Cry of Freedom*, 358–68.

Admiral Samuel du Pont successfully seized the South Carolina Sea Islands with the important naval base at Port Royal. Once established, the United States would never be dislodged from this beachhead off the South Carolina coast. At least some of the war would now be fought in the heartland of the South.[53] Although Lincoln could not know it at the time, this was the beginning of the shrinking of the Confederacy. The first half of the next year would turn out to be "one of the brightest periods of the war for the North."[54] In February, Roanoke Island was captured, and by the end of April the navy and army had captured or sealed off every Confederate port on the Atlantic except Charleston, South Carolina, and Wilmington, North Carolina. Ports such as Savannah, Georgia, remained in Confederate hands, but the rebels no longer had access to the ocean except through blockade runners, who had virtually no affect on the Confederate war effort.

In the West, the United States won a series of crucial victories, securing Kentucky for the Union. Although the Kentucky legislature had voted in September to stay in the Union, support for the Confederacy remained strong in the bluegrass state. The state's governor, Beriah Magoffin, had resigned to join the Confederacy. In November General McClellan had told General Don Carolos Buell, "It is absolutely necessary that we shall hold all the State of Kentucky" and to make sure that "the majority of its inhabitants shall be warmly in favor of our cause." McClellan believed that the conduct of the "political affairs in Kentucky" was perhaps "more important than that of our military operations." He wanted to ensure that the U.S. Army respected the "domestic institution"— slavery—in the state.[55]

McClellan's concerns were real. In late November about two hundred Kentuckians organized a secession convention and declared their state to be in the Confederacy. In December the rebel congress admitted Kentucky into the Confederacy. With more than 25,000 Confederate troops in the state, Kentucky was hardly secure.

---

[53] One of the important results of this was the liberation of thousands of slaves on the Sea Islands, many of whom would later be enlisted when the United States began to organize black regiments in late 1862. See David Dudley Cornish, *The Sable Arm: Negro Troops in the Union Army, 1861–1865* (W. W. Norton, 1966), and Willie Lee Rose, *Rehearsal for Reconstruction: The Port Royal Experiment* (Oxford, 1976).

[54] McPherson at 368 (cited in note 52).

[55] [General] George B. McClellan to Brig. Gen. D. C. Buell, Nov 7, 1861, *O.R.*, ser 2, vol 1:776–77.

All of this changed in a ten-day period in early February. On February 6, Ulysses S. Grant, until then an obscure brigadier general, captured Fort Henry on the Tennessee River in northern Tennessee. On February 16 he captured Fort Donelson on the Cumberland River along with more than 12,000 Confederate troops. These twin victories established a U.S. presence in the Confederate state of Tennessee and emphatically secured Kentucky for the Union. By the end of the month the U.S. army was sitting in Nashville, Tennessee, the first southern state capital to fall. Instead of Kentucky possibly going into the Confederacy, it was more likely that Tennessee would be returned to the United States.

On the other side of the Mississippi, in early March Confederate forces suffered a devastating loss at Pea Ridge in Arkansas. The Confederates, led by Earl Van Dorn, had planned to march into Missouri and eventually capture St. Louis. But Pea Ridge ended any chance of Missouri becoming a Confederate state. Instead, the outcome made it all the more likely that Arkansas would be brought back into the Union. A month later the United States won a major victory at Shiloh, in southwestern Tennessee. On the same day U.S. naval forces combined with the army to seize Island No. 10 in the Mississippi River, capturing more than 50 big guns and some 7,000 Confederate soldiers. In April a combined naval and army operation captured Memphis, and on May 1, General Benjamin Butler, who had developed the contraband policy while a commander in Virginia, marched into New Orleans.

This truncated history of the first months of 1862 illustrates how circumstances allowed Lincoln to begin to contemplate emancipation. By June he knew that the loyal slave states were unlikely to join the Confederacy. There would still be fighting in that region—especially horrible guerrilla warfare in Missouri—but by June 1862 it was clear that Kentucky, Maryland, Delaware, and Missouri were secure. So too was a good piece of Tennessee as well as the cities of New Orleans, Baton Rouge, Natchez, and smaller river towns in Mississippi, Louisiana, and Arkansas. There could be no more realistic fears that an emancipation policy would push Kentucky or Missouri into the Confederacy.

Lincoln now had a reasonable chance of implementing an emancipation policy for a substantial number of slaves. Even if the war ended with some part of the Confederacy intact, the president could break the back of slavery in the Mississippi Valley. Once free, these blacks could not easily be reenslaved.

By the spring of 1862 Lincoln had the third and fourth prerequisites in place for emancipation: security of the upper South and a reasonable chance of military success that would make emancipation successful. He was also moving toward the first prerequisite: a legal theory that would justify emancipation. The theory was not complete, but it had been developing since Butler discovered the legal concept of contrabands of war and brilliantly applied it to slaves. The First Confiscation Act had supplemented it. In March 1861 Congress prohibited the military from returning fugitive slaves, whether from enemy masters, loyal masters in the Confederacy, or masters in the border states. Any officers returning fugitive slaves could be court-martialed and, if convicted, dismissed from military service.[56] None of these laws or policies had attacked slavery directly. Freeing contrabands required that the slaves take the initiative of running to the army *and* that the army be in close proximity to them. The Confiscation Act only applied to slaves being used for military purposes. Most slaves fit neither category. But these policies showed that the national government was now secure in its understanding that it could implement an emancipation program. These policies also indicated that Lincoln was becoming comfortable with the idea that as commander-in-chief he could attack slavery. By the fall of 1862 Lincoln was convinced that there were "no objections" to emancipation "on legal or constitutional grounds; for, as commander-in-chief of the army and navy, in time of war, I suppose I have the right to take any measure which may best subdue the enemy."[57]

The second of the four prerequisites—insuring political support for emancipation—was still an open question in early 1862. But the nation was moving toward emancipation. On April 10 Congress passed a joint resolution declaring the United States would "cooperate with," and provide "pecuniary aid" for, any state willing to adopt a gradual emancipation scheme.[58] Most importantly, on April

---

[56] An Act to make an Additional Article of War, 12 Stat 354 (March 13, 1862). This law modified an important part of the Fugitive Slave Law of 1850, which had authorized the use of the military or the militia to return fugitive slaves.

[57] "Reply to Emancipation Memorial Presented by Chicago Christians of All Denominations," Sept 13, 1862, *CW*, 5:419–25 (quotations on 421).

[58] Joint Resolution No 26, 12 Stat 617 (April 10, 1862).

16, Congress abolished slavery in the District of Columbia and provided compensation for the masters. This law was consistent with Lincoln's long-standing understanding that the Constitution allowed Congress to fully regulate the District of Columbia. The president happily signed this law.[59] Fifteen years earlier he had been ready to move against slavery in the district through gradual emancipation, which acknowledged the Fifth Amendment claims of masters. Now he was able to act through compensated emancipation, which was also likely to survive a challenge on Fifth Amendment grounds.

In addition to providing payment to masters for the slaves, the D.C. emancipation law also provided money for colonization of former slaves in Africa or Haiti. Critics of Lincoln often have focused on this provision as proof of Lincoln's racism and his insincerity with regard to both emancipation and black rights. However, a serious analysis of this provision undermines such claims.

The law provided up to $100,000 for the colonization outside the United States of both free blacks already living in the district and the newly emancipated slaves. The operative language, however, was critical. The money was "to aid in the settlement and colonization of such free persons . . . as *may desire to emigrate* to the Republics of Hayti or Liberia, or such other country beyond the limits of the United States as the president may determine."[60] This language, which Lincoln had demanded, did not require or force anyone to leave the United States. Moreover, it allowed the president to prevent voluntary emigration if he "determine[d]" the destination was not suitable. The law also limited the amount to be appropriated for each emigrant to $100.[61]

This provision was clearly a sop thrown to conservatives and racists, who feared a free black population. In 1860 there were 14,000 blacks in the city, including about 3,200 slaves. The appropriation would have provided money for the colonization of only 1,000 blacks—less than a third of the newly freed slaves and less than 7 percent of the entire free black population of the city in

---

[59] An Act for the Release of Certain Persons Held to Service or Labor in the District of Columbia, 12 Stat 376 (April 16, 1862).

[60] Id at 378 (emphasis added).

[61] Id. Misunderstanding of the colonization bill is common. John Hope Franklin, for example, asserts that the law "provided for the removal and colonization of the freedmen," John Hope Franklin, *The Emancipation Proclamation* 17 (Doubleday, 1963), when in fact it did not provide for "removal" but merely allowed voluntary colonization.

1860. Moreover, by 1862 the black population in the city was much larger than 14,000, which meant that even a smaller percentage of the population could leave under the appropriation. Furthermore, the $100 was hardly an incentive for any free black or former slave to move to a new country. Not surprisingly, no record exists of *any* African American taking advantage of this offer. This law in fact may be unique in American history: the only time that Congress appropriated a substantial sum of money, to be given out to individuals, and no one applied to receive the money.

The political message of this law was significant. Congress, in an election year, was beginning to dismantle slavery. House members, who were to stand for reelection in the fall, were willing to run on a record that included voting to free some slaves. In June Congress abolished slavery in the federal territories, this time without compensation.[62] In doing so Congress completely ignored Chief Justice Taney's decision in *Dred Scott v Sandford*,[63] which specifically held that Congress could never abolish slavery in the territories. Congress was apparently not worried that the Chief Justice and his colleagues would have the audacity to undo their handiwork. This was one more incentive for the president to begin to think about a larger emancipation. It was in this context, with the war going relatively well, with the border states secure, and some emancipation taking place, that Lincoln began to work on the greatest issue of his lifetime.

V. POLITICAL SUPPORT FOR REMAKING AMERICA

As Congress moved to end slavery in the territories and the District of Columbia, Lincoln contemplated a much larger issue: ending slavery in the Confederacy. Before Lincoln could act, one of his generals once again began to move against slavery without authority. On May 9, 1862, Major General David Hunter, the commander of U.S. forces in the Department of the South, issued General Order No. 11, declaring martial law in his military district, which comprised the states of South Carolina, Georgia, and Florida. The General Order declared all slaves in those states to be free. Hunter justified this on the grounds that slavery was "incompatible"

---

[62] An Act to Secure Freedom to all Persons Within the Territories of the United States, 12 Stat 432 (June 19, 1862).

[63] 60 US 393 (1857). See Finkelman, 12 Lewis & Clark L Rev 1219 (cited in note 16), and Finkelman, *Dred Scott v. Sandford* (cited in note 18).

with a "free country" and undermined military operations and his imposition of martial law.[64]

Hunter had vastly exceeded his authority. Indeed, his action went well beyond the authority of any military officer. Even if Lincoln had wanted to support Hunter's program, he could not possibly have approved of a general acting in this manner without authority of the executive branch. Not only did Hunter lack authority for such an action, but he had not even consulted with his military superiors, the War Department, or the president. No president could have allowed a military commander to assume such powers and, not surprisingly, ten days later Lincoln revoked Hunter's order.[65]

This was not like the situation in Missouri in 1861. Lincoln did not have to placate border state slaveholders. South Carolina, Georgia, and Florida were already out of the Union. Nor would such an order cause Lincoln any great political harm. Most northerners were by this time ready to see the slaveocracy of the deep South destroyed, and Hunter's action was a major step in that direction. Politically, it would not have cost Lincoln much to allow Hunter to abolish slavery in South Carolina where the rebellion began. But the need to preserve executive authority and maintain a proper chain of command, if nothing else, forced Lincoln to act. He simply could not let major generals set political policy.

Even as he countermanded Hunter, Lincoln gave a strong and unambiguous hint of his evolving theory of law and emancipation. He rebuked Hunter for acting without authority, but he did not reject the theory behind Hunter's General Order: that slavery was

---

[64]

HEAD-QUARTERS, DEPARTMENT OF THE SOUTH, HILTON HEAD, S.C. May 9, 1862.

The three States of Georgia, Florida, and South Carolina, comprising the Military Department of the South, having deliberately declared themselves no longer under the protection of the United States of America, and having taken up arms against the said United States, it becomes a military necessity to declare them under martial law. This was accordingly done on the 25th day of April, 1862. Slavery and martial law in a free country are altogether incompatible. The persons in these three States—Georgia , South Carolina , and Florida—heretofore held as slaves, are therefore declared forever free.

DAVID HUNTER, Major-General Commanding. ED. W. SMITH, Acting Assistant Adjutant-General.

http://mac110.assumption.edu/aas/Manuscripts/generalorders.html.

[65] "Proclamation Revoking General Hunter's Order of Military Emancipation of May 9, 1862," May 19, 1862, *CW*, 5:222.

incompatible with both a free country and the smooth operation of military forces suppressing the rebellion. Instead, in his "Proclamation Revoking General Hunter's Order of Military Emancipation," Lincoln wrote:

> I further make known that whether it be competent for me, as Commander-in-Chief of the Army and Navy, to declare the Slaves of any state or states, free, and whether at any time, in any case, it shall have become a necessity indispensable to the maintenance of the government to exercise such supposed power, are questions which, under my responsibility, I reserve to myself, and which I can not feel justified in leaving to the decision of commanders in the field.[66]

Lincoln ended his public proclamation by urging the loyal slave states to accept Congress's offer of March 6, to give "pecuniary aid" to those states that would "adopt a gradual abolishment of slavery." He asserted that "the change" such a policy "contemplates" would "come as gentle as the dews of heaven, not rending or wrecking anything." He asked the leaders of the slave states—within the Union and presumably those who claimed to be outside the Union—if they would "not embrace" this offer of Congress to accomplish "so much good . . . by one effort."[67]

In hindsight, this document is a stunning example of Lincoln deftly and subtly shaping public opinion in advance of announcing his goals. By this time he was fully aware that none of the Confederate states were ever going to end slavery on their own, and that for the foreseeable future neither would the border states. But he was willing to continue to make conciliatory gestures, urging a peaceful and seemingly painless solution to the problem. This helped him to court conservatives, who might be opposed to federal action against slavery, while at the same time advocating abolition and preparing the public for an eventual end to slavery. He was offering a solution to America's greatest social problem with the least amount of social disruption. But he also hinted that there were alternative solutions. He did not exactly say he had the power to end slavery as commander-in-chief, he merely asserted that *if* such power existed, it rested with him, and that if he felt emancipation

---

[66] Id at 222–23.

[67] Id at 223.

had "become a necessity indispensable to the maintenance of the government" he was prepared to act against slavery.

Lincoln was preparing the public for what he would do. He was in no hurry. He was carefully laying the groundwork for public support and constitutional legitimacy, on the basis of military necessity. Lincoln the "commander-in-chief" had found the constitutional authority to end slavery that Lincoln the president did not have. Like any good courtroom lawyer, Lincoln was not ready to lay out his strategy all at once. He wanted to prepare his jury—the American public—for what he was going to do. He did not emphatically assert that he had the constitutional power to end slavery in the Confederacy, he merely raised it as a theoretical possibility. At the same time he made it unmistakably clear that if such power existed, it rested with him, and that he was prepared to use that power.

A series of events in mid-July converged to convince Lincoln that emancipation would have to come soon. On July 12 he met for the second time with representatives and senators from the upper South, urging them to endorse compensated emancipation (with federal help) for their states. He argued that by taking this stand the loyal slave states would help the war effort by showing the rebels "that, in no event, will the states you represent ever join their proposed Confederacy." Although by this time Lincoln did not expect the loyal slave states to join the rebellion, he apparently believed that voluntary emancipation in those states would be a blow to Confederate hopes and morale. He also urged the border state representatives and senators to act in a practical manner to salvage what they could for their constituents. He famously told them that the "incidents of war" could "not be avoided" and that "mere friction and abrasion" would destroy slavery. He bluntly predicted—or more properly warned—that slavery "will be gone and you will have nothing valuable in lieu of it." He also pointed out that General Hunter's proclamation had been very popular and that he considered Hunter an "honest man" and "my friend."[68] The border state representatives and senators did not take the hint, and two days later more than two-thirds of them signed a letter denouncing any type of emancipation as "unconstitutional." Eight border state representatives

[68] "Appeal to Border State Representatives to Favor Compensated Emancipation," July 12, 1862, *CW*, 5:317–18; Gienapp, *Abraham Lincoln and Civil War America* at 110 (cited in note 47); McPherson, *Battle Cry of Freedom* at 503 (cited in note 38).

then published letters of their own supporting the president.[69]

On July 14, the same day that the border state representatives denounced emancipation, Lincoln took a final stab at gradualism, although he doubtless knew the attempt would fail. On that day he sent the draft of a bill to Congress that would provide compensation to every state that ended slavery. The draft bill left blank the amount for each slave that Congress would appropriate, but provided that the money would come in the form of federal bonds given to the states. This bill was part of Lincoln's strategy to end slavery through state action where possible as a way of setting up the possibility of ending it on the national level. If he could get Kentucky or Maryland to end slavery it would be easier to end it in the South. This was also consistent with prewar notions of federalism and constitutional interpretation that the states had sole authority over issues of property and personal status. Congress reported this bill and it went through two readings, but lawmakers adjourned before acting on it.

Lincoln surely knew that this bill, like his meeting with the border state representatives, would not lead to an end to slavery in the upper South. Nevertheless, this very public attempt at encouraging the states to act to end slavery was valuable. Like his response to Hunter, Lincoln showed the nation that he was not acting precipitously or incautiously. On the contrary, he was doing everything he could to end slavery with the least amount of turmoil and social dislocation.

This proposed bill must also be seen in the context of Lincoln's actions on July 13, which was the day before he proposed the bill and the day after his meeting with the border state representatives. On July 13, Lincoln privately told Secretary of State William H. Seward and Secretary of the Navy Gideon Welles that he was going to issue an Emancipation Proclamation. This was not a sudden response to the border state representatives rejecting compensated emancipation. Had they accepted Lincoln's proposal it would not have affected slavery in the Confederacy, where most slaves lived. Indeed, Lincoln told Welles that for weeks the issue had "occupied his mind and thoughts day and night."[70] That was probably an understatement. Lincoln had probably been troubled by the issue

---

[69] CW, 5:319; Gienapp, Abraham Lincoln and Civil War America at 110 (cited in note 47); McPherson, Battle Cry of Freedom at 503 (cited in note 38).

[70] Lincoln, quoted in McPherson, Battle Cry of Freedom at 504 (cited in note 38).

since had been forced to countermand Frémont's proclamation, or maybe from the moment he first heard of Butler's contraband solution to runaways. Lincoln's conflicting views over emancipation—his desire to achieve it, his sense that the time was not right, and his initial uncertainty about its constitutionality—were surely evident in his response to Hunter's proclamation, which Lincoln announced on May 19—nearly two months before he spoke with Welles.

Up until this time Lincoln had stressed that he could not move against slavery until there was a fair prospect of securing the border states and winning the war. He had also framed his power to end slavery as inherent within his powers as commander-in-chief. By early July 1862 Lincoln believed he had a fair prospect of winning the war, he knew the loyal slave states were secure, and he had a coherent legal and constitutional rationale for emancipation. Ever the master politician, Lincoln suddenly shifted the argument for emancipation to one of military necessity. This was the key to gaining full northern support for what he was about to do.

Thus, he told Welles the issue was one of military necessity. "We must free the slaves" he said, "or be ourselves subdued." Slaves, Lincoln argued, "were undeniably an element of strength to those who had their service, and we must decide whether that element should be with or against us." Lincoln also rejected the idea that the Constitution still protected slavery in the Confederacy. "The rebels," he said, "could not at the same time throw off the Constitution and invoke its aid. Having made war on the Government, they were subject to the incidents and calamities of war."[71] Here Lincoln sounded much like Benjamin Butler in his response to Major Carey. Since that incident the administration had accepted the idea that the Fugitive Slave Clause of the Constitution could not be invoked by rebel masters. But why, Lincoln might have asked, was the Fugitive Slave Clause different from any other part of the Constitution? If rebel masters were not entitled to the protection of that clause, then they were not entitled to the protection of any part of the Constitution. Thus, Lincoln had found a constitutional theory that would be acceptable to most northerners. It might not pass muster with the U.S. Supreme Court, but that issue might not

---

[71] Id.

arise until after most slaves had been freed. More importantly, it would help secure northern public opinion.

The military-necessity argument is more complex. Lincoln did not begin to move toward emancipation until after the United States had had substantial military success in the first five months of 1862. Thus, emancipation was not a desperate act forced by military necessity. Rather, it was an act that could only be accomplished by military success. However, in framing its constitutionality, Lincoln argued simultaneously that emancipation grew out of military power—that is, his power as commander-in-chief—and that as commander-in-chief he could do whatever was necessary to win the war and thus preserve the Union. This too would garner public support. Lincoln might *know* that he should free the slaves for moral reasons and that he had the constitutional power to do so, but he also knew that he would have greater support in the North if his actions appeared to be tied to military necessity. Thus, the irony of emancipation emerged. Lincoln could only move against slavery when he thought he could win the war, but he could only sell emancipation to the North, and only justify it constitutionally, if he appeared to need it to win the war.

Four days after speaking with Welles and Seward, Lincoln signed the Second Confiscation Act into law.[72] This law was more expansive than the First Confiscation Act. The law provided a death penalty as well as lesser penalties—including confiscation of slaves—for treason and also allowed for the prosecution of "any person" participating in the rebellion or who gave "aid and comfort" to it. The law also provided for the seizure and condemnation of the property of "any person within any State or Territory of the United States . . . being engaged in armed rebellion against the government of the United States, or aiding or abetting such rebellion." This would include Confederate sympathizers in the border states as well as in the Confederacy. Two separate provisions dealt, in a comprehensive way, with the issue of runaway slaves and contrabands.

Under section 9 of the law any slave owned by someone "engaged in rebellion against the government" who escaped to Union lines or was captured by U.S. troops would be "forever free of their servitude, and not again held as slaves." Section 10 prohibited the military from returning any fugitive slaves to any masters, even those

---

[72] An Act to suppress Insurrection, to punish Treason and Rebellion, to seize and confiscate the Property of Rebels, and for other Purposes, 12 Stat 589 (July 17, 1862).

in the border states, unless the owner claiming the slave would "first make oath that the person to whom the labor or service of such fugitive is alleged to be due is his lawful owner, and has not borne arms against the United States in the present rebellion, nor in any way given aid and comfort thereto." Like the Washington, D.C., emancipation act, this law allowed for the colonization of such blacks "as may be willing to emigrate" to other lands. This was a sop to conservatives who feared black freedom, but it would not require anyone to leave the United States.[73] Significantly, unlike the D.C. emancipation bill, the Confiscation Act allowed colonization but did not appropriate any money for it.

The Confiscation Act was one more step toward creating public opinion that would allow emancipation. It also helped clarify the legal and constitutional issues, by once again affirming that under the war powers Congress, or the president, might emancipate slaves. The act did not, however, do much to actually free any slaves. The law provided numerous punishments for rebels, but their slaves would only become free after some judicial process. Had there been no Emancipation Proclamation or Thirteenth Amendment, the act might have eventually been used to litigate freedom, but it would have been a long and tedious process. The only certain freedom created from the act came in sections 9 and 10, which secured liberty to fugitive slaves escaping rebel masters. But this was not really much of a change from existing policy.

On July 22, five days after signing the act, Lincoln presented his cabinet with his first draft of the Emancipation Proclamation. The draft began with a reference to the Second Confiscation Act, and contained a declaration warning "all persons" aiding or joining the rebellion that if they did not "return to their proper allegiance to the United States" they would suffer "pain of the forfeitures and seizures" of their slaves.[74] This language would not appear in the final Proclamation. However, a few days after he showed this language to the cabinet, he recast it as a separate public proclamation.[75]

The rest of the first draft of the Proclamation focused on Lincoln's intent to urge Congress to give "pecuniary aid" to those states voluntarily ending slavery and "practically sustaining the authority

---

[73] Id.

[74] Emancipation Proclamation—First Draft [July 22, 1862], *CW*, 5:336.

[75] Proclamation of the Act to Suppress Insurrection, July 25, 1862, *CW*, 5:341.

of the United States." This was one more attempt to get the loyal slave states to end slavery. The final sentence of this draft proclamation finally went to the main issue. Lincoln declared that "as a fit and necessary military measure" he did "order and declare" as "Commander-in-Chief of the Army and Navy of the United States," that as of January 1, 1863, "all persons held as slaves within any state or states, wherein the constitutional authority of the United States shall not then be practically recognized, submitted to, and maintained, shall then, thenceforward, and forever be free."

This was the great change for Lincoln. He was now on record as believing that he had the constitutional power to end slavery in the Confederacy. Lincoln had solved the first precondition of emancipation. Kentucky, Missouri, Maryland, and Delaware were securely in the United States, and while their leaders were not ready to end slavery, they clearly would not be joining the Confederacy. The third condition had been met. The fourth condition had at least been partially met. With U.S. troops controlling most of the Mississippi Valley, a good deal of Tennessee, the islands off the coast of South Carolina and Georgia, and most southern ports closed by the navy, Lincoln knew that an emancipation program would be successful in freeing a substantial number of slaves, even if somehow a shrunken Confederacy survived. The only precondition that was left was the development of political support for emancipation. Here Lincoln was also close to achieving his goal. Congress had been moving toward emancipation; generals such as Hunter were pushing for emancipation; and once he proposed it to his cabinet, only the conservative Montgomery Blair, who was from a slave state, expressed reservations about emancipation. Blair did not oppose the concept, but did think it would cost the Republican Party votes in the fall elections. In the next two months Lincoln would work to lay the political groundwork for gaining greater public support for emancipation.

VI. PREPARING THE PUBLIC FOR THE INEVITABLE

For the rest of the summer Lincoln quietly shaped the political climate to create the necessary conditions for emancipation. Illustrative of this was his famous letter to the *New York Tribune* on August 22. In an editorial titled "The Prayer of Twenty Millions," Horace Greeley had urged Lincoln to end slavery. Lincoln responded with a letter, declaring his goal was to "save the Union," and that he would accomplish this any way he could. He would free some slaves, all slaves, or no slaves to save the Union. He also noted that this position was a description of his *"official* duty" and not a change in his "oft-expressed *personal* wish that all men every where could be free."[76]

The answer to Greeley was one more step to creating the political conditions for emancipation. Lincoln had now warned the nation that he would end slavery if it were necessary to preserve the Union. He was also now on record as asserting that he had the power to end slavery, although he did not spell out exactly what that power was or where in the Constitution he found it.

Lincoln had been quietly and secretly moving toward this result all summer. His letter to Greeley was a prelude to what he had already determined to do. No northerner could be surprised when he did it. Abolitionists could be heartened by having a president who believed, as they did, that "all men every where" should "be free." Conservatives would understand that they had to accept emancipation as a necessary policy to defeat the rebellion and save the nation.

On September 13 he replied coyly to an "Emancipation Memorial" from a group of Chicago ministers. He asserted that emancipation was useless without a military victory and would be "like the Pope's bull against the comet." He asked how he "could free the slaves" when he could not "enforce the Constitution in the rebel States."[77] Tied to this problem, he noted, was the possibility that emancipation would take "fifty thousand bayonets" from Kentucky out of the Union Army and give them to the Confederates.[78] Lincoln surely no longer believed this was the case, since Kentucky was firmly in the Union, but it underscored his long-standing belief that he had to make sure Kentucky was secure before he could move against slavery in the Confederacy. He also noted that he needed full public support to succeed. Thus, he urged the ministers to be patient. Emancipation could only come with military success and the ability to "unite the people in the fact that constitutional government" should be preserved. In passing, Lincoln also noted that he had the power, as commander-in-chief, to emancipate the slaves

---

[76] Lincoln to Horace Greeley, August 22, 1862, *CW*, 5:388–89.

[77] "Reply to Emancipation Memorial Presented by Chicago Christians of All Denominations," Sept 13, 1862, *CW*, 5:419–25 (quotations on 420).

[78] Id at 423.

in the Confederacy. Most importantly, perhaps, he also told these ministers that he had no "objections of a moral nature" to emancipation.[79]

Even as he responded to the ministers, evading any commitment and refusing to reveal his plans, Lincoln knew he had almost all his prerequisites on the table. To end slavery he needed the prospect of military success, the ability to secure the loyal slaves states, public support for black freedom, and a constitutional theory to justify his actions. In early September he had all of this except the first. The war had been going well since the previous December, but he needed a significant battlefield victory to have all his prerequisites in place. When he had that victory, emancipation would not be a "necessity" of preserving the Union, as he had said in the Greeley letter, but rather it would be the fruit of victory. The victory at Antietam was the last piece of the puzzle. He could now issue the Proclamation as the logical fruit of the military successes that had taken place since the previous December.[80]

On September 22 he issued the preliminary Proclamation, declaring that it would go into effect in one hundred days. He chose September 22 carefully, because it would be exactly one hundred days until January 1, 1863, thus tying emancipation with the new year. He now also had his constitutional/legal theory for issuing the Proclamation as he had explained in his letter to the *New York Tribune*.

He issued the Proclamation in his dual capacity as "President of the United States of America, and Commander-in-Chief of the Army and Navy." The purpose of the Proclamation was "restoring the constitutional relations" between the nation and all the states. The preliminary Proclamation authorized the enlistment of black troops and put the nation on notice that in one hundred days he would move against slavery in any place that was still in rebellion against the nation.[81]

On January 1, 1863, the final Proclamation was put into effect. Here Lincoln made the constitutional argument even more precise.

---

[79] Id at 424, 421.

[80] In hindsight it is of course clear that Antietam was not the knockout blow Lincoln was hoping for, and the end of 1862 and the first half of 1863 would be a period of enormous frustration for Lincoln, as the war went badly. But Lincoln could not know or foresee this when he issued the preliminary Proclamation.

[81] Preliminary Emancipation Proclamation, Sept 22, 1862, *CW*, 5:433; Proclamation No 16, 12 Stat 1267 (Sept 22, 1862).

He issued it "by virtue of the power in me vested as Commander-in-Chief, of the Army and Navy of the United States in time of actual armed rebellion." This was, constitutionally, a war measure designed to cripple the ability of those in rebellion to resist the lawful authority of the United States. It applied only to those states and parts of states that were still in rebellion. This was constitutionally essential. Lincoln only had power to touch slavery where, as he had told the ministers from Chicago, he could not "enforce the Constitution." Where the Constitution was in force, federalism and the Fifth Amendment prevented presidential emancipation. The document was narrowly written, carefully designed to withstand the scrutiny of the Supreme Court, still presided over by Chief Justice Taney. It narrowly applied only to the states in rebellion. It would not threaten Kentucky or Missouri and it would not threaten the constitutional relationship of the states and the federal government.

A careful reading of the Proclamation suggests that Professor Hofstadter was right. It did have "all the moral grandeur of a bill of lading." But, Hofstadter failed to understand the significance of a bill of lading to a skilled railroad lawyer, which is what Lincoln had been before the war. A bill of lading was the key legal instrument that guaranteed the delivery of goods between parties that were far apart and may never have known each other. A bill of lading allowed a seller in New York to safely ship goods to a buyer in Illinois, with both knowing the transaction would work. One contemporary living in Britain, Karl Marx, fully understood the highly legalistic nature of the Proclamation. Writing for a London newspaper during the war, Marx had a clear fix on what Lincoln had done, and why he did it the way he did: the "most formidable decrees which he hurls at the enemy and which will never lose their historic significance, resemble—as the author intends them to—ordinary summons, sent by one lawyer to another."[82]

So, in the end, when all the preconditions were met—the loyal slave states secured, military victory likely, political support in place, and the constitutional/legal framework developed—Lincoln went back to his roots as a lawyer and wrote a carefully crafted, narrow document: a bill of lading for the delivery of freedom to some 3 million southern slaves. The vehicle for delivery would be the army

[82] Marx, quoted in Phillip Shaw Paludan, *The Presidency of Abraham Lincoln* 187–88 (Kansas, 1994).

and navy—for which he was commander-in-chief. As the armies of the United States moved deeper into the Confederacy they would bring the power of the Proclamation with them, freeing slaves every day as more and more of the Confederacy was redeemed by military success. This was the moral grandeur of the Proclamation and of Lincoln's careful and complicated strategy to achieve his personal goal that "all men every where could be free."[83]

---

[83] AL to Horace Greeley, Aug 22, 1862, *CW*, 5:388–89.